IP '91, 39.95

37 ^{60}

FOX

UNDERSTANDING

G. B. Madison

UNDERSTANDING
A PHENOMENOLOGICAL – PRAGMATIC ANALYSIS

CONTRIBUTIONS IN PHILOSOPHY, NUMBER 19

Greenwood Press
Westport, Connecticut • London, England

Library of Congress Cataloging in Publication Data

Madison, Gary Brent.
    Understanding, a phenomenological-pragmatic analysis.

    (Contributions in philosophy, ISSN 0084-926X ;
no. 19)
    Bibliography: p.
    Includes index.
    1. Reality.   2. Rationalism.   3. Science and civili-
zation.   4. Technology and civilization.   5. Values.
6. Civilization—Philosophy.   I. Title.   II. Series:
Contributions in philosophy ; no. 18.
BD331.M33   110   81-4233
ISBN 0-313-22483-8 (lib. bdg.)   AACR2

Library of Congress Catalog Card Number: 81-4233
ISBN: 0-313-22483-8
ISSN: 0084-926X

First published in 1982

Greenwood Press
A division of Congressional Information Service, Inc.
88 Post Road West
Westport, Connecticut 06881

Printed in the United States of America

10 9 8 7 6 5 4 3 2 1

In truth, scientific knowledge [*la science*] is a great and very useful business. Those who despise it give evidence enough of their stupidity; but yet I do not set its value at that extreme measure that some attribute to it, like Herillus the philosopher, who placed in it the sovereign good, and held that it was in its power to make us wise and happy. That I do not believe; nor what others have said, that knowledge is the mother of all virtue, and that all vice is produced by ignorance. If that is true, it is subject to a long interpretation.

—Michel de Montaigne
Apology for Raymond Sebond

If human science refuses to understand that there is something which it cannot understand, or better still, that there is something about which it clearly understands that it cannot understand—then all is confusion. For it is the duty of the human understanding to understand that there are things it cannot understand, and what those things are.

—Søren Kierkegaard
The Journals

To my parents, Paul Ricoeur, and the people of Brazil in whose midst the idea for this book was first conceived

CONTENTS

UNDERSTANDING

INTRODUCTION

The latter half of the twentieth century represents the beginning of a new age in the history of humanity. This new era has been labeled, appropriately enough, the *electronic age,* for its most remarkable feature is the total transformation in human living patterns brought about by the development and spread of the electronic technology of instantaneous communication. In contrast to former times, when people for the most part passed their lives in isolation from and ignorance of their neighbors, the entire human race is today being resettled in one "global village," the result of developments in the technology of transportation and the electronic media. It is almost as if the human race were finally in a position to overcome the disruptive effects of the destruction of the Tower of Babel and reunite themselves in the fold of one single, self-conscious humanity. The development of the media, as described by Marshall McLuhan, seems to have furnished the practical means for realizing Teilhard de Chardin's utopian vision of a collective "noosphere,"[1]

The ideas of unity and uniformity, like those of democracy and equality, constitute the *mots d'ordre* of people of the electronic age and are at the basis of their collective ideology—the thought that inspires their action. And just as it was in America, "the most democratic country on the face of the earth," that, as Alexis de Tocqueville perspicaciously noted in the early 1800s, the ideas of democracy and equality were first translated into concrete action in such a way as to bring about a total and unprecedented transformation in the collective lives of people, so also it is in America that the new life-style of the electronic age has been first realized, and it is from America that it has, at an incredibly rapid rate, spread throughout the rest of the world.

Although to all appearances the ideals of unity and human togetherness are very noble ones indeed, they are not without certain pernicious effects.[2] Judging from what has actually taken place to date, it would seem that there

During 1976-1977 I was a Fellow of the Canada Council. I wish to thank the council for its generous financial assistance, which allowed me during this time to lay much of the groundwork for this book.

3

is a price to be paid for cultural unity, and this is the elimination of cultural diversity, or, put another way, the liquidation of the traditional cultures of the peoples of the world. Tocqueville was one of the first to note that the monotonous uniformity of American culture was becoming ever more of a world phenomenon: "Variety is disappearing from the human race; the same ways of acting, thinking, and feeling are to be met with all over the world."[3]

Indeed every year entire languages spoken by small communities throughout the world become, like rare animal species, extinct, and for much the same reason: the spread of technology and "global civilization." Many such languages survive only in the electronic warehouse of tape recordings.

When a people loses its language, it loses its culture as well. A people's culture is its system of values and the means whereby it orients itself in the world and achieves self-identity. Thus, were we to encourage a people to adopt, say, English as its working tongue, we would be imposing on them the thought patterns and outlook on reality peculiar to English; we would be imposing on them *our own culture*. As one linguist has remarked:

> To restrict thinking to the patterns merely of English, and especially to those patterns which represent the acme of plainness in English, is to lose a power of thought which, once lost, can never be regained. It is the "plainest" English which contains the greatest number of unconscious assumptions about nature. This is the trouble with schemes like Basic English, in which an eviscerated British English, with its concealed premises working harder than ever, is to be fobbed off on an unsuspecting world as the substance of pure Reason itself. . . . For this reason I believe that those who envision a future world speaking only one tongue, whether English, German, Russian, or any other, hold a misguided ideal and would do the evolution of the human mind the greatest disservice. Western culture has made, through language, a provisional analysis of reality and, without correctives, hold resolutely to that analysis as final. The only correctives lie in all those other tongues which by aeons of independent evolution have arrived at different, but equally logical, provisional analyses.[4]

When, in the altruistic attempt to "raise the standards of living" of the people of the Third World, we in the West export to them our science and technology, we are actually exporting to them our own culture, and thus technological aid serves as an instrument of cultural imperialism. For to employ this technology efficiently, a people must master and learn to think in its language of origin. Even when technological terms are translated into the native tongue (and this very often does not occur), the underlying thought patterns remain alien.

The language of journalism is a case in point. Some of the greatest successes registered in the technology of automatic or machine translation have been in the field of journalism, and the reason is not difficult to discover. Although a newspaper in Japan and one in the United States are written in Japanese and American, respectively, the way the language is used is in both cases nearly identical; newspaper Japanese and newspaper American are both species of one international language: journalese. Journalese is indeed the "plainest" of languages, as the linguist would say, and thus it is also one "which contains the greatest number of unconscious assumptions about nature." What one finds here between the various versions of journalese (Japanese, American, and the others) is a close isomorphism of vocabulary and even something of an isomorphism of structure—which is to say, a cultural isomorphism.[5] When one hears complaints about the ruinous effect of journalistic style on the English language, one can be sure that they are not without linguistic foundation.

The language of science poses even fewer difficulties for automatic translation than does journalese. In science it is irrelevant whether one speaks in English, Russian, Japanese, or French, for these different languages are, in this instance, merely different ways of saying the same thing. There is here in effect but one language in different guises. This is why translation of scientific texts poses no real problems. The language one translates from and the language one translates into are basically the same, that of the scientific mentality; "once equivalences have been set up, translation of science is so easy that more than one centre in America has started with scientific Chinese as one of the languages to try first in their programmes for machine translation."[6]

As in the case of journalese, science is eminently translatable into those languages that have worked out a scientific vocabulary for the simple reason that to do so one need not transgress any cultural boundaries. Science is homogeneous from culture to culture; it is in fact constitutive of one universal, international culture. But what does this mean? What is the nature of scientific universality? What is a "universal" culture? Ordinarily, to speak of different cultures is to speak of different value systems and world outlooks, ones that are not universal but particular.

Science is universal not because it is compatible with all of these different value systems but only because it expresses a single and single-minded approach to reality. Science, considered as a systematically organized body of knowledge, is but one value system among others and is universal only in the sense that it is to be found everywhere in the world that Western culture has implanted itself. "That modern Chinese or Turkish scientists describe the world in the same terms as Western scientists means, of course," one linguist says, "only that they have taken over bodily the entire Western system of rationalizations, not that they have corroborated that system from their native posts of observation."[7]

To the degree that alien cultures bodily take over the scientific-technological enterprise, they are abandoning their own traditional value systems in favor of one that is a product of our own culture.

Science and culture are simply not on an equal footing. Science is one and universal, but cultures are many and particular. This does not, of course, mean that something like a scientific culture is inconceivable. Our own culture has the dubious privilege of being close to achieving such a status, and there is no lack of individuals whose life goal is to eliminate the "archaic" in our culture altogether and completely infuse it with purely scientific values—vide B. F. Skinner.[8] And it must be admitted that there is no reason why one could not organize an innerly coherent world view around the scientific-technological enterprise. The important point to keep in mind is that such a culture would be merely one world view among others and therefore could not claim to have transcended cultural differences altogether. The sought-after unification of humanity, when it is conceived of in terms of the dominance of the so-called universal language of science and technology, is but another name for cultural genocide, the liquidation of alien cultures and their reduction to one culture in particular—our own.

When, through the technological means at our disposal, we communicate with foreign cultures, we inevitably tend to understand them in terms of our own scientific culture; we interpret their culture purely in terms of our own. Claims of a new global village notwithstanding, there is no genuine communication here, that is, contact with the other as other, in what is peculiar to him, but only reduction of the other to the same, to what is peculiar to us. We are often not unencouraged in this by the other, precisely, for, impressed with our technological successes, accomplishments, and sheer power, the other reciprocates by interpreting himself to us in our own terms. Just as it is often the exploited countries that have themselves solicited economic imperialism because of their desire to partake of the material abundance of the industrialized nations, so it is often the alien culture that freely submits to technological and cultural imperialism.[9] The electronic media today are among the prime instruments of this cultural imperialism. And cultural imperialism is the condition and the instrument of all other dominations.[10]

While in our culture we have become increasingly aware of the demands of natural ecology,[11] there is another type of ecology in regard to which we still remain generally insensitive: cultural ecology. A given culture is not unlike a natural biosystem in that it too is a structural and delicately balanced whole, and the abrupt introduction into it of foreign cultural elements can result in its total disruption and disintegration. Under the devastating influence of the Spanish conquistadores, the great Inca civilization vanished as abruptly and as completely as did the great herds of the American buffalo, what remains of both now is no more than so much "folklore" preserved for the distraction of tourists of the homogeneous electronic age. No express genocide intention need be operative to result in the annihilation of a culture. It can result from the best intentioned of foreign aid programs, for along with technical aid goes technical know-how and along with this the entire technological-scientific system of values and priorities, which we have created for ourselves. Accepting all of this as a package inevitably leads to tensions within the recipient culture, tensions between the new scientific values and the old cultural ones, cultural disruptions that tend to produce not a new synthesis but the complete disintegration of the culture as it existed before and its radical transformation along the lines of our own technological one.[12]

The spread of technology throughout the world no doubt is inevitable. It is indeed hard to see how any culture could successfully resist its onslaught in a time when the means of communication have become so highly developed and pervasive. And even if a given culture could totally isolate itself and put up an effective resistance, the result, given the ease of communication, would most likely be the most undesirable of societies—one of absolute tyrannical repression and totalitarian thought control. Cambodia under the Khmer Rouge after the American withdrawal and Iran after the fall of the shah furnish particularly salient examples of this kind of thoroughly irrational reaction to Western scientific-technological rationality. Technology can be rejected neither by other cultures nor by our own, and a fanatical resistance to it could, ironically, result only in the destruction of those values in the name of which the fight against technology is conducted—the freedom and dignity of the human person.

Thus although societies and cultures may be compared usefully to living organisms, this is only an analogy; cultures are not things, and what is of supreme importance is not society but the individual person. As one anthropologist pertinently remarks, "Societies are not organisms: they are not animals on the verge of extinction, and no one would wish to preserve traditional cultures in reserves, like nearly extinct animal species, regardless of the wishes of their members. What really matters are people, not societies."[13] This may appear self-evident to many of us, since it follows from the emphasis Christianity has always placed on the supreme importance of the individually existing human being, but it is something less than self-evident to an increasing number of people. There is, in fact, as typified by Marxist-inspired thought, which is preoccupied with abstractions such as "the proletariat" or "humanity" (a favorite title of many Communist newspapers), an increasing tendency today to stigmatize concern for individuals as such as being an instance of "individualism" and "bourgeois" thinking. And, indeed, as Tocqueville pointed out well over a century ago, even before Karl Marx made his appearance, the general tendency of our times, which is inspired by the egalitarian spirit, is to set Man up over and above individual men. Today, in a frantic attempt not to appear reactionary, even Christians are talking more about the transformation of society and less about human existence, more about social welfare and less about the salvation of the individual.

The individual cannot properly exist except in some kind of proper cultural and societal context; this is why the question of culture is of the utmost importance. However, that should not lead one—as it often does—into committing what Whitehead would have called the "fallacy of misplaced concreteness" by giving more importance to culture and society than to the individual. It is really frightful what atrocities can be committed against the human person, all in the name of abstractions such as culture, society, or even humanity.

The only way values having to do with the freedom and dignity of the person can be maintained is not through an impossible escape from technology but rather through a direct confrontation with it where the aim would be to break down the global scientific-technological cultural complex, to destroy the positivistic, materialistic, deterministic mentality associated with it, and to reintegrate technology as a means and science as an activity into a more comprehensive outlook and culture than the scientific-technological one.

In the case of alien cultures, the prognostic need not be as dismal as it is often made out to be. To be sure, with the ever-increasing generalization of technology, these cultures will be exposed to a very serious threat to their existence, and they will in fact survive and preserve their self-identity only at the expense of significant change and transformation. But change is a basic fact of cultural life—just as it is of biological life—and a basic characteristic of all civilizations, whether they are specifically "historical" or not. Confrontation and interplay—*polemos,* as Heraclitus would say—is the normal relation of one culture to another; "change and conflict are normal characteristics of social systems no less than equilibrium and harmony."[14] Were it ever written, the history of humanity and of human understanding would in fact be the history of cultural conflict and cross-fertilization. The question is not, therefore, whether cultures other than our own can avoid changing and undergoing transformation—for they cannot—but rather whether they can change in such a way as to preserve in the process a renewed self-identity, whether they can integrate the foreign and new into an enlarged understanding and reappropriation of the native and old. The question is whether they can revalorize the scientific-technological apparatus in the light of their own tradition. As the authors of a document prepared for UNESCO, dealing with technical assistance and cultural identity, state:

If the people themselves, steeped in the traditional wisdom of their scriptures, transform the new knowledge into a new expression of an ancient and beloved revelation, then the dangers of lack of spontaneity, falseness, manipulation and degradation are avoided. . . . a new synthesis will take place, which is organic because it has occurred within the same human organisms, which is harmonious because it is an expression of individual human beings' efforts to make sense of their own lives.[15]

Is it really possible, however, to divest the scientific enterprise of its vulgar materialism and to view it merely as an ensemble of techniques that could be used creatively, and thus differently, in different cultures?[16] The fact of the matter is that science as we know it and as it exists is bound up with an entire world view or system of values that took its present shape in the late Renaissance and early modern period and that is hostile to many of the older values of our culture, not to speak of other cultures. Our culture is very close to being a scientific culture—that is, not just a culture in which science is accorded a high value but where it tends to dominate and eliminate all other values and points of view. This is natural and perhaps inevitable given the claims and presuppositions of science, for science carries with it its own conception of truth. However many-sided it may be, truth is essentially one. And because truth, it is thought, is one, there can be basically only one mode of human understanding capable of discovering and expressing it. This, of course, is science. Underlying the scientific enterprise there is an operative presupposition as to what constitutes "knowledge." Knowledge is the representation of what reality is in itself, and it is "true" to the degree that it "corresponds" to the innate or essential structure of reality. This conception of knowledge at work in science prescribes a particular conception of reality. However many-sided it may be, reality is essentially one.

By its very nature, therefore, science is hostile to cultural diversity, for each culture represents a different conception of what reality is, and, from a purely descriptive point of view, there are as many "realities" as there are cultures. This violates the basic working premise on which science is built: the oneness of truth and reality.

The greatest danger facing Western culture is the ever-increasing technologizing of every aspect of life, as a consequence of which the notions of freedom and dignity are rendered ever more meaningless. "It is easy to boast of victory over ancient oppression," one social observer, Jacques Ellul, writes, "but what if victory has been gained at the price of an even greater subjection to the forces of the artificial necessity of the technical society which has come to dominate our lives?"[17] The "technological threat" so much spoken about by social writers is simply the translation of the working presuppositions of science into the practical sphere. For if the truth is one and if, by means of science, we think we have discovered it, then it is only "logical" that it should be universally and uniformly recognized and implemented. This requires that all priorities be dictated by the opinions of science and the needs of technology and that all nonscientific-technological values be relegated to a cultural no-man's-land. What Ellul says of technology is true of science as well.

> Technology cannot put up with intuitions and "literature." It must necessarily don mathematical vestments. Everything in human life that does not lend itself to mathematical treatment must be excluded—because it is not a possible end for technique—and left to the sphere of dreams.[18]

The greatest problem we face is, therefore, that of reconciling, within our own culture, the demands of science with other, more traditional values. This has been labeled the problem of the "Two Cultures."[19] What is the relation between so-called scientific facts on the one hand and humanistic, religious, and other, nonscientific values on the other hand? Western cultural imperialism—the problem of Other Cultures—cannot be effectively opposed so long as the conceptual imperialism of science and technology within our own culture is not recognized and opposed, so long, that is, as we do not deliberately confront the problem of the Two Cultures and determine for ourselves the proper place of science within human life as a whole, within, that is, the wider realm of creative, cultural values.[20]

Technologism and cultural imperialism pose extremely practical dangers, affecting as they do the way of life of everyone on this earth. But because they are the expression of a certain cultural orientation on our part and presuppose certain, if often unthematized, theories of knowledge and reality, they can be effectively opposed only if the underlying theories themselves are subjected to criticism. To criticize a theory is itself a theoretical endeavor, and thus our task is outlined. It is not an easy one.[21] We must attempt to discover reasons that can justify our opposition to technologism and scientism and must indeed demonstrate that rational understanding and action cannot be reduced to merely scientific knowing and technological activity.

If the dehumanizing tyranny of technology is to be resisted in the cultural realm, that is, the realm in which we actually live—in education, the organization of society, politics, economics—it is not enough merely to correct the more blatant excesses of technology (though this is indispensable). It is necessary to attack the very mode of thought that gives rise to these more obvious practical outcomes. The despoilment of the earth's irreplaceable resources, the economic exploitation of humans by humans, and the insidious spread of autocratic and uncontrollable bureaucracies: these are no accidents but the manifestations of a certain way of viewing the world and of acting on it, of a certain mentality that is the essence of modern technology. It is this basic mentality that needs to be countered.

It is necessary to become explicitly aware of the presuppositions of the technological enterprise in order to criticize them effectively. This is not easy, for presuppositions by their very nature are something of which one is not normally aware, for they are not *what* one is aware of but the *means* by which one is aware of or understands everything else. Our culture is very much a technological culture, and to the degree that it is so, we are insensitive to the underlying presuppositions of our culture. Most important, but also most difficult, is to become aware of these presuppositions so as to see that technology is but one way of coming to grips with existence, one particular value system among others, and that for this very reason, it cannot claim to be the only way of dealing with the world. It is important to realize that there are other values than technological ones, and these should determine the scope and limits of technology.

And let us make no mistake about it: the presuppositions of technology are not other than those of modern science. Scientific "knowledge" is in no way absolute or supreme but is merely the expression of one relatively narrow, as well as arbitrary, way of viewing the world and making sense of it. Scientific knowledge is nothing more than the expression of a certain intellectual technique: the scientific method. This technique has proven useful for certain purposes, but the failure on our part to realize its inherent limitations has had as its consequence the accelerating reduction of all cultural values to those of science. The ultimate outcome of this process can be none other than utter catastrophe, in both the physical and spiritual senses of the word. The only possible way the catastrophe can be avoided—if it can be avoided—and the only possible way that the ideals of human freedom and dignity can preserve some semblance of genuine meaning is through the recognition of values wider than those of science and technology and through the implementation of these values throughout our culture.

The goal of this book is not to elaborate and defend such values. It is more limited. The task before us is to become aware of the presuppositions of science and technology as such. Only in this way can a genuinely meaningful discussion of cultural values and priorities become possible. This task, though limited, will not be easy to carry out, for science and technology are the expression of certain epistemological and metaphysical options that are so thoroughly a part of our entire Western, rationalist tradition that normally we are not even aware of the fact that they are no more than arbitrary options. In order to make this apparent and in order to situate science properly within the wider realm of culture, we shall have to work out a theory of human understanding in general, a theory that will contrast at nearly every point with the generally accepted or orthodox theory. If such a theory can be formulated and rationally defended, then it will be possible to discern the limits of the scientific enterprise while at the same time acknowledging the undeniable importance of science as one way in which people can creatively express themselves.

My concern in this study is to situate science within the wider realm of creative, cultural values. This should perhaps be emphasized so as to avoid at the outset any possible misunderstanding, for it means that our concern will not be to effect a revolution or change of mind within science, considered in its own right as a mode (a system) of human understanding. We will not attempt to reconcile science and the humanities by advocating a new, "humanistic" science. Our concern is not to effect a change in science but rather a change in the attitude we as a whole—scientists and laymen alike—have toward science.

The dehumanizing effects of scientism can be effectively countered and perhaps neutralized when it is realized that science is, in its origin, as creative an endeavor as the other human cultural activities. Once this is fully realized—and once, as well, the true nature of creative understanding in general is realized—the limits of science must also be realized. In order to bring out fully the creative (and thus limited) nature of scientific understanding, we shall, in chapter 7 in particular, be led to distinguish between science as a body of established "knowledge," as a collection of "objective truths" (the way it is generally understood and taught in our schools and universities), and science as a human activity, as the free expression of the creative imagination.

The intent of this way of proceeding is not to effect a change in science, considered as a body of knowledge, as a particular epistemological system with its own essential makeup. In fact, my personal conviction is that science cannot and will not change, without ceasing to be what we essentially mean by "science." The science of tomorrow will not differ in any essential way from what it is today, what it was yesterday and the day before yesterday. This is not meant as an absolute statement; it means only that nothing in the history of science to date justifies one in supposing that science will change in its essential constituents or its underlying methodological presuppositions. What the history of the scientific enterprise reveals is a remarkable continuity in the matter of underlying presuppositions. One philosopher of science, Jules Vuillemin of the Collège de France, has pointed out a number of these presuppositions, and above all what is interesting from our point of view is that they are, as he maintains, basically none other than the underlying presuppositions of philosophical rationalism as instanced in thinkers such as Plato, Saint Anselm, Descartes, and Leibniz.[22]

This is extremely significant because it means that to contest the cultural imperialism of technological thinking, one must contest not only the presuppositions of modern science but also presuppositions fundamental to our entire Western intellectual tradition. This is what I meant when I said that the cultural imperialism of technology is the expression of a certain

cultural orientation on our part and presupposes certain, if often unthematized, theories of knowledge and reality and that these underlying theories
must by scrutinized. Exactly what these assumptions or implicit theories—having to do with the nature of reason and the nature of reality—are
will become apparent as we proceed with our inquiry.

It will also become apparent that, to a greater or lesser extent, these
preconceptions have been shared by the quasi-totality of the great thinkers
of the Western tradition (by "great" is meant "famous," "dominant,"
"well known," "celebrated," and so forth). So much is this the case that
the history of Western thought could be said to be, for the most part, the
history of rationalist thought. This means that as we proceed with this inquiry into the nature and scope of human understanding, we will find
ourselves obliged to undermine the foundations of the entire rationalist
edifice.

I am therefore in substantial agreement with Martin Heidegger's reading
of Western thought, which detects in it an inner and well-defined continuity. For Heidegger, modern science and technology is but the culmination
and ultimate logical consequence of Platonic rationalism.[23] I too believe
that modern science and technology are simply the end products of certain
fateful assumptions about human understanding and reality that were first
articulated by the ancient Greeks, and Plato in particular, and that there-
after were elaborated in the course of our intellectual history. Throughout
the whole of the Western tradition there is an amazing continuity of
thought, one most aptly labeled "rationalism."

Unlike Heidegger, however, I do not believe that the history of Western
thought is nothing but the history of rationalism (or what Heidegger calls
"metaphysics"). Ever since the ancient Greeks, from time to time, people
have protested against the dominant presuppositions of our rationalist
culture and have sought to expose its underlying prejudices. One thinks, for
instance, of Protagoras and Gorgias, who protested against the rationalist
dogmatism of Parmenides and the early Greek cosmologists; of Isocrates,
who was opposed to the rationalist metaphysics of Plato; of Sextus Empiricus, who criticized all dogmatic thought that preceded his time, stoicism
in particular; of Montaigne, who mounted an attack on rationalist thought
of the Renaissance from which modern science was to emerge; of Pascal,
who was opposed to Cartesian rationalism; of Kierkegaard, who attacked
Hegel's rationalist claims; of Nietzsche, who fought against more than two
thousand years of rationalist orthodoxy. These and other thinkers form
something like a tradition of their own, a properly anti-rationalist tradition.
The entire history of philosophy therefore can be looked upon as being
made up of two basic movements. First is the dominant current of rationalism and, within this current, a counter-current, which attempts to

bring us back to a more just appreciation of our powers and limits. Since rationalism constitutes the dominant current in the Western tradition, we may call the counter-current of anti-rationalism the counter-tradition.

It is to the members of this counter-tradition that we shall be looking for support in this attempt to overcome the rationalist presuppositions that serve as the theoretical basis for scientific and technological imperialism.[24] This, however, will not be without posing some difficulties. For one thing, academic philosophers often hesitate to accord the title of philosopher—and thus intellectual respectability—to some of these thinkers (Isocrates, Montaigne, and Pascal, for instance). For another, many of these anti-rationalist thinkers (Kierkegaard and Nietzsche, for instance) often have not themselves been altogether successful in avoiding some of the theoretical pitfalls of pure and simple irrationalism. Thus even though we will find welcome support in the history of counter-traditionalist thought, our task will not be an easy one, nor can it be assured of success at the outset.

This undertaking will be successful only if we manage to arrive at a viable theoretical alternative to rationalist theory. This means that our critique of rationalism itself must be eminently rational. Not only must we rationally discredit or "refute" rationalism, we must also set out a coherent theoretical alternative to it that is rational and convincing in its own right. Can one be a rational thinker and yet not a rationalist? The answer to this question remains to be determined. What readers will find in the pages that follow is a philosophical adventure with an uncertain outcome. We know what we want to do, but at this point we cannot know what our final position will be, nor can we assign it a proper name.[25]

Before embarking on this intellectual odyssey, a word of warning: it is likely that much of what I will say in my attempt to discredit rationalism will appear preposterous and absurd on first reading. When, for instance, I say that physical nature is an idea product of one particular mode of understanding (physical science) and for this reason cannot be used to explain all other modes of understanding and their idea products as well, readers may instinctively feel inclined to object that physical nature is, if anything, the producer of the understanding of it in us, not the product of it. It is, they might like to say, the concept or theory of it that is the product, not physical nature itself. Unfortunately, an objection such as this relies for its force on certain presuppositions as to the relation between reality and understanding that it is precisely the intent of this study to call into question and which it cannot therefore itself presuppose. Apparent difficulties in the text will thus often be due to the fact that what is said is unintelligible or unjustifiable in the light of the rationalist presuppositions with which we have all been imbued and which we all continue to hold to one degree or another (and which, moreover, it may be quite "natural" for us to hold). I accordingly request the readers' patience at times such as these when they feel inclined to reject my theses out of hand. As I develop my arguments and as readers continue to reflect on them, I hope that, through a cumulative effect, they will gain in persuasive power and that readers will eventually begin to question the validity of their inherited presuppositions. After all, is not philosophy just such a dialectical process of critical self-enlightenment?

NOTES

1. The following can serve as a typical example of the kind of views McLuhan has articulated:

> If the work of the city is the remaking or translating of man into a more suitable form than his nomadic ancestors achieved, then might not our current translation of our entire lives into the spiritual form of information seem to make of the entire globe, and of the human family, a single consciousness?

> Each mother tongue teaches its users a way of seeing and feeling the world, and of acting in the world, that is quite unique.

> Our new electric technology that extends our senses and nerves in a global embrace has large implications for the future of language. Electric technology does not need words any more than the digital computer needs numbers. Electricity points the way to an extension of the process of consciousness itself, on a world scale, and without any verbalization whatever. Such a state of collective awareness may have been the preverbal condition of men. Language as the technology of human extension, whose powers of division and separation we know so well, may have been the "Tower of Babel" by which men sought to scale the highest heavens. Today computers hold out the promise of a means of instant translation of any code or language into any other code or language. The computer, in short, promises by technology a Pentecostal condition of universal understanding and unity. The next logical step would seem to be, not to translate, but to by-pass language in favor of a general cosmic consciousness which might be very like the collective unconscious dreamt by Bergson. The condition of "weightlessness," that biologists say promises a physical immortality, may be paralleled by the condition of speechlessness that could confer a perpetuity of collective harmony and peace (*Understanding Media: The Extensions of Man* [New York, 1964] pp. 67, 83-84).

2. As, indeed, the ideas of democracy and equality are not without theirs. Tocqueville seems to have predicted our present technologically inspired consumer society in the early 1830s when he wrote:

> In democracies there is always a multitude of persons whose wants are above their means and who are very willing to take up with imperfect satisfaction rather than abandon the object of their desires altogether.

> The artisan readily understands these passions, for he himself partakes of them. In an aristocracy he would seek to sell his workmanship at a high price to the few; he now conceives that the more expeditious way of getting rich is to sell them at a low price to all. But there are only two ways of lowering the price of commodities. The first is to discover some better, shorter, and more ingenious method of producing them; the second is to maufacture a larger quantity of goods, nearly similar, but of less value. Among a democratic population all the intellectual faculties of the workman are directed to these two objects: he strives to invent methods that may enable him not only to work better, but more quickly and more cheaply; or if he cannot succeed in that, to diminish the intrinsic quality of the thing he makes, without rendering it wholly unfit for the use for which it is intended. When none but the wealthy had watches, they were

almost all very good ones; few are now made that are worth much, but everybody has one in his pocket. Thus the democratic principle not only tends to direct the human mind to the useful arts, but it induces the artisan to produce with great rapidity many imperfect commodities, and the consumer to content himself with these commodities (*Democracy in America* [New York, n.d.] vol. 2, bk. 1, chap. 10).

3. Ibid., vol. 2, bk. 2, chap. 17.

4. Benjamin Lee Whorf, *Language, Thought, and Reality* (Cambridge, Mass., 1972), p. 244.

5. Cf. Y. R. Chao, *Language and Symbolic Systems* (Cambridge, Mass., 1974), pp. 85, 150, 184; he says, for instance:

There are more and more recognized equivalences in journalistic, in sometimes barbarous styles, and this is one of the reasons why the news sections of current newspapers are easier to translate than the literary sections (p. 150).

Most projects for machine translation try for a start to limit themselves to the language of modern science and to some extent journalistic language, both of which, as we noted in connection with translation in general, belong to one international culture and have many fewer cases of multiple translational equivalencies (p. 184).

6. Ibid., p. 150.

7. Whorf, *Language, Thought, and Reality,* p. 214.

8. In his *Beyond Freedom and Dignity* (New York, 1971), the famous behavioral psychologist argues that "what we need is a technology of behavior" (p. 5). The answer to all social and cultural problems is to be looked for in a kind of social "engineering." The notion of human freedom or, as Skinner says, "autonomous man," "serves to explain only the things we are not yet able to explain in other ways. His existence depends upon our ignorance, and he naturally loses status as we come to know more about behavior." The task of a scientific analysis, he says, is to explain "the behavior of a person as a physical system" (p. 14). "Man is a machine in the sense that he is a complex system behaving in lawful ways, but the complexity is extraordinary" (p. 202). The traditional notions of freedom and dignity are archaic notions with which science can dispense. "What, after all, have we to show for nonscientific or prescientific good judgment, or common sense, or the insights gained through personal experience? It is science or nothing" (p. 160).

9. As one scientist from an underdeveloped country declared at a scientific congress:

"I come from an underdeveloped country, Venezuela, and we are shocked by the reaction against science. But we note that this reaction is restricted to a small corner of the world (the United States, and Europe, seen as a small peninsula of Asia!) and that, in fact 90 percent of the world's people still passionately desire science and a share in it as a source of human happiness; we even wish for pollution, as a sure sign of prosperity" (*Civilization and Science* [Amsterdam, 1973], p. 18).

10. H. de Varine defends this thesis in his book, *La Culture des autres* (Paris, 1975).

11. This awareness is not yet sufficiently great nor has it produced many truly significant results—witness the continuing reckless proliferation of nuclear reactors (which pose the greatest long-term threat to human and other life on this earth ever known) abetted by governments whose only concern is with "economic growth" and who do not care to understand how to cope with the dangers caused by radioactive wastes.

12. Under the spell of our technological civilization, leaders of the Third World countries have sought to set up capital-intensive, automated, large-scale industries. These industries provide jobs for a handful of people only and, in addition, demand a technical competence beyond that of the mass of the countries' inhabitants. The result is neglect of agricultural production (or concentration on large-scale production of cash crops for export, such that the country can no longer feed itself and must spend its hard-won foreign currency reserves or credit on imported food), the swelling of the cities with masses of displaced, unemployable

peasants, social anarchy and exploitation, crime, and spiritual alienation. No amount of foreign capital or technological expertise is capable of remedying this situation.

13. John Beattie, *Other Cultures* (New York, 1968), p. 274.

14. Ibid., p. 244.

15. Margaret Mead, ed., *Cultural Patterns and Technical Change* (New York, 1955), pp. 298-99.

16. This is the hope of the contributors to ibid.:

> It is realized that the technologies and inventions of modern science are themselves the outgrowth of a very particular historically limited type of culture—a culture in which the focus of interest has been upon the observable, the repeatable, the measurable. . . . An alien technology, supported by forms of education and inter-personal relations which are also alien, is likely to separate the practitioner of the new skill from his cultural roots. . . . Western-trained professionals carry about with them an enormous amount of cultural baggage which could very well be discarded. . . . Extraneous and culturally destructive effects can be avoided by stripping each scientific technique to the bone, to the absolute essentials which will make it possible for other people to learn to use it, and to handle it in a living, participating, creative way (ibid., pp. 293-94).

17. Jacques Ellul, *The Technological Society* (New York, n.d.), pp. 428-29.

18. Ibid., p. 431.

19. See C. P. Snow, *The Two Cultures: and a Second Look* (Cambridge, Mass., 1969).

20. I am thus in total disagreement with Snow's own analysis and recommendations in regard to the problem of the Two Cultures. Snow deplores the polarization between science and the "humanities" only because he sees in it a drain on our energies, which hinders us from tackling the major problem in the world as he sees it: eliminating the gap between the rich and the poor countries. What Snow failed to see was that an all-out, immediate industrialization of the Third World would mean the complete destruction of the distinctive cultures of these countries. It would mean the imposition on them of our own scientific-technological culture and would not leave them time to come to terms with science and technology in their own way and in terms of their traditional cultural values. Were we to follow Snow's advice and set aside the conflict between science and the humanities in order better to implement what he calls the "scientific revolution" (industrialization on a world scale), we would not have resolved the conflict and would not have discerned the proper place of science and technology within our culture as a whole but would simply have exported our problem to the rest of the world. We would, in fact, have forced the technological crisis on less-developed countries—where the people are even less in a position to confront the problem of the proper place of science and technology within life as a whole than we are (not having themselves experienced and grappled with the full cultural consequences of scientific-technological imperialism).

21. As Tocqueville accurately observed: "In the present age the human mind must be coerced into theoretical studies; it runs on its own accord to practical applications; and, instead of perpetually referring it to the minute examination of secondary effects, it is well to divert it from them sometimes, in order to raise it up to the contemplation of primary causes" (*Democracy in America,* vol. 2, bk. 1, chap. 10).

22. The definition of rationalism, for Vuillemin, is that it conceives of reason as the faculty for transcending experience by means of ideas. (Defined thus, it is obvious that modern science is in its own way as rationalist as classical, philosophical rationalism.) To conceive of reason thus is, according to Vuillemin, to recognize five characteristics of rationality:

> 1) There is a supra-sensible reality, separate from the sensible, constitutive of the supreme and immutable Reason.
>
> 2) This reality is the raison d'être is all reality. If the first rationalists conceived of it as excluding all multiplicity, by denying movement with Zeno and possibility with Diodorus, it becomes, from Plato on, the explanatory principle of all that is real in the phenomena themselves.

3) The intelligible principle guarantees the world its unity that reason grasps behind the veil of appearance and multiplicity. To rationally explain phenomena is thus to reduce them to a supra-sensible systematic unity, which alone is capable of unconditionally determining the totality of their conditions.

4) As soon as the rational principle no longer excludes diversity, it confers upon the universe a linear order of reality and perfection. Since any particular reality owes its being solely to this separated and pure principle, in which it participates as much as it is able, the ground of any imperfect reality can be found only in the perfection of the corresponding genus and, indirectly, in God. This principle of perfection has two consequences. It subordinates the science of phenomena to theology. It assigns to all derived realities a degree of perfection which is the measure of its perfection in the chain of beings.

5) As the *ratio essendi* of all reality the rational principle is also the *ratio cognoscendi*. In spite of its finitude, human reason possesses an innate virtue of being enlightened by the natural light; it thereby has access to truth and is able to unite, to the degree that it can, with the universal reason of which it is the image ("La raison au regard de l'instauration et du développement scientifiques," in Th. Geraets, ed., *Rationality To-Day/La rationalité aujourd'hui* [Ottawa: Editions de l'Université d'Ottawa, 1979], p. 68).

Also included in this volume is a short paper I wrote, "Pour une dérationalisation de la raison," which sets out in a succinct way much of the argument of the present work.

23. What we are here referring to as "rationalism," Heidegger designates with the term "metaphysics," and he says: "philosophy is metaphysics"; "metaphysics . . . is the legitimate completion of philosophy. . . . The end of philosophy proves to be the triumph of the manipulable arrangement of a scientific-technological world and of the social order proper to this world. The end of philosophy means: the beginning of the world civilization based upon Western European thinking" ("The End of Philosophy and the Task of Thinking," in *On Time and Being* [New York, 1972], pp. 55-59). William Barrett makes a similar point in a recent book on technique: "The whole of technology, as we know it, is the late, and maybe the final offspring of philosophy. There is not the least exaggeration in this judgment. It merely reports the simple historical course of things" (*The Illusion of Technique* [Garden City, N.Y., 1979], p. 26).

24. This is one of the main reasons why throughout this book I make numerous allusions to the work of other authors. These references are not for the sake of mere erudition but are intended to demonstrate that, contrary to possible first impressions, my position is not idosyncratic but is akin to or shares common elements with the thought of many other authors in the Western tradition and that, indeed, there is something like a counter-tradition of anti-rationalist thought running throughout the whole of this tradition.

25. What is perhaps the best name available from the history of philosophy for the position I will be defending is not a positive designation but a negative one. This name is *non-dogmatism*. Even though it is negative, it is nevertheless specific in that it is exclusive. In addition to excluding rationalism, it also excludes irrationalism. It is thus a better term than *anti-rationalism*, for an anti-rationalist position may be either rationally argued for (non-dogmatically) or irrationally (dogmatically) asserted. The true non-dogmatist asserts neither, with the rationalist, that "the Truth exists" nor that "reality has a well-defined meaning" nor, with the irrationalist (and relativist), that "there is no truth" or that "reality is meaningless." Non-dogmatism avoids—in principle, at least—the either-or (a term I shall be making much of in this study) of rationalism (absolutism) and irrationalism (relativism).

1 THE NOTION OF AN IDEAL LANGUAGE

Let us begin by boldly asserting a thesis in violation of all apparent scientific rationality: the understanding of the world characteristic of another culture cannot be adequately expressed in the language of Western science, for science is but one way of analyzing and understanding reality and for this very reason cannot legitimately claim to be universal. It is no more possible to translate without substantial loss of meaning the truths of various cultures into those of science than it is to translate fully one language into another. As Merleau-Ponty rightly remarked:

> The *full* meaning of a language is never translatable into another. We may speak several languages, but one of them always remains the one in which we live. In order completely to assimilate a language, it would be necessary to make the world which it expresses one's own, and one never does belong to two worlds at once.[1]

In what sense is perfect translation impossible? What does it mean to defend such a thesis? If we cannot fully translate foreign utterances into our own language, it would seem that we can never fully understand a foreign language or culture. Since our language will always be something of an obstacle to seeing exactly what is meant by a foreign utterance, the only way to apprehend precisely the meaning-intention of such an utterance would be to view it in terms not of our language but in its own linguistic and cultural context. Moreover, the impossibility of perfect translation would rule out as well the possibility of unambiguous communication between two languages or cultures. Thus it would seem that if in the attempt to reject scientific-technological imperialism one rejects the notion of perfect translation, one is forced into an even more undesirable position, into a kind of cultural and linguistic isolationism. In place of the universal community of mankind, which science claims to make possible and which was dreamed of by Teilhard de Chardin, one is condemned to an insurmountable parochialism and is forever excluded from Marshall McLuhan's "global village." Understanding and communication, it would seem, become impossible. One is apparently forced into a position of thoroughgoing *relativism,* not only in linguistic and cultural matters, but regarding the very notion of truth.

But it is not our intention to defend relativism. It could in fact be shown that relativism is logically contradictory. Like a dogmatic skepticism (for example, the skepticism of the Academy) which asserts that there are no truths but which, in asserting this, is actually asserting one truth and is thus contradicting itself, pure relativism is a logical impossibility. Is the relativist assertion that everything is relative itself a merely relative assertion? If it is absolutely true that everything is relative, then relativism is refuted and absolutism vindicated. If it is not absolutely true, absolutism is again justified. Moreover, logic aside, it is a fact that languages can be translated—they are every day in the United Nations—and that, through an interpreter, we can and do communicate with speakers of other languages (relativists have been known to give lectures with translation in foreign countries). Both the philosophical argument against relativism and the appeal to simple facts of experience regarding translation and communication are sufficient to refute the relativist thesis. Moreover, it is not only relatively easy to refute relativism, but one could make a good case for an opposing thesis: that any language qua language can and indeed must be translatable. That is, one could cogently argue for a definition of language according to which only those syntactical systems whose semantic value is capable of being taken up and reexpressed in a different syntax would count as meaningful language.

Support for such a view can be found in the thought of Charles Sanders Peirce, the founder of American pragmatism. He claims, on the one hand, that thought is essentially bound up with language[2] and, on the other, that the meaning of a proposition is another proposition.[3] That the meaning of a proposition is another proposition expresses his "triadic" conception of the symbolic function according to which a sign (term 1) not only refers to an object (term 2) but, in order to count as a sign at all, must in addition be related to a third term, which Peirce calls its "interpretant."[4] The interpretant of a given sign is simply *another sign,* which is capable of being substituted for the first sign in its relation to its object; it is thus a kind of commentary or gloss on the first sign. To the degree that a sign has any meaning, it must be possible to substitute another sign for it. If such a substitution is not possible, the sign in question actually has no meaning at all. What therefore accounts for a sign's truly being a sign—that is, having a meaning—is the fact that it can be interpreted by other signs. "Now the problem of what the 'meaning' of an intellectual concept is," Peirce says, "can only be solved by the study of the interpretants, or proper significate effects, of signs."[5] Thus the notion of an isolated sign (which is supposed to be meaningful), one without relation to other signs, is a nonsensical idea.

Not only, however, does a sign essentially refer to other signs that can serve to interpret it, but this process of interpretation is, for Peirce, an endless one. That there can be no final sign, no basic, unchanging meaning, necessarily follows from Peirce's general notion of a sign, for if, in regard to any given sign, the possibility of its having meaning lies in its being able to be interpreted by a second sign, then it is the same for the second sign; it too must be able to be taken up by a third sign, and the third by a fourth, and so on, as Peirce says, ad infinitum.[6] Thus, for Peirce, the possibility and indeed the necessity of our being able to translate or interpret any sign (concept) means also that there is and can be no final or perfect translation.

Peirce does in fact speak of a final or ultimate interpretant. But far from introducing a contradictory element into his theory of interpretation, the notion of a "final logical interpretant" rounds it out and gives it greater plausibility. When Peirce says that the process of interpretation or translation is infinite, he means that it is potentially infinite; no given interpretant can ever be "final" in the sense of not being likely to further reinterpretation. In this sense, the meaning of a sign is something "altogether virtual."[7] To say merely this is not enough, however. For, of itself, it would mean that at no given time does one ever possess the meaning of a sign; meaning would be something we never actually arrive at, and there would be an everlasting and unbridgeable gap between language and what it is about: reality. Thus Peirce requires something which, here and now, at any given moment, will assure something like a complete meaningfulness of signs even though this meaning will not be perfect in that it will not be immune to further change. He calls this "the living definition, the veritable and final logical interpretant," and he identifies it with habit: "Consequently, the most perfect account of a concept that words can convey will consist in a description of the habit which that concept is calculated to produce."[8] We will exploit this notion later in chapter 5 when we analyze understanding in terms of habit, so it is advisable that we take careful note of what Peirce is saying here. He defines habit in the following way, which has the merit of linking habit with *belief:* "Readiness to act in a certain way under given circumstances and when actuated by a given motive is a habit; and a deliberate, or self-controlled, habit is precisely a belief."[9] Since habits are nothing other than dispositions to act in a certain way and since beliefs are habits, it must be said that the "real meaning" of a sign or concept or proposition is nothing other than the kind of action to which it tends to give rise: "different beliefs are distinguished by the different modes of action to which they give rise."[10] Peirce also says, "The whole function of thought is to produce habits of action. . . . Thus, we come down to what is tangible and conceivably practical, as the root of every real distinction of thought, no matter how subtle it may be; and there is no distinction of meaning so fine as to consist in anything but a possible difference of practice."[11] It will be useful to keep this remark also firmly in mind, for in the rest of this book we shall be inquiring into many "subtle," highly theoretical, and complex issues—such as, in this chapter, the problem of an ideal language—but we should not lose sight of the fact that the ultimate import of these theoretical analyses is practical. Our entire criticism of rationalism and the conceptual imperialism of science and logic is motivated by the desire to defend a certain mode of human *praxis* that would be free from dogmatic intolerance.

Peirce's ideas on language, his "semiotic," as he called it, and, in particular, his notion of the interpretant seem to suggest that there is indeed a way of steering safely between the conflicting claims of relativism on the one side and absolutism or rationalism on the other. Perhaps it is possible after all to reject the notion of perfect translation and the concomitant notion that there is at bottom one proper way of understanding things and expressing their meaning—and indeed the notion that things or reality have a definable, self-same nature—without falling into the absurdities of relativism that would deny the possibility of translation altogether. If, like Peirce, we were to take a concrete, matter-of-fact, pragmatic view of things, we would have to say something like this: To say that an utterance has meaning amounts to saying that it can be re-expressed in a different way in a different language; if, faced with an utterance, we cannot say of it, "What that means is this," then, practically speaking, it does not make any sense to say that it means anything at all (for nothing is meaningful "in itself"; meaning is always meaning-for-someone). But if this is the case, it necessarily follows that what a culture means is itself a matter of interpretation; that is, one must reject the notion that meaning is something determinate to which, in principle, an ideal mode of expression corresponds. If we are to form a proper theory of human understanding, it is necessary to reject the notion of an ideal language.

The notion of an ideal language, a *lingua universalis,* is that prejudice which allows for something like a scientific imperialism—the reduction of other cultures to our own and the reduction of nonscientific aspects of our own culture to solely scientific categories. The problem of translation, of understanding and dealing with other cultures, as well as the problem of the Two Cultures (the problem of the relation between science and the humanities) is highly concrete and urgent. It has, however, a strictly theoretical aspect to it, for what is ultimately at issue is the proper theoretical way in which to view language, understanding (truth), and reality. And if the problem is to be satisfactorily dealt with on a theoretical level, it is necessary to find an alternative to the traditional theoretical interpretation of these matters.

The traditional view—which we shall henceforth refer to as the rationalist view—runs somewhat as follows. Language is essentially nothing more than a vehicle for expressing and transmitting a thought, which exists independently of language; thought is but a copy or representation of an independent reality. The truth-value of language is thus determined by its conformity or correspondence to thought, whose truth-value is itself determined by its conformity to reality. Reality is the ultimate criterion; it is determined by nothing outside of itself but simply is what it is (this is its formal definition), something fully determinate in itself. This view of things is found in Aristotle at the beginning of our intellectual tradition when he says that words are symbols for mental experiences. While languages vary among men, he says, the mental experiences they symbolize are the same; these latter, moreover, are images of things, which things are also the same for all.[12] In this traditional conception there are three terms:

reality (essence)$\longleftrightarrow$ thought (concept)$\longleftrightarrow$language (word).

When we move from the left to the right in this formula, we are dealing with the *order of determination* (it is reality that determines our knowledge in the sense that it is the "objective criterion" or measure for the correctness of knowledge, and it is knowledge that determines what we say, in the sense that the function of language is to conform faithfully to and "express" thoughts that are determinate and meaningful before being expressed in language). When we move from the right to the left, we have to deal with the *order of reference* (language refers to thought and thought refers to, is "about," or is directed toward reality). Corresponding to the first term is that branch of philosophy called *metaphysics,* to the second *epistemology,* to the third *logic.*

Given the formula and the traditional understanding of it as expressing the order of determination and that of reference, the metaphysics, epistemology, and logic of a given philosopher will all tend to be strictly interrelated. A certain kind of metaphysics will evoke a certain kind of epistemology and logic; a certain type of logic will call for a certain kind of metaphysics and epistemology, and so on, such that one can only artificially isolate one branch of philosophy from another. Traditionally, however, philosophers have sought to confer an aura of systematicity and necessity on their views and accordingly have singled out one branch of philosophy and have taken this to constitute a "first philosophy." The philosopher then attempts to show how all truths derive necessarily and rigorously from a certain basic starting point. This deduction is called a "demonstration." However, if metaphysics, epistemology, and logic all mutually imply one another, it would seem that there is no intrinsic reason why any branch of philosophy should be first and that, moreover, the notion of a first philosophy is itself a typical philosophical prejudice reflecting the very view that needs to be called into question: that there is a basic way of speaking about things and a "correct" understanding of them and that reality itself possesses a determinate nature.

In the modern period, under the influence of Descartes, epistemology—critique of knowledge—was taken to be the basic philosophical discipline. A revolution in starting points occurred, however, toward the end of the nine-teenth century, as a consequence of which the priority shifted from epistemology to logic. Attention was now focused on language and sym-bolism, and philosophy began to replay all of its old, familiar tunes in a new key. The figure most responsible for this shift was perhaps the German logi-cian, Gottlob Frege. Frege's critique of psychologism and the emphasis he placed on logic had extremely widespread consequences, which can be traced in the thought of leading figures of the twentieth century—Husserl, Russell, Wittgenstein, and many others.

The turn to logic and its coming to occupy the place of first philosophy is an expression of the realization of recent philosophy that the question about knowledge, and its relation to reality, cannot be divorced from, and indeed must explicitly focus on, the question of language and its relation to reality. What philosophy now took as its central theme was expression, symboliza-tion, and meaning. And one of the major effects of Frege's work was to revive interest in Leibniz's ambitious dream of a universal language, a *char-acteristica* or *mathesis universalis*—the belief Leibniz held in the possibility of a kind of conceptual algebra (an *ars combinatoria*), which would permit one to derive in a mathematical way all possible truths from a basic concep-tual alphabet expressing the atoms of thought (and, correspondingly, of reality).

In a truly Leibnizian spirit we find the phenomenologist Husserl, for in-stance, defending at the beginning of the century the idea of a universal grammar. The function of such an a priori science would be to discover the basic essence of language as such, the fundamental articulations of language, its universal invariants, without which language would not be language and which are more or less adequately realized in the various natural languages we speak. Such a science would enable one to understand how different natural languages express "the" categorical proposition, "the" plural, "the" hypothetical premise, and so on.[13]

Similarly, the search for an ideal language dominated the work of positivist-oriented philosophers such as Russell and Wittgenstein in the earlier part of this century. The motivating factor here is a basic distrust of traditional metaphysics—a feature characteristic of the times and shared by Husserl as well—which is thought to be vague and misleading. Both Russell and Wittgenstein see the antidote to metaphysical vagaries as consisting in, as Russell says, "a logically perfect language."[14] Such a language would be precise and univocal and would serve as a criterion for determining what can and cannot be meaningfully said; it would show "how traditional philosophy and traditional solutions arise out of ignorance of the principles of Symbolism and out of misuse of language."[15]

The logical task in regard to language is, Russell says, twofold. Logic must determine "the conditions for SENSE rather than nonsense in combinations of symbols" and "the conditions for uniqueness of MEANING or REFERENCE."[16] "A logically perfect language," Russell continues, "has rules of syntax which prevent nonsense, and has single symbols which always have a definite and unique meaning." Russell does not maintain that such an ideal language is easily realized, but he does insist, much as Husserl did in regard to his universal grammar, that language is meaningful only to the degree that it does indeed approximate this ideal language. As is easily seen, the two central notions in these remarks of Russell are sense and meaning or reference. They are both Fregean concepts, and it will be worth our while to take a closer look at them, for we may find that although on the surface the sense-reference distinction seems to furnish a useful conceptual tool for understanding what is involved in the symbolic process, on closer inspection the distinction will prove to be of rather dubious value.

For Frege, the meaning (*Bedeutung*) of a sentence or name is its reference, while the sense (*Sinn*) is the way in which the object referred to is actually thought of. Thus, for example, the two expressions ("names") *the morning star* and *the evening star* have the same meaning (*Bedeutung*), for they both refer to the same object, the planet Venus. The two expressions do not, however, have the same sense (*Sinn*), for they refer to Venus in different ways; the object referred to is thought of differently. Now it is, Frege says, the sense or "thought" that is translated when we translate a sentence from one language into another. Frege further distinguishes the sense or thought of an utterance from its coloring (*Färbung*), which, he says, is not of cognitive value and which is lost in translation, while it is the meaning or reference of an utterance that allows us to determine its truth-value. A meaningful utterance is true if that which, by means of its sense, the utterance means or refers to actually does exist. It is by means of sense that we can mean or refer to things, and it is the things themselves that will determine whether the meaning is true or false.

In all of this there seems to be a major presupposition: that the essence of language is to have meaning in the sense of having reference. Russell expresses this quite nicely when he says that "the whole function of language is to have meaning" and "the essential business of language is to assert or deny facts."[17] Although such a view seems disarmingly self-evident, it is actually quite far from being self-justifying. Is it indeed the case that language merely "refers" to a reality, which is independent of it and which can determine the truth or falsity of what is said about it? Are facts simply there to be discovered, independent of language?

Be this as it may for the time being, it is interesting to note some of the consequences that follow once one assumes that the whole business of language is to refer to facts. Once again Russell states the matter perfectly: "In order that a certain sentence should assert a certain fact, there must, however the language be constructed, be something in common between the structure of the sentence and the structure of the fact."[18] This, Russell says, is the "most fundamental thesis" of Wittgenstein's theory of language and meaning. It is also a fundamental belief of his own, holding as he does that there is an isomorphic relation between the structure of an ideal language and the structure of reality.[19] "For my part," he says, "I believe that, partly by means of syntax, we can arrive at considerable knowledge concerning the structure of the world"[20] Let us see how Wittgenstein develops this presupposition of the sense-reference distinction.

The fundamental intuition, as one might say (rather improperly, no doubt, this "intuition" being more of a prejudice or *idée fixe*), behind Wittgenstein's *Tractatus Logico-Philosophicus* is that language is a picture of reality.[21] Wittgenstein does not merely mean that a sentence is *like* a picture in some way or other; he actually means that a sentence *is* a picture of reality, in the most literal sense imaginable. To say that a sentence is a picture of facts is not, for Wittgenstein, to have recourse to a metaphor but to state a literal fact, or rather to take a metaphor literally, in dead earnest. Now if, like a photographic picture, language *represents* reality—if, that is, the essential function of language is to *refer* to reality—there must, Wittgenstein says, be a one-to-one correspondence between the elements of the picture (language) and that which it "depicts" (reality). This is to say that reality can be nothing more than the totality of facts representable by language. Just as a sentence (for Wittgenstein) is built up out of discrete *names,* so reality must be composed of simple *objects,* which, like names, can enter into possible combinations. This is Wittgenstein's version of Russell's "logical atomism," and the important thing to note is that this conception of reality as being built up out of simple, discrete objects (as the totality of such objects) is but a consequence of his particular conception of language and symbolism. Wittgenstein's example furnishes a striking illustration of the interdependence of a given logic and a particular metaphysics alluded to above, especially in view of the fact that Wittgenstein was never able to furnish examples of names and objects (unlike Russell who simply identified his atoms with sense-data) and in fact admitted that the postulate of simple objects was a purely a priori move, a purely "logical necessity."[22] Wittgenstein must assume the conception of reality he does in order to enable propositions to have a definite sense, that is, in order to justify his logic: "The demand for simple things *is* the demand for definiteness of sense."[23]

Susanne Langer gives voice to the same methodological prejudice when she writes: "It has become apparent that a proposition fits a fact not only because it contains names for the things and actions involved in the fact, but also because it combines them in a pattern analogous, somehow, to the pattern in which the named objects are 'in fact' combined. *A proposition is a picture of a structure—the structure of a state of affairs.'*[24] What is so seductive about this rationalist view as to the relation between language and reality is that (if one chooses to believe it) it affords assurance that reality is knowable and in this way satisfies a profound craving in the human soul, the craving for the security that comes from knowledge. If one believes that language mirrors reality, then, since it is easier to study sentences than the facts they represent, a logical analysis of language will serve to reveal the truth about reality.

It could easily be shown how the notion of an "ideal language," with its consequent implications for understanding and reality, dominates the thought of a positivist like Rudolf Carnap and, with appropriate differences, that of a phenomenologist like Husserl, but perhaps enough has been said to enable us to criticize this view. Although thinkers like Frege and Russell claim to be doing pure logic and in this way seek to confer unquestionable authority on their views,[25] their logic (theory of symbolism, language) is inseparable from a certain metaphysics (theory of reality) and epistemology (theory of understanding) and thus can be neither more nor less sound than this metaphysics and epistemology. It could be said that this theory of language presupposes a theory of reality, but this would not be strictly correct, since the term *presuppose* itself presupposes a certain conception of things according to which there is one unique basis from which all truths logically derive (this basis being the object of a first philosophy), and this one cannot maintain if one rejects the ideal language theory and the related (epistemological and metaphysical) concepts belonging to this idea-complex. The great difficulty in forming a consistent philosophical alternative to rationalism is that the very language and terminology one is most inclined to use is itself "contaminated" by the rationalist assumptions one wishes to reject. This, though, is as one would expect it to be if it is indeed the case, as the critic of rationalism must maintain, that meanings are not ideal entities to which words merely refer but are, on the contrary, essentially bound up with words and their use. If the latter is true, then words, having their own history, also have their own built-in meaning, which we are not free to determine with impunity. The problem that the critic of rationalism faces is that although he is attempting to use language to dispel certain illusions, this language is the source of the very illusions he is seeking to dispel. It is easy for the critic to be led by words into apparent inconsistencies, and it is easy for the rationalist thereby to refute his critic who, like the ancient sophist, Cratylus, is reduced to silence or at least to a piecemeal, guerrilla-type warfare with the consequent inability to provide a general, well-worked-out theoretical alternative to rationalism.

The task we have set ourselves is thus not easy, and nothing guarantees our success. This philosophical contest cannot, however, be avoided if we want to reject decisively cultural reductionism and scientific imperialism, for this can be done only if the notion—in whatever guise it might take—of an ideal language—the notion, that is, that meaning is basically univocal, that words can have a precise, determinate, and ideally proper sense—is itself rejected. But if it is rejected, the logician's insistence on "uniqueness of reference" and the notion that the whole business of language is to refer to facts must be rejected as well, for it is part of the same idea-complex. Ultimately the conception of reality assumed by ideal language theories— that reality consists of determinate facts that merely get discovered, that get mirrored in knowledge and expressed in language—must be rejected. (A sophisticated rationalist might say, not that determinate facts exist in reality in the mode of actuality, such that knowing them would be a purely passive matter, but that they exist in reality only in the mode of potentiality, such that a certain amount of invention in the way of concepts is necessary if one is to succeed in "discovering" them.)

A theory of translation, as the literary critic, George Steiner, maintains and indeed shows, is inseparable from and in a sense contains an entire theory of language.[26] A theory of language, it might be added, is itself a theory of understanding. And a theory of understanding is already a theory of reality. We have begun our attack on rationalism on the ground of translation; we shall not have finished until we have succeeded in working out an alternate theory of reality.

In recent decades the various ideal language theories set forth at the beginning of the century have tended to drop out of style in the philosophical world (both in Anglo-Saxon philosophy and on the Continent) and their proponents have been in constant retreat from their earlier positions. Their views, while not having been decisively refuted, have nonetheless come in for increasing criticism. The American philosopher, Max Black, for instance, has spoken out against "the vain hope of finding the true philosophical grammar."[27] His criticism, however, merely consists in pointing out the insuperable "difficulties that beset any serious effort to construct a universal grammar,"[28] and he does not question the assertion that the business of language is to state facts. More significantly, the later Wittgenstein decisively rejected his earlier views on language. Not only did his views change, but his loss of confidence in attaining an "unassailable and definitive" truth was accompanied by an aversion to the making of any general philosophical claims. The later Wittgenstein wishes to draw our attention to the relativity of all our beliefs,[29] but he fails or refuses to undertake what might be called a philosophy of relativity. Unlike the early Wittgenstein, the later Wittgenstein does not propose a theory of language, of understanding, and reality. However, we need such a theory if we are to reject decisively the ideal language theory and not merely to follow in the wake of philosophical fads that skip from one current topic to another and in the process neither fully justify nor decisively discredit anything.

After Russell and the early Wittgenstein, the work of Gödel, Tarski, and others in mathematical logic in the 1930's would seem to have demonstrated decisively the impossibility of any actual language's ever achieving complete universality in the form of a total and closed system. Even this, however, is not enough to disqualify the notion of a universal language qua ideal. And it is precisely the mark of a sophisticated absolutism or rationalism—one could cite the philosophies of Peirce and Husserl as examples of such a position—that although it recognizes the de facto impossibility of any given language's ever achieving universal status and any cognitive system's ever becoming a *science* in the full sense of the word (a total, systematic knowledge of a fully determinate reality, of the "totality of facts"), it nonetheless maintains, on the one hand, that the notion of a universal language is valid as an ideal or infinite goal, as that which confers a (teleological) meaning on our intellectual endeavors, and, on the other hand, that reality is itself fully determinate even though the language that would correspond to this reality and that would itself be universal and fully systematic is beyond our reach.

Although particular ideal language theories, such as those of Husserl and Russell, tend to die "the death of a thousand qualifications," the notion of an ideal language, the ideal of science, is, one might say, a phoenix that arises ever anew from its own ashes and is ever reincarnated in different forms. We have, for instance, recently witnessed the resurgence of the notion of "universal grammar"—understood as "a system of conditions on grammars," as "a highly restrictive schema to which any human language must conform"—in the rationalist linguistics of Noam Chomsky.[30] As one adversary of Chomsky confesses, "To most professional linguists today the question is less *whether* there are 'formal and substantive universals of language', but precisely *what* they are, and to what extent the depths at which they lie will ever be accessible to either philosophic or neurophysiological investigation."[31] Not only has Chomsky managed to provoke a new vogue in linguistics, but his influence has been felt in philosophy as well. Logicians and rationalists once again believe that it is professionally respectable to advocate ideal language theories.[32] It is not enough, therefore, to point out and insist on the de facto difficulties in establishing an ideal language. A genuinely philosophical or theoretical "refutation" of the rationalist ideal can only be one that succeeds in somehow discrediting the ideal qua ideal. This can be done only by working out an alternate theory, not just of language but, more basically, of understanding and reality.

One factor that compels us to protest against cultural and linguistic reductionism and motivates us in our search for a general theory of language, understanding, and reality that could serve as an alternative to the traditional view—the view that words refer to ideas, which refer to things or, vice-versa, that the truth-value of concepts is determined by their conformity to reality and that of language by its conformity to ideas, the view which lies behind the various ideal language theories but is also fairly well that of "common sense"—is our own human experience of the uniqueness of cultures and the impossibility of exactly reproducing the meaning-intention of one language in another language. This experience—well described by Steiner[33]—generally is common to those who have lived in another culture and have sought to understand reality by thinking in a foreign language that they have mastered (to the degree, of course, that it is possible for anyone to master fully a language not his own native one). Such a person will find it exceedingly difficult if not next to impossible to express fully the "foreign" in terms of the "native." Or again, on a purely intracultural level, a similar experience is had by those who, though they have committed themselves to the scientific view of things, nonetheless continue to experience a very deep appreciation for the view of life and reality afforded by religious or artistic expression; such people often experience a serious dilemma in reconciling their two approaches to reality.

It is one thing, however, to undergo an experience; it is another to give an account of it and to determine philosophically its significance. This is our task: we must discover reasons for rejecting the rationalist view of things. We are in need of an alternate theory, for a given theory can be refuted only by means of another theory. The theories of linguist Benjamin Lee Whorf may provide us with an initial impetus from which we may proceed to evolve a general philosophy of cultural and linguistic relativity—a philosophy that, like all consistent philosophies, will be universal but not rationalist.

Together with his teacher, Edward Sapir, Whorf formulated what has come to be known as the Sapir-Whorf hypothesis of linguistic relativity: that different languages embody different logics and that, accordingly, different languages express different understandings of reality. "Every language is a vast pattern-system, different from others, in which are culturally ordained the forms and categories by which the personality not only communicates, but also analyzes nature, notices or neglects types of relationship and phenomena, channels his reasoning, and builds the house of his consciousness."[34] What one calls "reality" is therefore relative to one's particular linguistic understanding or perception of it. In more detail, Whorf's "hypothesis" is that

the background linguistic system (in other words, the grammar) of each language is not merely a reproducing instrument for voicing ideas but rather is itself the shaper of ideas, the program and guide for the individuals's mental activity, for his analysis of impressions, for his synthesis of his mental stock in trade. Formulation of ideas is not an independent process, strictly rational in the old sense, but is part of a particular grammar, and differs, from slightly to greatly between different languages. We dissect nature along lines laid down by our native languages. The categories and types that we isolate from the world of phenomena we do not find there because they stare every observer in the face; on the contrary, the world is presented in a kaleidoscopic flux of impressions which has to be organized by our minds. We cut nature up, organize it into concepts, and ascribe significances as we do, largely because we are parties to an agreement to organize it in this way—an agreement that holds throughout our speech community and is codified in the patterns of our language. The agreement is, of course, an implicit and unstated one, BUT ITS TERMS ARE ABSOLUTELY OBLIGATORY; we cannot talk at all except by subscribing to the organization and classification of data which the agreement decrees.[35]

Whorf is expressing many of his basic ideas here; his overall position could perhaps be reconstructed in the following way. Understanding or thinking, he maintains, is a matter of perceiving or discerning relationships.[36] Unlike sensation, feeling, or intuition, thinking is essentially bound up with language.[37] The basic grammar or logic of our language dissects nature in a particular way; it therefore influences the way in which we think or understand reality. Language thus conceals or contains within itself an implicit metaphysics or view of reality (reflected in its logic or grammar). Philosophy (and science) is mainly a matter of making explicit this implicit and covert metaphysics, which is one with the language itself (and which is not, therefore, a matter of conscious awareness).[38] Different languages have, to a greater or lesser degree depending on their family memberships, different "logics" or "grammars."[39] From all of this follows the principle of linguistic relativity according to which "thinking" and "reality" refer not to intrinsically invariant entities but vary from culture to culture, from language to language. Thinking

follows a network of tracks laid down in the given language, an organization which may concentrate systematically upon certain phases of reality, certain aspects of intelligence, and may systematically discard others featured by other languages. The individual is utterly unaware of this organization and is constrained completely within its unbreakable bonds.[40]

In this view, it becomes impossible to speak of understanding or reality in any univocal and invariant sense.

Whorf's views furnish the means for formulating an at least prima facie plausible argument against the ideal language theories and the notion of perfect translation. For if it should indeed be the case that we tend to think according to what Whorf calls "a system of natural logic" and if, as he claims, this logic is, though seemingly self-evident, actually quite arbitrary, then the attempt to discover "an ideally perfect language," as Russell would say, or the underlying logic of language and thought corresponding to a basic structure of reality, would obviously prove to be radically misguided. The natural logic Whorf speaks of is that shared by the philosopher and the common user of language alike; it is the spontaneous but mistaken belief that language is only a means for expressing a thought that follows its own universally necessary laws, laws that are the same for all humanity and that are those of reality itself. Whorf writes:

> Natural logic says that talking is merely an incidental process concerned strictly with communication, not with formulation of ideas. Talking, or the use of language, is supposed only to "express" what is essentially already formulated nonlinguistically. Formulation is an independent process, called thought or thinking, and is supposed to be largely indifferent to the nature of particular languages. Languages have grammars, which are assumed to be merely norms of conventional and social correctness, but the use of language is supposed to be guided not so much by them as by correct, rational, or intelligent THINKING.
>   Thought, in this view, does not depend on grammar but on laws of logic or reason which are supposed to be the same for all observers of the universe—to represent a rationale in the universe that can be "found" independently by all intelligent observers, whether they speak Chinese or Choctaw. In our own culture, the formulations of mathematics and of formal logic have acquired the reputation of dealing with this order of things: i.e., with the realm and laws of pure thought. Natural logic holds that different languages are essentially parallel methods for expressing this one-and-the-same rationale of thought and, hence, differ really in but minor ways which seem important only because they are seen at close range. It holds that mathematics, symbolic logic, philosophy, and so on are systems contrasted with language which deal directly with this realm of thought, not that they are themselves specialized extensions of language.[41]

When Whorf speaks of the common-sensical distinction between grammar (which ensures "conventional and social correctness") and thinking or logic (which is "supposed to be the same for all observers of the universe"), one is reminded of the distinction made by Russell and Wittgenstein among others (Peirce had already formulated such a distinction[42]) between the grammatical form of a sentence and its logical form, and one is led to wonder if the "logical form of propositions" that Wittgenstein sought to lay bare is not perhaps but the one-sided thematization of the grammar of certain Western languages.

Also, if Whorf is correct in maintaining that language dissects reality in a particular way and that different languages do so differently, it would then follow that what the speakers of one language call a "fact" need not necessarily be a fact for the speakers of another language. This, however, would have a most important philosophical consequence: it would no longer be possible to maintain a clear-cut distinction between sense and reference. This distinction is valid only if there does exist a reality that is determinate in itself independently of language, such that the whole business of language is simply to refer to it. If, however, it is impossible to separate language and reality, if, that is, facts are relative to language, it cannot be maintained legitimately that the essential business of language is to state or refer to facts existing independently of it. One would then be forced to recognize that not only sense but reference as well is an essentially linguistic matter and that the sense-reference distinction is not absolute but merely relative, relative to particular languages. Whorf himself noted this consequence:

> That part of meaning which is in words, and which we may call "reference," is only relatively fixed. Reference of words is at the mercy of the sentences and grammatical patterns in which they occur. And it is surprising to what a minimal amount this element of reference may be reduced. . . . The context or sentence pattern determines what sort of object any word, in any language refers to. . . . reference is the lesser part of meaning, patternment the greater.[43]

Whorf gives as an example the Polish word for *tree*. Since this word also includes the significance "wood," only the context or sentence pattern can determine its "reference." There is therefore an essential dependence of "reference" on "sense."

Let us consider another example, this one borrowed from the famous Swiss linguist, Ferdinand de Saussure,[44] but used for our own purposes. Does the French word *mouton* have either the same reference or sense as the English word *mutton?* Historically or diachronically speaking, the English word is the "same" as the French, with only a difference in spelling. And yet the English word has neither the same significance nor exactly the same reference as the French word. The reason is that whereas in French there is only one word for designating the animal in question, in English there are two, *sheep* and *mutton*, the first meaning the animal on the hoof, the second the animal when served up for dinner. The English word *mutton* therefore does not refer to what the French word refers to, or, rather, it may (since *mouton* may mean the animal qua food), but the reference is a function of the sense, and the sense is determined diacritically by the constellation of other words in which it exists. This is of importance when it comes to translation, for if from language to language words do not have the same reference, it will be impossible to find an exact substitute for them. This is apparent in the case of the single English word *snow* and the many Eskimo words meaning what we for lack of equivalents are forced to call simply *snow*. *Snow* does not refer to what any of the Eskimo words refer to, and no strict translation that will capture the sense and reference of any one of the Eskimo words is possible in English; one can only give an approximate paraphrase in a case like this.[45]

This means that one does not simply see things that were already there, staring one in the face, waiting to be seen and described. Rather what one sees—the things themselves—is the result of interpreting one's immediate experience by means of a cultural-linguistic schema, and thus if one defines nature as the totality of what-is, *nature is relative to culture.* The facts that the words of a language refer to are the facts they are only because the words have the sense they do, and the sense they have is itself a function of the structure of that language.

This is especially obvious in the case of multivocal or polysemantic words, words with a multitude of possible "meanings." Such words, which are intrinsically ambiguous, constitute a veritable nightmare for the proponent of an ideal language, for in their case the sense-reference distinction breaks down altogether and the ideal of univocity is completely destroyed. An ideal language would actually require the elimination of all such words, for, as Russell says, "The first requisite of an ideal language would be that there should be one name for every simple, and never the same name for two different simples."[46] The sense-reference distinction is one with the distinction between name and fact (simple), but such a distinction (language-reality) cannot be maintained in the case of real languages. The world appropriate to an ideal language would not be an "ideal" world but, as Whorf points out, a "slave world of literal reference and humdrum prosaic details." The ambiguity and relativity of real language, far from being a defect to be overcome, is precisely that which allows for widening "the petty narrowness of the personal self's outlook."[47] Even science, when it is creative, is dependent upon the multivocal reality of words and operates with metaphor, so that even in the case of scientific understanding the sense-reference distinction is inappropriate and misleading; it is a conceptual tool of no real use when one wishes to analyze correctly the way in which understanding actually does function.

To discredit in this way the sense-reference distinction is to provide reasons for maintaining that perfect translation is impossible and that there can be no ideal language capable of expressing the "truth" in an unambiguous and univocal way. Just as the logical distinction between sense and reference conceals a certain metaphysics, so also does the notion of an ideal language. This is a metaphysics postulating that reality is itself of a fixed nature, is composed of distinct facts that are the same for all humanity (although certain people or cultures, "primitive" ones in particular, may not recognize the facts for what they are). Such a metaphysics may satisfy a basic psychological need for fixity and security (law and order), but it should not be accepted uncritically, and the argument against perfect translation has provided us with reasons for rejecting this metaphysics.

Only when we construct artificial languages and, in determining artifi-

cially the sense of words also lay down what they are to refer to, thereby dissecting reality in a particular way, is perfect translation possible. Then it is indeed the case that, as Wittgenstein says, "Definitions are rules for translating from one language into another."[48] In this case there is a one-to-one correspondence between the terms of the two languages, and correspondences of this sort are what get tabulated in two-language dictionaries. Once such languages are constructed and an interlanguage dictionary worked out, translation poses no problems at all; it becomes purely automatic and can be handled by a computer or a translating machine. The logic of human understanding is reduced in this case to something mechanical and uncreative; here the *calculus ratiocinator* becomes a veritable *machina rationatrix.* As Norbert Wiener, the father of cybernetics, perspicaciously remarked, "It is not in the least surprising that the same intellectual impulse which has led to the development of mathematical logic has at the same time led to the ideal or actual mechanization of processes of thought."[49] This is a highly noteworthy remark, since it confirms what we have been insisting on all along: the intimate and essential link between the scientific approach to reality and the increasing technologization and dehumanization of our culture.

When we return from the logical realm of artificial languages to the real world of cultural and linguistic pluralism, however, we find that translation is always only partial, is no more than a more or less appropriate paraphrase, and that what is expressed in one language or culture is never fully expressible in another. The English anthropologist, E. E. Evans-Pritchard, insists that "to understand a people's thought one has to think in their symbols."[50] And on the difficulty of translation he writes:

> The semantic difficulties in translation . . . are considerable enough between, shall we say, French and English; but when some primitive language has to be rendered into our own tongue they are, and for obvious reasons, much more formidable. . . . If an ethnographer says that in the language of a Central African people the word *ango* means dog, he would be entirely correct, but he has only to a very limited degree thereby conveyed the meaning of *ango,* for what it means to natives who use the word is very different to what "dog" means to an Englishman. The significance dogs have for them—they hunt with them, they eat them, and so on—is not the significance they have for us. How much greater is the displacement likely to be when we come to terms which have a metaphysical reference!

> For someone who has not made an intensive study of native institutions, habits, and customs in the native's own milieu (that is, well away from administrative, missionary, and trading posts) at best there can emerge a sort of middle dialect in which it is possible to communicate about matters of common experience and interests.[51]

In short, one can appropriately understand the meaning of a language or culture only by entering into that langauge or culture, for reality—what that language or culture "refers" to—is inseparable from it. These remarks of Evans-Pritchard should be taken seriously, for they are based not on the theories of a logician (curiously enough, a great many logicians as well as Chomskian linguists are monolingual only) but on the actual experience of a working, multilingual anthropologist. It is almost as if Frege had Evans-Pritchard in mind when he wrote:

> Nowadays people seem inclined to exaggerate the scope of the statement that a word can never be exactly translated into another language. One might perhaps go ever further, and say that the same word is never taken in quite the same way by men who share a language.[52]

Frege, of course, rejects outright such a notion. His reasons for doing so are worthy of consideration.

> If all transformation of the expression were forbidden on the plea that this would alter the content as well, logic would simply be crippled; for the task of logic can hardly be performed without trying to recognize the thought in its manifold guises. Moreover, all definitions would then have to be rejected as false.

Frege is right, of course. If we reject perfect translation, logic is severely constrained and limited in its range of applicability, and we can no longer operate everywhere with univocal definitions. If logic is to have universal validity, it must be maintained that there is but one thought (sense) that is expressed in a multitude of ways ("guises") and that "for all the multiplicity of language, mankind has a common stock of thoughts."[53] In addition it must be maintained that the function of language is to communicate what Frege, like others, calls "information." And if this is the case, one must be able to extract the information contained in one sentence and re-express it without loss in another sentence. All that would get lost in this process is the way the information, the sense or thought, is conveyed—what Frege calls the "coloring" of the thought. Coloring is, however, from a logical point of view, of merely "emotional" or "psychological" importance and therefore is irrelevant to the sense (which is something purely "logical").

Such indeed must be the case if logic is to have full sway. But just what does all of this prove? To say that the requirements for a logically perfect language are of such and such a sort does not, of itself, tell us anything about real language and how it functions. We can therefore agree with Frege that if perfect translation is impossible, this will impose a severe handicap on logic and will drastically reduce its usefulness as a tool for understanding reality. But then what this all really shows is only of how little use formal logic is when it comes to understanding reality.

The matter could be expressed differently by saying that the impossibility of perfectly translating natural languages does not make logic impossible any more than it prevents our inventing artificial, computer languages. But it does underline the artificiality of such languages and the limited validity of formal logic. Thus Frege's objection is actually an attempt to beg the question.

Actually Frege's objection is not so much logical as it is rhetorical.[54] Not only is he employing *petitio principii* as an eristic device, but he is also making use of a much more insidious sophistic debating trick. Frege's objection is a perfect example of the leading question, such as the classic, "Have you stopped beating your wife?" If we attempt to answer the question directly, we will be putting ourselves in an untenable position. That is, if we answer for instance, "Even though 'all transformation of the expression is forbidden,' still logic is not rendered completely impossible," we will be saddling ourselves with the thesis that translation is altogether impossible. But the logician can easily show that we are then speaking nonsense, for if meanings are not translatable at all, we can have no grounds for saying that there are any meanings to begin with. We will be placing ourselves in a kind of double bind, as when someone makes a great deal of effort to obey the doctor's order to relax. Frege's argumentative technique reflects very well the rationalist mentality in general, which operates with a vicious either-or. Either there is meaning, in which case it can be stated precisely and translated exactly, or there is no meaning at all. Either we accept the rationalist's assumptions, or we must commit ourselves to irrationalism. It is, however, this rigid either-or, this logical straightjacket, which we must refuse, just as we would have to refuse to answer the question, "Have you stopped beating your wife?" and would have to show instead why the question is utterly misleading.

It is necessary to discover a way of rejecting rationalism without falling into irrationalism and relativism or again, it is necessary to reject the notion that there is one reality and truth that is basically the same for all cultures without advocating a theory of complete equivocity.[55]

A number of unanswered questions still plague us. If perfect translation is not possible, how is it possible to understand another culture? Indeed does the word *understand* retain any meaning at all if perfect translation is not possible? Even though reasons have been found for rejecting the theses of rationalism, we have yet to spell out a viable alternative. We have, for instance, been led to say that to understand appropriately another culture, it is necessary actually to enter into it. And yet although the fact of linguistic relativity gives reasons for saying this, it would seem to lead into a kind of relativist cul-de-sac, for it would seem to follow that an anthropologist, for instance, must not only enter into the culture he describes but must also write his study of, say, Eskimo culture in Eskimo language. However, the result of this would be that we, in our culture, would never gain any understanding of the alien culture. A similar difficulty is suggested by Whorf's work. Whorf maintains that Hopi language conceals a metaphysics that is "properly describable only in the Hopi language."[56] And yet Whorf has managed to say—in English—a great deal about this metaphysics and in reading him we can, presumably, understand something about this world view and how it differs from our own. Is this not enough to indicate that there is something in common between the different cultures and which is being properly translated? Does this not indicate that, as Frege says, "for all the multiplicity of languages, mankind has a common stock of thought"?

Perhaps, though, the dilemma in which we find ourselves is of our own making. Perhaps, without suspecting it, we have let ourselves be caught up in a double bind after all. We are asking what it means to understand a foreign culture and how understanding is possible here, but have we questioned what we mean by understanding? Perhaps all of our difficulties stem from the fact that all along we have implicitly accepted as paradigmatic the traditional view of understanding, which we have nonetheless criticized, according to which to understand something is to form a picture or replica of it. This would indeed be enough to account for our dilemma, for understanding is surely an absolute impossibility if both of the following assertions are true: that understanding consists in the reduplication of an objective fact and that exact translation is impossible. In the case of translation, it has been argued that the transposition of a thought from one language to another is a matter of paraphrase and interpretation; one does not express the *same* identical thought—nor one totally different—but one that is somehow *like* the original, sufficiently like it to enable us to understand something of it. Perhaps, then, we can form a viable concept of understanding if the translation process itself is taken as a model.

Perhaps understanding is not a matter at all of reproducing a supposedly objective state of affairs ("reality") but is, rather, a matter of creative transformation, a matter of interpretation (of lived experience or statements about experience), of drawing likenesses and analogies. If this were the case, the fact that translation always involves a change and the emergence of a new thought that is not identical with but somehow like the original one would not be a hindrance or a limitation to understanding but rather the mark and proof of its limitless possibility. It would then have to be concluded that reality itself, that which is understood in a culture, far from being uncommunicable and meaningless, is infinitely interpretable and thus infinitely meaningful.

A rejection of the notion of a culturally invariant (univocal) truth and reality does not mean that we have to resign ourselves to a lesser and unfortunately imperfect degree of understanding. The ideal of univocity and scientific universality is not so much an ideal one should strive after as it is an illusion barring the road to any genuine understanding. The absolutism-relativism, univocity-equivocity distinction, like the sense-reference one, is a pseudo-distinction, a pernicious illusion of the understanding. To argue against absolutism almost invariably creates the impression that one accepts the ideal in principle and only maintains that it is never realizable in fact, whereas what the critic means is that the ideal itself is nonsensical. The critique of rationalism is almost universally misunderstood, for it is taken in terms of precisely that which it rejects.

This dilemma is of the same kind as that encountered by Husserl in his attempt to get others to understand the true import of phenomenology. Phenomenology almost invariably is taken to be a kind of denial of the "external" world; the phenomenological reduction brackets off the "real" world and leaves us with only our own "subjective" experiences—or so it is thought. In fact, of course, phenomenology is nothing of the sort, though the misunderstanding is inevitable, given Husserl's tactic, for he must start off from generally accepted beliefs: that there is a real world outside us, that consciousness is locked up inside of itself, and so forth. When he denies these beliefs, he is taken to be denying what these beliefs are beliefs in—an "external" world—whereas in fact he is not at all denying the world itself but merely attempting to form a better view of it (he is attempting to express better what might be called "our experience of the world"). The phenomenological reduction does not leave us with a lesser world; rather it reveals to us the real world—the world of our living experience, the world as we actually experience it, not a theoretical construct such as the external world—in all its plentitude, which formerly our natural beliefs prevented us from seeing. In phenomenology the real world is not denied; it is discovered for the first time. In suspending our beliefs, the phenomenological reduction frees our vision.

The natural objection at this point is to say that if what is being denied is not something real to begin with but only an illusion, why is this illusion so pervasive and deeply held? Surely an illusion as tenacious as this cannot be purely illusory. One might want to take as an example the Hindu thesis that the self is an illusion and does not really exist. It will be objected, with good reason, that if the self does not exist, it is exceedingly odd that it should be the source of so much difficulty when we try to get out of the belief that it does. How is it that something nonexistent and unreal can exert such a persuasive force? This logical objection may apply to Hindu thought, which postulates a kind of dogmatic monism (or non-duality), but it does not apply to the position being defended here. We are not saying that the belief in universality, in a culturally invariant reality, is unreal, only that it is wrong. It is in fact very real; it has been with philosophy since the very beginning and will no doubt continue on indefinitely. And if this is so, there must surely be good reasons for the belief. If it is an error, it must be a natural error. The illusion in question must be one that, to use Kant's words, is "inseparable from human reason, and which, even after its deceptiveness has been exposed, will not cease to play tricks with reason and continually entrap it into momentary aberrations ever and again calling for correction."[57] *Human understanding must be of such a sort that it invariably and naturally tends to misunderstand itself.*

This is not as preposterous as it might seem at first. The position that William James takes in his discussion of consciousness could serve as an illustration that will make more plausible our thesis concerning the natural tendency of understanding to misunderstand itself. In his major work, *The Principles of Psychology,* James maintains that the empiricist view of consciousness as consisting of stable, discrete, atomic units of sensation is false and that consciousness is instead a continuum and a "stream," a continuous flux.[58] If this is the case, though, how is it, James asks, that the empiricist error is so easily made and so widely held. The reason, he says, lies in the very nature of consciousness as he has described it. Consciousness is "intentional"; to have an idea is to have an idea-of-something. It is only natural, therefore, to want to describe consciousness in terms of that of which consciousness is conscious—things. Things, as we experience them, are relatively discrete and unchanging. "What wonder, then," James writes, "that the thought is most easily conceived under the law of the thing whose name it bears!"[59] As James observes, we are here misled by the nature of our language, and he suggests that different languages might be better guides for talking about consciousness,[60] although he does admit that "no existing language is capable of doing justice" to the multitude of possible relations between things, on the one hand, and thoughts about them, on the other.[61]

James's remarks are highly provocative. Were we to conceive of reality as a kind of "blooming, buzzing confusion," as he says, we could then say that for certain purposes it is useful to dissect this flowing reality in certain ways, and it is equally convenient to speak of thoughts as being structured in certain ways. It is useful, that is, to view reality as being composed of fixed, determinate entities and of thoughts as being equally fixed and determinate and, moreover, as being mirror images of the former. The important thing would be not to let ourselves be duped by our language. It seems, though, that philosophers—Locke and Hume, whom James criticizes for their insufficiently radical empiricism, could serve as examples—are prone to a special kind of ailment. Let us call it "inversion," the chronic tendency to always get things backward. We tend to perceive things as fixed and determinate entities, this is true. Therefore, so the rationalist argument goes, there must exist in reality fixed and determinate entities to be so perceived. We are, it is true, able to speak meaningfully. Therefore there must be fixed meanings to be spoken of. The list could be extended indefinitely. In all fairness, though, this is not an ailment peculiar to philosophers alone; it is shared by the man-in-the-street as well, just as is the "natural logic" Whorf speaks of. It is also the ailment that, in a more virulent form, afflicts behaviorists, cyberneticians of consciousness, and identity theorists who are led to say that humans are machines, that the mind is the brain, simply because people can be treated *as if* they were machines and language can be so distorted that all talk of mind can be arbitrarily reduced to brain talk.[62]

An adequate theory of human understanding will have to account for such misunderstandings. If the theory we intend to set out is to be successful, it will have to be able to account for the fact that it is not the generally and traditionally accepted theory and does not correspond to the "natural" view of things. That there is something fundamentally wrong with the traditional conceptions examined in this chapter would seem to be indicated by the fact that from Plato and his search for universal forms and "correct" names[63] to Russell and his quest for an ideal language, the advocates of these views usually cannot make good their claims to scientific precision and in fact very often proceed to add qualification upon qualification to them and, in effect, tone down their initial demands. If it were not for the fact that rationalists seem to take their professed beliefs seriously, one would be tempted to say of them, with Montaigne, "They do not want to openly express their ignorance and the imbecility of human reason, in order not to frighten children, but they reveal enough of it to us under the guise of a troubled and timorous science."[64]

That there is something fundamentally wrong here, something indeed perverse, is also indicated by the fact that this tradition constantly secretes a kind of "bad conscience" in the form of irrationalism. Irrationalism, it could be said, is the neurotic symptom that reveals the underlying disorder afflicting the mind and body of the rationalist tradition.[65]

If, however, it will be possible to formulate a theory of understanding that will account for why understanding invariably tends to misunderstand itself, it should be possible to counteract this misunderstanding so as to free ourselves from it. A genuine understanding of why we necessarily misunderstand understanding may be the means for liberation from the illusions of understanding.

NOTES

1. M. Merleau-Ponty, *Phenomenology of Perception* (London, 1962), p. 187.
2. C. S. Peirce, *Collected Papers* (Cambridge, Mass., 1931-1958). "All thought whatsoever

is a sign, and is mostly of the nature of language." (5:421). "The woof and warp of all thought and all research is symbols, and the life of thought and science is the life inherent in symbols; so that it is wrong to say that a good language is *important* to good thought; for it is of the essence of it" (2:220).

3. Cf. ibid., 5:427.

4. "A *Sign* or *Representamen,* is a First which stands in such a genuine triadic relation to a Second, called its *Object,* as to be capable of determining a Third, called its *Interpretant,* to assume the same triadic relation to its Object in which it stands itself to the same Object" (ibid., 2:274).

5. Ibid., 5:475.

6. Ibid., 2:303.

7. Ibid., 5:289.

8. Ibid., p. 491.

9. Ibid., p. 480.

10. Ibid., p. 398.

11. Ibid., p. 400.

12. Aristotle, *De Interpretatione* (New York, 1941), 1:16a3-8.

13. E. Husserl, *Logical Investigations* (London, 1970). See the Fourth Investigation.

14. B. Russell, Introduction to L. Wittgenstein, *Tractatus Logico-Philosophicus* (London, 1961), p. ix.

15. Ibid.

16. Ibid. (italics added).

17. Ibid.

18. Ibid.

19. Cf. B. Russell, *Logic and Knowledge,* "The Philosophy of Logical Atomism."

20. B. Russell, *An Inquiry into Meaning and Truth* (New York, 1940), p. 438.

21. Wittgenstein, *Tractatus Logico-Philosophicus,* 4.01.

22. L. Wittgenstein, *Notebooks 1914-1916* (Oxford, 1958), p. 60.

23. Ibid., p. 63.

24. S. Langer, *Philosophy in a New Key* (Cambridge, Mass., 1974), p. 68.

25. In the Preface to his *Tractatus,* Wittgenstein wrote, "The *truth* of the thoughts that are here set forth seems to me unassailable and definitive. I therefore believe myself to have found, on all essential points, the final solution of the problems."

26. G. Steiner, *After Babel* (New York, 1975), p. 279.

27. M. Black, "Language and Reality," in *Models and Metaphors* (Ithaca, N.Y., 1962), p. 16.

28. Ibid., p. 13.

29. See in particular Wittgenstein, *On Certainty* (New York, 1972).

30. See, for example, Noam Chomsky, *Language and Mind* (New York, 1972), p. 63. Chomsky expressly lays claim to "rationalism."

31. Steiner, *After Babel,* p. 105.

32. As an example, the Buffalo Logic Colloquium, in conjunction with the Philosophy Colloquium and the Linguistics Colloquium, announced that its meeting scheduled for April 30, 1975, would deal with the topic, "First Steps toward a Universal Language." The abstract of the proposed topic read as follows: "The quest for a 'universal base' underlying natural language lead *[sic]* linguists toward semantics and away from syntax. Thus we are lead *[sic]* to the notion of a formalization of the underlying thought of a discourse; and if we believe that the discourse reflects the thought and the thought reflects (however inadequately) the world we get into metaphysics which is a good place to be." Also typical of the new vogue is the title of a book that appeared in 1975: H. J. Robinson, *Renascent Rationalism* (New York: Macmillan, 1975).

33. Steiner, *After Babel,* pp. 115ff.

34. B. L. Whorf, *Language, Thought, and Reality* (Cambridge, Mass., 1972), p. 252.

35. Ibid., pp. 212-14; See also pp. 221, 240.

36. "The possibilities open to thinking are the possibilities of recognizing relationships and the discovery of techniques of operating with relationships on the mental or intellectual plane, such as will in turn lead to ever wider and more penetrating significant systems of relationships" (ibid., pp. 83-84).

37. Cf. ibid., p. 66. "These possibilities [of recognizing relationships] are inescapably bound up with systems of linguistic expression" (ibid., p. 84).

38. Cf. ibid., pp. 58, 81, 221. The well-known philosopher, Ernst Cassirer, was making much the same point when he wrote:

> All the concepts of theoretical knowledge constitute merely an upper stratum of logic which is founded upon a lower stratum, that of the logic of language. Before the intellectual work of conceiving and understanding of phenomena can set in, the work of *naming* must have preceded it, and have reached a certain point of elaboration. For it is this process which transforms the world of sense impression, which animals also possess, into a mental world, a world of ideas and meanings. All theoretical cognition takes its departure from a world already preformed by language; the scientist, the historian, even the philosopher, lives with his objects only as language presents them to him. This immediate dependence is harder to realize than anything that the mind creates mediately, by conscious thought processes. It is easy to see that logical theory, which traces concepts back to an act of generalizing "abstraction," is of little use here; for this "abstraction" consists of selecting from the wealth of *given* properties certain ones which are common to several sensory or intuitive experiences; but our problem is not the choice of properties already given, but the *positing* of the properties themselves. It is to comprehend and illuminate the nature and direction of *noticing,* which must precede mentally the function of "denoting" (*Language and Myth* [New York, n.d.], pp. 28-29).

39. "These automatic, involuntary patterns of language are not the same for all men but are specific for each language and constitute the formalized side of the language or its 'grammar'—a term that includes much more than the grammar we learned in the textbooks of our school days" (Whorf, *Language, Thought, and Reality,* p. 221).

40. Ibid., p. 256.

41. Ibid., pp. 207-8.

42. Peirce, *Collected Papers,* 5:399.

43. Whorf, *Language, Thought, and Reality,* pp. 259-61.

44. F. de Saussure, *Course in General Linguistics* (New York, 1959), pp. 115-16.

45. Cf. F. Boas, "On Grammatical Categories," in D. Hymes, *Language and Culture in Society* (New York, 1964).

46. Wittgenstein, *Tractatus,* p. x.

47. Whorf, *Language, Thought, and Reality,* p. 260.

48. Wittgenstein, *Tractatus,* 3:343.

49. N. Wiener, *Cybernetics* (Cambridge, Mass., 1961), p. 12.

50. E. E. Evans-Pritchard, *Social Anthropology and Other Essays* (New York, 1964), p. 79.

51. E. E. Evans-Pritchard, *Theories of Primitive Religion* (Oxford, 1971), pp. 12, 7.

52. G. Frege, *Translations from the Philosophical Writings of Gottlob Frege* (Oxford, 1970), p. 46n.

53. Ibid.

54. This is not meant as a criticism, for "rhetoric" is not meant here in its customarily pejorative sense. Since rhetoric is simply the art of persuasion, it is only natural that logicians should have recourse to it as much as anyone else when they wish to gain support for their logicist position. But that the logician who depends on rhetoric should turn around and reject rhetoric in favor of logic is grounds for criticism—of the logicist project. The very practice of the logician is enough to discredit the notion of a pure logic that he is rhetorically arguing for.

55. A further undesirable consequence of Frege's arbitrary distinction between sense and reference is that it sets up a rigid dichotomy between art and science. If we accept this (sense-reference) dichotomy we have to say that only science has truth-value, for poetic utterances, although they have a sense, are without reference (and according to Frege it is reference that allows for truth-value). "For poetic uses, it suffices that everything have a sense, for the scientific it is necessary that references are not lacking" (Frege to Husserl, May 24, 1891; "Frege-Husserl Correspondence," in *Southwestern Journal of Philosophy,* 5, no. 3 [Fall 1974]: these letters provide some of the clearest and most succinct of expositions of many of Frege's central concepts). We shall see in chapter 7, however, that science is not unlike art in the way in which it comes upon new "truths"; this also will serve to disqualify the sense-reference distinction.

56. Whorf, *Language, Thought, and Reality,* p. 58.

57. I. Kant, *Critique of Pure Reason* (London, 1963), A 298.

58. W. James, *The Principles of Psychology* (New York, 1950), vol. 1, chap. 9.

59. Ibid., 1:236.

60. Ibid.

61. Ibid.

62. See my article, "The Possibility and Limits of a Science of Man," *Philosophy Forum,* 14 (1976):351-66.

63. We shall consider Plato's rationalist views on language in chapter 6.

64. "Ils ne veulent pas faire profession expresse d'ignorance et de l'imbecilité de la raison humaine, pour ne faire peur aux enfans; mais ils nous la descouvrent assez soubs l'apparence d'une science trouble et inconstante." Michel de Montaigne, "Apologie de Raimond Sebond," in *Oeuvres complètes* (Paris, 1962), pp. 527-28.

65. Of irrationalism Heidegger has said: "Irrationalism is only the obvious weakness and failure of rationalism and hence itself a kind of rationalism. Irrationalism is a way out of rationalism, an escape which does not lead into the open but merely entangles us more in rationalism, because it gives rise to the opinion that we can overcome rationalism by merely saying no to it, whereas this only makes its machinations the more dangerous by hiding them from view" *(An Introduction to Metaphysics* [New Haven, Conn., 1959], p. 179).

2 | UNDERSTANDING ANOTHER CULTURE

Cultural imperialism and scientific-technological reductionism operate on the philosophical basis of a theory of understanding and language according to which the essential function of language is to refer to reality, reality being taken to be a fixed, determinate criterion that determines the truth-value of utterances or beliefs about it. From this view it naturally follows that there can be, at least in principle, a language that adequately describes or pictures reality, and this language—the "ideal language"—is usually taken to be that of science. Science, it is believed, gives us "objective information" about the "real world." A further consequence of this view is that different languages, to the degree that they communicate "information" about reality and state "facts," can be translated without any loss of meaning. To the degree that they cannot be so translated, they are deemed to be meaningless (of no informational value). Understanding is thus a univocal affair; it isolates and grasps the one identical meaning-content (the "thought," as Frege would say), which is merely expressed differently (with a difference of "coloring") in different languages. The cultural imperialism that this logicism—for that is what we may call it—tends to generate in practice can be effectively opposed only if the theories of understanding and reality involved are abandoned and alternate theories worked out.

This book seeks to suggest just such an alternate theory. If cultural imperialism is to be avoided, understanding cannot be taken as the apprehension of objective states of affairs; language cannot be thought of as merely the expression of determinate and univocal meanings, nor can reality be said to be one and invariant. Expressed more positively, this means that thought or understanding is always dependent on language (though not identical with it) so that differences in language reflect differences in thought, these differences being irreducible to a common, logical form. Reality itself is thoroughly pluralistic.

The true encounter with other cultures produces not so much harmony and contentment as confusion (a feeling of strangeness) and dislocation (alienation). Such an experience confounds, dazzles, bewilders, puzzles, amazes. The scientific name for this phenomenon is "culture shock." Such an encounter poses a threat to one's own mental and cultural equilibrium, to one's life in fact, for truly to encounter another culture in its otherness is to be made concretely and often painfully aware of the fact that there exist other equally possible ways of doing and seeing things, of ordering the world and coming to grips with life, ways often quite different and even at odds with one's own culturally habitual ones. In such an encounter one will either loose oneself, one's identity, in what is alien or come away enriched, better for the experience. What one can profitably learn from the experience of another culture is precisely the "relativity" of all cultures.

Cultures are essentially relative in that each culture is adequate to the needs and desires of that people of whom it is the culture, much as each language is adequate to express what the users of that language customarily wish to express. Cultures cannot be ranked in a linear or hierarchical order of perfection (a typically rationalist procedure), for each is, in its own way, incomparable and, in the scholastic sense of the term, "perfect": *"Intantum est autem perfectum unumquodque, intantum est actu"* ("But everything is perfect so far as it is actual").[1] Each is a structured whole that satisfactorily fulfills its purpose of bringing order out of chaos (indeed, if a culture were not satisfactory and perfect in this way, it would not have managed to exist in the first place). Each culture in its own way is thus as "logical" and as effective as any other, for each enables its members to live out their lives in a world of meaning. "As each culture is a whole, however sorely torn at the moment—whole in the sense that it is the system by which and through which its members live—in all relationships between cultures, each must be accorded dignity and value."[2]

The statement just quoted appears in a manual for the use of anthropologists and others having dealings with foreign cultures. It would therefore seem that the problem of cultural imperialism is not ignored by social scientists. Indeed the present-day state of affairs would seem to be the exact opposite. Most anthropologists today are at pains to be impartial, tolerant, and extremely respectful of cultural differences. Moreover, since the work of Bronislaw Malinowski, it has become not only an accepted practice but even something of a sine qua non for any aspiring anthropologist to spend time in the field, living with the native people who are the object of his study, mastering their language and learning their ways, participating—as much as it is possible for a scientific observer—in their daily life, attempting, in short, to play the part of participant observer. Two or three years of field work is now the obligatory rite de passage into the society of professional anthropologists. Instead of judging alien cultures from the outside in the light of Western culture, anthropologists make a deliberate and systematic effort to be what they like to call value free. Far from being absolutist and reductionist, the present tendency in scientific anthropology seems to be in the direction of some kind of cultural relativism.

That contemporary anthropology is insistent upon cultural relativity cannot be denied. It is no longer scientifically respectable to seek to impose Western standards of conduct on primitive peoples, or, indeed, to even speak of "savages" or of a "primitive" or "prelogical mentality," and anthropologists are often to be found in the forefront of the defense of native "rights." This new relativism together with the apparent attitude of tolerance, respect, and liberality, cannot, however, be said to constitute a viable methodological alternative to the old-style reductionism. In fact, it very likely represents a more subtle and insidious form of reductionism.

The most obvious defect of cultural relativism, though, is that it skirts the troublesome issue of normative judgments or evaluations. In their attempts to avoid imposing their own cultural standards on a foreign culture and in their attempts to describe a native people's beliefs and customs in their own terms and to make sense of them from their own point of view, anthropologists find themselves with no means of assessing and evaluating the practices they observe. One may indeed have liberal-minded qualms about judging alien customs from the point of view of one's own and coercing a native people to adopt Western practices concerning, for instance, marriage. What, however, is one to say of a cultural practice that involves ritual murder or infanticide? Is this too to be accepted in the name of a kind of cultural laissez-faire? Lévi-Strauss expresses very well the predicament that liberal-minded anthropologists find themselves in:

> If, in the first instance, we are threatened by obscurantism, in the form of a blind rejection of anything that is not our own, there is also an alternative danger: that of an eclecticism which bids us reject nothing at all, when faced with an alien culture. Even if that society should itself protest against the cruelty, the injustice, and the poverty which characterize it, we must not pass judgment. But as these abuses also exist among ourselves, how shall we have the right to fight them at home, if when they appear elsewhere, we make no move to protest?[3]

"Value-free" defenders of cultural relativity are involved in a serious contradiction of their own making. In regard to the alien culture they are staunch advocates of the right of the native people to order their lives as they see fit; here defenders are strict noninterventionists. When, however, they detect injustice and exploitation in their own society, they do not hesitate to assume the role of critic and denounce what they take to be economic, racial, or sexual discrimination. Supposedly they would in both cases invoke the same principle to justify this difference in attitude: the right to self-determination and self-realization—of individuals and groups within their own culture, on the one hand, and of different cultures, on the other. The fact remains, though, that their behavior is inconsistent in the two cases; they are, as Lévi-Strauss says, critics at home and conformists abroad.

This double standard of the cultural relativist is not only inconsistent but self-contradictory and self-defeating. The principle of universal, unqualified tolerance cannot be applied without the principle's negating itself. Primitive societies are often notably intolerant of other societies. Is one to tolerate this intolerance? If one does so, the same principle of universal tolerance will allow for our intolerance vis-à-vis them in the form of colonial exploitation. This is to say that the universal application of the principle of cultural laissez-faire logically results in a concrete state of affairs, which is the actual negation of what the principle supposedly stands for. Through this *reductio ad absurdum* it becomes apparent that the principle produces its own negation, that it contradicts itself.

Let us suppose the existence of a warrior society in which warfare and cannibalism constitute the basis of all social arrangements. Were a colonial government to prohibit this people's warring and feasting upon their neighbors, it would in fact destroy their social institutions and entire way of life. In a case like this the relativist and "tolerant" anthropologist is faced with an impossible choice: to admit the need for external intervention and control, in which case he is in effect consenting to the destruction of the society as it exists and is thereby violating his own principle of nonintervention and respect of their right to exist as they see fit; or else, knowing the socially disastrous consequences of external intervention, to oppose all such measures, but in this case he is condoning action on the part of the natives that is a blatant violation of the principle of respect for others that he professes. Nor can the relativist escape his dilemma by allowing for limits to the principle of tolerance and the right to exist as one sees fit. He cannot on his own methodological grounds legitimately allow for such limits, for the recognition of limits implies the recognition also that certain norms of behavior are somehow universally applicable, and such a recognition is logically incompatible with the thoroughgoing relativist thesis, which denies the existence of truths or principles that would be common to all cultures.

The dilemma of the thoroughgoing relativist is of the same sort as that of the radical ethical relativist. The latter—quite rightly—objects to the attitude of the ethical absolutist who maintains that standards of morality ("the moral law") are inscribed in a determinate human nature and who thereby gives license to anyone to impose intolerantly his morality on others, provided only that this is the "true" morality as prescribed by nature. Seeing that, like many primitive societies, most people in our society are intolerant of ways and practices that deviate from their own and that, furthermore, people generally take reality (nature) to be precisely that which they believe it to be, the worst forms of intolerance result in practice from the absolutist position. However, the ethical relativist fares no better;

in fact the result is the same, for in denying anything like a common human nature and in failing to provide for universal norms of some sort or other, the ethical relativist is in no position to proscribe the intolerant behavior of others and actually furnishes a good rationale for it.[4]

One further defect of cultural relativism bears noting. It could be wondered if the anthropologist who attempts to be value free and to avoid all judgment concerning the truth or falsity, rightness or wrongness of native practices and beliefs can ever truly understand the practices and beliefs in question—whether, that is, he can make sense of them in their own terms. To enter into the culture so as to understand it from within, he would have to abandon his noncritical and detached attitude; he would have to make the beliefs and practices his own. But then he would cease to be a "scientific" and "critical" observer.[5] Should, however, he remain an anthropologist, value free and detached, what assurance can he have that he has ever truly understood the native beliefs in their own terms? Does one sufficiently penetrate into a culture through the use of "informants"? What, moreover, is one to think of the customary anthropological practice of paying out "informant fees"? What exactly, one wonders, is the vlaue of "information" obtained in this way, if those who offer the information are motivated primarily by the money or other goods they will receive in return? What exactly is the anthropologist looking for anyway? Is he seeking to merely acquire information about native beliefs and practices, or is he attempting to penetrate the world projected and sustained by these beliefs and practices? If the latter, the use of informant fees would seem to be somewhat counterproductive and to be of no more use in gaining a lived understanding of the world view that inwardly sustains a people than paying for sexual favors would enable one to achieve an understanding of the intersubjective experience of "being in love."

What assurances can the anthropologist have that his informants are correctly informing him in the first place if he cannot directly compare their interpretations of native beliefs with his own empathetic interpretations of them? Is it not significant that informants often tend to be somewhat marginal in regard to their own society? When he was studying the Azande, Evans-Pritchard, an anthropologist who has attempted to a considerable degree to deal with the natives on their own terms, was unable to obtain much information from those who supposedly would be most knowledgeable about their own society, the aristocratic class, and had to rely instead on common citizens. As he says, "I found that, with rare exceptions, they were useless as informants, since they firmly refused to discuss their customs and beliefs, always directing conversation into some other channel, and that they contrasted in this respect with their subjects, who seldom objected, and were often keen, to furnish information."[6] More particularly, Evans-Pritchard encountered serious difficulties when he sought to gain information about the Zande corporation of witch doctors, which had its own esoteric life from which the uninitiated were rigorously excluded. He finally was able to gain what amount of information he did through the ruse of having his personal native servant accepted as a pupil by the witch doctors. He admits, however, that the witch doctors were aware of his intentions and that he was using his servant as "a sponge out of which I squeezed all the moisture of information which they put into it." This shows, as Evans-Pritchard himself confesses, "that in spite of the methods of investigation which I employed, my informants did not communicate their entire knowledge to me, even indirectly, and suggests that there were other departments of their knowledge which they did not disclose. This may have been the case."[7] Evans-Pritchard does not, however, entertain the possibility that his informants—aware of his intentions and hostile to them—could have been deliberately attempting to misinform and mislead him.[8]

Under these conditions, when those who are most in a position to know what they are talking about refuse to talk, one can legitimately wonder about the extent to which the anthropologist has really penetrated into and understood from an internal viewpoint those beliefs revealed to him by those who are talkative but only marginally knowledgeable or by those who may have reason to mislead him deliberately. As George Steiner observes, "If meaning is quite often kept from the outside questioner or communicated only in part, the whole issue of the status and extent of conveyed and translated sense remains open."[9] We are, all of us, so obsessed with the scientific (rationalist) notion of "truth" that we tend to think that the basic function of language is or should be to communicate "information," and we are frustrated when people use language to dissimulate their beliefs and actions. It is a fact, though, that people do use language as much to conceal as to reveal, and they often tend to prefer to speak in a roundabout, metaphorical, and ironic way rather than in a straightforward, literal, "scientific" way. Why is this? We must keep this question in mind.

The scientific anthropologist who genuinely attempts to understand the culture he is studying finds himself in a serious methodological dilemma. On the one hand, he can seek to understand the culture from within, taking it on its own terms. Although it is no doubt essential that anthropological work of any worth be based on a firsthand and sympathetic experience of the alien culture, this approach of itself leads into an impasse, for the outcome here would be that in refusing to make evaluative and comparative judgments concerning the customs and beliefs, the anthropologist becomes incapable of viewing them in any other terms than the native ones, which is to say that he has "gone native" and ceased to be an anthropologist. The anthropological (scientific) understanding of a primitive society is incompatible with actually being a primitive, just as the psychological understanding of a mentally disturbed person (of, that is, *his* world) is incompatible with actually being such a person (though, no doubt, the psychologist can profit from having himself at one time suffered from or had tendencies toward certain psychological disorders, and indeed one suspects that a good many psychologists chose their profession precisely because of the presence in them of such tendencies).[10]

The other horn of the anthropologist's dilemma is explanatory reductionism. If, instead of merely identifying empathetically with the primitive or alien society, he attempts to achieve a scientific understanding of it, he must employ explanatory techniques. He must, on the one hand, seek to discover casual factors that will explain customs and beliefs in terms that will surely be at variance with the reasons the natives themselves would propose, and he must, on the other hand, compare this society with others, which is to say that he must view it from the outside. Here the anthropologist remains an anthropologist, but his option for science forever prevents him from understanding the alien world in its own terms and makes of him a perpetual outsider. As one anthropologist remarks:

> In a basic sense social anthropology is essentially comparative, as all science is; comparisons are implicit in the very language which anthropologists use to describe other people's social institutions. When they speak of kings, princes and rulers, of fathers and sons, of priests and laymen, in the societies they investigate, they are implicitly assimilating these kinds of people to categories familiar to them from their own backgrounds.[11]

Here again we encounter the problem of language and translation. Indeed the problem of understanding an alien culture raises the whole question of rationality. What are the norms of rationality involved in understanding what is other? Are primitive beliefs in magic irrational, or do they have a rationality specifically their own? How can we understand the phenomenon of magic, which plays such an important role in the lives of primitives? Are we limited to evaluating magical practices and beliefs merely by means of the criteria implicit in them? Or is it perhaps the case that a belief in magic actually prevents us from truly understanding it, and that the only correct, rational evaluation of the phenomenon is one that compares it with science and technology, one, that is to say, that disqualifies it as a proper mode of understanding? How, in short, are we to understand the beliefs of another culture that appear to us as irrational?

In his desire to overcome his own cultural prejudices so as to understand the beliefs of another culture (that is, faced with the problem of rational criteria), the anthropologist is exposed to a powerful temptation. Aware as he is of the fact of linguistic relativity, he may think that he can avoid the danger of distorting the alien views if he does not simply translate them into his own native language, which carries with it its own way of viewing the world, but has recourse instead to a kind of "third language." This third language would have to be value free and impartial so as to serve as an objective means for critically assessing the rationality-value of various cultural beliefs. Such a language would permit the social scientist to understand, critically and objectively, not only other cultures but his own as well. This language is the language of science.

It is true, of course, our anthropologist will admit, that science is a Western invention, but he will argue that this does not restrict its range of applicability or detract from its intrinsic impartiality. Science, he will say, may be culturally emergent, but it is not culturally dependent. That is, though science is a product of our own culture, its peculiar characteristic is that it transcends this culture and strives to attain a universal vocation. Precisely because it transcends our own particular culture, we can use science as much to understand other cultures as to understand our own better.

A view similar to this is put forward by the editor of a recent collection of essays dedicated to the problem of rationality, of understanding other cultures.[12] B. R. Wilson attempts to do justice to the phenomenon of cultural relativity while defending the possibility of an anthropological science. He does not succeed. He acknowledges that the translation of the meanings of one culture into the language of another poses serious problems, but he does not believe that these problems are insurmountable. He admits that there is a sense in which the members of a primitive culture understand themselves better than any outsider ever could, but he also insists—as he must if anything like a social science (an explanatory discipline based on the scientific postulate of objectivity) is to be possible— that in another sense the members of a primitive society have "little or no chance of ever understanding" their society, presumably because they lack critical distance from the immediate phenomena.

> Obviously to make this latter statement is to claim that there are ways of interpreting the data about one culture into the terms employed in another, and the implication is that these are in some respects more comprehensive methods than have been available either in earlier periods of history or in other cultures. This is the claim on which social science, despite cultural relativism, despite the unwillingness to label other cultures as "primitive," necessarily rests.[13]

Wilson does not believe that in defending the possibility of exact translation and of objective understanding he is condoning the reduction of other cultures to our own, for the language of anthropology is not, he says, the value-ridden language of our own historical culture but is rather the value-free language of science: "the social sciences seek to order knowledge systematically in value-free, emotionally-neutral, abstract propositions."[14]

It is true, Wilson concedes, that the idea of science originated in our own culture, but this does not disqualify it from universal applicability, for science is value free even in regard to the culture of its origin. In other words, the unique characteristic of our culture is that it has allowed for the emergence of the notion of cultural relativity (such a notion, Wilson says, is not to be found in primitive cultures) and the impartial and objective study of cultural differences. The sociologist, therefore, "is in a better position than mediaeval man or primitive man to understand mediaeval and primitive society" because he "has a wider range of data, has become conscious of the importance of eliminating emotional and evaluative elements in his concepts and has a tradition of enquiry that uses such concepts and provides models of analysis."[15] This attitude of emotionless and evaluationless analysis is precisely "his 'cultural' inheritance."[16] Wilson writes:

> The attitudes of the western investigator are aspects of the cultural relativism that he has inherited as part of the posture of value-freedom that he has attempted to adopt in approaching other cultures. Part of the greater likelihood of understanding other cultures that he enjoys, when compared with men from those cultures, arises from the fact that cultural relativism is a possible perspective in his culture but not in theirs. What must be acknowledged, however, is that cultural relativity has its own inherent bounds precisely because of this. Other cultures are made understandable by ordering their concepts, beliefs, activities according to the premises of the tradition of Western social science. It cannot be escaped that the tolerance, ethical neutrality and detached curiosity about other cultures arise as the products of a particular culture at a certain stage of its development.[17]

Wilson says that the social scientist "need not regard *his* rational procedures as being more than the best way we know of investigating."[18] This is a strong assertion, but it is also ambiguous. No doubt the sociologist qua sociologist need attempt no more than to analyze cultural phenomena in purely scientific terms. But is this to say that the language of science is, without reserve, the best (even if this is qualified to mean the best as far as we know)? Is science, then, the universal, transcultural language, the true *mathesis universalis?*

Wilson tends to identify rationality with or, rather, reduce it to, scientific and technological rationality. The difference, he says, between primitive society and our own increasingly scientifically oriented society is simply that "the application of rational principles is far less extensive in simple society."[19] Our society is notably more rationally planned and controlled than is primitive society. This is surely true and cannot be disputed, but one can say that our society is more rational only if one equates rationality with nothing more than scientific control and techonological planning. Wilson again reveals his reductionist bent in regard to rationality when he says that

the ritual activities of people in simpler societies were "understandable em-
phathetically, poetically, mystically, and could not be communicated in a
set of rational propositions."[20] On this score a host of practices and beliefs
in our own culture—those which, such as religion, have managed so far to
resist technological-rational control—cannot be communicated either in a
set of "rational" propositions. Shall we therefore call them irrational or
prerational? It is apparent from Wilson's remarks that the ghost of Lévy-
Bruhl and his notion of a prelogical mentality continues to haunt the edifice
of social science. It is also apparent that though Wilson accepts the fact of
cultural relativity—or says he does—he is determined to discover an invariant, universal means of dealing with it, and this means is science.
Wilson's "recognition" of relativity is thus but a more subtle form of scientific absolutism and reductionism.

From a scientific point of view, Wilson's way of resolving the problem of
cultural relativity and of rational criteria no doubt is pointed in the right
direction; however, it leaves one question unanswered, and necessarily so,
since it is not a scientific question. This is the question concerning the status
of science itself. Is science the universal language that Wilson is making it
out to be? It is true that we can analyze our own culture by means of science
with as much "objectivity" as any other. This would seem to indicate that
science, and science alone, furnishes us with truly objective and culturally
independent or invariant knowledge. But what, one wonders, is the value of
such "value-free" knowledge? What relation does a sociological account
of, say, church-going in terms of what it socially accomplishes—the generation and maintenance of certain kinds of social rapports—have to do with
what people believe they are accomplishing in going to church and the
reason they would give for their activity? If for science the ritual practices
of a "more simple society" are non-rational, having merely "empathetic,
poetic or mystical" value, so also must be many beliefs and practices found
in our own culture. If it is deemed irrational or simply non-rational for a
primitive society to say of a twin that he is a bird—not *like* a bird but *is* a
bird—as the Nuer, a people of the southern Sudan, do,[21] what must one say
of that belief, which forms the heart of a ritual that itself is historically central to our culture—the ritual here being the Mass and the belief that of
transubstantiation? To say that wine becomes and is blood while still re-
maining wine (something that Catholics maintain) must be a totally irrational belief, on a par with the most primitive "superstition." Is there, then,
any way out of this scientific monopolizing of rationality? Indeed, is it even
the case that science is, as Wilson would have it, "value-free," "tolerant,"
"ethically neutral," "emotionally neutral"?

In his book on Zande witchcraft, Evans-Pritchard says, "Our body of
scientific knowledge and Logic are the sole arbiters of what are mystical,

common-sense, and scientific notions." He defines mystical notions as those "patterns of thought that attribute to phenomena supra-sensible qualities . . . *which they do not possess.*"[22] Again, he boldly states that "witchcraft is imaginary and a man cannot possibly be a witch."[23] Is it indeed the case, we ask, that science and logic are the sole arbiters of truth and that they alone can determine what are the "facts" and what are not—that, for instance, mysticism is wrong on its "facts"? What, after all, *is* a fact?

At the beginning of his book Evans-Pritchard states that much of the difficulty involved in a study such as his is due to "the complexity of the facts themselves."[24] This seemingly innocent turn of phrase actually conceals a methodological prejudice; it implies that the business of science is to describe "the facts," though it allows that this may not be a simple matter. Is it, however, the case that science consists in merely discovering so-called objective facts, that it impartially reveals "objective" truths that exist somehow *in rebus?* It would seem that Evans-Pritchard was bewitched by the claims of logic and in particular by the belief that language refers to facts, which are what they are independently of it. He speaks indeed in a very Russellian way when he says that confusion results from calling "the same thing by different names or different things by the same name."[25] It is evident that he is underestimating the importance of language and is in fact subscribing to a kind of picture theory of words:

> Terms are only labels which help us to sort out facts of the same kind from facts which are different, or are in some respects different. If the labels do not prove helpful we can discard them. The facts will be the same without their labels.[26]

In a like-minded fashion the famous American anthropologist, Clyde Kluckhohn, divides his study of Navajo witchcraft into two parts, the first entitled "Data" and the second "Interpretation." This division stems from Kluckhohn's assumption that "facts" and the "interpretation" of these facts can be fairly clearly distinguished and that whatever one's eventual attitude to Kluckhohn's own "interpretation" of the facts may be, one cannot but accept the "facts" themselves. Indeed he claims that the first part of his book deals with "sheer description" and merely states "what the facts are."[27] These "facts" he equates with "direct inductions from my field materials, together with an account of how they were obtained."[28]

In comparison with these remarks of Evans-Pritchard and Kluckhohn, Malinowski, whose work antedates that of the other two, would seem to have been more aware of the fact that science does not merely describe facts but actually interprets and constructs them when he wrote, "*Only laws and generalizations are scientific facts,* and field work consists only and exclusively in the interpretation of the chaotic reality."[29] If science does not merely sort out and describe preexistent, objective facts, but if, as Malinowski says, its "facts" are its own laws and generalizations, its own interpretive constructs and theories, how can it claim to be value free, that is *evaluation* free? If it is true that scientific models are akin to metaphors, it would seem that science is guilty of taking its metaphors literally. Moreover, it would seem that science suffers from the inversion syndrome in that when it is "tolerant," it seeks to accord a corner in the world of facts to mystical, empathetic, and poetic values, whereas the world of scientific fact is itself but the product of one way of evaluating, of valorizing the world and creatively interpreting and structuring the chaotic reality of our everyday lives.

If we wish to oppose scientific reductionism and the systematic application of technological "rationality" to our own and other cultures, we should perhaps not argue that certain areas of human life cannot be scientifically understood, for this would be to admit implicitly that science does furnish the sole and ultimate truth in regard to at least those areas where it applies. Instead we should attempt to show how science itself cannot claim a definitive status for itself because there are no facts in themselves and because science, like any other mode of expression, is but one means of creatively evaluating reality and constructing facts. The question concerning the place of science in the total realm of human activity and understanding would thereby gain in precision, for we would be asking not about what limited value we can accord to nonscientific forms of understanding but rather how science itself stands with regard to human understanding in general and what its limits are in this respect. The need for such a reversal in our question is well indicated by the following observations of W. T. Jones:

> Fifteen years ago, when I was writing *A History of Western Philosophy,* it became clear to me that the whole modern period—not merely in philosophy, but in every aspect of the culture—has been marked by an increasing tension between the new scientific view of man and the traditional humanistic view; and I concluded that the reconciliation of these conflicting views had become a matter of urgency, not merely for professional philosophers but for men and women everywhere. At the outset, however, I formulated the difficulty as the problem of finding a place for values in the world of fact. I did not make much progress until it occurred to me that this definition was culture-bound—was, indeed, a reflection of the predominance in our society of scientific ways of thinking. It makes as much sense to talk about the need of finding a place for facts in the world of values; indeed, in some cultures this would be the natural way of formulating my problem.[30]

In this respect one also thinks of the penetrating insights of Nietzsche into the evaluative, "perspectival" character of all knowledge—knowledge being for him interpretation and the creation of values.

Against positivism, which halts at phenomena—"There are only *facts*"—I would say: No, facts is precisely what there is not, only interpretations. We cannot establish any fact "in itself": perhaps it is folly to want to do such a thing. . . . In so far as the word "knowledge" has any meaning, the world is knowable; it is *interpretable* otherwise, it has no meaning behind it, but countless meanings.—"Perspectivism."

Form, species, law, idea, purpose—in all these cases the same error is made of giving a false reality to a fiction, as if events were in some way obedient to something. . . . One should not understand this compulsion to construct concepts, species, forms, purposes, laws ("a world of identical cases") as if they enabled us to fix the *real world;* but as a compulsion to arrange a world for ourselves in which our existence is made possible:—we thereby create a world which is calculable, simplified, comprehensible, etc., for us. . . . Our subjective compulsion to believe in logic only reveals that, long before logic itself entered our consciousness, we did nothing but introduce its postuates into events: now we discover them in events—we can no longer do otherwise—and imagine that this compulsion guarantees something connected with "truth." It is we who created the "thing," the "identical thing," subject, attribute, activity, object, substance, form, after we had long pursued the process of making identical, coarse and simple. The world seems logical to us because we have made it logical.[31]

Our consideration of the problem of understanding other cultures and the problem of standards of rationality in anthropology, while raising more questions than it has been able to answer, has nonetheless enabled us to approach somewhat nearer to our goal: a general theory of human understanding. It has become apparent that this intercultural problem is part of a more basic problem, a properly intracultural one. *The fight of other cultures to preserve their self-identity is inseparable from our own struggle to situate the world of science and technology within the wider universe of creative discourse.* This is to say that the problem of Other Cultures is but a wider aspect of the problem of the Two Cultures: the relation between scientific and humanistic thinking. This problem cannot be resolved until we have become clearer on how understanding, scientific or otherwise, functions.

In anthropology, when we seek to understand another culture, we must first attempt to penetrate into it so as to see it as much as possible as its members do and must attempt, initially, to describe it in its own terms.[32] This, however, is only the beginning. The purpose of an anthropological study of a cultural phenomenon such as sorcery is not to enable us to enter into that culture so as to become sorcerers ourselves. Rather we want to see the place of sorcery in the culture and, similarly, we want to know what is distinctive of the culture as a whole vis-à-vis other, perhaps related, cultures, and, ultimately, in what ways it differs from our own. At this point it becomes necessary to go beyond a merely internal and empathetic viewpoint—to the degree that such a viewpoint is ever attainable in the first place. An attempt must be made to explain or understand the culture scientifically, in a way no mere insider ever could. As one anthropologist says, "It is indeed a most important part of the social anthropologist's job to try to understand the distinctions consciously made by the people whose culture he is studying, but evidently his analysis may, and indeed must, go further. In the last resort their categories must be conceived in terms of ours, if they are to be intelligible to us at all."[33] Here different avenues open up, corresponding to different methodological options in anthropology. One may, for instance, attempt to give an account of cultural phenomena in terms of their social function and utility, or one may take a structuralist approach, or some other still yet. But all scientific accounts, of greater or lesser explanatory power, are ultimately reductionistic.

Functionalism, for instance, reduces the meaning of myth to its social function or usefulness. According to Evans-Pritchard, "Any section of society enjoying special privileges, whether magical or otherwise, produces its own mythology, the function of myth being to give sanction to the possession of the exclusive privileges."[34] This is akin to Malinowski's opinion that myth "is always made *ad hoc* to fulfill a certain sociological function, to glorify a certain group, or to justify an anomalous status."[35] In this case social anthropology becomes every bit as reductionist as the Marxian theory of culture or the Freudian theory of the person, for in all three cases it is being said that the "manifest content" of the phenomenon—of the myth, the culture, or the ego—is but the superficial symptom of an underlying and nonappearing cause and therefore should not be taken on its own terms. It is in effect being maintained that all consciousness is false consciousness and that the content of myth and other cultural products are but ideologies that mask an underlying reality.[36] To disclose this basic reality is to discover ultimate and true reasons and causes; it is to explain and to do science.[37]

On this score Lévi-Strauss is explicit and avowedly reductionist when he admits that he wishes to "study men as if they were ants"; he writes:

I believe the ultimate goal of the human sciences to be not to constitute, but to dissolve man. . . . Ethnographic analysis tries to arrive at invariants beyond the empirical diversity of human societies. . . . However, it would not be enough to reabsorb particular humanities into a general one. This first enterprise opens the way for others: . . . the reintegration of culture in nature and finally of life within the whole of its physical-chemical conditions.[38]

"This is an extreme reductionist argument," the British anthropologist, Edmund Leach, observes. For in the eyes of Lévi-Strauss (according to

Leach), "The structure of relations which can be discovered by analyzing materials drawn from any one culture is an algebraic transformation of other possible structures belonging to a common set and this common set constitutes a pattern which reflects an attribute of the mechanism of all human brains."[39]

When anthropology seeks to explain and give scientific reasons for beliefs and practices to be found in primitive cultures, it would appear, therefore, that it is confronted with a number of methodological problems that force it, irresistibly, in the direction of an increasingly crude and materialistic reductionism. The most current English-speaking school of anthropology seeks to explain cultural phenomena sociologically. It is thought that the existence of, say, magical practices and witchcraft beliefs in a given society has been sufficiently explained when these beliefs and practices have been related to and correlated with other features of the society in question, such as kinship systems or property ownership patterns, and an analysis of "concomitant variations" has been worked out. As Evans-Pritchard, an early practitioner of "social anthropology," expressed the matter, "It is one of the aims of social anthropology to interpret all differences in the form of a typical social institution by reference to differences in social structure. . . . differences in the form of the institution of magic, in particular between two societies, can be explained by showing the variation in social structure between these societies."[40] This type of approach wherein one aspect of a culture (or society) is "explained" by showing how it is tied in with other aspects of the culture (society), is modified by them, and varies with them, may be cleverly and imaginatively done, but its methodological defect is that it explains nothing at all about magic and witchcraft themselves; it does not enlighten us as to what magic is or about why people hold magical beliefs in the first place. At most it will "explain" why beliefs in witchcraft take one form in society A and another in society B or why, in society A or B, they change in a certain way over a period of time. Why people should believe, not in this or that form of witchcraft, but why they should believe in witchcraft at all—this sociology does not and cannot tell us.[41]

In an attempt to achieve greater explanatory power, anthropology may turn to psychology for assistance. Here, it would seem, we are better able to understand why people believe in magic to begin with. If so many peoples on the earth who have had no mutual contact hold remarkably similar beliefs, it can be due only to some innate feature of the human mind as such. Psychology, then, will account for the very existence of a phenomenon such as witchcraft, and not merely its external manifestations as in the case of sociology.

> In the last analysis, human nature conceived as a creative organism is the source and explanation of cultural processes. . . . cultural phenomena are in principle relative to the psychological organism that originates them.

. . . Hence cultures are to be explained primarily with reference to the nature
of the organism that originates them.[42]

Can one, however, legitimately conclude one's search for "explanation"
here?

What, after all, does it mean to speak of the human "mind" or of human
"nature"? Are not these concepts themselves in need of scientific clarifica-
tion? If one wishes to be a true scientist, must one not push on and seek to
discover truly "basic causes and determinants"? And where else could these
be found but in the material, physical makeup of the human organism? Is
not reference to the "mind" merely a way of talking about the brain, and is
not the brain a by-product of the evolution of matter? Must we not agree
with Lévi-Strauss that a true science of man—a genuine "anthropology"—
must ultimately be able to explain humans in terms of nature, in terms, that
is, of material, physical nature? Must we not agree that an explanation of
human practices is in fact, as Chomsky says of language, a matter ultimately for biology? The mysterious forces that magical beliefs speak of
surely can be reduced to a matter of human genetics. That about which people have always been concerned and that they have referred to by such terms
as soul, self, spirit, and mind, science now tries to tell us is nothing but the
evanescent by-product of neural activity. Nothing in culture was not first in
nature; culture is, in fact, nothing but nature and accordingly can be
understood in purely naturalistic terms.[43]

The science of man is thus thoroughly reductionistic when it seeks to furnish explanations. It was from a knowledge of anthropology but not qua
anthropologist that Edward Sapir, a past president of the American Anthropological Association, was speaking when he wrote:

The scientist of man has chief concern for science, not for man, and . . . all
science, partly for better and partly for worse, has the self-feeding voracity of
an obsessive ritual. We must give up our naive faith in the ability of the scientist to tell us anything about man that is not expressible in terms of the verbal
definitions and operations that prevail in his "universe of discourse"—a beau-
tiful, dream-like domain that has fitful reminiscences of man as an experiencing organism but is not, and cannot be, immersed in the wholeness of that
experience.[44]

We need not, however, object to scientific reductionism on the grounds
that certain aspects of our lives are thereby misunderstood or even totally
ignored and seek to limit the scope of social science and deny it recourse to
purely causal explanations, reductive though they be. For we would have to
accept the reductionist scientific verdict as to what things and people
"really" are only if, like the anthropologist in regard to his primitive culture, we took science merely on its own terms. If, however, all knowledge,

scientific or other, is evaluative and facts are themselves products of interpretation, we need accept as ultimate the scientist's account of things no more than the sorcerer's. Science is but one world view and one universe of discourse, as Sapir says, among others.

Peter Winch, a disciple of the later Wittgenstein who has dealt with the problem of understanding other cultures,[45] has rightly objected to Evans-Pritchard's treatment of Zande witchcraft on the grounds that it is marred by his uncritical acceptance of the belief in an independent and objective reality that is supposed to be revealed by science and logic. Evans-Pritchard, he says, is "wrong, and crucially wrong, in his attempt to characterize the scientific in terms of that which is 'in accord with objective reality.' "[46] Winch is wrong, however, in going on to draw a radical distinction between empathetic understanding and causal explanation and in suggesting that social science should limit itself to the former. He would maintain that human or social relations are an "unsuitable subject for generalizations and theories of the scientific sort to be formulated about them."[47] Indeed he holds that "the concepts used by primitive peoples can *only* be interpreted in the context of the way of life of those peoples."[48] This would rule out the possibility of any kind of social science of an explanatory sort (and it is hard to see what any kind of true science could be if it is not explanatory).

Winch objects to the explanatory approach to social reality because for him it is not reducible to physical reality. Wilhelm Dilthey's distinction between understanding and explanation that Winch completely takes over thus parallels here the distinction between man and nature. It is difficult to see, though, what justifies such a dualistic distinction other than its Cartesian lineage. If the distinction (man-nature; mind-body) is itself dubious, there appears to be no reason why science should not seek to explain not just natural phenomena (which Winch allows) but human phenomena as well—and in purely causal and explanatory terms. If Winch objects, and with cause, that such an approach does not do justice to human reality, we could just as well object that it does not do justice to nature either. The point is not there. It is rather that one cannot arbitrarily separate the human from the natural or, consequently, understanding from explanation. If a science of man is at all possible, it must surely seek to explain as much as it can.[49] Winch notwithstanding, Evans-Pritchard is surely, from a scientific standpoint, on the right track when he insists that science should not merely describe but must also seek to explain. As he says:

> Even in a single ethnographic study the anthropologist seeks to do more than understand the thought and values of a primitive people and translate them into his own culture. He seeks also to discover the structural order of the society, the patterns which, once established, enable him to see it as a whole, as a set of interrelated abstractions. Then the society is not only culturally intel-

ligible, as it is, at the level of consciousness and action, for one of its members or for the foreigner who has learnt its mores and participates in its life, but becomes sociologically intelligible. . . . the social anthropologist discovers in a native society what no native can explain to him and what no layman, however conversant with the culture, can perceive—its basic structure. This structure cannot be seen. It is a set of abstractions, each of which, though derived, it is true, from analysis of observed behaviour, is fundamentally an imaginative construct of the anthropologist himself. By relating these abstractions to one another logically so that they present a pattern he can see the society in its essentials and as a single whole.[50]

Lévi-Strauss remarks, more succinctly, "To reach reality we must first repudiate lived experience, even though we may later reintegrate it in an objective synthesis stripped of all sentimentality."[51]

Whether sociological explanation is explicitly causal or not, it is necessarily reductive, for it discovers "reasons" why people do the things they do, reasons of which they are themselves unaware, reasons "stripped of all sentimentality." The ultimate result of the scientific approach to humanity is thus to dissolve people into nature and to deny the uniqueness and irreducibility of human, lived experience—ultimately, as in the case of B. F. Skinner, to deny anything like human "freedom" and "dignity."

This is an outcome that we, like Winch, may not wish to accept as a final solution to the problem or the question, "What is man?" but we can oppose it effectively only if we adopt a different tactic from Winch's. We should not object to the attempt on the part of science to explain humanity but should instead raise a further question concerning the status of science itself as a human activity. If, as Evans-Pritchard admits, an anthropological explanation is "an imaginative construct of the anthropologist himself," we may better see both the value and the limits of science by situating it within the context of human understanding and imagination.

The problem comes down to this basically: the scientist qua scientist, anthropologist or physicist, does not know what he is talking about when he speaks of "reality." He does not know what he is talking about when like Lévi-Strauss he speaks of "reaching reality." But it is precisely an understanding of what we mean by "reality" that is the key to the whole disputed issue of reductionism—its possibility or impossibility, its desirability or undesirability. An anthropologist like Evans-Pritchard and a host of other social anthropologists after him are inevitably, whether they like it or not, reductionists, for they assume at the outset that magical forces are not real and that witches (those who exploit magical forces) cannot possibly exist. They will thus attempt to explain belief in magic and witches in terms of what for them is real—social relations. But what, after all, is reality? What makes one thing real and another thing unreal? What differentiates between the "real" and the "imaginary"? What is the "imaginary"? Is reality merely that which is observable? Hardly, for then science, which, as Evans-Pritchard admits, does not itself deal mainly with observable entities, would be as superstitious as magic.

Scientists always believe that what they have to say is "about" reality. Thus the usual discussion of reductionism turns on whether the object in consideration is real or merely apparent. Those who oppose the reduction of cultural phenomena to social phenomena accordingly will argue that culture has some kind of reality of its own over and above social relations; culture is not reducible to society. There can be a science of culture, as opposed to a science of society, David Bidney seems to be saying, only if there is an "objective reality" properly its own with which this science can deal or study.[52] In a confused and confusing piece of writing, Bidney declares himself an opponent of reductionism, but it is extremely difficult to grasp what this anti-reductionism actually amounts to. For, like his scientific colleagues, he does insist that "reality" is composed of different levels, such as the physical, the organic, the social, and the cultural. And he does say that from a "genetic, evolutionary point of view, all the ontological levels of nature are interrelated, since each higher level always depends on the lower level from which it has emerged."[53] If this is the case, surely one can understand a cultural phenomenon such as magic only by showing how it derives from the social and the physical, which is to say only by denying that there is something like magical, unnatural, nonphysical forces.

Often one happens onto truly worthwhile questions by reflecting obstinately on matters that others do not normally trouble themselves over—precisely because these matters are taken to be so self-evident that they are not thought to be worthy of question. Why then is it that anthropologists automatically and without a moment's consideration rule out the possibility of magic and witches? One unusually critical anthropologist observes:

> Our social sciences generally treat the culture and knowledge of other peoples as forms and structures necessary for human life that those people have developed and imposed upon a reality which we know—or at least our scientists know—better than they do. We can therefore study those forms in relation to "reality" and measure how well or ill they are adapted to it. In their studies of the cultures of other people, even those anthropologists who sincerely love the people they study almost never think they are learning something about the way the world really is. Rather, they conceive of themselves as finding out what other people's *conceptions* of the world are.[54]

Why is this? Why does the anthropologist who passes for being open-minded not even seriously entertain at least the possibility that people believe in magic and witches because there actually are such things? Surely it can only be because they are uncritically and unthinkingly taking for granted a certain conception of reality peculiar to themselves.

Social science could cease to be reductionistic vis-à-vis the beliefs of other cultures only if it broke with physical science and ceased to believe that what is basically real—the basic level of reality—is matter in evolutionary motion. But then social science would cease to be a part of what in our culture we mean by science. This should be enough to make us suspect that talk about reality is simply a shorthand way of expressing a certain belief about reality. Science postulates that reality is of such and such a nature, precisely because science is a particular kind of belief. Magic, being another set of beliefs, postulates a different kind of reality. The scientific notion of reality is therefore, one is tempted to say, a highly subjective and culture-bound notion.

What all of this would seem to indicate is that if we are ever truly to understand another culture, if we are, for instance, to understand belief in magic, we must first of all suspend our own scientific beliefs as to what reality is or is not. Reductionism is a form of dogmatism, and dogmatism can be overcome only by means of a kind of "phenomenological reduction" or what the third-century skeptical philosopher, Sextus Empiricus, called *epoche*. If we are to understand truly a belief system, we must study it purely as a system of belief and must suspend all judgment as to the reality or non-reality of what this belief purports to be a belief about.

The important thing, then, is to explore in more detail the basic structures of human understanding in its different modes. This is the only way of arriving at an appropriate understanding of what all understanding, from science to magic, seeks to understand in its own peculiar way: reality. It is the only means for arriving at a non-dogmatic metaphysics. We need to undertake a pragmatics of human understanding; that is, we need to analyze the workings of understanding so as to discern the ways in which it actually does function, and we need to do so transcendentally (or reflectively) by considering understanding in its own right, without regard to its "objective validity" (its "correspondence" to reality).

Our mode of approach must be phenomenological. In order to discern as best we can the actual structure and mode of operation of human understanding, we must apply the phenomenological reduction. We must suspend any prior conception we might have as to the ontological status of the objects of understanding (scientific, magical, or otherwise) and as to the relation between understanding and what is called reality so as to be able to analyze understanding and its various modes simply as they present themselves to our reflective scrutiny.

This methodological option will, it is to be hoped, enable us to steer a safe course between the extremes of rationalism and irrationalism, between absolutism and relativism. A thoroughgoing relativism is an unsatisfactory theoretical position because it cannot be properly argued for in the first place. It is therefore irrational. Not only is it self-contradictory from a purely logical point of view, and thus absurd (to say, "Everything is relative," makes about as much sense as to say, "Nothing is true"), it is also contradicted by our actual experience. The fact that if we try we can always communicate to some degree or other with members of other cultures and arrive at some understanding of the way they view things is enough to indicate that cultural relativity cannot be understood to entail complete and utter disparity. Human beings, after all, are not trees, intent merely on their own growth and oblivious to their near and far-off neighbors. Although translation from language to language and from culture to culture may never be perfect, still it is always possible (so much so that a language that could not be translated would not be a language at all). To say, therefore, that reality is thoroughly pluralistic cannot be taken to mean that there is not, in some sense or other, something that all cultures have in common, something that unites them in their very diversity. To say that reality is thoroughly pluralistic cannot mean that it is something totally different for each culture. Were this so, it would make no sense to speak of reality at all, and it would be necessary to say that reality does not exist or that it is totally meaningless. A thoroughgoing relativism entails ontological nihilism, and this we wish to avoid.

On the other hand, absolutism, which holds as Frege does, that for all the multiplicity of language, humanity has a common stock of thought and that, for all the diversity in beliefs as to the nature of reality, reality is yet one and the self-same for all people, is a fairly coherent and therefore rational position. Our opposition to it stems not so much from theoretical considerations as it does from practical ones, for the "logical" outcome of this kind of rationalism in the practical sphere is scientific-technological reductionism, and this, for practical reasons, is something we refuse to accept. Moreover, absolutist theory ignores the very real experience we have when we attempt to translate from other languages and cultures. To a greater or lesser degree we are always frustrated in these attempts, for although translation is always possible, it is never perfect. Absolutist theory is unacceptable, for an acceptable theory should be one that seems to fit our lived experience of things.

We must work out a coherent theory of cultural relativity and ontological plurality that rejects logical and scientific reductionism yet avoids the snares of relativism. This is why, after attempting in the following chapter to discern reflectively some of the basic characteristics that all systems of understanding have in common, we shall, in chapter 4, examine the concept of analogy to see if it can provide a viable theoretical alternative to both univocity (absolutism) and equivocity (relativism).

In the collection of essays on *Rationality*, Alasdaire MacIntyre, a critic of Winch who defends the view that science provides rational criteria for critically assessing beliefs of other cultures as well as the religious ones of our own and who defends the possibility of an anthropological science, is quite right when he says of his own position, "A Christian refutation of this paper would have to provide an alternative account of intelligibility."[5] It is just such an alternative account of intelligibility and, necessarily, of reality that this study will seek to provide.

NOTES

1. Saint Thomas Aquinas, *Summa Theologiae* (Alba, 1962), I, 5, 1.

2. Margaret Mead, ed., *Cultural Patterns and Technical Change* (New York, 1955), p. 299.

3. Claude Lévi-Strauss, *Tristes Tropiques* (New York, 1961), p. 384.

4. While we will wish later on (in chapter 4) to reject the notion of a determinate human nature, we will nonetheless, unlike the relativists, want to maintain that there is some sense in speaking of universal norms or the unity of reality. Our problem is this: although we wish to reject rationalist absolutism, we still want to justify a certain kind of universal validity for our statements. "Facts" may be relative to the mode of understanding or discourse one adopts, but surely this fact of the relativity of all facts is not itself relative but constitutes a universal truth.

5. J. Beattie, *Other Cultures* (New York, 1968), p. 87.

6. E. E. Evans-Pritchard, *Witchcraft, Oracles and Magic among the Azande* (Oxford, 1937), p. 13.

7. Ibid., p. 153. In his study of Navajo witchcraft, Clyde Kluckhohn has remarked on the difficulties involved in collecting information on the subject from even the common citizen: "The principal reason that so little is known of Navaho witchcraft is the extreme reluctance of the Indians to discuss the matter" *(Navaho Witchcraft* [Boston, 1967], p. 13). "The experience of many observers shows that one can have a good superficial knowledge of a Navaho group or know a number of Navaho individuals fairly well and hear relatively little about witchcraft" (ibid., p. 124). Again, with regard to the Nuer, Evans-Pritchard says, "They tend to be reserved in discussing religious matters, and it may even be said that a certain secrecy adheres to them; and those whom a European tends to know best, the younger men, have less an awareness of the sacramental role of cattle than the older people" *(Nuer Religion* [Oxford, 1974], p. 270). Frank Waters also makes some interesting observations on Indian secrecy in his study of the Navajo and Pueblo Indians, *Masked Gods* (New York, 1973), p. 273ff. *The penchant for secrecy seems to be well-nigh a universal phenomenon.* It is worth noting and recording the fact. It is also worth noting that the penchant for secrecy is not peculiar to "primitive" religion only. According to Saint Thomas, one of the reasons for the use of metaphor and sensible imagery in divine revelation is precisely to conceal the true meaning from unsympathetic unbelievers. "The very hiding of truth in figures is useful . . . as a defense against the ridicule of the unbelievers, according to the words, *Give not that which is holy to dogs* (Matt., vii, 6)" *(Summa Theologiae,* I, 1, 9, ad. 2).

8. Evans-Pritchard does make the following confession (or is it a cry of desperation?) when speaking of the Zande use of *asanza* (sing., *sanza*), their usual practice of speaking in a roundabout and deliberately misleading way and their "tortuous mind which prefers concealment and, when it expresses itself, circumlocution":

> It adds greatly to the difficulties of anthropological inquiry. Eventually the anthropologist's sense of security is also undermined, his confidence shaken. He learns the language, can say what he wants to say in it, and can understand what he hears; but then he begins to wonder whether he has really understood, when he sees how often Azande themselves take it for granted that what is said means something other than what is said, and when he cannot be sure, and even they cannot be sure, whether the words do have a nuance or someone imagines that they do, or wants to think that they do. One cannot

know what is going on inside a man. That is the meaning of one of the most quoted proverbs: *"i ni ngere ti boro wa i ni ngere ti baga?"* ("can one look into a person as one looks into a open-wove basket?") (*Social Anthropology and Other Essays,* [New York, 1964], p. 354).

9. G. Steiner, *After Babel* (New York, 1975), p. 355.

10. This could be compared with the reasons for becoming an anthropologist that Lévi-Strauss speaks of:

How can the anthropologist get free of the contradiction implicit in the circumstances of his choice? Under his very nose, and at his disposition, he has a society: his own. Why does he decide to disdain it, reserving for societies distant and different from his own the patience and devotion which he had deliberately withheld from his fellow-citizens? It is not by chance that the anthropologist is rarely on terms of neutrality with his own social group. Where he is a missionary or an administrator, he can be presumed to have identified himself so entirely with a certain order that all his energies are now given to its propagation. And when his professional activity takes place on the scientific or higher academic level, *objective factors in his past can very probably be adduced to prove that he is ill- or unsuited to the society into which he was born.* He has, in fact, become an anthropologist for one of two reasons: either he finds it a practical method of reconciling his membership of a group with his severely qualified acceptance of it—or, more simply, he wishes to turn to advantage an initial attitude of detachment which has already brought him, as we say, "half-way to meet" societies unlike his own (*Tristes Tropiques,* p. 381; italics added).

11. Beattie, *Other Cultures,* p. 47.

12. B. R. Wilson, ed., *Rationality* (New York, 1971).

13. Ibid., pp. ix-x.

14. Ibid., p. xii.

15. Ibid., p. xi.

16. Ibid., p. xv.

17. Ibid., p. xii. Is it perhaps significant that the ambivalent way in which Wilson recognizes cultural relativity here but then imposes on it "inherent bounds" is reflected in a stylistic inconsistency, for when he employs the term "Western" he at first writes it with a small "w" but then afterward with a capital one?

18. Ibid., p. xv (italics added).

19. Ibid., p. xvi.

20. Ibid., p. xvii.

21. Cf. Evans-Pritchard, *Nuer Religion,* pp. 131ff. Evans-Pritchard attempts to show how such a statement is not, as Lévy-Bruhl would have said, "prelogical"; he shows indeed how extremely sophisticated Nuer thought really is.

22. Evans-Pritchard, *Witchcraft,* p. 12 (italics added). Note incidentally how Evans-Pritchard spells "logic" here with a capital "L", as if to accord it some special, transcendent status or truth value.

23. Ibid., p. 119.

24. Ibid., p. 8.

25. Ibid.

26. Ibid., p. 11.

27. Kluckhohn, *Navaho Witchcraft,* p. 65.

28. Ibid., p. 6. One notable presupposition in Kluckhohn is his belief that "induction" furnishes one with uncontestable "scientific" facts. Apparently Kluckhohn subsequently had certain reservations about even the adequacy of his "facts"; cf. M. Marwick, "Witchcraft as a Social Strain-Gage" in Marwick, ed., *Witchcraft and Sorcery* (Baltimore, 1975).

29. B. Malinowski, *Magic, Science, and Religion* (New York, 1954), p. 238.

30. W. T. Jones, *The Sciences and the Humanities* (Berkeley, 1967), p. vii.

31. F. Nietzsche, *The Will to Power* (New York, 1968), ss. 481, 521. Nietzsche is admittedly difficult to understand. Although much of his thought was formulated with Kantian issues in mind, he must not be read in a Kantian sense and be taken to mean that "logic" applies only to the phenomenal world and not to the "real" world, the world in itself, which would be unknowable to us. His entire effort, on the contrary, was to discredit as a meaningless concept the notion of a "world in itself."

32. As one anthropologist makes a point of informing students, "An important contribution of social anthropology has been to demonstrate that the social and cultural institutions of societies remote from our own must be understood, if they are to be understood at all, through the ideas and values current in those societies, and not simply in our own terms. And this kind of comprehension is only possible when the investigator moves, usually literally as well as metaphorically, out of his own culture into the unfamiliar one which he wishes to understand, and 'learns' the new culture as he would learn a new language. (Often, indeed, the field anthropologist's first task is to master an unfamiliar tongue)" (Beattie, *Other Cultures*, p. x).

33. J. Beattie, "On Understanding Ritual," in Wilson, *Rationality*, p. 254.

34. Evans-Pritchard, *Witchcraft*, p. 21.

35. Malinowski, *Magic, Science, and Religion*, p. 125.

36. One anthropologist, while not wishing to embrace "an extreme functionalism," nevertheless writes, "I would interpret the witch [the belief in witchcraft] as expressing indirectly, on the level of fantasy, the powerlessness and dependency of the Indians [of Santiago El Parmar, Guatemala] experience on the level of socio-political reality." Benson Saler, "Nagual, Witch, and Sorcerer in a Quiché Village," in J. Middleton, ed., *Magic, Witchcraft, and Curing* (Garden City, N.Y., 1967), p. 98.

37. This is not to assert that functionalism, Marxism, Freudianism, structuralism, or any other particular aspirant for the title of human science is a valid form of science. They all lay claim to science, but whether they are adequately scientific is another question, which needs to be determined scientifically. Since it is an intrascientific question, it need not concern us here. For a critique of functionalism qua scientific explanation, see I. C. Jarvie, "Limits to Functionalism and Alternatives to It in Anthropology," in R. Manners and D. Kaplan, eds., *Theory in Anthropology* (Chicago, 1968).

38. C. Lévi-Strauss, *The Savage Mind* (Chicago, 1966), pp. 246-47.

39. E. Leach, *Lévi-Strauss*, (London, 1970), pp. 52-53. See also Levi-Strauss, *Tristes Tropiques*, p. 160, where he states that the totality of human customs is built up out of a finite number of elements, which it would be possible in principle to determine and to group together in a kind of periodic chart like the one for chemical elements.

40. Evans-Pritchard, "The Morphology and Function of Magic: A Comparative Study of Trobiand and Zande Ritual and Spells," in Middleton, *Magic, Witchcraft, and Curing*, p. 22. The following articles are also excellent examples of this type of approach: M. H. Wilson, "Witch-Beliefs and Social Structure" and S. F. Nadel, "Witchcraft in Four African Societies," in Marwick, *Witchcraft and Sorcery*.

41. In all fairness, Evans-Pritchard, unlike other, more extremist representatives of functionalism, does not believe that a cultural phenomenon (such as religion) is fully "explained" when it has been analyzed in sociological terms. See *Nuer Religion*, esp. pp. 285-86, 320.

42. D. Bidney, *Theoretical Anthropology* (New York, 1967), pp. xix, xx. Bidney nonetheless protests that such a view is not reductionist. The logic of his position is not readily apparent.

43. An anthropological position called "cultural materialism" is defended by M. Harris in *The Rise of Anthropological Theory* (New York, 1968):

> I believe that the analogue of the Darwinian strategy in the realm of sociocultural phenomena is the principle of techno-environmental and techno-economical determinism. This principle holds that similar technologies applied to similar environments tend to produce similar arrangements of labor in production and distribution, which

justify and coordinate their activities by means of similar systems of values and beliefs. Translated into research strategy, the principle of techno-environmental, techno-economic determinism assigns priority to the study of the material conditions of socio-cultural life, much as the principle of natural selection assigns priority to the study of differential reproductive success (p. 4).

Harris's tactic is apparent here; he is attempting to confer scientific respectability on anthropology by modeling it on biology (with not an insignificant amount of Marxist-inspired notions thrown in for good measure).

44. E. Sapir, *Culture, Language, and Personality* (Berkeley, 1970), pp. 182-83.

45. P. Winch, "The Idea of a Social Science" and "Understanding a Primitive Society," in Wilson, *Rationality;* see also Winch, *The Idea of a Social Science and Its Relation to Philosophy* (London, 1958).

46. Winch, "Understanding a Primitive Society," p. 80.

47. Winch, "Idea of a Social Science," p. 15.

48. Winch, "Understanding a Primitive Society," p. 95 (italics added).

49. See my article, "Le postulat d'objectivité dans la science et la philosophie du sujet," *Philosophiques* 1, no. 1 (April 1974). Of course, social reality is a much more complex phenomenon than physical reality. In dealing with the social we must take account of the attitudes of the subjects being studied and their reactions to the fact of their being studied, a problem that physics does not face, though something of an analogue could perhaps be found on the subatomic level where the nuclear physicist has to take account of the reaction of the particles to his observation of them. Accordingly the method of a social science will have to be more elaborate and complex than that of the physical sciences. See Lewis White Beck, "The 'Natural Science Ideal' in the Social Science," in Manners and Kaplan, *Theory in Anthropology.*

50. Evans-Pritchard, *Social Anthropology,* pp. 148-49; see also pp. 61-62.

51. Lévi-Strauss, *Tristes Tropiques,* p. 62 (translation corrected).

52. Bidney, *Theoretical Anthropology,* p. xxxviii.

53. Ibid., p. xviii.

54. P. Riesman, "A Comprehensive Anthropological Assessment," in D. Noel, *Seeing Castaneda* (New York, 1976), p. 52.

55. A. MacIntyre, "Is Understanding Religion Compatible with Believing?" in Wilson, *Rationality,* p. 76.

3

SEPARATE REALITIES: MAGIC VERSUS SCIENCE

The true world is that as revealed by science. Only the language of science and logic is meaningful and true; it accordingly furnishes the common denominator for the analysis of all other languages or modes of discourse. Such is the position that the rationalist is led to as a consequence of his desire for an objective criterion of rationality, for definiteness of reference, and fixity, univocity of meaning. The result of this identification of truth with scientific truth and meaning or of rationality with the language of science and logic is the reduction of all other forms of expression, in other cultures as in our own, to the supposedly universal language of science. "It is," as the scientific rationalist says (B. F. Skinner, in this case), "science or nothing."

Against this dehumanizing reductionism the antiscientific relativist rightly protests, for he knows from his own personal experience that there is more in the world and in human life than is ever dreamed of by science. Objecting to the scientific monopoly on meaning and truth, the relativist retaliates by decentralizing rationality and by fragmenting it into a multitude of different languages or "ways of life," each one of which, he says, possesses its own "logic" and truth-value. As Winch does, he will say that "intelligibility takes many and varied forms" and there is no "norm for intelligibility in general."[1] In this, however, he is merely perpetuating, and even compounding, the error on which rationalism rests: the error of equating reality with the particular world projected or expressed by a language. In relativism the one world of science becomes the many, disparate worlds of a host of different ways of life. Rationalism was able to allow, theoretically, for the possibility of understanding the other and for translation, albeit at the price of a ruthless reductionism. In relativism, however, translation is rendered simply impossible since there is now "no norm for intelligibility in general." No understanding of the other is possible now short of becoming the other. The practical consequences of relativism are thus every bit as undesirable as those of rationalism, for if it is impossible to us to understand another culture, then there is surely no point in trying to do so. Because translation and communication are impossible, one can now ignore the other and in fact impose one's own views on the other in good conscience.

Most relativists would not wish to endorse this consequence, but nonetheless it is the one that logically follows from the denial of norms for intelligibility in general. This is perhaps why one rarely, if at all, encounters an out-and-out relativist; nobody, one imagines, could be quite so naive as to cut the ground from under his own feet willingly by taking on all the contradictions that are the inevitable outcome of a thoroughgoing relativism. Indeed relativism can be maintained as a philosophical position only because relativists at one point or another sidestep the logical consequences of their position and are inconsistent. A position such as that of the later Wittgenstein, for instance, which tends to deny universal criteria of any sort and substitutes for this the vague notion of "family resemblances," is possible only so long as it is not stated as a theory (and Wittgenstein scrupulously avoids all tendencies to anything like a general theory). Relativism thus leads a parasitical life on the margins of rationalism, protesting against its vices but unable to formulate a proper *theory of its own.*

It is, however, necessary, as MacIntyre rightly noted, that a refutation of rationalism provide an alternate theory of intelligibility. And the theory must be able to lay claim to some kind of universal validity; it must offer a norm for intelligibility in general. We say that a person's life is senseless, pointless, if there is no unity to it. The same must apply to human life as a whole. What constitutes its unity? All beliefs are beliefs about reality; all cultures have their "myths"—such as our "science"—that lay claim to truth. What then is reality, truth? Is it possible to formulate a theory about reality that is not rationalist, that does not reduce it to the limits of any one particular culture or language? This would be possible only if reality is not linked in an isomorphic fashion to any one language or way of life but is seen as transcendental in regard to all. If all cultures and modes of expression are "equally true" and if reality is yet somehow "one," then reality must be transcendental in regard to culture and language. Terms such as *meaning, truth,* and *reality* must be, from culture to culture, from language to language, neither absolutely univocal nor purely equivocal but somehow analogical and must point to an underlying analogical unity in reality, an *analogia entis,* as the medievals would have said. A viable alternative to rationalism, one that seeks to account for the undeniable fact of relativity, must seek to view reality as something transcendental, transcultural, translinguistic. If reality is indeed common to all cultures and modes of expression—if they are all in their own way "true"—while being identical with none, then we can hope to form an adequate theory of reality only by discovering what is analogically common to all cultures and modes of expression. To do this we must adopt a transcendental approach to the question of reality and truth by reflecting on human understanding itself, its scope, and limits.

We shall attempt to discern reflectively the various modes of human understanding in their actual working. To do so, it will be necessary to suspend judgment as to whether they are "true" in the sense of adequately expressing reality. To suspend judgment in this regard is to bracket all questions as to what reality really is in order to be able to describe and analyze human understanding as such, without regard to the intended object of understanding, "reality."

When we take as our object of inquiry human understanding itself, it immediately becomes apparent that what is common to all cultures and modes of knowing and is basic to each (what, in other words, is universal) is the creative act. Through expressing themselves creatively and constructing various systems of meaning, people come to some understanding of themselves and achieve what they call "truth." The creative act also, however, gives rise to a plurality of different and dissimilar cultures and thus to what might be called a plurality of different and dissimilar truths. In order to understand how there can be something like a common truth in spite of the plurality of cultural truths, it is necessary to re-examine the nature of the creative act itself.[2]

In a way culture and creativity are synonymous. Culture is both the condition for and the consequence of the creative act. This might seem to be contradictory, for it might appear that cultural and linguistic plurality is more of a hindrance than a help to creativity. Because cultures are numerous and diverse, they are also partial, or limiting and constricting. People are sometimes heard to complain of the restraints placed on them by their culture, their times, their vehicle of expression. The ideal would seem to be to transcend all cultural and linguistic barriers so as to be free to do and say all that one wanted. Such a freedom would, however, be a freedom from everything and consequently a freedom for nothing. It would in fact be pure chaos, the infinite void of pure possibility where nothing is possible, precisely because everything is possible.

It is, then, as though the possibilities open to humans are, ontologically speaking, so infinitely enormous that people cannot even begin to act and to create and to understand unless they first somehow delimit their possibilities. This delimitation and the laying down of particular rules, particular structures of action, and modes of expression is the definition of culture. A given culture is nothing other than a particular system of rules and constraints. Importantly, however, rules and constraints are not the opposite of freedom and creativity, for freedom and creativity become real, as opposed to merely ideal, possibilities only when there are structural forms within which or in terms of which one can operate. As one composer has observed, "It is not sufficient to have the whole world at one's disposal—the very infinitude of possibilities cancels out possibilities, as it were, until limitations are discovered."[3]

To know or understand something (in the sense of having positive, determinate knowledge of it) is to be able to classify it, to be able to situate it within a certain context or system, to be able to say of it, "This is an instance of that" (this is the traditional definition of judgment: subsuming a particular under a universal). (From this it follows that it is impossible to have positive knowledge of the world or reality as a whole. With what could it be compared, and within what wider context could it be situated?) To express oneself meaningful is to follow the rules of a certain linguistic or conceptual "game," and games are precisely finite, structured, and rule-governed modes of behavior: "All coherent thinking is equivalent to playing a game according to a set of rules."[4] The great man of antiquity, who was honored by his community because he made action possible and life meaningful, was the law giver, the constitution framer, such as Lycurgus and Solon. The delimitation of possibility in the form of cultural particularity at one and the same time narrows possibilities and opens up horizons of action and meaning, and so were it not for the limiting structures of culture, meaning, and thus truth, would be completely inaccessible to people, for, faced with an infinite ocean of possibilities, they would have nothing actual to grab hold of and no ground on which to anchor their endeavors and would simply drown in this immense, formless sea.

From the point of view of culture and creative expression, reality could be said to be a kind of chaos of undifferentiated possibilities. (This must be understood as a characterization that we are temporarily adopting in order to facilitate an analysis of human understanding. After we have worked out a theory of understanding we will be able to return, in chapter 9, to the properly metaphysical question of the "nature" of reality and will be able to determine what, properly speaking, it can and cannot be said to "be.") Now if reality itself is somehow "chaotic," human understanding must be a selective activity, which confers some semblance of order on this welter of pure possibility.

To understand, it must be said, is to interpret; to perceive something is to see it as some thing. We never hear auditory stimuli or see raw sense data; what we always hear and see are certain things, which the language we speak has already named for us. Chaos, the absence of determinations, cannot be perceived and repels the mind. The act of understanding is thus precisely that: an act, an activity. We do not passively perceive a reality already there, for what (ontologically, not epistemologically) is initially there, what initially exists for us, what reality in the first instance is is not any actual thing but any number of possible "things." A system of knowledge or a science thus in a sense creates its object by structuring chaotic reality in a certain way. In the words of one writer:

The world does not present itself to us neatly packaged into cultural events, psychological events, biological events or physiochemical events; nor does it present itself to us in terms of "levels of reality" or "natural phenomena." It comes to us as a stream of concrete events which are "just what they are." Out of the countless properties associated with any given event, the ones that are selected out for special concern will depend upon one's theoretical interests and scientific purposes. Since language is by its very nature abstractive—and all knowledge about the world if it is not to remain private must be stated in propositional form—we can never exhaust the total "concreteness" of an event. Nor is it the purpose of any theoretical science to faithfully reproduce "reality," either in whole or in part. We are, in effect, constantly engaged in a process of theoretical selecting-out, and it is for this reason that the notion of "pure" description is a chimera. To put it in a slightly different way, while there may be one "reality," there are many different kinds of questions which one can address to that reality and in consequence many different ways of conceptualizing it. And since this reality is never grasped directly, but only through our conceptualizations of it, the nature of reality turns out to be as varied as there are different theoretical formulations of it. We cannot somehow get behind our concepts to a non-conceptualized "real" world. The point of all this is that the *logical* independence of a science is not based upon having its own separate "chunk of reality" with which to deal—for this is not true of any science. Rather, it is based upon the fact that it has a set of distinct questions or problems which are its special concern, and that in seeking answers to these problems it has developed a body of distinct terms and concepts (which determine its subject-matter), as well as laws and theories (which organize and explain its subject-matter).[5]

This basic fact regarding the selective activity of consciousness was already pointed out by one of the greatest of American philosophers, William James, and it formed the basis of his philosophy. "Each science," he said, "arbitrarily carves out a field from the scheme of things in which to lodge itself."[6] In a more general vein he writes:

Out of what is in itself an undistinguishable, swarming *continuum,* devoid of distinction or emphasis, our senses make for us, by attending to this motion and ignoring that, a world full of contrasts, of sharp accents, of abrupt changes, of picturesque light and shade. . . . reasoning is but another form of the selective activity of the mind. . . . the mind is at every stage a theatre of simultaneous possibilities. Consciousness consists in the comparison of these with each other, the selection of some, and the suppression of the rest by the reinforcing and inhibiting agency of attention. . . . The mind, in short, works on the data it receives very much as a sculptor works on his block of stone. In a sense the statue stood there from eternity. But there were a thousand different ones beside it, and the sculptor alone is to thank for having extricated this one from the rest. Just so, the world of each of us, however different our several views of it may be, all lay embedded in the primordial chaos of sensations, which give the mere *matter* to the thought of all of us indifferently.[7]

Since the time of James, work in the psychology and physiology of the senses has amply demonstrated that even in the case of sense perception, one does not merely form passive copies of a supposedly determinate reality but actively participates in the very constitution of what one sees. As Gestalt psychology has shown, the eye is already something of a free and discriminating ("mindful") agent; it is in fact impossible to separate eye and mind radically.[8] "Perception," Gadamer appropriately remarks, "always includes meaning."[9] Percept is inseparable from concept, and there is no such thing as a pure or mere sensation any more than there can be a word or language that is purely denotative (referential) and not also, in its very function of denotation, connotative. The eye already "thinks" (interprets) what it sees, and the reality that it presents to the mind is one that the mind has already accredited in advance. As the historian of science, Thomas Kuhn, observes, "What a man sees depends both upon what he looks at and also upon what his previous visual-conceptual experience has taught him to see. In the absence of such training there can only be, in James's phrase, 'a bloomin' buzzin' confusion.' "[10] James himself says, "Sensations and apperceptive ideas fuse here so intimately that you can no more tell where one begins and the other ends, than you can tell, in those cunning circular panoramas that have lately been exhibited, where the real foreground and the painted canvas join together."[11] And a more recent philosopher, Nelson Goodman, referring to recent research in psychology and on the relativity of vision remarks:

> There is no innocent eye. . . . Not only how but what it sees is regulated by need and prejudice. It selects, rejects, organizes, discriminates, associates, classifies, analyzes, constructs. It does not so much mirror as take and make; and what it takes and makes it sees not bare, as items without attributes, but as things, as food, as people, as enemies, as stars, as weapons. Nothing is seen nakedly or naked.
>
> The myths of the innocent eye and of the absolute given are unholy accomplices. Both derive from and foster the idea of knowing as a processing of raw material received from the senses, and of this raw material as being discoverable either through purification rites or by methodical disinterpretation. But reception and interpretation are not separable operations; they are thoroughly interdependent.[12]

This might be thought to be a somewhat awkward way of putting the matter, for in saying that it is impossible to separate eye from mind radically or that sensation and conception, reception and interpretation are inseparable, one seems to be admitting that there are indeed two elements in all cognition, which, however, are always bound up together and can never be separated, whereas in fact this two-element theory of understanding must be denied. This awkwardness is unavoidable, for as is always the case in human understanding, a new theory can be formulated and understood only by contrasting it with a previously accepted and current theory. No theory is determined by a supposed relation to reality (such that it would be "reality," "what is really the case in point of fact," which prescribes or even "validates" a proper theory about it). Instead a theory, like a semantic unit within the sphere of language, receives its determination and specificity—its meaning—from its opposition to other theories.

The theory that must here be opposed and rejected is the one that conceives of the mind as a kind of two-tiered device for receiving and processing "information." This is the central theory of empiricism, which takes up the scholastic dictum, *nihil est in intellectu quod non prius fuerit in sensu,* and conceives of the mind as simply a mechanism for combining and associating—according to certain determinate psychological laws that James Mill for one attempted to spell out—the "raw data" of the senses. And it is also the theory of Kantian epistemology, which differs from classic empiricism only in the conceptual twist it gives to it. Here the mind is not just a transmitter of information but is instead an active transformer of information.[13] This underlying and constantly presupposed distinction between sensation and intellection (and between understanding and reality as well), however, must be rejected.

In his attempt to work out a new philosophy of language and to overcome views of language of the sort I criticized in chapter 1, the literary critic, I. A. Richards, is forced into dealing with basic problems in the theory of understanding and, referring to James also, is led to much the same conclusion we are aiming at. Just as he wishes to deny that words merely "refer" to extralinguistic realities, which are what they are independently of language (a belief he aptly labels the "Proper Meaning Superstition"), so also he realizes that he must deny that there are in the mind anything like "sensations":

> That sounds drastic but is almost certainly true if rightly understood. A sensation would be something that just was *so,* on its own, a datum; as such we have none. Instead we have perceptions, responses whose character comes to them from the past as well as the present occasion. A perception is never just of an *it;* perception takes whatever it perceives as a thing of a certain sort. All thinking from the lowest to the highest—whatever else it may be—is sorting.[14]

And later, when talking about metaphor, he makes the following remark, which should be kept in mind because it points to the inseparability of perception and expression and implies that both are but different aspects of the imagination: "The processes of metaphor in language, the exchanges between the meanings of words which we study in explicit verbal metaphors, are super-imposed upon a perceived world which is itself a product of earlier or unwitting metaphor."[15] Perception is itself "metaphorical"; all seeing is a seeing-as.[16]

Thus perception and imagination are activities that differ only in degree; the real and the fictive are both children of the mind. Some fictions are more tenacious and are backed up with more intersubjective and cultural sanctions, and these are the ones we call "realities." Out of what we have seen Whorf refer to as the "kaleidoscopic flux of impressions which has to be organized by our minds," we pick out certain strands while ignoring others and then proceed to weave these strands together to form a unified fabric, which we then call "reality"; this is the work of the productive imagination. The activity of the storyteller who, out of the overabundant profusion of human acts, selects just those which are to count and who then proceeds to work them up into a coherent story, conferring thereby a meaning on them and on a human life: this is the basic paradigm of all mental activity.

The selective and discriminating character of human understanding is apparent even in science, itself a cultural and, originally, creative game. Modern science would never have arisen had people not devised the scientific method, which is a deliberate attempt to narrow one's perspectives and eliminate all "distracting" sensory solicitations. The true scientist knows that he must exclude from his field of vision and forget (abstract from) the incredible richness of nature, which so fascinates the painter and poet, if he is to get down to any serious scientific business. There is nothing to be criticized in this; the narrowing of the field of vision is indispensable to the scientific project, and a botanist who, like some Wordsworth, let himself revel in the beauty of a flower in a meadow would never arrive at a scientific knowledge of the plant.[17] Stephen Toulmin, a philosopher of science, says:

> To talk, in the philosophy of science, of theoretical physics falsifying by abstraction, and to ask for the facts and nothing but the facts, is to demand the impossible, like asking for a map drawn to no particular projection and having no particular scale. In epistemology, too, to argue that our everyday concepts falsify by abstraction or are necessary conditions of experience, with the suggestion that one thereby points to a defect in our conceptual equipment or to an unfortunate limitation on our capacity for experiencing, is to evince a similar misconception. If we are to say anything, we must be prepared to abide by the rules and conventions that govern the terms in which we speak: to adopt these is no submission, nor are they shackles. Only if we are so prepared can we hope to say anything true—or anything untrue.[18]

In short, as Gerald Holton, physicist and historian of science, remarks, "We are always surrounded by more 'phenomena' than we can use, and which we decide—and must decide—to discard at any particular stage of science.''[19] And as Holton points out, selection in science operates at three successive levels: in regard to the "facts," which the scientist isolates and which then constitute the "data" of his problem; in regard to the type of hypothesis he will have recourse to in order to "explain" the facts; and in regard to the explanatory method he chooses to follow in "testing" his hypothesis.[20]

Wordsworth himself would never have stopped to marvel over his daffodils had he not excluded from his field of vision a multitude of possible details of interest perhaps to the florist or to the farmer but not to the poet. As Henry James, the novelist brother of William James, remarked in the preface to *The Spoils of Poynton,* life is all inclusion and confusion, and art is all discrimination and selection. Both art and science operate a rigorous selection and choose to call "real" only that which they deem important. They differ, of course, on what this shall be.

If, then, understanding arises through the selective and constructive activity of consciousness, we can formulate a basic law that appears to apply to all modes of understanding. *All systems of understanding, all products of human expression, have a bipolar nature: they are both revealing and concealing.* To select certain things and deem them important is to ignore other things as irrelevant. Just as there is an inescapable dialectic between limits and creativity, between rules and freedom, just as this dialectic is characteristic of the creative act itself, so also is there a dialectic in the creative product, in any particular culture or any particular literary or scientific work. Because the creative act is rendered possible by the limitations imposed on the context in which it arises, that which is expressed in this act bears the mark of these limitations. What is said is said only because other things that could have been said were not said but were ignored. If indeed one is to say something, one must not try to say everything. If a writer spends his entire life writing, it is because the "definitive work" is not possible, because no one can say everything. One of the most difficult things about writing is the discipline it takes to refrain from saying all those things that press in on one and demand to be expressed. The writer must learn—and it is not easy—to ignore his feeling that, as the novelist Thomas Wolfe said (*The Story of a Novel*), everything has not only to be used but also to be told and nothing can be implied.

Human understanding is always cultural and historical, which is to say partial and finite, and no one "truth" can exhaust the reservoir of possible truth (of what could be said and held to be true). It thus could be said that all human truths are but the expression of an understanding which is a finite grasp of what Anaximander called τὸ ἄπειρον, the Infinite, a limited understanding of the Unlimited, a circumscribed awareness of the All-Encompassing. All language both shows and conceals; creative expression is an endless game of hide-and-seek.

In the remainder of this chapter we shall reflect in more detail on this dual characteristic of human understanding. We shall concentrate first on those features of truth systems by means of which they allow for some measure of positive understanding—for the formation of viable meanings—and then we shall attempt to see how all understandings also conceal as much as they reveal, how, in other words, understanding necessarily tends toward misunderstanding.

We are inquiring into the general characteristics of human understanding, and because we wish to situate the world of science within the larger universe of creative discourse, it is advisable to begin not by opposing scientific and nonscientific understanding but rather by seeing what they have in common. Only in this way can we hope to succeed in discovering the proper limits of science. Because science, like art and religion, is a human activity and not a gift made by the gods, it is doubtful that there can be any truly radical difference between these different modes of understanding. As one of the most outstanding physicists of our time, Werner Heisenberg, remarked, "Science is made by men, a self-evident fact that is far too often forgotten. If it is recalled here, it is in the hope of reducing the gap between the two cultures, between art and science."[21]

Just then as we have to reject as an unwarranted assumption that begs the question, the claim of the positivists that only science gives us truth, so also we cannot maintain as self-evident that science has no truth-value but only technological usefulness. Nevertheless this latter position is espoused by that most outstanding thinker, Martin Heidegger, who lists art, politics, religion, and philosophy as ways in which truth happens but expressly excludes science from this list: "By contrast, science is not an original happening of truth, but always the cultivation of a domain of truth already opened."[22] There may be some validity to Heidegger's claim, but if we take a purely reflective view of the different modes of understanding and abstract for the time being from the question of their "truth"—if, that is, we suspend all judgment as to their reality status—perhaps we may see that they all exhibit the same general structures. And as a consequence we may see that far from being a useful distinguishing criterion, truth itself needs to be redefined in light of the way understanding actually functions.

Now whether our object is science or religion, it is evident, from a reflective point of view, that in either case human understanding, to the degree that it seeks to be positive knowledge, is characterized by the fact that it tends toward the construction of a system. Consciousness is selective, and what it selects it must work into some pattern or arrangement. A statement of whatever sort can lay claim to truth only if it is meaningful, and it has meaning only by belonging to a certain frame of reference, a certain matrix of thought or universe of discourse. It is the frame of reference—the system—that, as a set of rules, prescribes the way in which the statement is to be interpreted. Thus it is that we speak of the grammar of religious discourse or the logic of science.

All positive knowledge tends to take the form of a system. This is perhaps most apparent in the case of science; it is not only science, however, but all positive knowledge *as such* that is systematic, for to say that one "knows" something is simply another way of saying that one knows how to situate it in regard to a given context. Not to be able to situate something, to classify it, is not to know it. One may marvel or wonder over the unknown and unfamiliar, but when one has come to know it, all wonder has disappeared; knowledge begins in wonder, but wonder dissolves in knowledge. "Mere facts" thus do not exist in any determinate sense, for what the eye cannot interpret and classify, it does not and will not "see." Pure chaos is as unperceivable as sheer nonsense is unthinkable. In the case of science, a "fact" becomes a scientific fact only when it is capable of being integrated and explained in terms of a general scientific theory or frame of reference. In some cases this can be done only by altering the theory in question so as to produce a more inclusive system. But were there no system, there would be no facts and, a fortiori, no discovery of "new" facts. As Thomas Kuhn observes, "In science . . . novelty emerges only with difficulty, manifested by resistance, against a background provided by expectation. Initially, only the anticipated and usual are experienced even under circumstances where anomaly is later to be observed."[23]. No number of "anomalous facts" are capable of falsifying a scientific theory until they are themselves structured by an alternative theory.

To understand, therefore, means to transform chaos into order and to construct a system of meaning. Here there is no difference between the mind of the primitive aborigine and that of the modern scientist. The "primitive" mind, as Lévi-Strauss has shown, functions in substantially the same way as the scientific mind; it is the phenomena to which they apply themselves that serve principally to distinguish them.[24] "All men by nature desire to know," Aristotle wrote at the beginning of his treatise on metaphysics, and this is confirmed by Lévi-Strauss who finds in primitive people "a genuinely scientific attitude, a sustained and always watchful curiosity, and a desire for knowledge for its own sake."[25] And the primitive expresses knowledge in the same way as does the scientific anthropologist who studies him: by establishing detailed classifications or "arrangements," as Lévi-Strauss says, and constructing complex systems of meaning. No utterance can be said to express knowledge unless it is part of a general system of meaning—no more than any sound can be said to be a word unless it is part of a general system of linguistic, phonetic values.

To the degree that understanding is an understanding of anything—that is, is positive, revealing—it is systematic; it tends, with greater or lesser success, to assume the form of a system. Another basic characteristic of all bodies of knowledge should in addition be explicitly noted. All systems, like living, organic beings, are closed systems of meanings. As William James observed, "A system, to be a system at all must come as a *closed* system, reversible in this or that detail, perchance, but in its essential features never."[26] It may be that no actual system can ever achieve complete closure, but it nonetheless is the case that all systems are systems only to the degree that they are closed, self-sufficient universes of discourse.

This is most obvious in the case of science where the ideal is that of a total, exhaustive, and systematic body of knowledge, a total knowledge of the totality, the cosmos. "The ultimate ideal of any science is the formulation of a comprehensive and systematic theoretical structure, i.e., a set of highly interconnected, hierarchically ordered and 'logically closed' theoretical propositions."[27] Lévi-Strauss writes, "The entire process of human knowledge thus assumes the character of a closed system."[28] And he sees in the most modern forms of science that tend toward this status of a closed system a vindication of the deepest motives and desires of primitive thought.

Thus it follows that there can be no such thing as an "open" system; an open system is a *contradictio in adjectivo*. Apologists for science like to claim that their system is an open one, but this is a false and misleading claim. What is true is that one system may be more flexible than another, but all that this means is that one system may be better capable of ingesting and digesting new experiences than another. All systems have a built-in safety device mechanism whose function is to suppress whatever might serve to challenge and overthrow the system.

One can discern in art, as well as in science, the desire for totality, closure, and absoluteness. Proust's great work, *A la recherche du temps perdu*, is one such attempt to achieve the status of a closed system. The book doubles back on itself and is the story of itself, of how the author came to write it; it ends at the moment when the author begins to write the book and in this way forms a giant circle. The perfect work, in science as in art, is self-grounding and self-sufficient; it forms a circle, the most perfect of all forms, for a circle is, by definition, closed and complete, with neither beginning nor end; it is unlimited. In painting too, one often comes across the "closure phenomenon," as when the painter paints himself in the act of painting or when, as in Van Eyck's "Marriage," the entire scene is concentrated and re-expressed in a mirror within the painting itself that reflects the entire painting. In such instances it would seem that artists, as Merleau-Ponty remarked, are "claiming that there is a total or absolute vision, outside of which there is nothing and which closes itself over them."[29] The true artwork, such as a statue or a piece of music, stands on its own, serves no ulterior purpose, and expresses nothing but itself.

It could thus be said that the mark of perfection of any mode of understanding or system of knowledge is the degree to which it approaches the status of a tautology—that is, the degree to which it achieves closure and self-sufficiency. Let us see in more detail how this is the case in regard to two quite distinct yet equally definite systems of understanding (which may not be as radically different as is commonly thought): magic and science.

A very persistent way of characterizing magic—found in Lévi-Strauss as much as in Frazer, albeit with certain significant differences—is to say that magic is primitive science (*la science sauvage*). Or, as Malinowski says, "Both magic and science show certain similarities, and, with Sir James Frazer, we can appropriately call magic a pseudo-science."[30] Thus the difference between modern science and primitive magic is that between legitimate and illegitimate science. Magic is illegitimate science because it has not yet freed itself from superstition; it posits occult and unverifiable forces and does not seek to explain phenomena in terms of natural, observable causes.

But to speak of magic as a form of superstition is to prejudice, to prejudge, the issue at the very outset and thereby to exclude the possibility of any meaningful comparison between magic and science, for the word *superstition* intrinsically is pejorative and has no real meaning apart from "not being in accord with the facts"; for all practical purposes, the word is simply a synonym for *unscientific*.[31] The dictionary defines *superstition* as "any belief or attitude that is inconsistent with the known laws of science or with what is generally considered in the particular society as true and rational."[32]

If, then, in attempting to classify magic and science, one says that the former is superstition, one is actually saying nothing at all, merely that magic is not science, that it is not true, that he does not agree with it. But because in primitive society magic is not superstition, from the primitive's point of view, it would be our science that is superstitious. One person's science is another's superstition. To attempt to distinguish between science and magic by an appeal to the truth, to "agreement with the facts," will not get us anywhere because what people take to be the facts varies according to their beliefs. People often marvel over how primitives are able to get by as well as they do and have for so many thousands of years with the extremely rudimentary "scientific" knowledge they possess and the positive handicap of so many "false" beliefs, such as that sickness and death are due to witchcraft and not to natural and controllable causes. What we should marvel over is not this, however, but the very fact that people do express their wonder in this way. Because most people, victims of our own culture, assume that science is knowledge of the "facts," they find it difficult to imagine how belief in magic can be maintained when magic is so obviously incompatible with science and thus, supposedly, in error as to what "really" is the case. How can magic work, how can its falsity not be apparent, when it so blatantly contradicts the facts? Or, as Malinowski asks, "Plausible though the fallacious claims of magic might be to primitive man, how is it that they have remained so long unexposed?"[33]

To ask this kind of question, however, is to prevent oneself totally from understanding what magic is (and what science, too, is for that matter). To talk about "facts" and to try to distinguish between magic and science in this way is to fall victim to a thoroughly spurious issue. A scientific "fact," such as an atom is, after all, no more observable and no more "factual" than something like witchcraft substance (a substance in the body of witches that makes them witches). We will not succeed in discovering how belief in magic is possible (or science either) as long as we concentrate on the interpretive constructs of magic—the "facts," such as the witchcraft it is meant to deal with—and ignore how it actually functions as a mode of human understanding, so let us look first at magic and then at science purely as systems of understanding.

Magic and the belief in witchcraft[34] is indeed like science in that it seeks to explain, to make intelligible, to understand, certain evident facts of experience (the facts to be explained through magic are those relating to sickness, misfortune, and death), and it does so in the only way it is possible to understand anything: through constructing a system of meaning. The great merit of Evans-Pritchard's classic study of witchcraft among the Azande of the south Sudan is that it shows in ample detail how magical practices and belief in witchcraft constitute a coherent system. "For the Zande mind," he says, "is logical and inquiring within the framework of its culture and insists on the coherence of its own idiom."[35] This is perhaps the most interesting observation in Evans-Pritchard's study, and it is of the utmost importance for our own comparison of magic and science. Belief in witchcraft and magic is no less logical than belief in science.

Witchcraft is a system of meaning that allows the Azande to explain events that call for an explanation—those that go against normal expectations—and explanation here (as in science) consists of reducing the strange and unexpected to what is familiar and already known. For example, a man plants his eleusine crop correctly and cares for it properly, but the crop fails. The question he asks and that demands an explanation is, Why should his crop fail when he did everything necessary to ensure its success and when those of his neighbors have succeeded, and why should it fail this time when it has not at others? The reason for such a failure cannot be merely technical because technically everthing necessary had been done to ensure the success of the crop. Now, a Zande knows that witchcraft is an ever-present possibility—this is a first principle in his system of thought—and so he does not hesitate to attribute the unexpected event to a known cause: witchcraft.

As another example, an old granary collapses and injures those sitting beneath it. The Zande knows that it was an old, weak structure, and he observes that termites had been eating away at its supports and that it was likely to collapse anyway. He does not deny all of this, but for him it is not a sufficient explanation, for the question remains as to why the granary should have collapsed at exactly the moment when he was sitting under it, at this time and not some other, on him and not someone else. Termites and aged wood may be the occasion or the condition for the granary's collapsing, but they cannot be its cause or provide a sufficient reason. In response to our assertion that they do furnish a sufficient explanation, the Zande could well reply with the words of Socrates: "Fancy being unable to distinguish between the cause of a thing and the condition without which it could not be a cause! It is the latter, as it seems to me, that most people, groping in the dark, call a cause—attaching to it a name to which it has no right."[36]

To say, as we would, that it was mere chance that accounts for the event would not satisfy the Zande. Chance does not explain anything; it is not an answer but the absence of an answer; it is precisely what is in need of an explanation. The true cause of the event can be only witchcraft. The belief in witchcraft does not contradict or violate what we would call natural causation. Evans-Pritchard writes:

> Zande belief in witchcraft in no way contradicts empirical knowledge of cause and effect. The world known to the senses is just as real to them as to us. We must not be deceived by their way of expressing causation and imagine that because they say a man was killed by witchcraft they entirely neglect the secondary causes that, as we judge them, were the true causes of his death.[37]

What witchcraft explains is precisely what "natural" or "secondary" causes cannot account for. The true cause of misfortune thus being known to the Zande, he consults the *benge* or poison oracle to corroborate his assessment of the situation and to discover which witch is responsible for his misfortunes. When he has this information, he can persuade the witch to withdraw his influence or, if the witch has already succeeded in killing a relative of his, he can apply vengeance magic to kill the witch in turn.

The important thing to note is that belief in witchcraft, oracles, and magic constitutes a coherent system, indeed, a total system, wherein every part buttresses every other part. Suspecting that witchcraft is directed against him, a man will consult the oracle to discover the identity of the witch. The oracle will either confirm or deny that witchcraft is operative in this case. If it recognizes the presence of witchcraft, it will reveal the name of the witch. The man will then confront the witch and attempt to persuade him to withdraw his evil influence. Normally the accused will not deny his being a witch and will agree to "cool down," as the Azande say, his witchcraft. The matter usually ends there.[38] Interestingly in thus admitting his "guilt," the witch has validated the oracle's designation of him as a witch and has thereby reinforced the whole system.

But surely, it will be objected, a man knows whether he is a witch and whether he has done a witch's deed, and if he knows that he is not a witch, he will know that the oracle is wrong and will thereby be led to cast doubt on the whole system. This does not happen. First, even if a man denied being a witch, this would in no way affect other people's beliefs in the institution of witchcraft, for they would say he was lying. More importantly, witchcraft, according to the terms of the Zande system, is not something a man may choose or not choose to practice and is not a matter of mere malevolent intention; witchcraft is biologically inherited and a man may be a witch without knowing it. Indeed the way that a man comes to know he is a witch is when the oracle designates him as such. The existence of witches and the validity of the divining oracle are thus mutually self-confirming. The system cannot be disproved; it is self-validating.[39]

The most interesting aspect of witchcraft and magic as a system of belief is its tautological character. This accounts for its perfection as a system and for its long and entrenched existence in the history of the human race. Because witchcraft is a total explanation of reality, it possesses the peculiar feature that it can assimilate even that which would tend to contradict it; it can account for its own failure to explain particular cases, for the poison oracle, the highest court of appeals in the system, at times makes unacceptable predictions—predictions that do not work out in fact—just as, in science, an experiment—the highest court of appeals for us—sometimes fails to demonstrate what it was meant to demonstrate. The interesting feature of the system, though, is that it can explain even these contradictions. Indeed the contradictions serve to reinforce the system, for they can be explained in terms of the system itself; facts that seemingly would validate an alien system, such as that of science, nonetheless can be translated into and thus understood in terms of the system's own conceptual framework. Evans-Pritchard writes:

> Azande observe the action of the poison oracle as we observe it, but their observations are always subordinated to their beliefs and are incorporated into their beliefs and made to explain them and justify them. Let the reader consider any argument that would utterly demolish all Zande claims for the power of the oracle. If it were translated into Zande modes of thought it would serve to support their entire structure of belief. For their mystical notions are eminently coherent, being interrelated by a network of logical ties, and are so ordered that they never too crudely contradict sensory experience but, instead, experience seems to justify them.[40]

The conceptual framework of witchcraft provides a number of ready explanations for seeming failures of the oracle. The operator, for instance, may not have observed the necessary taboos prior to the consultation. Or the poison may not be genuine (the operator can verify this by asking the oracle at the outset, "Poison, are you good?"). Or, witchcraft may be opertive and may be corrupting the oracle (here too the operator may ascertain whether this is the case by asking the oracle an appropriate question). The operator may be incompetent. Something may have happened after the oracle gives its prophecy to alter the course of events (this could have been avoided if subsequent consultations of the oracle had been made). In the case of a lesser oracle, the termites oracle, the oracle may give a bad answer deliberately if it is consulted too often about the same matter, a practice it finds bothersome. In short, there is no lack of alternative explanations within the system itself capable of explaining any apparent breakdown of the system. "Paradox though it be," Evans-Pritchard observes, "the errors as well as the valid judgments of the oracle prove to them its infallibility."[41] To say, for instance, that the oracle did not work correctly because it had been bewitched is a means of confirming the total system of witchcraft belief of which the oracle is a part. "Thus," Malinowski says, "the failures of magic can always be accounted for by the slip of memory, by slovenliness in performance or in observance of a taboo, and, last but not least, by the fact that someone else has performed some counter-magic."[42]

Some people in Zandeland are skeptical of the claim of witch doctors and the pronouncements of oracles. The Azande are no more naturally credulous than any other people and manifest the same spectrum of belief ranging from gullibility to skepticism to be found anywhere. But even skepticism serves to reinforce belief in the system. "Azande are only sceptical of particular oracles," Evans-Pritchard points out, "and not of oracles in general, and their scepticism is always expressed in a mystical idiom that vouches for the validity of the poison oracle as an institution."[43] Again, a Zande may have severe doubts concerning the competence of a given witch doctor and may in fact suspect him of trickery for the sake of personal profit; he may even doubt the integrity of any number of witch doctors with whom he has had dealings, but this will not lead him to doubt the validity of the institution of witch doctor:

> Indeed, scepticism is included in the pattern of belief in witch-doctors. Faith and scepticism are alike traditional. Scepticism explains failures of witch-doctors, and being directed towards particular witch-doctors even tends to support faith in others.[44]

In spite of their belief in magic, however, the Azande, contrary to what might be thought, do not ordinarily behave much differently from Westerners. Like us, most of their time is taken up with the day-to-day routine of making a living and relaxing when they have the time. They are not constantly invoking oracles, practicing magic, or looking for witches. "It is true that some people perform [magical] rites more often than others, but the performance is never more than an occasional break in routine activities of daily life."[45] Azande, in short, lead for the most part the same humdrum kind of existence that people everywhere do. A Zande may not even take witch doctors at all seriously, just as in our society a number of believers are only nominally such and turn toward their church only in moments of crisis. "I have noticed," Evans-Pritchard remarks, "that men who frequently spoke with a measure of contempt about witch-doctors have made speed to visit them when in pain."[46] The same is true of many people in our society who delight in pointing out the corruption, avarice, and inefficiency of the medical profession but do not hesitate to consult a physician when they fall ill.

The Azande believe in their witch doctors for the same reason we believe in our medical doctors: like us, they have little or no choice in the matter. Witchcraft is never seriously called into question because the Azande know of no other system that could take its place. Evans-Pritchard insists that "they reason excellently in the idiom of their beliefs, but they cannot reason outside, or against, their beliefs because they have no other idiom in which to express their thoughts."[47] He writes in more detail:

> There is no incentive to agnosticism. All their beliefs hang together, and were a Zande to give up faith in witch-doctorhood he would have to surrender equally his belief in witchcraft and oracles. A seance of witch-doctors is a public affirmation of the existence of witchcraft. It is one of the ways in which belief in witchcraft is inculcated and expressed. Also, witch-doctors are part of the oracle-system. Together with the rubbing-board oracle they provide questions for the poison oracle which corroborates their revelations. In this web of belief every strand depends upon every other strand, and a Zande cannot get out of its meshes because this is the only world he knows. The web is not an external structure in which he is enclosed. It is the texture of his thought and he cannot think that his thought is wrong.[48]

If one's logic is that of witchcraft, it is no more possible to be persuaded that the alien logic of scientific explanation is more valid than it would be for a scientist to allow for the validity of witchcraft. Science and technology may succeed in the long run in supplanting magic, but they cannot disprove it. Is it not significant that magical beliefs continue to exist—underground—in our own society?

A system as such cannot be falsified. One will find reasons for rejecting a given system only when one has already subscribed to another system. From Evans-Pritchard's descriptions, it is obvious that magic involves circular reasoning. It cannot be criticized for this, however, since circular reasoning is not a defect in any system qua system. Indeed all systems of belief are circular, including science, as the scientist, Michael Polanyi, has shown, on the basis precisely of Evans-Pritchard's presentation of Zande witchcraft.[49] Systems are circular and complete in themselves for they are attempts to discover an underlying order in the world; they are attempts to construct a unified cosmos out of chaos.[10] All knowledge tends to take the form of a system, and all systems are circular and tautological.

Although Evans-Pritchard was never able to overcome his prejudice that magic is false because it contradicts science, it is nevertheless the mark of his integrity as an anthropologist that he was still able to recognize the persuasiveness and viability of the system. Speaking of the rubbing-board oracle, he says that he attempted to "trap the oracle" by asking it very specific questions that could be easily tested, such as, "Will it rain tomorrow?" "The oracle would answer, 'I do not know.' When I asked it questions in more general terms, as the Zande does, it gave me straight affirmative or negative replies, and usually correct ones."[51] Again, in regard to the poison oracle he says:

> I always kept a supply of poison for the use of my household and neighbours and we regulated our affairs in accordance with the oracle's decisions. I may remark that I found this as satisfactory a way of running my house and affairs as any other I know of.[52]

And in general:

> When we see how an individual uses them [Zande notions] we may say that they are mystical but we cannot say that his use of them is illogical or even that it is uncritical. I had no difficulty in using Zande notions as Azande themselves use them. Once the idiom is learnt the rest is easy, for in Zandeland one mystical idea follows on another as reasonably as one common-sense idea follows on another in our own society.[53]

One further aspect of the system of witchcraft and magic should be noted because it will enable us better to compare science with magic. Let us consider the shaman or witch doctor himself, who stands in relation to witchcraft and magic much as the scientist does in relation to science. Like scientists, witch doctors form a profession and closed corporation; they share in a body of esoteric knowledge and techniques unknown to laymen and are a key factor in reinforcing general belief in the system of witchcraft. It would thus seem that if anyone is in a position to know if witchcraft and magic is or is not at bottom a hoax, it would be the witch doctor. Invariably the question is raised as to whether witch doctors really do what they claim to do or whether they cheat. This is of the same sort as the question as to whether magic is true or merely superstitious, and, like it, it has no easy answer. Let us see why.

The role of the shaman or witch doctor is twofold: divination and curing. We shall concentrate on the latter. A witch doctor cures a sick person by extracting from his body a foreign substance, such as a piece of charcoal or a small insect, which is supposed to be the cause of the illness. He will, for example, suck at a part of the patient's body and when he has succeeded in extracting the object, he will show it to the patient, presenting it as the cause of the illness; this extraction is usually sufficient to effect the cure. Does the witch doctor really remove such a substance from a person's body, or is it merely a matter of trickery? Evans-Pritchard was able to discover that the witch doctor performs this feat by means of clever sleight of hand; he will, for instance, conceal the object he pretends to be removing in his mouth beforehand. Much of the apprenticeship involved in becoming a witch doctor involves the learning of a vast repertory of such "tricks."

It seems that the question as to whether the witch doctor is a cheat is easily answered. And yet the curious fact is that although the witch doctor knows perfectly well the tricks of his trade, he himself firmly believes in the genuineness of his profession. How is this possible? Is the witch doctor merely deluding himself? This is what Evans-Pritchard thought:

> The Zande witch-doctor, in spite of his extra knowledge, is as deep a believer in magic as his slightly less-informed fellows. At first I used to think that to some extent he understood the folly of his divination and leechcraft, but after a while I began to realize how little he really understood. He knows that he cheats laymen but does not know how he is cheated by his own ignorance. . . . They know that their extraction of objects from bodies of their patients is a fake, but they believe that they cure them by the medicines they administer. . . . Here, as everywhere, we are confronted with the same tangle of knowledge and error. . . . They display an intellectual acuteness which might have expressed itself in scepticism and disillusionment were they not enclosed in the same network of thought, the same web of witchcraft, oracles, and magic, as are laymen.[54]

To say, as Evans-Pritchard does, that witch doctors are the victims of the very delusions they practice on others and fall prey to the same "superstitions," to use one of his own terms, is too simplistic an answer and thus unacceptable. It is as if one were to equate the witch doctor with a theatrical magician who was as much taken in by his own feats of prestidigitation as his audience, for, in a strict sense, the witch doctor does not cheat—at least no more than do our own medical doctors who prescribe useless medicines and perform unnecessary surgery because they know their patients will be satisified with nothing less. When a witch doctor produces an object from his mouth while persuading his patient that it came out of his body, he knows that this act itself constitutes cheating, but he would say that, all things considered, he is not really cheating at all. He will justify himself by saying perhaps that he must rely on these tricks since his magic is not as powerful as that of other witch doctors, especially those of former times who really could perform the feats that he, with his lesser competence, must merely mimic. Here the witch doctor is able to admit to the dubiousness of certain of his practices, though without calling into question the institution of witch doctor. His admission of fraud is expressed in such a way that it actually reaffirms the validity of magic and magicians as such.

More importantly, the witch doctor will say that the more spectacular of his feats, such as the extraction of objects, is not essential to what he is doing. The real cure does not consist of removing an object from the patient's body but is effected, rather, by means of the witch doctor's magical medicines. The removal of an object is merely a gimmick for popular consumption. Because the cause of illness is spiritual in nature, the cure is equally spiritual; no material object can be "shown" as the cause of the illness. The witch doctor, however, is an astute psychologist who knows that ordinarily people want a performance and will not be fully satisfied unless they are provided with something tangible. In catering in this way to popular demand, he is behaving no differently from our medical doctors who prescribe placebos, and there is no more reason to say that the witch doctor is acting in bad faith and is lying to himself about the validity of magic than there would be to say of our doctors that they thereby doubt the validity of scientific medicine or that their practice in itself invalidates medical science.

One of Evans-Pritchard's informants stated:

> When the man has recovered people say that indeed witch-doctors are skillful healers, whereas it is the medicine which really cures people, and it is on account of medicine that people recover when they are treated by witch-doctors. The people think that healing is brought about by the extraction of objects, and only witch-doctors know that it is the medicine which heals people. The people themselves do not learn the truth because only witch-doctors know it, and they keep it a secret.[55]

Because the essence of witch doctory lies in the use of magical medicines, the fact that witch doctors do in fact make use of tricks when dealing with ordinary people does not demonstrate the falsity of witch doctory as such. If witch doctors were mere tricksters, they would not be able to justify themselves in their own eyes, but they do believe in their system and one witch doctor will consult another for treatment when he falls ill. Of course, in such cases they, like their Western counterparts, dispense with the tricks and other "inessentials".

On the basis of his encounters with shamans (*manangs*) in Borneo, E. Fuller Torrey, an accredited psychiatrist working for the National Institute of Mental Health in the United States, writes:

The question arises whether *manangs* are "honest" in what they do. Early missionary accounts especially ridicule them as frauds and expose the tricks they use to get blood on the dagger [used to kill the offending spirit responsible for the loss of the patient's soul, the cause of his disorder], etc. My conversations with three of them convinced me that while they are not above trickery, they use it in the belief that they are helping the patient. They have absolutely no doubt that the patient's soul is lost, and they believe that anything which will assist in its retrieval is not dishonest. Other observers confirm this view of their authenticity.[56]

Only if one is assessing shamanism from the outside, from the point of view of another system, can one say that the shaman cheats, for in terms of his own system he does not really cheat. Lévi-Strauss takes a more sophisticated position than Evans-Pritchard when he writes that "fraud is cosubstantial with magic and, strictly speaking, the sorcerer never 'cheats.' "[57] What, however, justifies Lévi-Strauss in maintaining that magic as a whole is a fraud? And how can Evans-Pritchard say that the faith of the Azande is "without foundations"[58] and that, although they otherwise display "intellectual ingenuity and experimental keenness," they nevertheless remain "blind" to the "failures" of their system to explain reality?[59] Surely magic can be said to be a failure and so much superstition only when it is assessed from the point of view of science. But what validates this scientific assessment? Can it be scientifically demonstrated that science gives us a true picture of reality? Is the way the scientist justifies his faith in science that different at bottom from the way the witch doctor justifies his faith in magic? Let us take a closer look at science as a system of belief.

Magic may have its myths, but science, that self-proclaimed demythologizer, is not without ones of its own. Even, and especially, if it is thought that magic is a kind of primitive science, it is often said that magic is a pseudoscience because it explains things in terms of unverifiable, occult, or supernatural forces. Science, on the other hand, gives "true" explanations since it deals with "real" factors, with natural, verifiable, and, it is even said sometimes, observable causes. Of course the assertion that science deals only or primarily with observable entities is utterly false, as most scientists would no doubt concede. An electron, for example, is a theoretical entity and cannot be observed in any ordinary sense of the word. The scientist, however, would want to say that even though it is a theoretical entity, a hypothetical construct, it nonetheless refers to something real. But what is reality? What does it mean to speak of reality in a case like this when what is "real" necessarily transcends all possible direct experience?

Perhaps it will be said that we have not grasped the meaning of a "hypothetical construct." This designates a postulated entity (a reality), which, though not definable in terms of observable entities, is nonetheless essentially and logically related to these. An electron, to stick with our example, is "real" because it—or, more precisely, the atomic theory—furnishes a logical and coherent account of the way observed things appear to function. But could one not say as much for witchcraft? Certainly, as we have seen, the belief in witchcraft as a force constitutes a perfectly logical and coherent way of explaining observable phenomena. Moreover, to postulate witchcraft as the true cause of events does not in any way contradict ordinary experience. Like atomic theory, witchcraft does not deny observable facts (such as the fact that termites had eaten away at the granary supports) but rather complements them and provides the missing link. Why, then, should belief in atoms be deemed "realistic" while belief in witchcraft be labeled "superstitious"? The one belief is no more and no less systematic, on the whole, than the other. The natural objection at this point is to answer, because the system of science is true whereas that of magic is false. That means that scientific theories can be verified, can be shown to be true, whereas those of magic cannot. Magic, though, cannot be falsified if one operates within this system. Can science be falsified—scientifically? Let us see.

There are two great myths concerning science. The first is the myth of the empty head. According to this widely held fiction, the scientist is an impartial observer of things who merely records without preconceptions what he sees and is thereby led, by the process of induction, to formulate a theory, one "suggested by the facts themselves." What is in question here is the logic of scientific discovery (we shall return to this issue in chapter 7). The other great myth has for its idol the scientific experiment, and this is the one we shall be particularly concerned with at this point.[60] It is the experiment that determines whether a scientific theory is true or false; the purpose of the experiment is to verify (or falsify) theories.[61] The experiment is thus the highest court of appeals in science, and its verdicts are always final—because they reveal the way things really are—or at least this is what the myth says. From this point of view, witchcraft would be false because it cannot be experimentally verified.

Were this myth true, we could expect the scientist to abandon a given theory as soon as it is contradicted by an experiment: "one does not hesitate, *for the sake of a single experiment*, to undertake a complete reconstruction."[62] But this rarely happens. The scientist is no more inclined to abandon his theories simply because the experiment turns up anomalies than the Zande is led to surrender his belief in witchcraft simply because the poison oracle contradicts itself. And, like the Zande, the scientist has various secondary explanations he can call on to justify the failures of his experiments: perhaps the experiment was not performed properly; perhaps the results were not interpreted correctly; perhaps the initial data were not representative enough; perhaps some outside force was interfering with the closed setup of the experiment. When Michelson's experiment failed to demonstrate the existence of ether drift, scientists did not for this reason cast doubt on the very notion of the ether. As one scientist typically remarked, "This experiment may have to be explained away."[63] Anomalies usually can be accounted for if the scientist is clever and patient enough, and he can always dismiss the anomaly as being "due to unknown sources of error." Polanyi observes:

> The process of explaining away deviations is in fact quite indispensable to the daily routine of research. In my laboratory I find the laws of nature formally contradicted at every hour, but I explain this away by the assumption of experimental error. I know that this may cause me one day to explain away a fundamentally new phenomenon and to miss a great discovery. Such things have often happened in the history of science. Yet I shall continue to explain away my odd results, for if every anomaly observed in my laboratory were taken at its face value, research would instantly degenerate into a wild-goose chase after imaginary fundamental novelties.[64]

In the final analysis, it is the scientist himself, relying on nothing but personal judgment and the common consensus of colleagues, who must decide what is to count as evidence against a theory and what not. "There is a residue of personal judgment required in deciding—as the scientist eventually must—what weight to attribute to any particular set of evidence in regard to the validity of a particular proposition." "Agreement with experiment will therefore always leave some conceivable doubt as to the truth of a proposition and it is for the scientist to judge whether he wants to set aside such doubt as unreasonable or not." "He is himself the ultimate judge of what he accepts as true."[65]

It is thus exceedingly difficult for any amount of factual data to disprove a theory or discredit an interpretive schema—and the more basic the theory, the more it is immune to falsification—since "what the facts are," that is, what one thinks the facts are, is itself determined by the schema. Let us consider an extremely fundamental theory, more philosophical perhaps than scientific, that all reality is material or, conversely, psychical. Bishop Berkeley is known for having denied that matter exists at all; to be, he said, is to be perceived, and all reality exists only in the mind. To many this seemed preposterous, and Dr. Johnson, for one, thought he could refute it by observing that if the bishop were to stub his foot on a rock, he would soon enough be convinced of its material reality. This, of course, did not constitute a refutation of Berkeley's theory since Berkeley was not denying "facts," such as that rocks exist and produce certain effects, but was rather attempting to explain what it means to say that they exist; and what it means to say that they exist is that they are or can be perceived, *esse* is *percipi*. Dr. Johnson himself was guilty of the argumentative blunder known as *ignora-*

tio elenchi; he was confusing the issue at stake and was being irrelevant. Berkeley was not denying the obvious fact that material things appear to exist; he was only asserting that their reality is their appearance. Johnson's appeal to the pain-inflicting rock thus can actually be used to support Berkeley's thesis. Facts enter into an interpretive construct only through their meaning, which is to say that they can never prove or disprove anything. There are, for instance, a veritable host of "facts" concerning extrasensory perception, but these are not yet "scientific" facts because currently no general scientific theory can adequately "explain" them.

"Facts" cannot refute Berkeley's idealist thesis. The apologist of science perhaps will say that this is because it is a philosophical and not a scientific theory or hypothesis. This objection, though, is irrelevant, for scientific theories, if they are basic enough, are equally irrefutable. Such for instance is the case with Newton's First Law of Motion: all bodies remain at rest or in uniform rectilinear motion unless compelled by impressed forces to change their state. This can only be assumed to be true; it can be neither proven nor disproven, for as the philosopher of science, Norwood Hanson, points out, it is "not an experimental issue; it concerns the organization of concepts."[66] As Poincaré would have said, important scientific hypotheses cannot be falsified for the simple reason that they are definitions. To say, for instance, that a freely falling body accelerates in a constant fashion is only to state what one has chosen to understand by "freely falling body." Were an experiment to come up with an instance of a falling body that did not appear to accelerate in a constant fashion, it would be dismissed as irrelevant to the hypothesis; one would say that the body was not falling freely. Scientific statements are theoretical statements; contrary to myth, they are not "empirical."

Again, the operative notion of modern science—that reality can be explained in terms solely of matter in motion (mechanism and quantitative analysis)—is what the physicist, Gerald Holton, would call a "thematic hypothesis": a belief that "by its very nature is not subject to verification or falsification."[67] All of science is secretly guided by such "thematic presuppositions" that can be neither proved nor disproved by experimentation and appeal to "facts." It could thus be said of believers (dogmatists) in general, whether they be scientists or shamans, that they "admit only such facts as can be explained by their own theories, and dismiss facts which conflict therewith though possessing equal probability."[68] Even more, facts that conflict with a theory are not even recognized as facts.

The real purpose of the scientific experiment is not so much to verify a theory as to show its viability. If on the whole a theory is coherent and possesses explanatory power—that is, if it can be used to coordinate a large number of observations and if, when translated into an experiment, it does not seem to be grossly contradicted by any particular observation (minor difficulties in adjusting the theory to fit currently accepted "facts" can be ignored as insignificant)—then it will be said to be "true." Of course, if a great number of anomalies build up, the scientist gradually will be led to cast suspicion on his theory and may begin to look about for another theory. If the matter that the theory covers is basic, he may even recognize that a fundamental readjustment of the entire system of science is called for, as when in the earlier part of this century the viability of classical, Newtonian physics was cast into doubt. The important thing to note, how-ever, is that no amount of contrary "evidence" will induce a scientist to abandon his theory *unless he knows of an alternative theory that can take its place.* Thomas Kuhn has emphasized this point in his remarkable book on scientific revolutions: "once it has achieved the status of paradigm, a scientific theory is declared invalid only if an alternate candidate is available to take its place."[69] Just as the Zande has no choice but to believe in witch-craft, no matter how many times the oracles contradict themselves, since without this system of meaning he would lose all power of understanding and coping with reality, so also the scientist cannot let go of his belief in science because that is the only system he knows.

Skepticism is a vital element in science because it allows for a certain open-mindedness and the ability of the system to evolve. A rigidly dogmatic scientist would never question his beliefs, and science would not progress. Scientific open-mindedness is not, however, without its limits, for there is one thing that a scientist cannot doubt: the institution of science itself. We could thus apply to science the very remarks Evans-Pritchard made about witchcraft, if only we make the appropriate word changes: "Scientists are only sceptical of particular theories, and not of science in general, and their scepticism is always expressed in a scientific idiom that vouches for the validity of science as an institution." Again: "Indeed, scepticism is included in the pattern of belief in science. Scepticism explains failures of theories, and being directed toward particular theories even tends to support faith in others." As in witchcraft, in science everything hangs together, and no amount of adverse experiments could ever conceivably invalidate science itself; there is here, as Evans-Pritchard said of witchcraft, "no incentive to agnosticism." The scientist, it would thus appear, is as much a prisoner of his (closed) system as the Zande is of his, there being nothing within the sys-tem that could ever warrant disbelief in it. The scientist, Jacob Bronowski, suggests as much:

> The most modest research worker at his bench, pushing a probe into a neuron to measure the electric response when a light is flashed, is enmeshed in a huge and intertwined network of theories that he carries into his work from the whole field of science, all the way from Ohm's law to Avogadro's number. He is not alone; he is sustained and held and in some sense imprisoned by the state

of scientific theory in every branch. And what he finds is not a single fact either: it adds a thread to the network, ties a knot here and another there, and by these connections at once binds and enlarges the whole *system*.[70]

Were an observer from another culture or another planet (a kind of inverse Evans-Pritchard) to do fieldwork among Western scientists and were he to watch them performing their experimental rites, consulting them as the Azande do their oracles, and more often than not, as Polanyi says, explaining away deviations that frequently contradict the laws of nature they profess, he might get the idea that scientists are basically cheats. It would, of course, be necessary to disabuse him of this overhasty judgment, for although some scientists are no doubt fraudulent and operate primarily for personal gain and although many physicians are quacks, nonetheless most scientists genuinely believe in science just as most doctors genuinely believe in the efficacy of medical science. Our inverse Evans-Pritchard will admit to this and will allow that scientists are hapless victims of their own system, a "tangle of knowledge and error." However, another extraplanetary observer, an inverse Lévi-Strauss this time, will point out that scientists cannot really be said to be cheats, voluntary or involuntary; "fraud," he will say, "is cosubstantial with science and, strictly speaking, the scientist never 'cheats.' "

Some philosophers of science in the positivist school would want to say that systems of belief such as witchcraft or even psychoanalysis are unscientific, are in fact false, for the simple reason that they are unfalsifiable. The system of witchcraft or magic is said to be false because no conclusive experiment could ever be conducted within this system, which could conceivably disprove the existence of witchcraft. Thus the "principle of falsifiability" is seen as a complement to the principle of verifiability and as the criterion that allows for distinguishing valid (scientific) from invalid (unscientific) systems. However, such a principle is incapable of accomplishing what its advocates claim for it; it cannot show that science is a correct and true system and that magic is false, for there is no possible scientific experiment that could ever conceivably show up the falsity of science as a system. As systems of belief, magic and science are equally valid (true) because they are equally redundant or tautological.[71] Polanyi admits this:

> The stability of the naturalistic system which we currently accept . . . rests on the same logical structure [as the beliefs of the Azande]. Any contradiction between a particular scientific notion and the facts of experience will be explained by other scientific notions; there is a ready reserve of possible scientific hypotheses available to explain any conceivable event. . . . The process of selecting facts for our attention is indeed the same in science as among the Azande.[72]

The closed and total nature of systems such as magic and science is precisely what enables their adherents to ascribe truth-value to them. And the fact of the matter is that the redundant nature of the system will both justify the system in the eyes of its adherents and invalidate it for someone outside of it. Only when one ceases to believe or simply does not believe in a system will its all-inclusive interpretive ability seem to be suspect instead of as evidence of its truth. A former Marxist such as Arthur Koestler will, after he has broken with communism, cite as one of his reasons for this break just precisely that which, while he adhered to Marxism, constituted for him proof of the system's truth: its ability to provide a total explanation of things. Thus, as Polanyi points out:

> The attribution of truth to any particular state alternative [view of the universe] is a fiduciary act which cannot be analysed in non-committal terms. . . . there exists no principle of doubt the operation of which will discover for us which of two systems of implicit belief is true—except in the sense that we will admit decisive evidence against the one we do not believe to be true, and not against the other.[73]

To say, therefore, that a system such as science is true amounts to no more than saying that one is persuaded of its validity, and the means of persuasion here is the systematic and tautological nature of the belief itself. Explanation (demonstration) amounts to no more than persuasion, and what is "true" is simply what one believes (to be true). In his famous article written in 1872, "The Fixation of Belief," Charles Sanders Peirce expressed this matter about as well as it ever has been since:

> Hence, the sole object of inquiry is the settlement of opinion. We may fancy that this is not enough for us, and that we seek, not merely an opinion, but a true opinion. But put this fancy to the test, and it proves groundless; for as soon as a firm belief is reached we are entirely satisfied, whether the belief be true or false. . . . The most that can be maintained is, that we seek for a belief that we shall *think* to be true. But we think each one of our beliefs to be true, and, indeed, it is a mere tautology to say so.

The object of belief, what belief is belief in, goes by the name of "reality." Thus, to different beliefs correspond different realities. Reality therefore is essentially pluralistic and relative.

It is evident that the world systems of magic and science are quite different and even incompatible, but it is also evident that they are not all that unalike in the way in which they function. Both systems are similar from a formal point of view, and believers in magic and science tend to justify their views in a similar fashion and are, in their own systems, every bit as rational and "logical" as the other. It would therefore seem that human understanding functions everywhere in a way that is analogously the same. We shall, accordingly, deal explicitly with the topic of analogy in the following chapter. Now, though, we are in a position to answer a question raised by the last chapter: whether belief in magic is "rational." The answer is that it is rational, for it meets all the criteria of rationality. *That is rational for which a persuasive rationale can be given.* If one can convincingly make sense of a belief, it is rational. And making sense of a belief is nothing more than coherently relating this belief to other beliefs that one also holds and that tend to make up something like a general system of belief. To be sure, a consequence of this is that a belief may be fully rational in terms of one system but totally irrational in terms of another. (Belief in magic is indeed irrational from the point of view of science; it does not make good "scientific sense.") But this does not in any way affect the intrinsic rationality of the belief itself.

One lingering question clamors for immediate consideration and no doubt should be dealt with even though we are not yet in a position to do it full justice: whether science, in spite of its formal likeness to magic as a system, is not a "better" system than magic. Science may not be intrinsically more rational than magic, but, even so, is it not a fact that it is more "true"? Peirce thought so.[74] And Polanyi, who argues for their formal similarity, nonetheless certainly appears to think so as well, and in this he is no doubt typical of nearly everyone in our culture, open-minded though they otherwise be. After saying that the "process of selecting facts for our attention is indeed the same in science as among the Azande," Polanyi immediately added: "But I believe that science is often right in its application of it [the process of selecting facts], while Azande are quite wrong when using it for protecting their superstitions."

Now the problem is this: given what he has said concerning the fiduciary character of all world views, what possible criteria can Polanyi have for objectively distinguishing a true system from a false one? How can he legitimately characterize the Zande system as superstitious? The Zande system is, as he admits, every bit as true for them as science is for us, and so what justifies us in maintaining that our system of belief is truer than theirs? Frazer was able to say that "the scientific theory of the world is the best that has yet been formulated" because he unquestioningly accepted as true the modern dogma of evolution.[75] Evolution, however, is a theoretical notion of science and thus cannot—if a vicious circle is to be avoided—be used to justify science itself. To argue for the supreme validity of science as a system from the scientific fact of evolution would be another instance of tautological reasoning.

To be sure, in our society belief in magic could rightly be labeled "irrational" and "superstitious" since ours is a predominantly scientifically oriented and technologically controlled society and one cannot successfully operate in it by means of magic. But, is our society better than a primitive one? One might, like the behaviorist, B. F. Skinner, want to use the notion of survival value as a criterion for assessing cultures. In this view, our society would be more successful (better) than primitive ones since it is more complex and powerful, has a higher gross national product, its members tend to be physically healthier and less prone to disease, live longer and are more numerous (we have achieved a high population growth); in any physical confrontation our society would overwhelm any primitive society. These, however, are all technological considerations and cannot be used to justify technology as a way of life and of understanding the world.

The fact that our society is technologically superior to primitive societies does not of itself constitute a proof of even so much as its better survival value. On the contrary, there is every reason to fear that we may perhaps not be in a position to control our own means of control—technology—and may in fact cease to exist, either though global warfare or through overexploitation of natural resources. Perhaps to this it will be retorted that although technology may not ensure our survival and may in fact constitute a threat to it, it nevertheless makes for more dynamic and adventurous living and has lifted us out of the historical stagnation in which primitive societies have been plunged from time immemorial. One can legitimately wonder, however, why restlessness should constitute a higher value than living in harmony with one's environment, and just where is it that "progress" is supposed to get us in the long run. Of itself, what good does it serve to survive for an additional thousand, ten thousand, or one million years when everything ultimately will fade away into the featureless nothing out of which it arose in the first place?

One further objection against ascribing as much truth-value to magic as to science is worth considering because in the minds of most people it is the most obvious and irrefutable of all. The objection is this: the fact that science "works" is proof enough that it is true, to the exclusion of all other modes of understanding that seek to pass themselves off as true knowledge. Is not the fact that science issues in successful technology sufficient proof for the truth of science? Is not technology itself the living proof of science? The fact of the matter is, however, that magic also "works." Indeed, it could be laid down as a general principle that *any sufficiently developed belief system is bound to work*. The reason is that a theory is a guide to action; it orients our action in a certain direction and guides it along certain lines, all of this to the exclusion of other possible directions and lines. It is therefore only natural that the theory is subsequently confirmed by action, since the action itself is made possible by the theory. Hannah Arendt has taken note of this highly interesting but usually ignored feature of human understanding:

> While technology demonstrates the "truth" of modern science's most abstract
> concepts, it demonstrates no more than that man can always apply the results
> of his mind, that no matter which system he uses for the explanation of natural
> phenomena he will always be able to adopt it as a guiding principle for making
> and acting.[76]

It is extremely difficult, therefore, to see how it could be maintained that
science is better, more rational, or truer than magic in any absolute sense of
the terms. In our culture we say that magic is superstitious because it posits
supernatural or occult entities and forces, but could it not perhaps be the
case that primitive people show precisely that they still understand something we have forgotten: that there is, in some sense or other, another
dimension to human existence than the merely natural or technological?

In his study of the Trobriand Islanders, Malinowski pointed out that the
natives have recourse to magic only in special circumstances—what others
have termed "limit situations"—when they find themselves in emotional
predicaments or when they undertake feats that tend to go beyond the limits
of the competence of their everyday technology, such as when they embark
on a fishing expedition on the high seas and not merely in the calm island
lagoons. Magic reveals itself to man "in those passionate experiences which
assail him in the impasses of his instinctive life and of his practical pursuits,
in those gaps and breaches left in the ever-imperfect wall of culture which he
erects between himself and the besetting temptations and dangers of his destiny."[77] In invoking magic the primitive is able to overcome dread and
despair and confront the perils of the great unknown; magic "enables man
to carry out with confidence his important tasks, to maintain his poise and
his mental integrity in fits of anger, in the throes of hate, of unrequited
love, of despair and anxiety."[78]

Primitive man, however, does not attempt to do through magic what he
can do through technology:

> He knows that a plant cannot grow by magic alone, or a canoe sail or float
> without being properly constructed and managed, or a fight be won without
> skill and daring. He never relies on magic alone, while, on the contrary, he
> sometimes dispenses with it completely, as in fire-making and in a number of
> crafts and pursuits. But he clings to it, whenever he has to recognize the im-
> potence of his knowledge and of his rational technique.[79]

This is important; it shows that magic performs a function that transcends
the scope of science and technology. This is, properly speaking, a religious
function. Malinowski's belief that magic is simply a means for allowing
"pent-up physiological tension to flow over" prevented him from seeing
this function and led him to conclude that the magical act is simply a
"substitute action," stemming from an inability to perform a "real action"

by means of science and technology.[80] But Malinowski's examples indicate something else. Magic is not a substitute for technology but a complement to it. The magical rite is a way of saying something like, "Do your best and, as for the rest, trust in God."[81] Magic enables people to cope with that over which science and technology can have no possible control—such as one's inevitable death—and enables them to carry on when science and technology let them down. *Magic thus frees a man from dependence on what he does know, from science and technology, from being controlled by his own means of control.*

It would thus appear that perhaps primitive man expresses in his magic an understanding of things that we have lost sight of, an understanding of the supreme importance to man of reconciling himself with the uncontrollable and the unknowable, with fate and fortune. Through magic, the primitive has access to a range of meaning inaccessible to us—to science and technology—for here that which is beyond the limits of his knowledge and control is not merely absurd and meaningless. Because magic enables people to face up to and accept their fate, it makes of their lives something more than "a tale told by an idiot, signifying nothing," and even death has its significance in life. When one realizes the religious significance of magic, one need no longer be astonished, as Malinowski was, "that 'savages' can achieve such a sober, dispassionate outlook in these matters [health, disease, the threat of death] as they actually do."[82]

The very fact that technology can be taken as the "proof" of science should be enough to lead us to have second thoughts about the cultural priority we in our age have accorded to science, for the uncontrolled implementation of technology is leading us headlong into an ever more undesirable state of affairs.[83]

In regard to two instances—magic and science—we have seen how people come to some understanding of the world and how they do so by interpreting their experience and ordering it according to a particular frame of reference. A frame of reference constitutes a coherent system of meaning and provides a total explanation of things. One can accept as true only that which is accredited by one's system of belief, and reality can be only what one's system says it is. This might possibly appear to be trivially true, but like so many other seemingly self-evident things—for instance, the fact that there is a world and not simply nothing at all—it is worth reflecting on. First, it implies not only that reality is thoroughly pluralistic but also that systems, being total explanations, are, as systems, mutually exclusive. One cannot believe in both at the same time; the situation is that of an either-or: believing in one system requires a letting go of the other. As models of reality, magic and science are incommensurable. The situation is indeed that which Socrates is referring to when, alluding to Protagoras's thesis that "whatever at any time seems to anyone is true to him" (a thesis we are ourselves prepared to adopt), he says, "When one thing is entirely different from another, it cannot be in any respect capable of behaving in the same way as that other. . . . We are not to understand that the thing we speak of is in some respects the same though different in others, but that it is entirely different."[84]

Understanding therefore conceals as much as it reveals, for if the mark of a system whereby it allows for stability and thus for understanding is that it is relatively impervious to threats to itself from the outside, then any system of meaning has its limits and intrinsically is incapable of recognizing that which transcends these and which, interpreted otherwise, could justify another, rival system. Is it not significant that for someone who holds to a given conceptual schema—magic, science, Freudianism, Marxism, or some other—its ability to explain everything and to handle all objections is precisely the mark of its truth-value, whereas for one who does not hold to this particular schema, these qualities are the sure indication of its falsity? Does this not indicate that terms such as *knowledge* (*science*), *superstition*, and *ideology* are merely relative? *Science* will be that system which one believes in and assents to; *superstition* and *ideology* will refer to rival systems that one does not accept.[85]

While what we have seen in this chapter regarding science as a system of belief and its similarity in this respect to magic does not constitute (and is not intended to constitute) a refutation of science, it should nonetheless incline us to adopt a very skeptical attitude toward all scientific theories—indeed to all theories—that claim to reveal what nature or man "really" is. We are now in a position to confront the question raised toward the end of the preceding chapter concerning the status of science as an explanation of reality. We now have reasons for refusing to accept the verdict of science—whatever it be and especially if it claims that humans are nothing but sophisticated machines for processing information—as final or even supreme. This is not to say that we have grounds for doubting the validity of science; we do not simply mean to say that the scientific view of things is wrong.

One can legitimately say that a theory or system is wrong only if one can defend in its place an alternate theory or system that would be, supposedly, the right one, in the sense of claiming to express "what reality really is" (magic is wrong only for someone who believes in science or some other rival system). One can doubt something—in the sense of holding it to be false—only if one does not doubt everything, only if one's doubts are anchored on something that one tacitly believes in. Universal doubt is not possible. Ordinary skepticism always operates in a basic context of accepted belief. The magician or the scientist can be skeptical of one aspect of his general system of belief only if he presupposes others; in fact to doubt any part of the system is to reaffirm the system as a whole. No belief system can ever radically call itself into question (this is another way of saying that no belief system can ever demonstrate its overall truth as a system), and the reason is that if, working within the frame of reference of a system, one were, *per impossibile*, to doubt the system as a whole, one would thereby have destroyed the very meaning of the concepts and terms with which one is attempting to question the system. Total doubt is meaningless; it is like attempting to move an object by means of a lever that rests on no fulcrum.

To be exact, it must be said that doubting is not the simple absence of belief but rather a mode of negative belief; it is belief expressed in the negative form.[86] To say, "I doubt that," is the same as saying, "I believe that that is not true," and one can believe that something is false only if one believes that something else is true. To doubt something is a positive action, and one can doubt *this* only if one believes *that,* just as one can apply pressure on an object and push it away from oneself only if one can exert a counterthrust on another object that is fixed and gives one the necessary footing. As William James rightly insists, "We never disbelieve anything except for the reason that we believe in something else which contradicts the first thing. Disbelief is thus an incidental complication to belief."[87]

We could thus doubt—in the sense of disbelieving—the validity of science and reject it as false only if we invested our faith in a rival system. But what other system could win our loyalties? Magic is an unlikely candidate for our belief since, after science, it is hardly possible, assuming that it would even be desirable, to adhere in good faith to the magical view of things. The intent of this chapter was not, however, to argue for the superiority of magic over science, nor is the purpose of this book as a whole to provide an alternate or rival world view to that of science. Rather our aim has been to play off one system (magic) against another (science) in such a way as to bring out the characteristics of belief and belief systems as such.

Perhaps now we are in a position to see that belief is in fact the normal state of human consciousness. *To be conscious is to believe.* "Consciousness of the world," Husserl says, "is consciousness in the mode of certainty of belief."[88] Or as James expressed the matter, "Belief is thus the mental state or function of cognizing reality."[89] To be conscious is to be conscious of something, and the object of consciousness is what is called a reality. Now since to be conscious of or to "know" something is synonymous with believing, reality, which is the object of consciousness, is an object of belief. What people call reality is, in short, a belief object and is relative to the way in which it is intended or believed in: "The way in which the ideas are combined is a part of the inner constitution of the thought's object or content."[90]

James remarks, interestingly enough, how it is possible for belief to be "pathologically exalted." "One of the charms of drunkenness unquestionably lies in the deepening of the sense of reality and truth which is gained therein.''[91] This intensification of belief—of the sense of reality—is at its greatest in drug-induced states of altered consciousness (James refers to intoxication by nitrous oxide). Under the influence of drugs, ''a man's very soul will sweat with conviction, and he be all the while unable to tell what he is convinced of at all.'' What is interesting about altered states of consciousness like these in which the mind, freed from absorption in the usual and usually petty objects of its concern, displays a boundless credulity is the way they suggest that the mind in its primitive state may be nothing but undifferentiated, overflowing belief, which, like the Freudian libido, is ready to attach itself to and deem real whatever objective content presents itself or is suggested to it. If this is true, it would follow that one cannot completely cease to believe without also ceasing to be conscious. Radical doubt becomes impossible. Belief is a tendency, and it is innate; doubt or disbelief (unlike James I am using these terms synonymously) is an activity and is learned; it is the fruit of long experience (*sensu stricto* an ''experience'' always involves a challenge to one's habitual beliefs and is never without notable limits).

If we cannot radically doubt—and cannot, accordingly, demonstrate the absolute validity of any belief system—we can nevertheless become aware of our beliefs as such. To see that a belief is a belief is to see also the limitations of the belief (it is to see that the belief is a belief and not knowledge). We cannot choose not to believe, but we can free ourselves from living naively in our beliefs.[92] To see that science is a system of belief is therefore sufficient to answer the question dealt with in the last chapter, whether we must accept as true and decisive the scientific view of man. There is, we see now, no reason why we should. Science is but one system of belief among others, and there is no compelling reason why one should believe in it rather than in another.

Not only are the claims of physical or social science to a true and definitive account of things thoroughly discredited in this way when we realize that all ''knowledge'' is but belief, but the very ideal of science becomes suspect. ''Science'' in the traditional sense simply means ''true knowledge of reality''; any system of understanding—philosophical, theological, or scientific in the modern sense—can attempt to claim for itself (and usually has) the title of science. But because all systems of belief tend to be tautological, no system can conclusively demonstrate its validity (its correspondence to reality), and thus no system can ever prove that it is indeed science. This being the case, *the very notion of science appears as an illusive will-o'-the-wisp, as an illusion and an idol of the understanding*. In fact, the notion that there is a determinate, fixed reality to which corresponds, at least ideally, a perfect knowledge (a science) appears to be a purely polemical conceptual device used in defending one's own beliefs and in attacking those of others.

We can no longer accept unquestioningly as something self-evidently true the traditional philosophical (Platonic) distinction: *doxa-episteme*, belief-knowledge ("science"), for, as we have seen, all fixed beliefs take themselves to be true (to be "knowledge"), or, conversely, all knowledge is basically doxic, is, as Polanyi would say, of a fiduciary nature. Like the sense-reference distinction, the belief-knowledge distinction is empty because it corresponds to no experiential, actual reality; it is in fact a mystification of the true nature of human understanding. Moreover, another traditional philosophical conceptual couple, the appearance-reality distinction, must also appear as highly suspect because it goes hand in hand with the distinction between belief and knowledge. The distinction between appearance and reality is a purely eristic one since by *reality* one means the object of one's own belief (which one believes to be not a belief but knowledge) while one calls (mere) appearance the object of those beliefs of others that differ from one's own. Although they are basic to our intellectual tradition, these are all distinctions we can no longer subscribe to if we reject the distinction between science and superstition. These terms correspond to nothing absolute but are purely relative; there is no *science* without *superstition*, and vice-versa, since the terms are used only to justify one's own beliefs in the face of those of others.

The originating context of the various distinctions between appearance and reality, belief and knowledge, science and superstition, as well as the individual concepts themselves, is the need people have always felt to defend their beliefs or world views (systems of understanding) in the face of alien and thus threatening beliefs. Proving, demonstrating, explaining, arguing are all instruments of persuasion. They are the means whereby the adherents of a given system of understanding justify to themselves their belief in the system and the means also whereby the adherence of others is solicited. It is thus fully appropriate that in this book we should have been led to raise the question of human understanding, its scope and limits, within the context of intercultural relations and, specifically, with regard to the problem caused by the confrontation of science with non-Western cultures. And we are now approaching the point where we may realize the basic absurdity of the very ideal of science. This ideal would be absurd, self-contradictory, because although it arises and can arise only within a situation of epistemic and cultural plurality—through the effort of people to arrive at one belief that will be able to lay claim to "truth" and thus to express "reality"—it nonetheless has as its necessary consequence the suppression of such a plurality. Science, which cannot arise and exist except in a situation of epistemological plurality, cannot tolerate this plurality since its logic tells it—with its principle of noncontradiction—that two views cannot both be true if both purport to express reality and yet differ markedly and are mutually exclusive in what they say about reality. An ideal that has as its necessary consequence the denial of that which renders it possible in the first place is surely absurd.[93]

It would thus appear that plausible reasons have been discovered for maintaining that all ideal language theories are misguided. There can be no ideal language, no language or system of understanding that can demonstrate that it is the perfect (or the best) expression of true reality, since no system is ever capable of justifying itself. All language, the medium of understanding, is, like understanding, as falsifying as it is revealing. We can cease to be the dupes of our language only if we realize this. The ideal of science, of a universal language, is an error, but it is a natural error that is spontaneous to us. Are we capable of understanding that?

Since, when it is a question of discerning what reality really is, error is natural, we cannot hope to succeed in understanding reality unless we can cope with our own tendency to misunderstand things and decisively reject the temptation to want to know—to achieve a science of reality. The tactic we must follow, and which indeed we have been implicitly following all along, thus becomes clearer: we wish to work out a theory of reality. But we have seen that reality is something very elusive. Every system believes that it has gained access to reality, but if there are as many realities as there are systems of belief, "reality" becomes a purely equivocal term with no meaning at all. Meaning can be ascribed to this term and our own metaphysical endeavor can be viewed as meaningful only if it is recognized that reality—taken in a sense that remains to be determined—transcends all possible understandings of it, and in this way preserves its oneness. For only if reality is somehow one can it be and be meaningful. The most terrible of all questions now arises: in our attempt to counteract the desire for science, are we not removing the very ground from under our feet? Are we not, by insisting on the transcendence of reality, forcing ourselves into a position that will prevent us from saying anything? Are we not committing ourselves to a thoroughgoing skepticism?

NOTES

1. P. Winch, *The Idea of a Social Science and Its Relation to Philosophy* (London, 1958), p. 102.

2. In a paper read at the VIII Congresso Interamericano de Filosofia, Brasilia, November 1972, "Science and the Multiplicity of Cultures," A. Wojciechowski rightly pointed this out:

The indeterminateness and endless variety of possibility of creative acts, proper to the human person, play a decisive role in the process of culture. They account for the unpredictability of cultural developments on the one hand, and the richness and variety of cultural forms and manifestations on the other hand. The plurality of cultures cannot be explained without taking into consideration the nature of the creative act. The reasons of the plurality of cultures constitute also a barrier to generalizations in the scientific study of culture. Moreover, it may be safely assumed that any attempt to do away with this plurality by an insistence on the common characteristics of men and by the use of technical means of communication will not be successful.

3. R. Sessions, "Problems and Issues Facing the Composer Today," in *Problems of Modern Music,* ed. P. H. Lang (New York: W. W. Norton, 1962), p. 31.

4. A. Koestler, *The Act of Creation* (London, 1970), p. 31. To explain something in the sense of giving its cause is to play a kind of intellectual game. As the philosopher of science, N. Hanson, remarks, "Cause-words resemble game-jargon. . . . The entire conceptual pattern of the game is implicit in each term" *(Patterns of Discovery* [Cambridge, 1972], p. 61). In his now classic work, *Homo Ludens* (Boston, 1970), J. Huizinga put forward and defended the insightful thesis that culture is a form of play or game.

5. D. Kaplan, "The Superorganic: Science or Metaphysics?" in A. Manners and D. Kaplan, eds., *Theory in Anthropology* (Chicago, 1968), pp. 24-25.

6. "Chaque science découpe arbitrairement dans la trame des faits un champ où elle se parque." W. James, "La notion de conscience," in *Essays in Radical Empiricism* (Gloucester, Mass., 1967), p. 209.

7. W. James, *The Principles of Psychology* (New York, 1950), 1:284-88.

8. The great merit of Gestalt psychology is to have articulated and emphasized the following characteristics of perceptual understanding:

1. Perceptual fields are organized, structured.
2. Perceptual fields are structured into a figure and a ground.
3. All perceptual forms tend toward closure.
4. All such forms are more or less stable and resistant to change.
5. Different forms tend to coalesce into larger, more articulated ones.
6. Forms are meaningful.
7. What is important in a form is not its component parts but the overall structure; the parts may change without the structure's being altered.

A good exposition of Gestalt psychology is Wolfgang Köhler's *Gestalt Psychology* (New York, 1959). Köhler, though, follows the general reductionist trend of the social sciences in thinking that psychology is a matter of biology.

9. H.-G. Gadamer, *Truth and Method* (New York, 1975), p. 82.

10. T. Kuhn, *The Structure of Scientific Revolutions* (Chicago, 1970), p. 113.

11. James, *Essays,* p. 30.

12. N. Goodman, *Languages of Art* (Indianapolis, 1978), pp. 7-8.

13. For a modern version of the Kantian position, see Susanne Langer, *Philosophy in a New Key* (Cambridge, Mass., 1974), esp. p. 42.

14. I. A. Richards, *Philosophy of Rhetoric* (New York, 1965), p. 30.

15. Ibid., pp. 108-9.

16. Hanson discusses the interpretive nature of perception in *Patterns of Discovery,* chap. 1, but he does not go as far as we shall wish to go and does not identify all seeing with seeing-as (see p. 19), and this is because he does not realize that, in the case of human consciousness, not only scientific knowing but also simple sense perception is thoroughly conditioned by language. He tends in the traditional way to dichotomize vision, which he says is essentially pictorial, and knowlege, which is fundamentally linguistic (p. 25).

17. In his study, *La formation de l'esprit scientifique,* (Paris, 1969), G. Bachelard takes as his guiding theme the notion of *epistemological obstacle* and attempts to show, through a wealth of concrete examples drawn mostly from the eighteenth century, that the modern scientific method and mentality is a very recent phenomenon and how it came to exist only when people gradually and with much difficulty overcame their natural ways of thinking. As a good example of the type of mentality that must be overcome before an analysis can become scien-

tific, I quote from Bachelard the following criticism of Newton by an eighteenth-century, prescientific-minded writer; the author (Louis Castel) in effect is criticizing Newton for ignoring the richness of nature as it reveals itself to us in our direct prescientific experience. It is obvious to us today that such a criticism—which we can fully sympathize with, since it is an attempt to call into question the conceptual imperialism of the scientific approach to reality—nevertheless completely ignores what the scientific endeavor actually is and must be.

> Les couleurs du Prisme ne sont que des couleurs fantastiques, spéculatives, idéales, et à la pointe de l'esprit et des yeux. . . . Comment en n'y mesurant que des angles et des lignes, M. Newton s'est-il flatté de parvenir à la connaissance intime et philosophique des couleurs. . . . En fait de couleurs, il n'y a d'utile et de substantiel même, que les couleurs des peintres et des teinturiers. Celles-ci se laissent manier, étudier et mettre à toutes sortes de combinaisons et de vraies analyses. Il serait étonnant et cependant il est assez vraisemblable que Newton a passé toute sa vie à étudier les couleurs, sans jamais jeter les yeux sur l'atelier d'un Peintre ou d'un Teinturier, sur les couleurs mêmes des fleurs, des coquilles, de la nature (p. 230).

18. S. Toulmin, *The Philosophy of Science* (New York, 1960), p. 129.

19. G. Holton, *Thematic Origins of Scientific Thought* (Cambridge, Mass., 1973), p. 55.

20. Ibid., pp. 92-93.

21. W. Heisenberg, *Physics and Beyond*, (New York, 1971), p. vii.

22. M. Heidegger, "The Origin of the Work of Art," in his *Poetry, Language, Thought*, (New York, 1971), p. 62.

23. Kuhn, *Structure of Scientific Revolutions*, p. 64.

24. The same point is made by Max Gluckman in his review of Evans-Pritchard's work on the Azande: "In quoting Evans-Pritchard to show how beliefs in witchcraft affect Africans' behavior and thought, I have emphasized that often their minds work in the same logical patterns as ours do, though the material with which they think is different, so that it is clear that if they were given the same education and cultural background as we have, they would think with the same materials and in the same way as we do." "The Logic of African Science and Witchcraft," in M. Marwick, ed., *Witchcraft and Sorcery* (Harmondsworth, England, 1975), pp. 330-31.

25. C. Lévi-Strauss, *The Savage Mind* (Chicago, 1966), p. 14 (translation corrected).

26. W. James, *The Will to Believe* (New York, 1956), p. 13.

27. Kaplan, "The Superorganic" p. 30.

28. Levi-Strauss, *Savage Mind*, p. 14 (translation corrected).

29. M. Merleau-Ponty, "Eye and Mind," in *The Primacy of Perception* (Evanston, Ill., 1964), p. 169. Albert Camus gives an interesting description of this phenomenon in the section entitled, "Rebellion and Art," in his book, *The Rebel* (New York, 1956). He observes how art in general, and the novel in particular (Camus refers to Proust), seeks not to reproduce nature or life but to transform it by giving it a cohesion and unity it lacks in our everyday experience of it. "The aim of great literature," he says, "seems to be to create a closed universe or a perfect type" (p. 259). "The essence of the novel lies in this perpetual alteration *[correction]*, always directed toward the same ends, that the artist makes in his own experience" (p. 264). "The most definite challenge that a work of this kind can give to creation is to present itself as an entirely *[un tout]*, as a closed and unified world" (p. 267).

30. B. Malinowski, *Magic, Science and Religion* (New York, 1954), pp. 86-87.

31. One can then rightly expect that scientific treatments of superstition will often be pointless and trivial since they will tend to be nothing more than a veiled apology for science. Such is the case with the book of one British professor of psychology, Gustav Jahoda, *The Psychology of Superstition* (London, 1969). After casting about unsuccessfully for an "objective means" of distinguishing "superstition" from other types of belief and action, Jahoda finally decides that he will use the word "in the sense of the kind of belief and action a reason-

able man in present-day Western society would regard as being 'superstitious' '' (p. 10). Jahoda thus assumes that superstition is one particular kind of belief and so fails to see that any belief can qualify as superstition provided only that there is someone to disagree with it. Jahoda's study thereby is deprived of any real value at the very outset, and it predictably consists in no more than tallying up various scientific "explanations" that can account for why so many people hold the beliefs they do. The unspoken assumption behind all of Jahoda's book is that science furnishes the ultimate criteria for distinguishing the true from the false. Only science can verify its theses (p. 143). But because Jahoda wishes to be an "open-minded" scientist (he spent some time in Ghana where he learned "a healthy respect for their [medicine men and fetish priests] skill and insight," whence his interest in superstition "as a psychological problem"), he refused to issue a blanket condemnation of superstition and does not advocate that we should strive to eliminate it completely. From "an evolutionary perspective," superstition may have "positive survival value" (p. 145). The tendency toward superstition is part and parcel of our psychological makeup and should not therefore be viewed as "abnormal." But even though—here Jahoda takes his distance from fellow rationalists of former times—we can never overcome it completely, he nevertheless concludes his book with a pious scientific exhortation: "educators need not be discouraged from their efforts to wean men away from harmful or even useless superstitions" (p. 147). Jahoda's book is, in sum, a good example of "well-meaning," "open-minded" scientific self-righteousness. We would have no objection to his pointing out the folly of other peoples' beliefs if he did not so seriously ignore the folly of his own.

32. *Webster's New World Dictionary of the American Language* (Cleveland: World Publishing Co., 1956).

33. Malinowski, *Magic, Science and Religion,* p. 82.

34. As Evans-Pritchard shows in regard to the Azande, belief in magic is part of the basic belief in witchcraft. "Zande magic can no more be appreciated than Zande oracles unless we consider its relationship to Zande notions of witchcraft. Take away belief in witchcraft, and magic and oracles become, in the main, a meaningless rigmarole" *(Witchcraft, Oracles and Magic among the Azande* [Oxford, 1937], p. 439).

35. Ibid., p. 42.

36. Plato, *Phaedo,* 99b (Tredennick, trans. [New York, 1961]).

37. Evans-Pritchard, *Witchcraft,* p. 73.

38. A condensed presentation of Evans-Pritchard's discussion of this matter in ibid. can be found in his article, "Witchcraft amongst the Azande," reprinted in Marwick, ed., *Witchcraft and Sorcery.*

39. For a study of the way in which a person accused of witchcraft or sorcery ends up by genuinely believing himself to be a witch, see Lévi-Strauss, "The Sorcerer and His Magic," in *Structural Anthropology* (New York, 1963). The phenomenon at work here is the same as that in evidence in the infamous Moscow trials of the 1930s where the "unjustly" accused actually came to believe themselves guilty.

40. Evans-Pritchard, *Witchcraft,* pp. 319-20.

41. Ibid., p. 330.

42. Malinowski, *Magic, Science and Religion,* p. 86.

43. Evans-Pritchard, *Witchcraft,* p. 350.

44. Ibid., p. 193. Evans-Pritchard also writes:

> I particularly do not wish to give the impression that there is any one who disbelieves in witchdoctorhood. Most of my acquaintances believed that there are a few entirely reliable practitioners, but that the majority are quacks. Hence in the case of any particular witch-doctor they are never quite certain whether reliance can be placed on his statements or not. They know that some witch-doctors lie and that others tell the truth, but they cannot at once tell from his behavior into which category any witch-doctor falls.

They reserve judgment, and temper faith with scepticism. . . . I have heard even witch-doctors themselves admit that not all members of their corporation are reliable and honest, but only those who have received proper medicines from persons qualified to initiate them (p. 185).

45. Ibid., p. 425. Of the Navajos, C. Kluckhohn says, " 'The average Navaho' does not talk about witchcraft as much nor behave with respect to witchcraft as much as one is likely to think on just finishing an intensive discussion of that subject. . . . In many Navaho local groups witchcraft is probably less significant as a determinant of behavior than the reading of this book may suggest" (*Navaho Witchcraft,* p. 123). Of our own culture it could also be said that scientific theories and methodology determine most people's actual behavior much less than an outsider, familiar with our literature, might conclude. Another anthropologist writes, "It is often said by Europeans claiming to know something about tribal life that the African lives in perpetual dread of sorcery. It is true that he regards sorcery as an ever-present danger. But he is no more obsessed by fear of it than is the average inhabitant of a large city in Western Europe obsessed by fear of being involved in a traffic accident. Both are dangers that must be faced almost daily; but just as we can avoid a collision by exercising caution, so do the Tswana [a people of Botswana] believe that it is possible to protect oneself against sorcery" (I. Schapera, "Sorcery and Witchcraft in Bechuanaland," in Marwick, *Witchcraft and Sorcery,* p. 114).

46. Evans-Pritchard, *Witchcraft,* p. 191.

47. Ibid., p. 338.

48. Ibid., pp. 194-95.

49. In his admirably presented résumé of Evans-Pritchard's findings, Polanyi indicates three ways in which witchcraft constitutes what we have called its tautological status and suggests that these features are to be found in science as well: the circularity of the system, the auto-matic expansion of the circle in which an interpretive system operates, and the principle of sup-pressed nucleation. See *Personal Knowledge,* pp. 288-92.

50. Although Frazer thought that magic was a "mistake" and illusory, he did hold that "science has this much in common with magic that both rest on a faith in order as the under-lying principle of all things." For Frazer with his nineteenth-century evolutionist views, science stems from magic and constitutes progress over it in that it explicitly postulates "what in magic had only been implicitly assumed, to wit, an inflexible regularity in the order of natural events, which, if carefully observed, enables us to foresee their course with certainty and to act accor-dingly." He says in addition: "Every great advance in knowledge has extended the sphere of order and correspondingly restricted the sphere of apparent disorder in the world, till now we are ready to anticipate that even in regions where chance and confusion appears still to reign, a fuller knowledge would everywhere reduce the seeming chaos to cosmos" *(The New Golden Bough* [New York, 1959], p. 649). Lévi-Strauss fairly well shares this view but attacks Frazer's opinion that the primitive merely projects his fancies onto the world and is not a careful observer of natural phenomena. The difference for Lévi-Strauss between magic and science does not so much lie in the practitioners as in the levels of reality to which they apply themselves; see *Savage Mind,* chap. 1.

51. Evans-Pritchard, *Witchcraft,* p. 367.

52. Ibid., p. 270.

53. Ibid., p. 541.

54. Ibid., p. 255.

55. Ibid., pp. 235-56.

56. E. F. Torrey, *The Mind Game* (New York, 1972), p. 113.

57. Lévi-Strauss, *Savage Mind,* p. 221

58. Evans-Pritchard, *Witchcraft,* p. 336.

59. Cf. ibid., pp. 338-39.

60. Another myth concerns the status of the scientist within the system of science. It is often

said that the scientist is a disinterested seeker after truth and that his only motives are to discover the truth of the matter and that the truth is the only authority to which he submits himself. In this he is unlike the witch doctor who is not interested in the truth but only in perpetuating superstitious dogma. This myth of science is, however, a pure mystification. Referring to the views of Preuss, Marett, Hubert, and Mauss, Malinowski seeks to show the difference between science and magic by saying, "Science is born of experience, magic made by tradition" (*Magic, Science and Religion*, p. 19). Of course, this is plain nonsense. As for the matter of experience, magic is born from experience as much—or as little—as is science; witchcraft is no more unexperienceable than are electrons. Similarly science is every bit as traditional as magic; there would be no science were the tradition of scientific inquiry not scrupulously passed on from one generation to another. Again Malinowski writes, "Science is guided by reason and corrected by observation, magic, impervious to both, lives in an atmosphere of mysticism." But we have seen that the believer in magic is every bit as rational as the scientist and no more impervious to observable facts of experience than he. "Science is open to all, a common good of the whole community, magic is occult, taught through mysterious initiations, handed on in a hereditary or at least in every exclusive filiation." Sheer nonsense. It is true that a popular, vulgar knowledge of science is widely diffused throughout our society; but as Evans-Pritchard has most clearly shown, virtually every Zande knows a great deal about magic and can operate and interpret the oracles. In fact the gap separating the ordinary Zande's body of magical knowledge from that of the professional witch doctor is immensely smaller than that separating the scientific knowledge of most people from that of the professional scientists. (Scientists, like the clergy of former times, refer to all nonscientists as laymen. August Compte was amazingly accurate when he predicted that scientists would be the high priests of the new Order of Reason.) Science is as much a matter of "mysterious initiations" as is magic. One becomes a recognized scientist only when one publicly demonstrates that one has mastered a set of interrelated concepts, "a particular *constellation of explanatory procedures*" as Toulmin says (*Human Understanding*, 1:160) and shows one's ability to apply these appropriately in various practical situations. And conformity to current scientific dogma is rigidly enforced in the scientific community. One will be listened to only if one possesses respectability and authority, and these are gained by publishing in prestigious journals and writing widely accepted textbooks. One is entitled to wonder if the coercive pressure in the scientific community to "think right" is not even stronger than in shamanistic corporations, which often tend to be rather loosely knit. Science, Polanyi has said, is democratic; but when was a scientific issue ever settled by ballot? To try, like Polanyi, to justify the Protestant religion by likening it to science and thus to democracy (see *Science, Faith and Society*, p. 57) betrays an incredible degree of naiveté.

61. The classic positivist position is that only those statements count as scientific that can be empirically verified. Some writers on science maintain, however, that scientific statements can never be conclusively verified; at the most they can only be falsified. Thus Karl Popper formulates the criterion for science in this way: *"it must be possible for an empirical scientific system to be refuted by experience"* (*The Logic of Scientific Discovery* [New York, 1968], p. 41).

62. The statement is by Joseph Petzoldt, a disciple of Mach and the founder of the *Zeitschrift für positivistische Philosophie;* it is cited by Holton, *Thematic Origins*, p. 276. The essay in question, "Einstein, Michelson, and the 'Crucial' Experiment," should be consulted in its entirety because Holton, on the basis of extensive and detailed historical research, refutes, in the case of Einstein, the positivistic myth of the primacy of the experiment.

63. Holton, *Thematic Origins*, p. 267. Regarding the occasional failure in their treatment of patients experienced by both shamans and Western psychiatrists, Torrey writes:

> Therapists in all cultures tend to blame their patients for their failures. In Western therapy it is usually ascribed to the patient's being "unsuitable for therapy," having "too rigid defenses," not being able "to give up his symptoms," etc. In other cultures it

is usually blamed on a taboo broken by the patient or his family, and therapists end most healing sessions by invoking enough taboos to insure their being broken, thus leaving themselves an excuse for failure (*The Mind Game,* p. 39).

64. Polanyi, *Science, Faith and Society,* p. 31.

65. Ibid., pp. 30, 31.

66. Hanson, *Patterns of Discovery,* p. 96. Hanson goes on to say (p. 98): "The possible orderings of experience are limitless; we force upon the subject-matter of physics the ordering we choose."

67. Holton, *Thematic Origins,* p. 53.

68. Sextus Empiricus, *Pyrrhoniarum hypotyposeon* ("Outlines of Pyrrhonism"), 1:183.

69. Kuhn, *Structure of Scientific Revolutions,* p. 77. Although he means to abstract from the "history," "psychology," and "sociology" of science and pretends to a "straight logical" account of science according to which a science is a deductive system that can be falsified only if one of the lowest-level hypotheses in the system is refuted by experience, the positivistic philosopher of science, R. B. Braithwaite, does say, in a way that anticipates Kuhn:

> The scientific deductive system which physics has gradually built up by incorporating the original deductive systems of Galileo and his contemporaries has developed by the rejection of hypotheses when the system which included them led to the prediction of observable results which were found not to be observed. But exactly which hypothesis was to be rejected at each point was a matter for the "hunch" of the physicist. Generally speaking, a hypothesis was not rejected until an alternative hypothesis was available to take its place. . . . The process of refuting a scientific hypothesis is thus more complicated than it appears to be at first sight (*Scientific Explanation* [Cambridge, 1968], p. 20).

70. J. Bronowski, *The Identity of Man* (Garden City, N.Y., 1971), p. 43. It is precisely *this* fundamental similarity between science and magic—the fact that the scientist is as much a prisoner of his closed system as is the magician—which is not perceived by Robin Horton in his otherwise excellent article, "African Thought and Western Science," in B. R. Wilson, ed., *Rationality* (New York, 1971). In the first part of his article (the best part, from my point of view), Horton admirably points out the many similarities between scientific explanation and traditional religious thought in African societies. He shows here how "most of the well-worn dichotomies used to conceptualize the difference between scientific and traditional religious thought" (intellectual versus emotional, rational versus mystical, reality oriented versus fantasy oriented, empirical versus nonempirical, and so forth) do not apply; he maintains that they are pseudodifferences that block all understanding of traditional thinking (p. 152). He shows very well how the relation between African religious thinking and common sense or ordinary experience is of the same sort as between science and common sense in Europe.

After having discredited these pseudodifferences, Horton pinpoints the real difference, as he sees it. For him the "key difference" is that "in traditional cultures there is no developed awareness of alternatives to the established body of theoretical tenets; whereas in scientifically oriented cultures, such an awareness is highly developed." In short, "traditional cultures are 'closed' and scientifically oriented cultures 'open' " (p. 153).

Our reflection in this chapter on the relation between magic and science shows that this is simply not so. Indeed to draw such a distinction, as Horton does, is no doubt to fall victim to the most well-worn pseudodichotomy of all. Horton refers to two of the Evans-Pritchard passages I have cited ("There is no incentive to agnosticism," and "they reason excellently in the idiom of their beliefs, but . . .") in an attempt to show how, unlike science, traditional thinking cannot question itself. But we have seen that this is basically no less true of science. Both science and magic are systems of belief; science is thus no less dogmatic (or "superstitious") than is magic. (And one wonders if in fact magic or traditional religious thought is not much less inflexible and much more open to revision and development than it is usually made out to be.) Horton says that the tenets of religious belief are "sacred" (p. 154), but an impartial observer of scientists and their attitudes toward the exigencies of the scientific method would have to say the same of the basic tenets of science. The typical scientist believes no less than the typical witch doctor does that his system expresses something "real," that it reveals something about the "nature of reality."

The reason for Horton's blindness in this matter is fully apparent in this article and well worth noting. Horton must hold that science is a more "objective" system than magic, for if he were to abandon his own faith in science he would have to abandon his belief in a fixed, determinate, and supremely knowable reality—and this he is not prepared to do. Horton says that one important difference between science and religious thinking lies in the fact that in the latter, but not in the former, "any challenge to established tenets is a threat of chaos, of the cosmic abyss, and therefore evokes intense anxiety" (p. 154). But if this is a characteristic of magic, it is no less a characteristic of science, and Horton gives the most perfect de facto demonstration that it is that one could hope for. For if magic and science are on an equal footing, he says, the result, "intolerable in the extreme," is a kind of ontological pluralism that undermines the scientific "search for order" and "human beings can expect to find no sort of anchor in reality." It is obvious that Horton perceives magic as a "challenge" to science (just as a magician would perceive science as a threat to his belief system) and that his defense of science is a means of warding off the "anxiety" evoked by "the threat of chaos," this "horrific prospect" (p. 157). His motives in defending science are thus the same as those of someone who defends magic.

71. This fact is completely ignored by the philosopher-anthropologists I. C. Jarvie and J. Agassi, who, although they reiterate Evans-Pritchard's statements on the irrefutability of magic qua system, nevertheless fail to see that science itself is no less of a tautological system than is magic. They accept without question the myth of scientific open-mindedness and self-criticism and even go so far as to say, in a typical positivist fashion, that contrary to magic, science holds "irrefutability" to be a defect in a system. Of course positivistic scientists do criticize magic (for instance) for not being "falsifiable," but what they fail to see is that science itself is no less "irrefutable" than is magic. Cf. their joint article, "The Problem of the Rationality of Magic," in Wilson, *Rationality,* p. 192.

72. Polanyi, *Personal Knowledge,* pp. 292, 294.

73. Ibid., p. 294.

74. In "The Fixation of Belief" Peirce distinguished between different ways of assessing beliefs and selecting among them and ended up by maintaining that the scientific method is the best way for doing so. This was a fateful move; it was also to prove fatal to pragmatism as a philosophical movement. It was fateful, for to a very great extent it oriented the pragmatic movement in a particular direction: pragmatism tended to become the philosophical justification of science, indeed the handmaiden of science. This is what proved to be fatal. In attempting in the area of social and political thought to equate the "democratic process" with the scientific method (a good example of this approach is Sidney Hook's *Reason, Social Myths and Democracy* [New York, 1966]), pragmatism paved the way for its eventual bankruptcy and failure as an organized philosophical movement. As is becoming increasingly apparent to all thinking people, democracy has nothing to do with science, and the reason is that science has nothing to do with questions relating to fundamental value choices; science cannot determine what is the "good life." In fact the unbridled application of the scientific method in all areas of our social, political, and cultural life increasingly is resulting in a very undesirable state of affairs and, not the least, in the withering away of political freedom.

75. Frazer, *New Golden Bough,* p. 649.

76. H. Arendt, *The Human Condition* (Chicago, 1958), p. 287. The text continues: "If, therefore, present-day science in its perplexity points to technical achievements to 'prove' that we deal with an 'authentic order' given in nature, it seems it has fallen into a vicious circle, which can be formulated as follows: scientists formulate their hypotheses to arrange their

experiments and then use these experiments to verify their hypotheses; during this whole enterprise they obviously deal with a hypothetical nature." Thus, when science seeks to justify itself, it is caught up in a vicious circle.

77. Malinowski, *Magic, Science and Religion,* p. 81.

78. Ibid., p. 90.

79. Ibid., p. 32.

80. Cf. ibid., pp. 80-81.

81. Saint Ignatius of Loyola is reported to have said that when one acts one should count on oneself alone, as if God did not exist, while remembering all the while that everything depends on His will. This is in a sense what primitive man does.

82. Malinowski, *Magic, Science and Religion,* p. 32.

83. See appendix II, "Magic, Science, and Religion."

84. Plato, *Theatetus,* 158c (Cornford trans.).

85. Cf. Maurice Lagueux, "L'usage abusif du rapport science/idéologie," in *Culture et langage.* (Montreal, 1973). Lagueux says: "Est scientifique la théorie que je choisis de soutenir et idéologique ce qui paraît s'y opposer" (p. 228).

86. That doubt is not the opposite of belief but is, rather, a particular mode of belief, Husserl makes amply clear in his *Ideas,* sec. 106, "Affirmation and Negation together with their Noematic Correlates."

87. James, *Principles of Psychology,* 2:283.

88. E. Husserl, *Experience and Judgement* (Evanston, Ill., 1973), sec. 7, p. 30.

89. James, *Principles of Psychology,* 2:283.

90. Ibid., p. 286.

91. Ibid., p. 284.

92. The becoming aware of one's beliefs qua beliefs, a development whereby one frees oneself from living naively in them, is nothing other than what Husserl referred to as the "phenomenological reduction" or *epoche.*

93. Lest the rationalist wish to accuse us of inconsistency in that while we claim to reject rationalism we nevertheless continue to make use of rationalist notions (in that we are using the principle of noncontradiction, which is itself a rationalist principle), to refute rationalism, this much needs to be said: We are not using the principle of noncontradiction or any other rationalist principle to prove anything; we are merely attempting to show how rationalism itself is inconsistent and unfaithful to its own first principles, wishing thereby to show up the basic "absurdity" of rationalism. We would be inconsistent only if we claimed to know more than the rationalist claims to know about reality. Our tactic here is not unrelated to that of Diogenes the Cynic who, when Plato defined man as a featherless biped, turned the whole Platonic doctrine of essential natures to ridicule by producing in response a plucked chicken and saying, "There is Plato's man for you." Or, to draw another, related analogy, our tactic is basically that of Sextus Empiricus who, by means of dialectical and rational argument, showed that dogmatism or what we would call rationalism cannot uphold any of its basic tenets without falling prey to internal contradictions.

4 ANALOGY AND REALITY

It is necessary to reject rationalism. Although rationalism asserts that reality has meaning, it holds that this meaning can, in principle at least, be captured by a science (human or divine, as the case may be). Rationalism thus results, in practice, in dogmatic intolerance and, in our day and age, in scientific-technological totalitarianism. Totalitarianism (even the political variety) can be successfully combated only if one rejects that notion which serves as the condition for the intelligibility of reality according to rationalism: the notion of the *totality*—that is, only if one rejects the rationalist assumption that reality is a cosmos, a well-articulated and thus knowable whole, only if, in a word, one rejects the very ideal of a science of reality.

The traditional alternative to rationalist absolutism is relativism. Relativism recognizes that reality is irreducibly pluralistic and can be interpreted in many different ways, all of them entitled to be called true. Relativism rejects the myth of the cosmos and encourages tolerance, but it does so at an extremely high cost. The price to be paid is the loss of meaning altogether. Reality in fact ceases to be meaningful since it is no longer one (in any meaningful sense of the term); the ways in which it is understood in different cultures and universes of discourse are irremediably many and thus equivocal. No two cultures, no two peoples, mean the same thing by "reality," which is to say that "reality" no longer means anything.

If one wishes to maintain that reality is indeed meaningful in some proper sense of the term (and not by a mere equivocation) and is thus the possible object of a metaphysics, but if one also wishes to escape from the dangers of rationalist absolutism that postulates that this meaning is expressible in one particular mode of discourse (if, that is, one wants to overcome dogmatism), it would seem that one is obliged to defend two theses conjointly: (1) reality is somehow "one" (in opposition to relativism), and (2) reality transcends all possible understandings of it, that is, all belief systems (in opposition to rationalism). One must therefore argue for the unity of reality—a unity of meaning—while at the same time insisting that this meaning is never univocal—expressible in an ideally correct and definitive way—and can never be the object of a science. Such a position has rarely been defended in the history of Western thought, and one can legitimately wonder if it is even possible to defend it rationally.[1] This is what we propose to consider in this chapter by reflecting in more detail on the question of analogy.

Like the concepts of univocity and equivocity, the notion of analogy is, in a sense, highly theoretical, and to examine it is to engage oneself in a highly theoretical inquiry seemingly far removed the original questions from which we started out. Nonetheless this inquiry is necessary if we are to discover a means of working out a theoretical alternative to rationalist absolutism on the one hand and irrationalist relativism on the other. What we are able to learn about analogy will, moreover, prove useful when we turn to an examination of metaphor in an attempt to discern the way in which creative understanding functions.

Before turning to analogy, however, an attempt should be made to draw out the main implications of the preceding chapter, for only in this way will we be able to measure the gravity of the problem facing us and so realize the imperative need to find a way out of it—by means, let us hope, of the notion of analogy. The previous chapter has serious implications regarding two basic notions that are central to any metaphysics and theory of understanding: reality and truth.

In regard to reality, it has been seen that different systems of understanding, such as magic and science, construe reality differently. What reality is for a believer in magic is not what it is for a believer in science. If, then, we retain our transcendental approach to the question of reality and view it purely in terms of human experience of it, it must be said that *to different beliefs correspond different realities*. "What the facts are" or what reality is is a function of the mode in which it is intended, is dependent on and relative to the particular system of understanding one happens to adopt (or to be enculturated into). The way people perceive reality is determined by the way in which they approach it, on their frames of reference or universes of discourse. From an experiential or transcendental point of view—the only point of view allowable when it is a question of reflecting on human understanding of reality as such—I. A. Richards expresses the matter perfectly when he says, "The fabrics of our various worlds are the fabrics of our meanings."[2]

This view accords with that of Whorf, with the theory of linguistic relativity. To say that the fabric of reality for any given person is the fabric of his meanings is to say that it is the fabric of his language or universe of discourse, for meaning is inseparable from language (though not reducible to it). To different languages correspond, therefore, different realities. Whorf's teacher, Edward Sapir, expressed the matter in this way:

> It is quite an illusion to imagine that one adjusts to reality essentially without the use of language and that language is merely an incidental means of solving

specific problems of communication or reflection. The fact of the matter is that the "real world" is to a large extent unconsciously built up on the language habits of the group. No two languages are ever sufficiently similar to be considered as representing the same social reality. The worlds in which different societies live are distinct worlds, not merely the same world with different labels attached.[3]

A world or a reality is precisely what a belief is a belief in; it is what is projected by any particular system of understanding. Since a person will take to be real what his system of belief posits as reality, it is irrelevant whether one speaks of a world system or just simply of a world; there is no practical difference between the two, just as there is no such difference, as Peirce remarked, between a belief and a true belief. Now since the world system or system of belief of the shaman is incompatible with that of the scientist, the world of the shaman or someone who believes in shamanism is quite simply another world from that of the scientist. The fact that they seek to gain understanding by adopting different symbolic schemas inexorably condemns them to separate worlds.

There can be something like worldwide, unambiguous communication only for people who live in the same world. However, people would all share the same world only if they shared the same world system. This means that the scientific ideal of a world community is possible only if there is one world system. It is possible only through the elimination of cultural plurality and the reduction of all worlds to the one world of science.

There is not one world, however, but many worlds. Because each culture or universe of discourse is a world, or projects its own, there are as many worlds as there are cultures. A world is nothing other than the ensemble of rules and conventions according to which a people plays out its life and exercises its creativity. A "man of the world," as the saying goes, is someone who moves with ease within his own culture and is an accomplished player in the game of life. And each culture is itself composed of a multiplicity of subworlds: the world of the child, the world of the artist, the world of the madman, the world of the religious believer, and so on.

It might be objected at this point that nonetheless there is one "really real" world, which is common to all of these "merely cultural" worlds, this being the universe of physical reality. However differently people view the world, it is still a fact that they all live in the same physical world, on the planet Earth, the third planet in the solar system. If this were indeed so, cultural pluralism would not entail ontological pluralism—as we have been arguing that it does—and it would be possible to arrive at a basic science of reality—physical science—wherein the term *reality* enjoys a fixed, precise, and univocal meaning. The objection does not hold, however, because people do not mean the same thing by *reality*. Physical, material reality exists only as the idea product of the physical sciences; it exists only for the scientist or for someone who subscribes to this particular world view. Atoms, the universal building blocks of reality according to science, have the same epistemological and metaphysical status as witchcraft substance, the basic element in the world system of magic and witchcraft. Therefore it cannot be maintained that physical nature is any more "objective" than any other conception of reality. On the contrary, all systematically developed views of reality are equally objective (although some views may be less rigid than others and more self-critical). By definition all beliefs are objective, since it is the nature of a belief that it posits as "real" (objective) that which it is a belief in. Belief, as James said, is nothing other than "the mental state or function of cognizing reality."

To attempt to escape from ontological pluralism by positing physical nature as that which is universally real and which includes in itself all the different cultures and world views held by people would simply be another instance of the inversion syndrome. It would represent the error of attempting to explain understanding in terms of something that itself is a product of a particular form of understanding. In this case the idea product (physical nature) of merely one mode of understanding (physical science) would be used to explain all other modes of understanding and their idea products as well.[4]

The conclusion that must be drawn is that reality (qua objective correlate of belief) is irremediably pluralistic and relative. *There are a multitude of separate realities and possible worlds* and, Leibniz notwithstanding, it cannot be said that one world in particular is the best of all possible worlds, unless, of course, one's purposes are merely polemical and one wishes to do no more than persuade someone else to adopt one's own particular and limited view of things. If, however, this is so, does it make any sense to attempt to work out a metaphysics of reality? Should not this attempt be abandoned as a meaningless search after a mere fiction? Before we come to grips with this formidable question, let us set out the implications of the previous chapter regarding the other key notion in any metaphysics and theory of understanding: truth.

The traditional definition of truth is that it is the correspondence of ideas with reality: *veritas est adequatio intellectus ad rem*. This definition may be retained, but, if so, it must be revised to take account of our critique of the traditional conception of reality as that which is what it is, one and the self-same, fully determined and "univocal" in itself. For if reality is thoroughly pluralistic and if truth is correspondence to reality, truth itself must be thoroughly relative. We have found that it is impossible to say that science is any truer than magic in any absolute sense of the term; science could be shown to be truer than magic only if it could be shown that the reality it posits is more real than that of magic. But this is impossible. Therefore it must be concluded that just as there is an irreducible plurality or realities, so also is there a multitude of truths. No belief or statement can be unequivocally true or true in any absolute sense since there is no univocal sense to the term *reality*.

How then are we to conceive of truth? Truth, it is said, is the property of certain beliefs or propositions that are "meaningful" and that "agree" with what actually is "the case." This definition, too, can be retained if we are clear as to what constitutes meaning, reality (what is the case), and agreement.

For a statement to be true—and truth is said primarily of things said, that is, statements—it must, before it can ever be said to agree with anything, be meaningful. (I cannot justifiably say of a statement that means nothing to me that it is true since I have no idea of what I am talking about when I say this.) Just as a word can have meaning only as part of a language, so also a statement can have meaning only as part of a general system of belief. To say, for instance, that radioactive nuclides of cobalt 60 have a half-life of 5.29 years means nothing apart from the notion of atoms, electrons, the periodic table, and the like, which altogether constitute the system of belief of physics. When a statement is formed in accordance with the grammar of a particular universe of discourse, it is automatically meaningful because it says something possible about a world held to be real. To be meaningful is the same as to be possibly or potentially true.

A statement becomes actually true when the state of affairs it posits as possible is accepted as being itself actual—that is, when it is actually believed in and is no longer merely entertained as a candidate for belief (as a mere hypothesis). A proposition, as Protagoras would have said, is true only when someone believes it. "Agreement with reality" thus means (pragmatically speaking) agreement among the users of a particular language in regard to how they will apply it. Since reality is nothing other than what people, sharing a common belief system, believe in (since it is what is postulated in a common consensus), truth is no more than agreement among these people as to the various tenets of their belief. To say that a proposition is true amounts, therefore, to no more than this: that it accords or fits in with what is already taken to be "true," with an already accepted belief system. Truth is always "cultural" and "contextual."[5]

This non-rationalist conception of truth allows for a proper understanding of two correlative notions having to do with truth and reality—definition and essence—for the question of truth involves the question of definition and the object of a definition is an essence. A statement can be true only if it asserts something of something (the something asserted may be a quality, a quantity, an action, existence or nonexistence). Now one way of asserting something of something is to say, "This is X" (if we are not stating a definition but asking for one we say, "What is X?"). To say that something is X is to define it, for a definition is a statement of what something is. Now "what something is" is its essence, its *quidditas* or whatness. The rationalist maintains that it is the essence of a thing that determines its definition: *ratio quam significat nomen, est definitio* ("the essence expressed by the name is the definition").[6] But on the basis of what we have so far discovered about the way understanding functions, it is something else that must be said. It must be said that a definition is the result of an act of defining. And what is it to define? It is, as the word itself indicates, to delimit. To define is *definire,* combining the words *de* ("from") and *finis* ("boundary," "end"). To define something in such a way as to see it as an instance of something else, as an X (species and difference, *per genus et per differentiam:* "man is a rational animal"), is an activity wherein we introduce distinctions into the kaleidoscopic flux of experience, separate certain things from other things (delimit them), and combine these imaginative groupings into orderly classifications. To define is, in effect, to interpret; it is a creative act of the understanding. Definitions cannot therefore be said to be incorrect except inasmuch as, in regard to a particular universe of discourse, they violate its generally accepted conventions.

Now definitions provide us with essences, and so it must be said that an essence is simply the product of an act of interpretation or evaluation. "What the facts are" is determined by the way in which we evaluate or creatively interpret our experience; facts and essences are the products of values and interests. William James was saying something very much like this when he wrote:

> Every way of classifying a thing is but a way of handling it for some particular purpose. Conceptions, "kinds," are teleological instruments. No abstract concept can be a valid substitute for a concrete reality except with reference to a particular interest in the conceiver. The interest of theoretic rationality, the relief of identification, is but one of a thousand human purposes. When others rear their heads, it must pack up its little bundle and retire till its turn recurs. The exaggerated dignity and value that philosophers have claimed for their solutions is thus greatly reduced. The only virtue their theoretic conception need have is simplicity, and a simple conception is an equivalent for the world only so far as the world is simple—the world meanwhile, whatever simplicity it may harbor, being a mightily complex affair.[7]

Nietzsche was even more insistent on rejecting "essences":

> There are no "facts-in-themselves," for a sense must always be projected into them before there can be "facts."
>
> The question "what is that?" is an imposition of meaning from some other viewpoint. "Essence," the "essential nature," is something perspective [*sic*]

and already presupposes a multiplicity. At the bottom of it there always lies "what is that for *me?*" (for us, for all that lives, etc.)

A thing would be defined once all creatures had asked "what is that?" and answered their question. Supposing one single creature, with its own relationships and perspectives for all things, were missing, then the thing would not yet be "defined."

In short: the essence of a thing is only an opinion about the "thing."[8]

Such then are the conclusions to which we are led concerning reality, truth, definition, and essence. One can rightfully wonder if they are not of such a sort as to undermine completely any attempt, such as our own, to say something truthful about reality. Must the attempt to work out a metaphysics of what-is be abandoned as a hopeless and vain pursuit? Must it be assumed that the term *reality* is purely equivocal and that there is no Reality (here spelled with a capital to indicate that which would be common to all realities), only a plurality of disparate realities?[9] It must be conceded that if there are no fixed essences, there can be no exact definition, in univocal terms, of reality. Does this mean, however, that it is meaningless to speak (truthfully) of a Reality over and above the plurality of realities? Is the metaphysical question, "What is Reality?" a nonsensical one?

It must be denied that there is anything like an identical reality, one that is the same for all people, and this has to be denied since it is the only way in which to combat rationalism effectively and the theoretical and practical totalitarianism stemming from it. Although we denied that there are fixed, univocal essences and maintained that reality is thoroughly pluralistic, we did not say that these realities have nothing at all in common with one another. Indeed the very fact that it is possible to speak of *different* realities implies that the term *reality* has some sort of common meaning, else how could one begin to distinguish among its different instances or modes? If in each case reality meant something totally different—if the term were completely equivocal—the search for a true understanding of Reality would have to be abandoned at this point, and, indeed, what has already been said about ontological pluralism and relativity could not even have been said. What is called for, therefore, is a more thorough reflection on the implications of our own critique of rationalism, for if ontological relativity is at all defensible, it can be so only if reality does not necessarily entail equivocity and relativism.

Now the only conceivable alternative to both univocity (rationalism) and equivocity (relativism) is analogy. Because analogy seems to be the only way out of the dilemma we find ourselves in—rejecting rationalist absolutism without falling into relativism—it must be explored in more detail. Perhaps the concept of analogy will provide us with a theoretical justification for speaking not of the same reality or of purely different realities but of similar realities, and in this way open up the way to a metaphysics of Reality.

The major problem confronting any metaphysics is that of working out and justifying an appropriately and specifically metaphysical mode of discourse. In our case it is the problem of finding a means for talking about Reality (as the common element in all realities), which does not thereby give rise to the belief that Reality has a definite essence that can be fittingly expressed in a univocal, exact definition; it is the problem of reconciling unity and difference in such a way as not to reduce either one to the other. The only conceivable manner in which this could be accomplished is by means of analogy. A. Nemetz pinpoints the problem:

> It seems that it makes no causal difference whether one says that analogical discourse is necessary because reality is analogous, or whether one says that when reason attempts to discursively account for its own pluralism, the result is necessarily analogical. . . . I think the metaphysics of knowledge centers on the question of how reason can account for its own inherent pluralism.[10]

One has no choice but to maintain that Reality itself is somehow analogous if one's goal is to work out a metaphysics on the basis of a theory of understanding, which views understanding as inherently pluralistic. Reality itself must be analogous if it is possible to say anything about it and all languages or modes of understanding are relative. To the "multivocity" of language must correspond an analogy of being. The question is whether analogy is itself a viable notion and constitutes a genuine alternative to both rationalism and relativism (univocity and equivocity), a true *via media.*

The Thomist school of philosophy—the only one to have reflected systematically and extensively on the question of analogy—distinguishes, according to one traditional classification, three kinds of analogy: analogy of attribution, metaphorical analogy, and analogy of proper proportionality.[11] Ignoring for the time being metaphorical analogy, let us see if either analogy of attribution or that of proper proportionality is able to provide a satisfactory means for conceptualizing the unity in difference that must exist between the different systems of understanding and the realities corresponding to them.[12]

In analogy of attribution (or analogy of proportion, as it is also called) one particular term is predicated of many different subjects. It might seem that this is the kind of analogy implied by the statement that different cultures or belief systems intend in their own unique way one Reality. One would then say that "objectivity validity," "truth-value," or "reality" is something analogously common to differing cultures or belief systems. Is "reality" really the common term here, though—something with a definite meaning in itself and merely referred to differently by different modes of understanding? Let us recall the traditional example. The term *healthy* is said of a living organism, medicine, and urine. In this form of analogy the term applies most properly (*formaliter,* as the medievals put it) only to living organisms; this is the *ratio propria,* the proper meaning. By extension, it can be said of medicine, in that this is the cause of health, and of urine, as a symptom of health. It is thus obvious that in analogy of attribution the various uses of the term presuppose and are grounded in a *ratio communis,* a common meaning, which is itself univocal; the term conserves one and the same basic meaning throughout its different uses. This amounts to saying that the term *healthy* applies unequally to the things of which it is predicated. In analogy of attribution there is always a *prime analogate* (for example, living organism). As Cajetan, the sixteenth-century commentator of Saint Thomas says, "There is diversity of relationships, but the term of those relationships is one and the same."[13] Were we to take analogy of attribution as our model, we would then have to say that notwithstanding the diversity of belief systems, there is one and the same reality, which they all intend in their differing ways, and we would also have to say that differing belief systems express reality unequally and that the "proper" meaning of reality is the one expressed by one belief system in particular.

Because analogy of attribution is applicable only to those instances where different terms (analogates) are directly related to one and the same univocal notion, it is obvious that it will not suit our purposes, for we cannot say that the reality posited by one system of belief is any more real or true than that of another. Reality is not a univocal term that is merely used analogously; it is analogous in itself. If there is a plurality of realities, there cannot be a direct relation between the belief systems that posit these realities, such that one could rank them on a descending scale according to the degree to which they "correspond" to reality.

This means that the relation between belief systems is not a relation of proportion (a relation between terms)—*analogia secundum convenientiam proportionis*—but of proportionality (a relation between proportions)—*analogia secundum convenientiam proportionalitatis.* To paraphrase Cajetan, there is a diversity of relationships, and the term of those relationships is not one and the same. The only common element between, for instance, science and magic is the way in which each intends its own reality; that is, what is analogous is not something like reality but rather the kind of relation that obtains between each belief system and its own particular reality. The realities in question (scientific and magical) are themselves incommensurate, but the systems of magic and science function in a like way in that while they posit different realities, they both posit their realities as, for instance, existent realities.

It would seem, then, that the form of analogy we are looking for is analogy of proper proportionality. Plato furnishes us with an example of this kind of analogy when he writes, "As the good is in the intelligible region to reason and the objects of reason, so is this [the sun] in the visible world to vision and the objects of vision."[14] This form of analogy would seem to be a highly promising candidate for conceptualizing what is common to all systems of understanding, since here the thing predicated (for example, reality) is said to be analogical in itself and not merely in its use, as in analogy of attribution. Thus if the term *healthy* is predicated of different things according to an analogy of attribution, the term *vision* is predicated of different things (such as the eye and the mind) according to an analogy of proper proportionality. In analogy of proper proportionality the analogue (such as reality) applies to each analogate (system of belief) not unequally, as in analogy of attribution, but properly and equally. What is common here is not the thing itself that is predicated ("reality"), but rather the likeness in question has to do with the kind of relation that each of the two things bears to what is predicated of them: corporeal vision is to the eye what intellectual vision is to the mind; the reality of witchcraft substance is to magic what the reality of atoms is to science. As Jacques Maritain notes, "In this case, what is signified by the concept, inasmuch as it is one (even though it is so only in a unity of proportionality) is intrinsically and formally in each of the analogates."[15] Witchcraft substance is as real for magic as atoms are for science; neither is more real than the other; "reality" applies equally to both, even though it means something entirely different in either case. And as Maritain also says, quoting John of Saint Thomas:

> "Analogia proportionalitatis [propriae] dicenter quorum nomen commune est, ratio vergo significata eadem secundum similitudinem seu convenientiam proportionum [et in utroque formaliter et vere praesens]." The sense in which the analogue belongs intrinsically and formally to each of the analogates is purely and simply diverse (*ratio significata est simpliciter diversa*), yet the same under a certain aspect (. . . sed eadem secundum similitudinem *proportionum*), in that it implies like relations to terms that are alike even though essentially different—relations that are registered in the very nature of the analogical concept. . . . as Cajetan says, it [analogy of proper proportionality] alone constitutes a true analogy, the others being called by that name only in an improper sense.[16]

The concept of analogy of proper proportionality therefore seems to be the concept we need in order to defend our rejection of both absolutism (univocity) and relativism (equivocity). It enables us to say to the relativist that cultural relativity, which is undeniably a fact, must nevertheless not be conceived of in such a way as to imply that different belief systems are "purely and simply diverse" and have absolutely nothing in common and that the concept of reality has no common meaning among cultures. On the contrary, all belief systems are "about" or "signify" one and the same thing, reality, which is therefore "intrinsically and formally in each" of them. To the absolutist, however, it enables us to say that reality is only "analogically" common to all belief systems. When "reality" is predicated of different belief systems, it is done in the mode of proper proportionality: different such systems are alike in that they have similar relationships to their respective realities, which themselves are therefore "alike even though essentially different." Only analogy of proper proportionality constitutes a true analogy; only it provides a genuine alternative to both univocity and equivocity.

Has not this discovery of a means of conceiving of analogy that does not reduce it to univocity legitimated our search for a metaphysics of reality that would be neither rationalist nor relativist? It would have only if it is admitted that analogy is a meaningful notion alongside univocity and equivocity, only if it is admitted that it is indeed a viable middle way between the two. This, however, is not always readily conceded.

Analogy is a highly unstable notion, such that even when attempts are made to defend it, it can slip through one's fingers, leaving one with nothing to show for one's efforts. This invariably happens when, in a misguided search for "scientific" rigor, an attempt is made to formalize or mathematize analogy of proper proportionality.[17] Traditionally analogy of proportionality, which says, for example, that one belief is "true" in a way that is somehow similar to the way another, quite different belief is "true," even when "true" or its correlate "reality" does not have the same meaning, is schematized as $a:b::c:d$. This already looks like a mathematical formula. The "is" of ordinary language (a is to b as c is to d) has been translated (and thus changed) into the abstract symbols ":" and "::". Instead of saying, "One belief is true in a way analogous to the way another belief is true," one says: $b_1:t_1::b_2:t_2$. "Similar to" or "analogous to" is an intrinsically vague notion, and so if one is looking for scientific, logical, "exactitude," one can conceive of "similar to" only as a mode—and a deficient or weak one at that—of "identical with." For logic, "is" in a case like this means " $=$."

However, to have recourse to " $=$ " ($\frac{b_1}{t_1} = \frac{b_2}{t_2}$) is to transform analogy of proper proportionality into analogy of attribution, for the " $=$ " reduces t_1 and t_2 to merely different modes of T.[18] Or again, were one to mathematize the already formal $a:b::c:d$, one might write, $\frac{2}{4} = \frac{3}{6}$. But the result of this is to curtail analogy drastically, for what this mathematical ratio expresses can be reduced to the simple concept of the half; $\frac{2}{4} = \frac{3}{6}$ reduces to $\frac{1}{2}$. In a formalist account of analogy, "truth" becomes univocal once again.

Even an author who disavows this formalist type of approach shows how pervasive it is as a tendency of the human mind and how he is himself a victim of it when he writes of the traditional notion of proper proportionality as presented by Cajetan (in an attempt to "expose it"):

What is really being said here is that two or more things are similar in similar respects; and when one asks how the respects are similar, one is told that such a question cannot be asked in this case. This is not an ordinary similarity but a proportional one, and irreducibly proportional so that the proportion cannot even be granted the relative invariance of a mathematical function, for that would introduce a sameness. But can we ask "similar" or "similitude" to be ready at our call when we have cut their moorings? Can we honestly invite a term like proportional to carry the burden of a new and unique usage when we have severed its mathematical spine?[19]

Our author is indeed correct when he says of analogy of proper proportionality that—if it has any meaning at all—it is "irreducibly proportional" and "that the proportion cannot even be granted the relative invariance of a mathematical function, for that would introduce a sameness." What, however, justifies him in saying that in this case "similar" and "similitude" have "cut their moorings"? From what have they cut themselves? The implication is that they are thereby mutilated notions and merely a degenerate form of "sameness." He in fact says that in analogy of proper proportionality, "proportional" has "severed its mathematical spine." What, though, justifies him in maintaining, or at least in uncritically assuming, that the true meaning of "similarity" is mathematical "identity"? This would seem to be a purely logicist, rationalist prejudice. It is in fact frankly stated as such by an author who was not merely an unwitting victim of logicism but was himself a professed rationalist, Edmund Husserl. Husserl says:

An improper use of identity in the case of like things, refers us back, through its very impropriety, to a proper use of the same term, i.e., to an identity. We find in fact that *wherever things are "alike," an identity in the strict and true sense is also present.* We cannot predicate exact likeness of two things, without stating the respect in which they are thus alike. Each exact likeness relates to a Species, under which the objects compared, are subsumed: this Species is not, and cannot be, merely "alike" in the two cases if the worst of infinite regresses is not to become inevitable. If we specify the respect of our comparison, we point by way of a more general class-term to the range of specific differences among which the one which appears in our compared members is to be found. . . . Not every Species has of course an unambiguous verbal expression, and so at times a suitable expression for a "respect" is lacking, and to state it clearly might be difficult. We none the less keep it in view and it governs our talk of "alikeness." *It would of course appear as a total inversion of the true state of things, were one to try to define identity, even in the sensory realm, as being essentially a limiting case of "alikeness."* Identity is wholly indefinable, whereas "alikeness" is definable: "alikeness" is the relation of objects falling under one and the same Species. If one is not allowed to speak of the identity of the Species, of the respect in which there is "alikeness," talk of "alikeness" loses its whole basis.[20]

Husserl's logicist thesis is thus that "alikeness" is merely a weak form of "identity," that it has no meaning apart from identity, that wherever an "alikeness" is present, an underlying identity can always be found. Exact likeness or identity, however, is made possible by the fact that there are fixed species or essences (Husserl even believed that essences could be clearly intuited by means of a special kind of sight, which he called *Wesenschau*). Husserl allows that our language may sometimes fail us and that to a particular species there may not always correspond an appropriate verbal expression, but he insists that there must be species and identity if language (all "talk of 'alikeness' ") is to have any meaning.

This is a remarkable text, for it embodies most of the logicist or rationalist prejudices we have already commented on in preceding chapters. Husserl's conception of language is strictly traditional: language merely mirrors a reality which is what it is, fully determinate in itself, apart from language. All knowledge consists in conforming our vision to fixed essences.[21] If anything has any meaning, this meaning must be precise and univocal.

To the degree that the exact likeness that Husserl speaks of is to be found anywhere in this imperfect world of ours, it most surely exists between these views of his and those of Frege discussed in chapter 1. Frege too attempted to derive metaphysics from logic and to view reality in the light of the methodological postulates of logic. There must be univocal meanings that are perfectly translatable, he said, if logic is to be able to perform its functions. But all that this shows is of how little use formal logic is when it comes to understanding reality. Husserl's mode of argument is identical with that of Frege (and is every bit as much of a question begger). He is saying that language can have no meaning if there is not something apart from it to "mean," to "refer to," something fixed and determinate; without essences language "loses its whole basis." Why, one might well ask, however, should there be a "basis" to everything? What justifies one in positing total intelligibility, perfect, exact meaning anyhow, apart from the obvious fact that it is psychologically comforting? Or, as James asks, "Why should anywhere the world be absolutely fixed and finished?"[22]

Husserl's own remarks could easily be turned against him by a critic of essences such as Nietzsche who could say that all of Husserl's argument is a case of wishful thinking. Husserl posits essence and identity for the simple reason that it is in his interest as a logician to do so. Far from demonstrating what Husserl thinks they do, these remarks show just the opposite—that meaning is never perfect and univocal but always the product of our imperfect human understanding, which eagerly strives after meaning and, in its frustration at never finding it whole, posits identity as a limiting case of its own vague, analogical, metaphorical way of grappling with things. The "total inversion" Husserl speaks of is precisely the one that rationalists like

Frege and himself are guilty of; they seek to explain human understanding in the light of an ideal, which exists only as a product of human imagination. Their very mode of argument derives from this inversion, as when they confront us with a vicious either-or, saying that either there is no meaning at all to language or language is merely a way of expressing perfect, univocal meanings. But the either-or is an instance of logical thinking—it is the law of excluded middle—and therefore cannot be used to justify the logicist view of things. Logic, like science, is a mode of human understanding, and thus it cannot claim that its idea products, such as that of species, or its laws—identity, contradiction, excluded middle—are those of reality itself. As Montaigne so well observed, "Whatever we're lectured to about, whatever we learn, we must always remember that it's man who gives and man who receives; it's a mortal hand which offers it to us and a mortal hand which accepts it."[23]

From a strictly human, mortal point of view, is there anything more absurd than to say that analogy ("similarity") must be understood in the light of identity and not, as we would want to say, the other way around, since, as Husserl himself argues, identity is wholly indefinable whereas "alikeness" is definable? Isn't this the most superb instance of all of getting the cart before the horse—explaining the definable in terms of the indefinable, explaining what is known in terms of what cannot be known? As Sextus Empiricus would have said, Husserl is "proposing to decide and establish the less questionable matter by the more questionable, which is absurd."[24] Like Aristotle's owl, human understanding may be half blind to what really is, but is this any reason to let ourselves with our poor eyesight be led around by someone who is totally blind, who explains the dimly known in the "light" of the completely unknown? What a logical treatment of analogy shows is nothing other than the limits of logic.[25]

The inability of logic to give a proper account of analogy demonstrates that analogy can be a meaningful notion only if there is not a realm of essences, of pure, fixed, univocal meanings, only if the analogical "is" is not reducible to the mathematical " = " and "alike" to "identical," "similar" to "same."

We all know what we mean when we say that something is "like" something else. Someone who wants to know what something is ("What is X?") does not ask, "What is its essence?" but, rather, "What's it like?" In doing so, he is, from a rationalist's point of view, acting "shamelessly" by trying to explain what something is like when he does not yet know what it is.[26] The rationalist notwithstanding, however, it is a fact that we all know how to reason by analogy, how to use and understand highly complex similies, analogies, and metaphors; we are not, all of us, like Husserl, mathematicians capable of intuiting essences. To explain analogy in terms of identity is

thus to explain the familiar in terms of the unfamiliar. What indeed does
" = " mean anyhow? Just what is an "exact" likeness, a pure identity? How
can two things be "equal," the "same"? If they are the same, how can they
be different, which they must obviously be if they are two? To this the rationalist might answer, To say that they are equal or the same is only to say
that they are identical in a certain respect, not in every respect. This,
however, still leaves the question open as to what "identity" actually
means. Analogy may not be an easy notion to understand on the conceptual
level, but it is not, like identity, a sheer mystery. Identity, it could even be
said, is intrinsically meaningless—perhaps, indeed, all purely univocal concepts are—since it is nothing but analogy pushed to its unthinkable limits.

Admittedly analogy is ambiguous (and this is enough to account for the
aversion logicians have for it since they generally abhor the vague and ambiguous), but if it is ambiguous, it is nonetheless systematically ambiguous.
Even Aristotle, the founder of theoretical logic, finds analogy or "thinking
by example" indispensable as when, to express what he means by his highly
abstract concepts of potentiality and actuality, he says that "potentiality is
like sleeping in the way that actuality is like waking."[27] Analogy is a basic
trait of our lives of understanding, just as time is a basic given of our human
experience, and, like time, it poses no less of a problem when we try to
understand it theoretically. As Saint Augustine remarked:

> In our conversation, no word is more familiarly used or more easily recognized
> than "time." We certainly understand what is meant by the word both when
> we use it ourselves and when we hear it used by others. What, then, is time? I
> know enough what it is, provided that nobody asks me; but if I am asked what
> it is and try to explain, I am baffled.[28]

Paraphrasing Augustine, we could say, What in conversation is more
familiarly used or more easily recognized than analogies? We certainly
understand what is meant by them. What, then, is analogy? I know enough
what it is, provided that nobody asks me, but if I am asked what it is and try
to explain, I am baffled.

The fact that analogy resists logical formalization and is hard to define
theoretically is no reason for rejecting it as a meaningless notion, in the
same way as some Eleatic might want to deny the existence of time since it is
virtually impossible to conceive of in terms of his rigid logic. Because we are
constantly using analogies and making ourselves understood thereby, we
can deny their meaningfulness only if we deny the meaningfulness of our actual lives. If logic is incapable of properly conceptualizing analogy and if
analogy is a basic trait of our understanding, the conclusion to be drawn is
not that analogy is meaningless but rather that logic has severe limitations.
This would seem to be the most judicious conclusion because people con-

stantly use words analogously, and understand one another, even though they may be unable to specify exactly and unambiguously what they mean (although if they are allowed to clarify their analogy by means of further analogies they usually do just fine). Analogy points to the existence of a practical kind of knowledge, which is quite untranslatable into logicist, rationalist concepts. This fact must be kept firmly in mind because it can serve as a constant reminder that something is fundamentally wrong with the rationalist way of thought and its entire conceptual framework.

If understanding and reality are to be understood properly, what is called for is a non-rationalist mode of thought capable of grasping conceptually that which we, in our practical lives, accomplish with instinctive ease. In order to understand analogy we need a mode of thinking that is not logical but, so to speak, analogical; we must base our metaphysics and theory of understanding not on the logicist interpretation of language and understanding—not on what language and understanding ideally are—but must instead derive them from the way people actually do use language and do understand. Or as I. A. Richards has insisted in speaking of metaphor: "We must translate more of our skill into discussable science. Reflect better upon what we do already so cleverly. Raise our implicit recognitions into explicit distinctions."[29]

"Philosophy's vocation," Paul Ricoeur has remarked, "is to clarify by means of concepts existence itself."[30] This is what we shall be attempting to do in the next three chapters where our concern will be to conceptualize the way understanding actually does function, after which we shall attempt to conceptualize the ontological implications of the concepts worked out in an attempt to understand understanding. By then we should have discovered what can be known and said about reality and what cannot.

But already it is possible to discern in a general way what is analogously common to all cultures and universes of discourse. What is common or universal is the experiential fact that all people attempt to understand their lives through creative expression or discourse in which analogy plays a key role. What is common and universal is this human praxis. The worlds we construct thereby differ from one another and may even be totally incommensurable (as are the worlds of magic and science), but the situation in which we all find ourselves and which we attempt to clarify in our diverse ways is analogously one.

What all people share is therefore not a common world but a similar situation: the *human condition*. They are all confronted with the mystery of birth, the enigma of death, sexuality, and the need for recognition, the obligation of devising ways of living in an inimical, opaque and often hostile environment. Different cultures or worlds are the result of the different ways in which people have sought to deal with the whence, whiter, and wherefore of existence. It is this lived-through human situation that analogously binds all cultures together and not an "objective" nature, for "nature" is something that exists only in and through culture. Nature (or world) is what gets constituted according to the way in which people choose to come to grips with the riddles of life.[31]

This means that the common element in cultures is not something that is expressed, as such, in any culture. In other words, although the human situation is common to all people, different cultures perceive this situation differently, and they give different interpretive responses to it, ones that often have very little in common. Thus the common element is not to be found on the level of symbolic expression (for what is to be found here are different "worlds" or "realities"); it exists rather at the level of lived experience that has not yet been articulated. *The error of logicism is that it ignores this extralogical or extralinguistic basis of all language and logic;* it moves solely on the level of theory and ignores practice.

Logic is concerned solely with language and signs; it does not and cannot deal with what language is "about": experience or reality. When a logician does talk about these things he has no other option, qua logician, but to conceive of them "logically," by projecting onto them the characteristics proper to language, logically conceived (*vide* Frege or the early Wittgenstein who argue in effect that extralinguistic reality must have such and such characteristics if logic is to be possible). Logicism is unable to understand analogy precisely because it looks for the common element on the level of logic or language, a level of experience that has been conceptualized already. The truly basic question for any metaphysics of reality is the question concerning the relation of language or theory, on the one hand, to experience or practice, on the other. It is this question that logicism ignores, and necessarily so. We, however, cannot afford to ignore it; indeed only by confronting it head on will it be possible—if it is at all possible—to work out a non-absolutist, non-rationalist metaphysics.

Philosophy is a form of discourse, one that calls itself rational, and thus if we say with Montaigne, "I always call reason that semblance of discourse that everyone forges within himself," it becomes imperative to inquire, by means of discourse, into the relation between discourse and what it is about, between discourse and prereflective or lived, preverbal experience.[32] The ultimate task of understanding is to understand the relation between itself and its object, that mute experience underlying and motivating all attempts at understanding and expression and in which understanding seeks to discover some semblance of meaning.

Analogy is an unstable, fragile notion, which disintegrates when forced into the procrustean bed of logical formalism. But it is also true that it eludes the feeble grasp of relativism and escapes through its too loosely drawn logical nets, and it will be instructive to see how and why this is so.

Just as Husserl served as a good example of the logician's reductive approach to analogy, so may the position of the later Wittgenstein illustrate the inadequacies of relativism as a philosophical attempt to understand analogy; Wittgenstein is, in fact, as nearly perfect an antithesis to Husserl as one could wish for.

In opposition to the kind of logicism to be found in Husserl's project of a universal grammar and, indeed, in opposition to his own earlier position, which similarly sought to discover the "general form of propositions"[33] (the universal essence of language), the later Wittgenstein recognizes the irreducible pluralism of all languages and the relativity of all meaning. He now rightly objects to the logical straitjacket of univocity and recognizes that what different uses of the same word have in common is often not something that could ever be rigidly formalized. Instead of the universal form of language, the later Wittgenstein speaks of "family resemblances" in effect his way of saying "analogy" (a term he avoids, however, perhaps because it is not colloquial enough for an "ordinary language" philosophy and because he wants "to bring words back from their metaphysical to their everyday use").[34]

In considering a particular instance of the "What-is-X?" question Wittgenstein introduces his notion of family resemblances. The question is, What is language? Wittgenstein attacks his own erstwhile notion that there is a universal form of language and says that language has many different forms, such that it is impossible to say what the essence of language is.

> Instead of producing something common to all that we call language, I am
> saying that these phenomena have no one thing in common which makes us
> use the same word for all—but that they are *related* to one another in many
> different ways. And it is because of the relationship, or these relationships,
> that we call them all "language."[35]

We know, or believe we know, what it means to have one thing in common, but what does it mean to say that there is no such common element here but rather that all of these different "languages" are called languages for the simple reason that they are "related to one another in many different ways"? Is this a satisfactory answer to the question, What is language? or is it rather the evasion of an answer? Wittgenstein tries to explain himself by turning to the example of games. What is a language? is the same sort of question as, What is a game? So, what is it which makes a game a game?

There are board games, card games, ball games, Olympic games and others, but what is common to them all? Wittgenstein answers, "If you look at them you will not see something that is common to *all*, but similarities, relationships, and a whole series of them at that."[36] There is "a complicated network of similarities overlapping and criss-crossing: sometimes overall similarities, sometimes similarities of detail."[37] In short, there is no essence "game," but games "form a family."[38] No one feature or group of features is common to all games; there are only overlapping similarities, which Wittgenstein calls "family resemblances," since "the various resemblances between members of a family: build, features, color of eyes, gait, temperament, etc., etc. overlap and criss-cross in the same way."[39] We must not seek to discover what binds all games together but should merely take note of their multifarious similarities, of the self-evident and indisputable fact that they are related: "We must do away with all *explanation*, and description alone must take its place."[40] Wittgenstein admonishes us, "Don't think, but look!"[41]

To think, however, is precisely what we want to do here. We have for the most part no trouble in doing what Wittgenstein admonishes us to do: to "look" and to recognize relations. This is not a philosophical problem. It is, however, a philosophical problem to say what is involved in the perception of similarity and to think the matter over so as to arrive at a concept of similarity, and supposedly philosophy is what Wittgenstein is trying to do (having entitled his book *Philosophical Investigations*). To be sure, Wittgenstein entertains another idea of philosophy. In philosophy, he says, one should not draw conclusions; philosophy should only state "what everyone admits."[42] It would seem, however, that the important thing, if one is doing philosophy, is not just to state the obvious but to reflect on it and to think what it means, what is involved in it, and what is presupposed by it. The important thing is to be able to translate skill into knowledge, to form an adequate theory of practice.

In his appeal to practice, Wittgenstein skirts the philosophical problem of analogy. He does not attempt to show how the What-is-X?" question can be answered analogously but quite simply rules this question out ("don't think, but look!"). The "logic" of his position is curious and seems to be this: because it is impossible to discover any one feature that is common to all language (all language games), the question, What is language? should be abandoned. For an opponent of logicism this is indeed an extremely odd way of going about things, for the logic here is none other than the either-or logic of logicism. In his reaction against rationalism, Wittgenstein, it would seem, is still conditioned by its logic; though discredited, the ideal of univocity still continues to be operative, only now in a negative way. Instead of saying, as he did before, that there is a general form of propositions, Wittgenstein now says that there is no such form. He is not, therefore, so much proposing an alternative to rationalism as he is merely turning it inside out (or upside down, as Marx did with Hegel); the thought of the second Wittgenstein is merely an inverted rationalism.

Instead of saying, or attempting to say, what is analogously common to all instances of a general concept such as game, Wittgenstein merely enumerates—correctly (but how? what is his guide?)—instances or examples of games.[43] It is as if, when we wanted to know what X was and asked someone, he answered, "This is an X, and that too, and also this other thing, but what X is, don't ask me." It may indeed be difficult to say what X is, what, for instance, time is, but does this mean that it is wrong-headed to attempt to do so? Must this ingrained human tendency to search for general concepts (a tendency that sets us apart from the beasts) be uprooted from our being and be deemed perverse?[44]

We have objected to the rationalist's identification of meaning with reference, with the notion that the meaning of a word is the thing to which the word refers or is the relation between word and thing, for here there is no way of accounting for analogy (except by reducing it to some form of univocity). But neither does Wittgenstein offer an account of analogy. Although he rightly rejects the notion that meanings can be absolute and that what is common to all instances of X can be stated in a precise formula, he does not attempt to show how to *conceive* of meaning analogously. Quite to the contrary, he berates our "craving for generality"[45] and proceeds in effect to reduce meaning to action. The meaning of an utterance is neither what it refers to (an objective state of affairs) nor is it the thought (meaning-intention) that accompanies the utterance but is rather its use: "The meaning of a word is its use in the language."[46] In the midstream of his philosophical career Wittgenstein switches metaphorical horses and in the place of the picture image of the *Tractatus* now likens language to a tool: "Look at the sentence as an instrument, and at its sense as its employment."[47]

The consequence of all this is an extreme conventionalism. The meaning of a term is nothing more than the way it is used. To understand a meaning is purely and simply to be able to act in an appropriate manner. Meaning is determined by practical use, and nothing more.

Of course, this conventionalism is not for all that an outright nominalism.[48] Unlike a straightforward nominalist, Wittgenstein is not saying that what all games have in common is merely the fact that they are all called games (that all they have in common is the name *game*). There may not be any common "essence" game; nevertheless it is not a purely arbitrary convention that classifies different things as games. The metaphor of the tool is helpful here, for a tool is what it is because of the use for which it is destined. We invent tools for certain purposes, and it is the interrelationships of these purposes that determines the relations between the tools. So it is with language. What gives a certain unity to our use of terms is the modes of behavior of which they themselves are a part. As Wittgenstein says, "The *speaking* of language is part of an activity, or of a form of life."[49]

It might seem that by this insistence on "forms of life" Wittgenstein has taken account of just what logicism ignored: the extralinguistic, presymbolic experience of meaning that motivates and calls forth all language. But this is not the case. Wittgenstein's forms of life may be preconceptual, but they are not presymbolic. The use and behavior that invests language with whatever meaning it may have are particular uses and modes of behavior, ones that are already highly structured. They embody a kind of practical, unthematized, yet already articulated knowledge; they are what Polanyi might call "tacit" forms of knowing. What Wittgenstein means by "use" or "forms of life" falls on this side of what could be called the expression-experience duality (on the side of expression), where expression (understanding) itself is subdivided into thematic or theoretical and practical.

The arbitrary conventionalism that Wittgenstein was able to avoid when he rejected fixed referents by locating in actual practice the reason for similarity between linguistic meanings is thus reintroduced on the level of practice itself. For *what is it that accounts for similar forms of life?* I may have no trouble in grasping the meaning of utterances by members of my own linguistic and cultural community because we all share in a common form of life, but how can I possibly make sense of cultural behavior that differs radically from my own? If nothing is analogously common to different forms of life themselves, there is no way for me to understand another culture, and the result is a thoroughgoing relativism. All one can say is that to different forms of life correspond different meaning systems. If, however, we say that to different uses correspond different meanings, we run into a difficulty reminiscent of the one found in Whorf when he says that different languages embody different metaphysics and that, for instance, the Hopi language conceals a metaphysics that is "properly describable only in the Hopi language." But the curious fact of the matter is that Whorf was able to say, in English, a lot about the Hopi metaphysics, which is to say that his actual practice served to contradict his theory or, at least, to indicate that it had severe limitations.

On Wittgenstein's own grounds, it is impossible to escape relativism, for it is impossible to find reasons for forms of life (that is, it is impossible to discover something more basic than a mode of behavior, something that motivates it and makes it intelligible). Wittgenstein cannot handle this question, and this is perhaps why he rules it out and belittles it as meaningless. Philosophy, he says, can only describe the actual uses of language; it cannot give any reason or foundation for them.[50] We simply have to accept "forms of life" as an ultimate given.[51] Confronted with a form of life, all that can be said is, *"This language-game is played."*[52] "The question is not one of explaining a language-game by means of our experiences, but of noting a language-game."[53]

It is, however, a fact of experience that we can do more than merely note different language games and that even a radical difference in modes of behavior does not prevent us from achieving some understanding of another form of life quite alien from our own. We do not react to foreign ways of life in the same way as we do to, say, exotic species of animal life. The only way out of the dilemma would be to recognize that there is something that all people share in common, something that is to be found neither on the level of explicit meaning nor even on the level of practical behavior and "tacit" knowledge but deeper still.

We have seen how Wittgenstein castigates the "craving for generality." In accordance with his behavoristic-like orientation, he also denounces the view that somehow a state of understanding intervenes between, for instance, hearing an order and executing it or the view that action is grounded in mental states; this he calls "a general disease of thinking."[54] Whereas in the *Tractatus* he maintained that the true essence of a thing is not immediately apparent, is in fact hidden beneath the surface and must be discovered or dug out through careful analysis,[55] the later Wittgenstein holds that everything is out in the open and needs only to be noticed. For him the task of philosophy is merely to describe what is plainly visible. It is precisely this methodological prejudice that prevents him from working out a theory of analogy and from seeing that the meaning of words is something analogically common to them all.

Words and language have an intrinsic generality that mere particular modes of behavior lack. Terms such as *love, respect*, and *recognition* can be used to characterize or interpret all sorts of behavioral patterns that have, from a purely observational point of view, little or nothing in common. To reduce language to (linguistic) behavior (even when behavior is taken in a wide sense and not merely in the narrow "behavioristic" sense) and to confuse meaning with use is to destroy language and meaning by eliminating their necessary generality. It is as if one were to confuse the word (or concept) *leaf*, which is something general and universal, with the actual leaves of all the different species of plants, which obviously do not have any one feature in common. If one wishes not merely to describe how people use words but to discern how it is that words mean, why it is they have a kind of universal mode of existence, one must look deeper than mere use, for although the use of language is obviously a form of behavior, the meaning of language is not. To understand this meaning, one must look for the common intention behind the multifarious uses.[56]

Intentions are not observable. They are, in fact, the supremely hidden element in all discourse. Never can I observe another person's intentions; all I see and hear are his actions and utterances. It is not surprising, therefore, that, given his methodological (behavioristic) bias, Wittgenstein is reluctant to allow for the existence of meaning-intentions: "Nothing is more wrongheaded than calling meaning a mental activity!"[57]

Wittgenstein is correct when he rejects the notion that words describe intentions, as if language were something that merely accompanied intentions. Just because meaning-intentions are not observable, however, or are not "inner mental states" does not mean that they do not exist as something irreducible to use and to overt behavior. It does not mean that intentions do not somehow transcend their expression. While Wittgenstein is correct in saying that "our criterion for someone's saying something to himself is what he tells us and the rest of his behavior,"[58] his error is to confuse the criterion of meaning with meaning—the how we know something with the what it is that we thereby know. The criterion of meaning is something observable; meaning itself, however, is not observable. Although meaning-intentions cannot be described, they can and must be interpreted, on the basis of what one says and does (even my own intentions I can truly know only when I have spoken and acted them out). Meaning is not natural but cultural, and like all other things cultural, such as social institutions, it is not, unlike behavior, something that can be seen and thus described; it can only be inferred from behavior. As one anthropologist very aptly remarks, "Ideas and values are not given as data; they must be inferred."[59]

Wittgenstein writes, "When I think in language, there aren't 'meanings' going through my mind in addition to the verbal expression: the language is itself the vehicle of thought."[60] Although one may not agree with rationalism when it says that language merely reflects a thought that is fully determined in itself, is one to go to the opposite extreme and reduce thought to language, to "verbal behavior"? Is there not something like a meaning-intention that somehow precedes expression and of which one is, in some vague way, directly aware? Surely it is possible to agree with Wittgenstein when he says that an "intention is embedded in its situation, in human customs and institutions,"[61] without for all that denying that one can mean and intend to say something before he has actually said it. William James, to whom Wittgenstein alludes in this context, describes the phenomenon of intending with much less prejudice than Wittgenstein when he writes:

> What is that first instantaneous glimpse of some one's meaning which we have when in vulgar phrase we say we "twig" it? Surely an altogether specific affection of our mind. And has the reader never asked himself what kind of a mental fact is his *intention of saying a thing* before he has said it: It is an entirely definite intention, distinct from all other intentions, an absolutely distinct state of consciousness, therefore; and yet how much of it consists of definite sensorial images, either of words or of things? Hardly anything! Linger, and the words and things come into the mind; the anticipatory intention, the divination is there no more. But as the words that replace it arrive, it welcomes them and calls them right if they agree with it, it rejects them and calls them wrong if they do not. It has therefore a nature of its own of the most positive

sort, and yet what can we say about it without using words that belong to the later mental facts that replace it? The intention *to-say-so-and-so* is the only name it can receive.[62]

As this text of James admirably points out, the intention-of-saying-so-and-so is an altogether peculiar phenomenon. On the one hand, the meaning-intention or, as James says, the anticipatory intention, precedes and motivates expression and is a particular (determinate) intention because it calls forth certain words and rejects others that present themselves and yet, on the other hand, nothing can be said of it without using the words that subsequently replace it. A curious fact indeed! Meaning cannot properly or fully exist—or be described—apart from language, and yet it is not reducible to verbal behavior either.[63]

If this indicates anything at all, it most surely is that language is a very peculiar sort of phenomenon that cannot be properly understood if one approaches it merely as an instance of observable behavior or as part of the "natural history" of humanity, as Wittgenstein says. Language has not only an outside but also an inside. The Greek definition of man as ζῶον λόγον ἔχον is not merely a zoological description of human behavior or of a physical feature characteristic of the human race in the way that the ability to fly is characteristic of birds.[64] Birds fly, but they do not appear to mean anything thereby. Humans speak, and their speech means something. Language is not only the visible manifestation of a particular way of life, as wings are for birds, but it is also the means whereby people come to some understanding of the meaning of their way of life and, perhaps, of the common meaning of any possible way of life and of being in general. Unlike other modes of behavior, language is self-reflective. It is not only an activity that people engage in, like the mutual grooming of monkeys; it not only signifies something, as grooming does, but is the self-awareness of signifying and thus the self-consciousness of a meaning-intention.

Language is more than a mere mode of behavior or way of life, for it is the means whereby a way of life can become conscious of itself and of the fact that it seems to be the expression of something more basic than itself. There is an intention to speak, and this is basically the intention to say what-is, the meaning of experience, of things themselves, of being. One who does not take this extralinguistic and extrabehavioral element of language into account will never understand what language is and how different languages can intend one meaning or express differently a common intention and, failing to understand this, will not understand how there can be something like Reality over and above the plurality of realities.

Beyond both theoretical and practical understanding (this latter corresponding to Wittgenstein's "forms of life"), beyond the manifest world of expression, there is the shadowy, obscure realm of experience, which motivates and gives rise to expression and out of which emerges the "need to speak," to which all people bear witness in their multitudinous and manifest ways of life and diverse language games. In this dark country resides the intention of language—what it refers back to, means to say. What exactly the relation is between "experience" and "expression" will concern us later. It suffices for the time being to have taken note of the difference between the two and of the fact that there is something like a meaning-intention that transcends language (qua behavior or performance) and is irreducible to it (though not, of course, as rationalism would have it, separable from it). This is the true and ultimate "referent" of language.

This critique of relativism has enabled us to rehabilitate the notion of reference in a non-rationalist context and in so doing has justified, in principle at least, the attempt, which is metaphysics, to say something about the unique referent of all languages: Reality. Although one must agree with relativism that meanings are not, as rationalism thinks, determinate entities that determine knowledge and language, one nevertheless cannot simply reduce meaning or what language means to language and its use. There is a meaning-intention—the "intended," *l'intenté*, as Paul Ricoeur says[65]— which relativism ignores but also which rationalism totally misconstrues. Only by passing through the relativist critique of rationalism and then turning around and subjecting this critique to a critique of its own is a truly "alternative account of intelligibility," as MacIntyre says, and a nondogmatic metaphysics, which is to say, a theory of reality as something analogous in itself, possible.

What is valid and worth retaining in Wittgenstein is his critique of rationalism, but as is the case with many other critiques (that, for instance, of Herbert Marcuse who adroitly exposes the mystifications of scientific-technological thinking but proposes nothing definite and constructive in its place), Wittgenstein does not provide us with a satisfactory alternative to the well-conceived but erroneous epistemology and metaphysics of rationalism. If one is merely describing the USE of language, conventionalism is the only correct way of accounting for established meanings. It is not "essential natures" or "intelligible species" that give words their meaning; rather the literal or "proper" meaning of a term is simply the one that a linguistic community accepts as proper; it is the customary meaning. Wittgenstein furnishes an altogether satisfactory account of how language games are played.

But how one plays the game and what the game itself is are two different questions. When one is merely describing how language functions, one need not allow for anything like "intentions" since they are in no wise observable (and thus describable) as such and are, in fact, from an observational standpoint, one with modes of behavior and situations. If, however, one is looking for reasons as to why different games are not merely called games but are all instances of "game" (and this Wittgenstein must do if he is not to fall into nominalism), he cannot appeal merely to practice because this is a circular explanation and thus no explanation at all. What prevents Wittgenstein from going beyond a ruinous conventionalism is his methodological prejudice: his belief that philosophy must eschew the "hidden." This aversion to the hidden is one more exemplification of Wittgenstein's overreaction to his own earlier rationalism, for it is not evident that the hidden must be an essence, something that is determinate in itself and that determines language from the outside, that the hidden is incompatible with "use." The hidden may be quite indeterminate in itself; it may be, that is, not univocal but analogical. The reason for Wittgenstein's inability to work out a theory of analogy, for his inability to discover anything common to all instances of games, lies in the fact that he looks for similarities on the level of the manifest or the already expressed (albeit unthematically) and ignores that hidden dimension of experience that gives rise to expression and that binds all language games and ways of life together analogically.

Against analogy of proper proportionality it is sometimes said, in an attempt to expose or discredit the notion, that it does not really explain anything or furnish genuine reasons. It does not function as a genuine heuristic device, which would allow one to derive something as yet unknown from the already known. Although it looks like a mathematical formula, it is not one, and thus nothing can be done with it. To say that different cultures are in an analogy of proper proportionality ($\frac{a}{b} = \frac{c}{d}$) is not to say anything at all; either one already knows both cultures, and thus necessarily also their reality correlates (four terms), or one knows only one (two terms), that is, one knows either just two terms or else four terms, but one cannot know three terms and not the fourth, such that one could derive the unknown fourth from the known three. A theory of analogy therefore will not allow one to arrive at new knowledge or make predictions.[66]

This is entirely true. A theory of analogy is not a scientific explanation and is of no use in predicting what types of culture are likely to be found in various parts of the world or the way in which a particular culture is likely to evolve. Analogy does not explain why a given culture has taken on the form it has. From the point of view of science or causal analysis, the question why or how cultures are the type of cultures they are (why, for instance, culture A is matrilineal and patriarchal rather than matrilineal and matriarchal) is in no way answered by saying that cultures are characterized by the way in which they articulate common human concerns and intentions. What analogy does account for is our own ability to understand other cultures and to communicate with them.

Only the existence of a basic analogical relation between cultures can explain the fact that when we are thrown into a different and exotic culture, we always end up by understanding it. This phenomenon cannot be accounted for by saying that we are able to grasp the meaning of a foreign language by means of the behavior or way of life of its speakers. It is not the case that "the common behaviour of mankind is the system of reference by means of which we interpret an unknown language."[67] This is not the case, for there is no such thing as a common behavior of all people. Behavior—even such a basic act as eating and preparing food—often differs tremendously from one culture to another; in fact one is inclined to say that the more basic and common the behavior (such as eating, sex) the more it tends to differ from culture to culture. It is not, then, in terms of behavior that one understands the meaning-system of another culture or its language; on the contrary, it is behavior that puzzles us and needs to be understood.

One cannot understand the behavior in terms of the language (although this is no doubt what the rationalist would want to do) because the meaning-system is even more inaccessible than the overt behavior, nor can one understand the language by reference to the behavior. If, therefore, there is not something more basic than both meaning-system and behavior, one would never understand another culture. But the fact is that one does. Wittgenstein says, "If a lion could talk, we could not understand him."[68] This, however, should be turned around to read, If a lion could talk, then we could indeed understand him. We could surely succeed eventually in understanding even a Martian or some other extraterrestrial creature, provided only it could talk. This, in any event, is the working hypothesis and the operative faith (assuming that they could understand us) of the American space agency when it includes taped statements of human intentions in its interplanetary exploratory craft.

When we encounter an alien and strange mode of behavior, we succeed in understanding it or in making it intelligible to ourselves by interpreting it, though not necessarily in a fully self-conscious way. To make intelligible is in Latin *intelligere;* it is *inter legere*—to read between the lines and to make explicit the hidden intention. A certain bizarre custom suddenly becomes intelligible when we realize that it is their way of expressing what we, for our part, would express differently, in a different behavior; we realize that their intentions and our own are, the differences in appearance notwithstanding, the same. A good example is the one used by Montaigne (which he himself borrowed from Herodotus).[69] What behavior could be more abhorrent to us than eating our own fathers? And yet the ancient people who behaved in this fashion looked upon their curious practice as a mark of affection and esteem, for they thereby gave their fathers the most worthy and honorable sepulcher possible: their own bodies. They transformed themselves into living relics of their fathers and regenerated their dead remains by integrating them into their own living flesh. It is easy to imagine, Montaigne says, how abominable and cruel our custom of throwing our parents' bodies into the earth, there to corrupt and be eaten by worms, would appear to them.

In a case like this, the modes of behavior are utterly unlike one another, and yet it can be said that they both express the same intention: that of loving one's parents and honoring the dead. Thus, it is not because a mode of behavior seems natural to us or because we have a tendency to act in the same way that it is intelligible to us. On the contrary, even when we have understood the behavior in question, it may still disgust and repulse us. But in spite of this, we can still understand that it expresses in its own way the same intention or meaning that we express quite differently. There is a common analogical element among all cultures, but this element does not itself appear in the formula $\frac{c_1}{r_1} = \frac{c_2}{r_2}$, for it is the hidden element, that of intention. How indeed could we ever understand other cultures if it were not that different cultures are simply different modes in which people come to grips with the questions of life that are common to all (and that as common questions point to common meanings)? Only if, beneath the diversity of culture, there is a common analogical element, can one truthfully say with Montaigne, *"Rien d'humain ne m'est étranger"* ("Nothing human is foreign to me").

To deny intention or some basic, pre-expressive element common to all people is to deny that life has any meaning (in any meaningful, universal sense of the term). Life is reduced to a mere aimless game, indeed to a medley of senseless games guided by no transcendent purpose; it is reduced in fact to a confusion of unrelated tales told by a bunch of idiots and signifying nothing.[70]

Thus if the effect of logicism is to render our lives meaningless, the consequence of relativism is the same. Given its overly rigid criteria of intelligibility, logicism can make no sense of the ambiguous, yet systematic, understanding embodied in our praxis and prereflective behavior. Relativism does recognize this level of expressive meaning, but it cannot account for it because it does not recognize and account for itself; the relativist position is one of theory and not mere praxis. Like many other philosophers, Wittgenstein makes the fatal error of not taking into account in his theory the implications of his own theoretical praxis. He is like a philosopher who maintains the thesis of the "primacy of the practical," who says that the practical takes precedence over theory but who simultaneously overlooks the fact that the practical cannot be purely and simply primary over theory, since it is precisely by means of his own theory that the practical is accorded primacy; that the practical is primary is itself a theory. Philosophy, in the case of Wittgenstein, even goes so far as to take on a dangerous suicidal tendency. The purpose of philosophy here is to eliminate itself; it arises, he says, when "language goes on holiday"[71]; philosophical problems are diseases that must be eradicated: "The philosopher's treatment of a question is like the treatment of an illness."[72] But if philosophical problems arise out of the "misuse" of language and are illnesses, human existence itself can be described only as a pathological condition that should be cured, since what properly makes people human is that they possess a desire for the truth, which leads them to ask "What-is-X?" questions. Theory and the "craving for generality" are the specific marks of humans, and not to ask "philosophical" questions and to "misuse" language in this way is to be something less than human. A computer, if it is rightly programmed, will not fail to use language "correctly," but a computer is not human. It may not be within our power ever to discover the truth and to achieve a science of Reality; this is the presumptuous ideal of rationalism that wishes to transform humans into something more than they actually are, but not to seek the truth is not to be human. To say that theory is absurd, as Wittgenstein in effect does, is to say that human life is absurd.[73]

Wittgenstein recognizes that the rationalist belief in a culturally invariant reality is an error, but he fails to see that it is a natural error. He rightly says that concepts "are the expression of our interest"[74] but fails to see that if this can indeed be said to be true, it cannot be the last word. We may never be able to eradicate our tendency to believe—our penchant for dogmatism—and may not be able to transcend our own limited realities, but this does not mean that the notion of Reality that all people hold is meaningless. Rationalism may be wrong-headed, as Wittgenstein says, but relativism is mindless (unmindful of itself as an exercise of mind). It is up to us to discover why understanding invariably tends to misunderstand itself. Only if this can be understood will it be at all possible to understand what understanding misunderstands: Reality.

In the preceding chapter, magic was played off against science in an attempt to bring out the general features of all modes of understanding or belief systems. This chapter has employed a somewhat similar tactic; relativism has been played off against rationalism to arrive at a proper theoretical understanding of analogy in an attempt to discover a notion that would allow one to reconcile pluralism with universality. It is time to spell out our conclusions and sum up our argument. A word of warning, however, is in order. What follows are merely the implications that emerge out of a dual critique of rationalism and relativism; they are not "conclusions" in the strict logicist sense since they have not been demonstrated or proved in any proper sense of these terms. They merely represent the position one must take if one refuses both rationalism and relativism. They cannot be "proved," but the remainder of this book should be able to justify them by showing that they are the only means for understanding the way in which understanding actually functions.

Analogy can be a meaningful theoretical concept, a viable middle way between univocity and equivocity, only if that which is supposed to be analogous is not reducible to that which actually gets expressed, either in a properly theoretical mode or as a form of life. This can be stated with the aid of diagrams where:

    l = language, universe of discourse, culture, belief-system, and so forth.

    r = reality, world (the correlate of an l).

    R = Reality (the universal or analogical element common to all r's).

    L = the ideal language that adequately expresses R.

Different cultures (belief systems plus their reality correlates) are related to one another in an analogy of proper proportionality. According to the traditional formula, this would be symbolized as:

(1) $l_1:r_1::l_2:r_2$.

Logicism shows that this formula is reducible to:

(2) R

l_1 l_2 l_3 etc.

Moreover, since the different l's are directly related to or expressive of one and the same reality, it is possible to pass from one to the other or to substitute one for the other without loss of meaning; perfect translation is possible between the different l's, which is also to say that the different l's are reducible to a common, ideal language, L:

(3) R

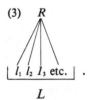

L

Relativism points out that to reduce in this way analogy of proper proportionality to analogy of attribution is to deny analogy altogether by reducing it to a mode of univocity. Pluralism can be safeguarded and can be meaningful only if different l's are not directly related to R, indeed, only if R is not something that any l can have direct access to or directly refer to, which is to say only if L is not possible. Relativism thus realizes that the formula, $l_1:r_1::l_2:r_2$, does not work. It rightly points out the inappropriateness of the "::" or "=" and as a consequence denies that there is any one feature common to all l's. The result is:

(4) $l_1 \text{———} r_1$
$\quad l_2 \text{———} r_2$
$\quad l_3 \text{———} r_3$
$\quad$ etc.,

where there is no general term (R) that binds all the successive units together into one whole. Hence R loses all meaning here and disappears from the picture altogether.

If one accepts neither one nor the other of these outcomes (3 or 4) and if one wishes to affirm the meaningfulness of R (and thus the possibility of metaphysics) while not reducing it to a univocal notion, one must not allow it to figure directly in the diagram. Thus instead of the absolutist formula (2), one would have to write:

$$(5) \quad \frac{R}{\begin{array}{c} r_1 \; r_2 \; r_3 \;\; \text{etc.} \\ {\Large /\;\;|\;\;\backslash\;\;\backslash} \\ l_1 \;\; l_2 \;\; l_3 \;\;\; \text{etc.} \end{array}} \; .$$

And instead of the relativist formula (4) one would have to write:

$$(6) \quad \begin{array}{l} l_1 \text{———} r_1 \\ l_2 \text{———} r_2 \\ l_3 \text{———} r_3 \\ \\ \quad \text{etc.} \end{array} \quad \Big| \quad R.$$

That this represents a genuine alternative to both the absolutist and the relativist positions is indicated by the fact that formulas 5 and 6 express the same thing.[75] Diagram 6 indicates that there is something common to all l's and r's, but the line " $|$ " indicates also that this common element transcends anything to be found in any one l and r set. Similarly, diagram 5 indicates by the line " ___ " that different r's are not merely aspects of one and the same thing.

It is indeed a persistent temptation to want to reconcile a pluralism of understanding with the meaningfulness of that which is understood (R) by saying that it is not nature or reality that is relative but only our culturally influenced views of it. Culture is merely a truth-limiting factor; the facts are what they are, though what a culture or society holds to be true (cultural truth) will vary and be relative from one culture to another, since a given culture acts like a filter, which, while permitting one to take note of certain aspects of reality, screens out others from view. According to this theory cultural limitations are not truth destroying, for it is still possible in principle to achieve a knowledge of the totality (R) by combining the various partial truths or "aspectual" insights of different cultures into a comprehensive whole. This however, is precisely what needs to be denied.

Various cultures (*I*'s) are not merely parts or aspects of one overriding whole, which could be the object of a system or science. Such a view is incompatible with a genuinely analogical conception of reality. Instead of "aspects" or "parts," it would be more appropriate to speak of "perspectives" and to say, with Nietzsche, that all knowledge is "perspectival," for this lets it be understood that there is indeed some one thing (if only analogously one) that is variously perceived (through different cultural perspectives), while at the same time it does not imply that this thing could ever be grasped "whole," apart from its various, limited perspectives: "As if a world would still remain over after one deducted the perspective!"[76] Indeed, the notion of a "totality of perspectives" (or of a "totalization of perspectives") is quite meaningless; as Merleau-Ponty points out in his well-known study of perception, an object viewed from everywhere at once is the definition of an object viewed from nowhere at all, in sum, a nonobject.[77]

All of this raises once again, however, the question asked at the end of the last chapter: if Reality transcends all cultures or languages, what can be said of it? If understanding is inseparable from language, how can one understand anything about that Reality which transcends language? How can one possibly get some insight into Reality (as that which is analogously common to all cultures) if it is not reducible to expression? We shall begin to tackle this question in the next chapter. Already, though, it is obvious that nothing can be said of Reality and that metaphysics, as a form of rational discourse, is impossible if it is the case that language is incapable of dealing with that which transcends it—if, in a word, the unsayable cannot be said. There is no reason, however, apart from logical prejudice, why this should be assumed to be the case. There is no reason why we should not continue our search for Reality, for, as Heraclitus remarked, "If one does not expect the unexpected one will not find it out, since it is not to be searched out, and difficult to compass."[78]

NOTES

1. It is true that Aristotle defended a notion of analogy, but he did not work out a "sufficiently analogical" concept of analogy; see note 18 below.

2. I. A. Richards, *The Philosophy of Rhetoric* (New York, 1965), p. 19. Richards later writes, "The world—so far from being a solid matter of fact—is rather a fabric of conventions, which for obscure reasons it has suited us in the past to manufacture and support" (pp. 41-42).

3. E. Sapir, *Culture, Language and Personality* (Berkeley, 1970), p. 69.

4. It is an instance of what William James called "the stock rationalist trick of treating the *name* of a concrete phenomenal reality as an independent prior entity, and placing it behind the reality as its explanation." "There never was a more exquisite example," James says, "of an idea abstracted from the concretes of experience and then used to oppose and negate what it

was abstracted from" ("Pragmatism's Conception of Truth," in *Pragmatism and Other Essays* [New York, 1963], pp. 97, 101).

5. The dogmatist will perhaps object to this way of viewing truth and will want to assert that if a statement is "true" it can only be because it "corresponds" to or "represents" an "objective state of affairs," which is what it is "independently" of our knowing anything about it. In affirming this, however, the dogmatist is talking about something of which he knows nothing (this is the usual failing of dogmatists) in that it transcends, by definition, human experience. *As a matter of fact*, we accept as true that which we do not doubt (as Pierce pointed out). Speaking from a strictly human point of view (the only legitimate point of view for a reflective human), truth is simply what is accepted as such; it is a characteristic of all firmly held beliefs. If one is to apply consistently the transcendental (phenomenological) approach to philosophical problems (such as that of truth), one must bracket all transexperiential claims (such as truth being the correspondence to an extraexperiential state of affairs); one must subject them all to a pitiless *epoche* and simply describe, as best one can, what they amount to *in practice* (pragmatically speaking).

6. Saint Thomas Aquinas, *Summa theologiae* (Alba, 1962), I, 13, 6; Thomas is referring here to Aristotle (*Metaph.*, 1012a23).

7. W. James, "The Sentiment of Rationality," in *The Will to Believe* (New York, 1956), p. 70.

8. F. Nietzsche, *The Will to Power*, (New York, 1968), sec. 556.

9. W. T. Jones, with whom we have found ourselves in considerable agreement, nevertheless, says, "I reject the notion of a single Reality (with a capital 'R') and propose to replace it with the more viable notion of a plurality of realities (lower-case)" (*The Sciences and the Humanities* [Berkeley, 1967], p. 145).

10. A. Nemetz, "Metaphysics and Metaphor," in R. Houde and J. Mullally, eds., *Philosophy of Knowledge* (Philadelphia, 1960), pp. 319-20.

11. Cf., for example, Jacques Maritain, *The Degrees of Knowledge* (New York, 1959), appendix II. Of course, in Saint Thomas the problem of analogy arises and is discussed in a theological context (this is perhaps no accident, however; indeed, one can wonder if it is not precisely some kind of theological or, as in the case of Aristotle, metaphysical interest—as opposed to merely logical concerns—that calls forth the problem of analogy in the first place). Thomas's problem was to show how one can meaningfully talk of God, without thereby negating His transcendence. A term such as *wise* cannot have totally different meanings when predicated of both humans and God, else it would mean nothing to say of God that He is wise, and the ultimate consequence would be a sheer agnosticism. Nor can the term have identically the same meaning, for this would destroy the difference between man and God, and the result would be anthropomorphism. The meaning must be neither univocal nor equivocal but analogical. That the problem of predicating names of God is, logically, of the same sort as predicating terms such as *true* of different cultures or world views is indicated by the fact that Thomas's formulation of the problem can serve to describe our own problem if the term *different cultures* is substituted for *God* and *creature:* "Univocal predication is impossible between [different cultures]. . . . Neither, on the other hand, are names applied to [different cultures] in a purely equivocal sense, as some have said. . . . Therefore it must be said that these names are said of [different cultures] in an *analogous* sense, that is, according to proportion" (*Summa theologiae*, I, 13, 5).

12. Unlike analogy of attribution—where one term (such as *healthy*) is predicated not univocally and yet properly of two different things (for example, a living organism, medicine), in metaphorical analogy one term (for example, *smiling*) is predicated properly of one thing (a person) but improperly and by equivocation of another (such as a meadow). Thus people say that to speak of a "smiling meadow" is a "mere" metaphor, since a meadow cannot "really" smile. That metaphor is an improper analogy—an analogy of improper proportionality—is a

rationalist prejudice, which we shall criticize in chapter 6. Metaphor cannot be properly understood in the context of a philosophy of essence (in rationalism, which posits a determinate reality); to take metaphor seriously is automatically to abandon rationalism. Metaphorical analogy is the odd man out in traditional discussions of analogy, and we are accordingly ignoring it for the time being. But since metaphorical analogy is based on analogy of proper proportionality (to speak of a "smiling meadow" is a shorthand way of saying that "the field in the beauty of its flowering is like to the beauty of the human smile by proportionate likeness" [*Summa theologiae*, I, 13, 6]), a reconsideration of metaphor is likely to have important retroeffects on the notion of analogy which this chapter, ignoring metaphor, will arrive at. It is important to keep this in mind. For the rationalist, analogical predication is based on resemblance. *What if, however, the resemblances that analogy of attribution articulates are what first get created by means of metaphor?* Readers are entitled to expect something of a reversal of the problem in the following chapters. If they think they detect a strange undertow in the following discussion, they are entirely correct.

13. Cajetan, *The Analogy of Names* (Pittsburgh, 1959), chap. 2, par. 8, p. 15.

14. Plato, *Republic* (New York, 1961), VI, 508b.

15. J. Maritain, *The Degrees of Knowledge* (New York, 1959), p. 419.

16. Ibid., p. 418.

17. For a recent attempt at a formal, logical defense of analogy, see I. M. Bochenski, "On Analogy," *Thomist* 2 (1948): 424-47.

18. Analogy of proper proportionality gets reduced to analogy of attribution (that is, it is reduced to merely a special mode of univocity) when, as is sometimes done, one takes the following famous text of Aristotle as expressive of the way there are many but related senses of "being": "There are many senses in which a thing may be said to 'be,' but all that 'is' is related to one central point, one definite kind of thing, and is not said to 'be' by a mere ambiguity" (*Metaphysica* [New York, 1941], 1003a33, Ross trans.). That this is analogy of attribution is evident from the example that immediately follows, that of "healthy." Thus although he pays lip-service to the plurality of the meanings of being ("There are many senses in which a thing may be said to 'be' "), Aristotle in the end reduces all these meanings to a common meaning, which is itself univocal ("but all [these meanings] refer to one starting-point")—the universal, basic meaning being that of "substance" ("substance" then functioning exactly like "healthy"). Aristotle therefore cannot be said to have steered a successful course between equivocity and univocity. In all fairness to Aristotle, he does not use the term *analogy* to describe this kind of relation between terms. He reserves ἀναλογία, which Ross translates as "proportion," for a *relation between relations;* for example, sight is to the eye as reason is to the soul. Cf. *Ethica Nicomachea* (New York, 1941), 1131a30ff. And the reason for his failure is also evident in the same paragraph; he cannot properly conceive of analogy because his express goal is a unified *science* of being ("not only in the case of things which have one common notion does the investigation belong to one science, but also in the case of things which are related to one common nature; for even these in a sense have one common notion. . . . everywhere science deals chiefly with that which is primary, and on which the other things depend, and in virtue of which they get their names"). Aristotle's "essentialist" prejudice ("common natures" which determine names) is evident here also. Indeed, the whole passage from which we have been quoting is a fine example of the conceptual framework of rationalism.

19. D. Burrell, *Analogy and Philosophical Language* (New Haven, 1973), pp. 14-15.

20. E. Husserl, *Logical Investigations* (London, 1970), pp. 342-43 (italics added).

21. In *Cartesian Meditations* (The Hague, 1960), Husserl writes (sec. 34, p. 71), "The eidos itself is a beheld or beholdable universal, one that is pure 'unconditioned'—that is to say: according to its own intuitional sense, a universal not conditioned by any fact. It is *prior to all 'concepts'*, in the sense of verbal significations; indeed, as pure concepts, these must be made to fit the eidos."

22. James, "Humanism and Truth," in *Pragmatism,* p. 180.

23. "Quoy qu'on nous presche, quoy que nous aprenons, il faudroit tousjours se souvenir que c'est l'homme qui donne et l'homme qui reçoit; c'est une mortelle main qui nous le presente, c'est une mortelle main qui l'accepte" (M. de Montaigne, "Apologie de Raimond Sebond," in *Oeuvres complètes* [Paris, 1962], p. 546).

24. Sextus Empiricus, *Pyrrhoniarum hypotyposeon* [Outlines of Pyrrhonism], II, 33.

25. It is interesting and highly instructive to note that Husserl himself seems to have had serious second thoughts about the validity of the logicism to be found in his early *Logical Investigations* (1900). In a very late work, *Experience and Judgment* (pub. 1939), Husserl (via Langrebe, his assistant and the actual compiler of the book) asks the following question, which is obviously meant rhetorically: "How can the nature of the superior be clarified by a return to the inferior?" (sec. 6, p. 28). Husserl's thesis here is precisely that the "superior" (for example, identity) is in fact understandable only in terms of its grounding in the "inferior" (such as likeness). The logician, Husserl says (sec. 10, p. 45), deals not with original experience but with "idealizations," with "nothing more than a garb of ideas thrown over the world of immediate intuition and experience, the life-world," and he mistakes the former—the abstract—for the latter—the concrete.

26. Cf. Plato, *Theaetetus* (New York, 1961) 196d, Cornford trans.: "Doesn't it strike you as shameless to explain what knowing is like, when we don't know what knowledge is?"

27. Aristotle says (speaking of actuality and potentiality), "Our meaning can be seen in the particular cases by induction, and we must not seek a definition of everything but be content to grasp the analogy" (*Metaphysica* 1048a35-7). It is almost as if Aristotle had, like Oedipus, "one eye too many" to be a good, consistent rationalist. And to complicate the Oedipus analogy even further with Freudian imagery, it could be said that the reason for his cross-eyed vision and split personality is that he was never able to carry through in a determined way the ritual murder of his intellectual father, Plato. Instead of decidedly abolishing Plato's essences, Aristotle for the most part merely brought them "down to earth" (leaving eternal, immaterial, immovable substance as the object of a divine Science).

28. Saint Augustine, *Confessions,* trans. R. S. Pine-Coffin (Penguin Books, Hamondsworth, 1961). XI, p. 264.

29. Richards, *Philosophy of Rhetoric,* pp. 94-95.

30. P. Ricoeur, *Freedom and Nature* (Evanston, Ill., 1966), p. 17 (translation corrected).

31. Cf. M. Merleau-Ponty, *Phenomenology of Perception* (London, 1962), p. 432:

To our assertion . . . that there is no world without an Existence that sustains its structure, it might have been retorted that the world nevertheless preceded man, that the earth, to all appearances, is the only inhabited planet, and that philosophical views are thus shown to be incompatible with the most firmly established facts. But in fact, it is only intellectualist, abstract reflection which is incompatible with misconceived "facts." For what precisely is meant by saying that the world existed before any human consciousness? An example of what is meant is that the earth originally issued from a primitive nebula from which the combination of conditions necessary to life was absent. But every one of these words, like every equation in physics, presupposes *our* prescientific experience of the world, and this reference to the world in which we *live* goes to make up the proposition's valid meaning. Nothing will ever bring home to my comprehension what a nebula that no one sees could possibly be. Laplace's nebula is not behind us, at our remote beginnings, but in front of us in the cultural world.

That "nature" is a meaning and therefore is understandable only in terms of culture becomes obvious as soon as one performs the phenomenological reduction and adopts a transcendental-pragmatic point of view.

32. "J'appelle tousjours raison cette apparence de discours que chacun forge en soy." Montaigne, "Apologie de Raimond Sebond," in *Oeuvres complètes,* p. 548. Isocrates had already made much the same point:

The power to speak well is taken as the surest index of a sound understanding, and discourse which is true and lawful and just is the outward image of a good and faithful soul. With this faculty we both contend against others on matters which are open to dispute and seek light for ourselves on things which are unknown; for the same arguments which we use in persuading others when we speak in public, we employ also when we deliberate in our own thoughts; and, while we call eloquent those who are able to speak before a crowd, we regard as sage those who most skillfully debate their problems in their own minds (*Nicocles*, 7-9).

33. Cf. *Tractatus Logico-Philosophicus*, 4.5.

34. L. Wittgenstein, *Philosophical Investigations* (Oxford, 1963), par. 116.

35. Ibid.

36. Ibid., par. 66.

37. Ibid.

38. Ibid., par. 67.

39. Ibid.

40. Ibid., par. 109.

41. Ibid., par. 66.

42. Ibid., par. 599.

43. In par. 135 Wittgenstein says, "Asked what a proposition is—whether it is another person or ourselves that we have to answer—we shall give examples and these will include what one may call inductively defined series of propositions. *This* is the kind of way in which we have such a concept as 'proposition.' "

44. When the later Wittgenstein says, "don't think, but look!" one is reminded of the statement by the early Wittgenstein, "What we cannot speak about we must pass over in silence" (*Tractatus*, 7). The later Wittgenstein is, albeit for other reasons, no more able to formulate and utter a theory of analogy than was the early Wittgenstein.

45. L. Wittgenstein, *The Blue and Brown Books* (Oxford, 1968), p. 17.

46. Wittgenstein, *Philosophical Investigations*, par. 43. However, in a typical Wittgensteinian fashion and in line with his constant avoidance of general statements, Wittgenstein qualifies this assertion with a preceding clause: "For a *large* class of cases—though not for all—in which we employ the word 'meaning' it can be defined thus:"

47. Ibid., par. 421.

48. This is the thesis defended by R. Bambrough in his article, "Universals and Family Resemblances," in G. Pitcher, ed., *Wittgenstein, the "Philosophical Investigations"* (London, 1968).

49. Wittgenstein, *Philosophical Investigations*, par. 22. He also writes, "To imagine a language is to imagine a form of life" (par. 19).

50. Cf. ibid., par. 124.

51. "What has to be accepted, the given is—so one could say—forms of life" (ibid., par. 226).

52. Ibid., par. 64.

53. Ibid., par. 655.

54. Wittgenstein, *Blue and Brown Books*, p. 143.

55. See Wittgenstein, *Philosophical Investigations*, par. 92, for a statement of the kind of position adopted in the *Tractatus*.

56. Wittgenstein rightly objects to the superficial thesis of empiricism that the meaning of a term is the mental image (idea) that the word evokes in our minds. If a universal meaning, the meaning "horse," for instance, were an image or "mental picture" of those features that all horses possess in common, it would, in order to cover all possible horses, have to be an extremely vague and indefinite image, to the point of not being the image of anything at all. Images are particular entities, and how could a particular entity ever be a universal? Meanings

certainly are not mental entities of this sort, and Wittgenstein is to be commended for throwing out all of this cheap mental bric-a-brac. But while his own answer to the questions of universals—use—does give a better account of what in fact is involved when we speak and has the great merit of getting away from "mental imagery" and airing out the stuffy attic of the empiricist mind, it does not really account for meaning as something intrinsically general any better than did empiricism; it merely shifts the locus of the problem. General meanings are still confused with particular things, in this case observable modes of behavior. The error of empiricism and Wittgenstein's error are basically the same. It is the error of supposing that mind or meaning is somehow (through introspection for empiricism, by means of behavioral observation for Wittgenstein) open to view. Mind and meaning are not visible entities, however, but are rendered accessible and made intelligible only through language, which is to say that language itself is not a mere sign indicator or label attached to determinate things but is the way in which the invisible, "hidden" realm of meaning is made present in the visible world. Meanings cannot be described (as can an image, presumably, or a mode of behavior); they can only be interpreted, much as the psychoanalyst interprets the unconscious through its overt manifestation in dreams and slips of the tongue.

57. Wittgenstein, *Philosophical Investigations*, par. 693.

58. Ibid., par. 344.

59. J. Beattie, *Other Cultures* (New York, 1968), p. 28.

60. Wittgenstein, *Philosophical Investigations*, par. 329.

61. Ibid., par. 337.

62. W. James, *The Principles of Psychology* (New York, 1950), 1:253.

63. It would be interesting and instructive to compare Wittgenstein and Merleau-Ponty on meaning-intention. The orientation of Wittgenstein is strikingly similar to that of Merleau-Ponty, who is at pains to deny the rationalist claim that language is merely the mirror of thought and that thoughts exists in their own right prior to expression. And just as Wittgenstein in his critique of rationalism tends to reduce the meaning of language to its use, so Merleau-Ponty tends to reduce it to gesture and bodily behavior. There is, however, an essential difference between the two, which is instructive from our point of view, for, unlike Wittgenstein, Merleau-Ponty hesitated to deny the existence of meaning-intentions. It is as though he tacitly realized that the outright rejection of meaning-intentions is no more satisfactory a solution than the rationalist hypostatization of meaning. For a detailed consideration of Merleau-Ponty's significantly ambiguous treatment of this question, see my study, *The Phenomenology of Merleau-Ponty* (Athens, Ohio, 1981), pp. 114-19.

64. That *logos*—language and its good use—is the most characteristic and noble trait of man in relation to the rest of creation is a constant theme in the greatest of the ancient Greek rhetoricians, Isocrates; cf. esp. *Nicocles*, 5-10; *Panegyricus*, 48-51; *Antidosis*, 257, 294.

65. P. Ricoeur, *The Rule of Metaphor* (Toronto, 1977).

66. Perhaps it is a feeling of inferiority vis-à-vis the scientist that accounts for the fact that a theologian, R. Garrigou-Lagrange, argues, surprisingly, that analogy of proper proportionality *does* have but one unknown term; cf. his *God, His Existence and Nature* (London, 1949), p. 288.

67. Wittgenstein, *Philosophical Investigations*, par. 206.

68. Ibid., p. 223e.

69. Montaigne, "Apologie de Raimond Sebond," in *Oeuvres complètes*, p. 565.

70. Unlike relativism, rationalism appears to assure meaning to life, but this is indeed only an appearance, for its postulation of universal intelligibility and determinate essences makes a mockery of our human experience of contingency, adversity, and uncertainty, the very substance of any real life. To say that meaning is something fixed and determinate is in effect to say that as human, finite knowers, we are mere puppets in the hands of an absolute knower. If there are absolutist "essences," human freedom and creativity are vain words.

71. Wittgenstein, *Philosophical Investigations,* par. 38.

72. Ibid., par. 255.

73. The inner contradiction in Wittgenstein's philosophizing is perceived by A. M. Quinton; see his article, "Excerpt from 'Contemporary British Philosophy,' " in G. Pitcher, ed., *Wittgenstein, the "Philosophical Investigations"* (New York, 1968). Wittgenstein's actual behavior gives the lie to his own theory and bears witness to the naturalness of man's theorizing and his craving for truth and generality, for, knowing that he was to die of cancer, Wittgenstein nonetheless continued to work on his posthumously published book, *On Certainty,* up to April 27, 1951, the day he was taken violently ill, dying two days later. Either Wittgenstein led an absurd life and died an absurd death, or his life and his theorizing had a meaning his own theory is unable to account for.

74. Wittgenstein, *Philosophical Investigations,* par. 570.

75. The consequences of this view of things concerning the notions of sense and reference could be diagrammed as follows:

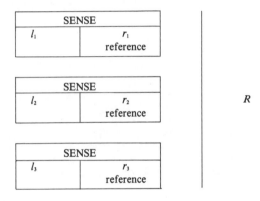

76. F. Nietzsche, *The Will to Power* (New York, 1968), sec. 567.

77. As Merleau-Ponty says, speaking of the "total" object, whose existence he denies, "Our perception ends in objects, and the object once constituted, appears as the reason for all the experiences of it which we have had or could have. For example, I see the next-door house from a certain angle, but it would be seen differently from the right bank of the Seine, or from the inside, or again from an airplane: the house *itself* is none of these appearances; it is, as Leibniz said, the flat projection of these perspectives and of all possible perspectives, that is, the perspectiveless position from which all can be derived, the house seen from nowhere. But what do these words mean? Is not to see always to see from somewhere? To say that the house itself is seen from nowhere is surely to say that it is invisible!" (*Phenomenology of Perception,* p. 67).

78. G. S. Kirk and J. E. Raven, eds. and trans., *The Presocratic Philosophers* (Cambridge, 1966).

5 MODES OF UNDERSTANDING

In order to defend the possibility of a metaphysics or theory of reality that does not ignore the inherent pluralism of understanding (that is, a non-dogmatic, non-rationalist metaphysics), I attempted in chapter 4 to show how the concept of analogy constitutes, at least in theory, a middle way between rationalist absolutism (univocity) and anti-rationalist relativism (equivocity). The only metaphysics possible on the basis of, and compatible with, epistemological pluralism is one that views reality (being) as being itself inherently analogical, and a genuinely analogical conception of reality (a true *analogia entis)* is possible only if one rejects both rationalism and relativism, for neither of these positions is capable of conceptualizing analogy.

The aim of this and the following chapters is to show that analogy is the only proper concept with which to understand both understanding and reality. Of the three ways open to thought, only the way of analogy can lead thought to a successful issue, beyond dogmatism on the one hand and absurdity and irrationalism on the other. In the next two chapters we shall see how analogy is basic to all understanding, how, that is, the perception or creation of analogies and likenesses is the central function of all understanding, how all understanding is imaginative and metaphorical. As a preliminary to this, this chapter attempts to clarify the basic senses in which one can be said to have an understanding of reality; how, in addition, one comes to understand another reality (another culture); and how, finally, one can come to understand something about not just a particular cultural reality or a number of such realities but Reality itself—the hidden, analogical element in all realities.

How does understanding arise? In what does it consist? What is it? How does it function? Understanding is perhaps the most difficult thing to conceptualize, and understandably because it is that which is closest to us; in the reflective act of self-understanding, subject and object, knower and known, are one and the same. Understanding is in fact that which we ourselves are. One might therefore wonder if it is any easier to understand understanding than it is to jump over one's own shadow. If it is true, as I have insisted all along, that understanding necessarily tends to misunderstand itself, is this not enough to invalidate and render impossible any attempt at genuine self-understanding that would be free from the illusions of understanding? Not necessarily. The natural error of understanding consists in its taking the object of its believing for reality. This is natural, for it is impossible for understanding to do otherwise, to be anything else but belief, but it is a presumption (*"la présomption de la raison,"* as Merleau-Ponty would say) and an error, for understanding can never prove that what it believes to be reality is indeed reality itself (that is, Reality). Were it our purpose to understand understanding in the sense of understanding the true relation that supposedly obtains in fact between understanding and true reality, our's would indeed be a hopeless task. But this is not our goal; we are not attempting to overstep the bounds of experience but only to interrogate experience itself. In this attitude of interrogation, we must ask with Montaigne, *Que sçay-je?* What exactly is it that I know? We must attempt to draw up an inventory of what we do know, on the basis of our actual, lived experience.

Now we do not really know what reality "in itself" is and what understanding "in itself" is—what the nature of the mind is—and we do not know what objective relation obtains between the two, assuming, indeed, that there are two things here that stand in some sort of objective, external relation to one another. If we are honest with ourselves, we will recognize that here we run up against an inscrutable mystery. The mystery stems from the impossibility for a reflecting subject to overstep the limits of his experience in such a way as to determine cognitively the "objective" relation that supposedly obtains between experience and "reality." If we are to achieve some degree of clarity, what we need most is a method, which means a way of proceeding. We shall accordingly seek to follow through with the program announced at the end of chapter 2. We shall attempt to give an account of understanding as it presents itself to our reflective scrutiny once we have suspended all judgment as to its ontological status (its relationship to what people call reality), with the sole aim of arriving at a pragmatics of understanding—an account of the way it functions. Although the way people conceive of understanding and its relationship to reality varies and although they differ in what they say it is, to someone who suspends judgment as to these epistemological and ontological claims, certain constants do seem to be apparent.

On the one hand, "understanding" seems to imply a transitory and heightened awareness—let us call it *insight*—as when one suddenly exclaims, "Ah, now I see." This is the *Eureka!* experience. But the term also connotes an already acquired, abiding, and merely passive disposition of which one is only marginally aware, as when one says of someone, "He understands what he's supposed to do." In this second sense, to say that a person understands is simply to say that given the occasion he will be able to perform a specific task (whether manual or intellectual—the difference is of little importance) in an "appropriate" manner, even though, were he asked, he might not be able to say how he accomplishes it. It is in this sense that the great majority of people understand a language. Speaking and understanding a language presupposes a great deal of intelligence and is a highly complicated business, but most people who accomplish this feat with instinctive ease have little or no active understanding of what is involved. Understanding in this sense is thus a form of "tacit knowing" or of behavior "know-how"; it is the ability or competence to perform. It is, in short, habit. As such it stands opposed to understanding in the first sense, insight. Habit is passive understanding, whereas insight is active understanding.

It is important to keep in mind that understanding in the active sense never occurs alone or exists by itself, as in a void; insightful understanding always occurs on the basis or in the context of an already acquired, habitual understanding. Habit, while opposed to insight, is the necessary basis for all insight; habit is both the enemy and the ally of insight. This is to say that habit and insight stand in a dialectical relationship to each other, and this dialectic constitutes the total phenomenon of understanding.

The habitual is the acquired. It is the readiness, tendency, or disposition to perform certain actions or to behave in a certain way. It is understanding that has become automatized or mechanized. Habit refers to those actions, often highly complex, that, as a result of practice, one can perform routinely and without conscious attention, such as speaking a language, solving a stock arithmetical problem, driving a car, or playing a piano. Habit, in the strict sense, should be opposed to instinct. An instinct is not an acquired or learned tendency but an innate one. Those animals whose behavior patterns are predetermined by their biological makeup and who act in rigid and invariable fashion are said to operate by instinct, whereas those—the invertebrates—that display a certain flexibility in their behavior, that adopt their responses to their changing environment (qua individuals, not simply as a species), are said to act by intelligence, the ability of the individual to form new behavior patterns (new habits) and to vary old ones. A dog that is more trainable than another is said to be more intelligent than the other, and, by this standard of trainability—the ability to acquire new habits—dolphins are said to be immensely intelligent. But of all the animal species, humans are the most intelligent, for they, most of all, are "creatures of habit." There are in people no "pure" instincts of any significance; what otherwise would pass for instinct is in people transformed to a greater or less degree by the force of habit. And of all the animals, people are the ones whose behavior patterns differ the most from one group of individuals to the next. This is why people are above all cultural animals. In the last analysis, habit is culture.

Habit is a kind of second nature. What we do by force of habit we do naturally, which is to say, without thinking. Thus habit stands opposed to conscious thinking. As James put it, *"Habit diminishes the conscious attention with which our acts are performed."*[1] This is the whole point of habit: by enabling us to perform certain acts in a thoughtless, quasi-mechanical way, habit relieves us of having to think through each step in the act and thus allows us to perform it more efficiently and more rapidly. The curious fact is that it is precisely because people are to such a great extent creatures of habit and behave for the most part almost like mindless automatons that they are also thinking beings. Because habit relieves us of having to think about those innumerable acts that we must perform every day, it frees us to think about other matters over and above the routine affairs of our daily lives. As the very enemy of conscious awareness, habit is also, paradoxically, its ally. Again, as James remarks, "The more of the details of our daily life we can hand over to the effortless custody of automation, the more our higher powers of mind will be set free for their own proper work."[2] Between habit and awareness there is the same dialectic as that between rules and freedom. Free and creative—"mindful"—activity is possible only within the already structured context of established habit. Human freedom is the freedom to alter one's habits and to acquire new constraints. Creative thinking is the name for this process.

Understanding in the active sense of insight arises only when an established habit becomes problematic. When we run into difficulty in performing an accustomed action, we are brought up short and made expressly aware of the action itself. We experience a form of puzzlement; the normal course of events becomes questionable. Thinking is nothing other than the response to this state of perplexity, to the experience of difficulty and resistance. Habit and insight vary, then, in an inverse ratio. As Arthur Koestler observes,

> Consciousness may be described in a negative way as the quality accompanying an activity *which decreases in proportion to habit-formation*. The transformation of learning into routine is accompanied by a dimming of the lights of awareness. We expect, therefore, that the opposite process will take place when routine is disturbed: that will cause a change from "mechanical" to "mindful" behaviour.[3]

Thinking, or what Koestler here calls "consiousness," consists of a reassessment of one's previously acquired habit and is the attempt to restructure it in such a way as to avoid further frustration. Both the scope and intensity of insight—thinking—will vary according to the degree of resistance and frustration experienced. In most cases it will be restrained and/or short-lived and will involve no more than a minor readjustment in behavioral patterns, as when one accustoms oneself to driving a new car or branches out from playing a piano to playing an organ. In other cases, as when one undergoes a religious or ideological conversion or adopts a revolutionary scientific theory, it will be intense and/or long and drawn-out and will result in a thorough reordering of one's accepted, habitual beliefs. But in all such instances understanding is actively at work, *regardless of whether the thought process is fully conscious of itself.*

Active understanding begins, then, when a situation becomes problematic and one's usual responses fail to achieve the expected result. It ends when the state of perplexity dissolves and a new habit has been formed; it ends, therefore, in "a dimming of the lights of awareness," as Koestler puts it. The total phenomenon of understanding is thus an incessant alteration of habit and insight, of machine-like and mindful behavior, and it is impossible ever to equate understanding with either one or the other of its opposed moments or to say that one is more basic than the other.

It is true that in one sense habit is prior to and thus more basic than insight since insight or creative thinking arises only when previously established habits prove inadequate and break down. But in another sense thinking is more basic than habit since habits arise out of acts of thinking—which is what we mean when we say that habits are learned and, as a mark of intelligence, are opposed to instinct—and are merely the fossilized remains of acts of insight that have long since vanished. Habit is the living memory of awareness; it is, paradoxically, only as habit that understanding in the active sense can exist over a period of time and as something more than a momentary flicker in the dark. And yet habit is the enemy of insight. To say that all thinking is for the sake of habit—as some pragmatists sometimes seem to be saying—is to say that people are nothing more than sophisticated automatons, kinds of computers with the special ability of being able to reprogram themselves. What, however, makes people human—that is, "mindful" beings—and what assures our spiritual dignity is our power of intellectual insight—a power or ability that the medievals "thingified" and turned into a "faculty" to which they gave the name *intellecuts agens*. We are more than a mere machine, more than a mere automaton or creature of habit, and yet what spiritual awareness we do enjoy is never "pure," can never exist apart from habit. We are not mere machines—and yet not angels either.

Thus if it is a mistake to say that thinking is for the sake of habit, it is equally wrong to say that insight is an end in itself or can ever exist as a permanent state of mind. Against Aristotle, against Saint Thomas, and against rationalism in general, it must not be maintained that our *summum bonum* consists in pure contemplation. Contemplation is not for the sake of action, but action is not for the sake of contemplation either. Active understanding—intellectual insight, contemplation—is not an end in itself; it is not itself an end but has its end, in the literal sense, in the new praxis to which it gives rise, a praxis, however, that is the result of insight and is destined in its turn to falter and give rise to renewed insight. The total phenomenon of understanding is thus a Heraclitean flux of awareness and habit; it is the rhythm of their ebb and flow. Awareness or insight is something that is ever being born and ever dying anew; it exists fully only when one is in between established habits or states of acquired understanding.

What does it mean, in the context of a particular culture or belief system, to speak of understanding? All active understanding arises out of a ground of established habit or accepted belief. Now the set of habits or beliefs shared to a greater or lesser extent by all the members of a group constitutes what, in a quasi-anthropological sense, could be called its *culture*.

A culture is composed of a basic level of unthematized beliefs, which is nothing other than "common sense" (common sense being a culture's lowest common denominator and also what might be called an unsophisticated and somewhat less than fully coherent world outlook) and a higher level of theoretical beliefs such as those of magic and science. It is composed, in other words, of a world of immediate everyday experience (as interpreted according to an unreflective schema) and a world (or worlds) of explicitly theoretical entities, which is more or less anchored in the former. There is no point at which a commonsensical understanding changes over into a theoretical ordering of experience. "Common sense" already generalizes and "theory" is a matter of degree only. There is a natural tendency on the part of understanding to elaborate ever more highly structured systems of belief, and, as theory progressively outstrips common sense, it has a retroeffect on it; certain theoretical beliefs "sediment" or "flow back" into common sense, transforming it in the process. For this reason, common sense varies from time to time and from place to place; it is not "natural" but "cultural."

Common sense is a kind of generalized fore-understanding of reality, and it has its own language, which all members of a culture use much of the time and many all of the time. This language and the passive understanding it embodies is quite sufficient for most of one's dealings with one's world. Common sense provides or constitutes a ready-made schema with which to interpret daily happenings and events. When, however, an unexpected event occurs, something out of the ordinary, something that goes against one's usual, habitual expectations, common sense or the stock-in-trade of one's habitual interpretations may very likely prove inadequate to account for the occurrence, and the result is a form of puzzlement. At such a time one's habitual understanding is called into question and one begins to think.

This process of thinking or active understanding is the same for someone who on the basis of everyday experience adheres to the magical view of things as it is for someone who on the same basis believes in science.[4] When common sense or one's habitual, everyday world interpretation falters, one turns to the higher-level belief systems of explicit theory. For many peoples this is the system of magic; for us it is, increasingly, the system of science.[5] The important thing to note is that *thinking occurs only as a response to the experience of anomalies* (and one might wish to add that the mark of great thinkers is that they are particularly sensitive to anomalies and open to experiencing them). The Azande are not for the most part preoccupied with magical entities or occult forces; they turn to magical theories only when their usual everyday, commonsensical responses to a problematic situation, such as an illness, prove inadequate.[6] In our culture we turn to science and its theoretical constructs for the same reason. When the flow of immediate, unreflective living (common sense) is interfered with and becomes problematic, one seeks to discover what is amiss; one seeks actively to understand one's situation.

Understanding in this active sense consists of reflecting upon the situation in which one was formerly thoroughly immersed; it consists, therefore, in viewing one's immediate world from a different vantage point. This is to say that in order actively to understand the world to which one has become accustomed but which has now become problematic, one must view it in the light of another world. Thus in order to understand one's immediate experience, one posits or constructs certain theoretical entities with which to interpret this experience.[7] In order to understand what it means that one is experiencing difficulties, one has recourse to an interpretive, theoretical schema that will explain what is occurring. One constructs or turns to another world in order better to understand this world. This other world may be the world of magical entities (witchcraft substance and the like) or the world of scientific entities (atoms and the like). And as R. Horton observes, "In both cases reference to theoretical entities is used to link events in the visible, tangible world (natural effects) to their antecedents in the same world (natural causes)."[8] The function of theory is to explain, to confer some semblance of order on the world of our ordinary, lived-through experience so as to make it intelligible.

Thinking, therefore, has for its basic function to link up or tie together one item of experience with another in such a way as to produce a unified fabric (a unified belief system), which is then held to be the fabric of reality itself. The function of theory in this regard illustrates perfectly the thesis of I. A. Richards: "The mind is a connecting organ, it works only by connecting and it can connect any two things in an indefinitely large number of different ways."[9] This connective activity of the mind is an activity of the *imagination*. Active understanding is nothing other than an exercise of the imagination.

The higher-level belief systems or worlds of magic and science are the results of active (inventive, imaginative) understanding, and when one is learning one's way about in them, one can be said to be thinking. However, recourse to magical or scientific theory soon becomes itself a matter of mere unreflective *praxis*. Understanding—explaining—one's immediate experience in terms of the theoretical entities of science or magic becomes itself a routine matter, a habit, a form of passive understanding. When one "gets the hang" of magical or scientific explanation—when one has mastered the "rules of the game"—one can have recourse to them and apply them in a quasi-mechanical fashion, "without thinking." For someone for whom the world of scientific entities (such as, atoms) has become as real, which is to say habitual, as those of ordinary experience (such as, tables and chairs), science is no more than glorified or sophisticated common sense.

Although a theoretical belief system, such as a system of religious dogma, is the result of acts of insightful understanding or of creative thinking, for its initiates and official representatives, its priests, it is usually no more than a higher-level form of passive understanding, which has as much the force of habit as does common sense. The same is true of science as well. As Thomas Kuhn has pointed out, most of the work in science is routine, uncreative work in which one refines and applies ever more widely already accepted scientific theories, or what Kuhn calls "paradigms":

> Mopping-up operations are what engage more scientists throughout their careers. They constitute what I am here calling normal science. Closely examined, whether historically or in the contemporary laboratory, that enterprise seems an attempt to force nature into the preformed and relatively inflexible box that the paradigm supplies. No part of the aim of normal science is to call forth new sorts of phenomena; indeed those that will not fit the box are often not seen at all. Nor do scientists normally aim to invent new theories, and they are often intolerant of those invented by others. Instead, normal-scientific research is directed to the articulation of those phenomena and theories that the paradigm already supplies.[10]

"Normal science," Kuhn says, "does not aim at novelties of fact or theory and, when successful, finds none."[11] One becomes a scientist in the same way one becomes a witch doctor: by mastering a set of beliefs and explanatory techniques. And scientific understanding is for the most part a passive affair, a matter of habit, a routine ability like that of the accomplished piano player. Heidegger is thus quite right when he says, "Science does not think"[12]—if by "science" here one means normal science. But then this is just as true of "normal" religion and "normal" magic—and even of "normal" philosophy.

What Kuhn calls "extraordinary" science does "think," however, in the same way that "extraordinary" religion thinks. One has only to reflect on the development of Hebraic monotheism in the hands of those exceptional individuals, the prophets, or of the rational evolution of the Greek pantheon through the work of the poets to realize what mystification it is when a believer in the rival belief system of science asserts that only science progresses. Religious systems evolve, and for the same reason that scientific ones do: in an attempt to make the system more comprehensive and to enable it to deal with an ever wider range of novel experiences. Scientific revolutions occur for the same reason as revolutions in pantheons: in order to make the system more coherent and to streamline it. It is as proper to speak of religious "discoveries" as it is of scientific discoveries, and in both cases the reason for the occurrence of these system-revolutionizing changes is the same: the experience of anomaly. In science, as Kuhn says, "Discovery commences with the awareness of anomaly, i.e., with the recognition that nature has somehow violated paradigm-induced expectations that govern normal science."[13]

Only when the theoretical system tied in with common sense itself proves inadequate, only when, that is, the theory itself falters or breaks down, does one begin to think in the fullest sense of the term—creatively. Thinking or active understanding, on the higher level of theory, is the response to a "paradigm crisis" and involves the creation of a new, revised paradigm. This active understanding amounts to basically nothing other than a change in vision. One no longer sees the world in exactly the same way after the act of creative understanding—after the construction and adoption of a new paradigm—as before. In active understanding one's vision of the world changes, and because there is no practical difference between a world system and a world, the world itself undergoes a creative transformation. Kuhn is thus correct and is not merely indulging in hyperbole when he says:

> When paradigms change, the world itself changes with them. . . . In so far as their [scientists'] only recourse to that world [of their research engagement] is through what they see and do, we may want to say that after a revolution scientists are responding to a different world.[14]

In regard, therefore, to any given world or reality (of common sense or theory), active understanding consists in the active reorganization of that world. To understand actively is not to form a passive copy of an already existing world but to transform actively such a world; here one does not conform to but rather transforms a given world. Intracultural understanding has, then, as its end the construction of a new reality, a new belief system, on the basis of and in relation to an old one.

A world is transformed when it is viewed in a new way. Active understanding is seeing the old and familiar in a new and strange light. As Nietzsche remarked, "Not that one is the first to see something new, but that one sees as *new* what is old, long familiar, seen and overlooked by everybody, is what distinguishes truly original minds.''[15] Such a seeing is what is meant by creative insight. In the next two chapters we shall attempt to understand the actual mechanisms by which active, insightful understanding operates, that is, the nature of the creative act. To sum up the present discussion we can say that in regard to any given system of belief or reality, understanding is of a dual nature. As passive understanding, it consists of the mastery of an interpretive schema, whether of common sense or of a higher, theoretical sort, and is the ability to operate with ease and competence within this schema, within a generally accepted belief system, with regard to a specific reality. As active understanding, though, it consists of the reorganization of this schema (of common sense or theory); it involves interpreting a given world anew, in seeing it otherwise than before. Intracultural active understanding, which is inseparable from creative insight, always involves the "misuse" of a currently accepted idiom, its disorganization and reorganization in a new way, and when one creatively reinterprets a world, it is not only one's vision of the world—its meaning—that changes, but the world itself undergoes a "coherent deformation." Thus understanding is basically a case of metaphorical vision, a case of "seeing-as." A given, accepted world is simply a dead or trivialized metaphor, but one that can always be revitalized in active, creative understanding. Or, as Wallace Stevens says, "Reality is a cliché from which we escape by metaphor."[16] In active understanding, a particular belief system is semantically extended and reshaped; a world, a semantic reality, grows and is transfigured.

If the object of intracultural (or, more precisely, intrasystematic) understanding is a particular reality (which is conformed to in passive understanding and transformed in active understanding), the object of intercultural understanding is another reality, another well-articulated belief system different from and, to some degree, opposed to one's own. The question that arises here is accordingly, How does one understand another culture, another reality? This is the central question raised, but not answered, in chapter 2. The condition for understanding another culture is the same as for understanding or coming to understand (active understanding, thinking) in general: the experience of anomaly. Before one can come to understand another culture, one must first experience it as other, as something strange and perplexing.

This might seem self-evident, yet it is worth insisting on the point, for it is quite conceivable that, as often happens with tourists and soldiers, one could be thrown into another culture without fully realizing the fact. This is because it is in general only natural for consciousness to ignore that which falls outside its accustomed categories of interpretation. The first step in understanding another culture is thus the realization that what is involved here is not merely a variation on one's own categories (as when an American tourist, say, categorizes a Third World country as "quaint" and "under-developed" and thereby sees it as a deficient mode of his own technological civilization) but a wholly different set of categories.

Coming to understand another culture is like coming to understand an-other language. In both cases it is necessary to realize that what one is deal-ing with is not merely variations on the rules of the game one is used to playing but another game altogether. Just as one normally tends to think that one's native language expresses things the way they really are and con-forms perfectly to the intrinsic flow of thought, such that a different way of forming a sentence, with, as in German, the verb at the end, appear odd,[17] so one tends to look upon one's culturally habitual way of doing things as the "normal" and "natural" way. One normally tends to identify one's culture with nature itself. In order to understand another culture, it is first necessary that one perceive the other culture as *other*, which is to say as equally normal in its own right (and, of course, this means also that one must perceive one's own culture as somehow "unnatural").

Thus in intercultural understanding the anomaly that provokes thought is not of the same sort as in intracultural understanding. The anomaly here is not some kind of "freak event," a phenomenon or a number of phenomena that do not fit into one's habitual interpretive schema; it is not merely an event in experience but rather a different interpretation of experience that constitutes the anomaly. Here one's categories are challenged not by an event that cannot be assimilated but by a different set of categories. This constitutes a much more serious crisis for understanding, for it is not merely this or that tenet of one's belief system that is being challenged but the en-tire system.

To be made aware fully and concretely of another belief system means that one has appreciated its logic, which means also that one has realized that one's own belief system cannot claim for itself a unique and absolute status and in this sense is arbitrary. At such a time one experiences not only frustration and perplexity, as when a chance event resists interpretation, but something like horror and anxiety, for one is threatened with the loss of one's belief system, which is to say that reality itself (what one takes reality to be) begins to disintegrate. One is threatened with chaos and absurdity, the total loss of understanding and of the means for living in one's world.

It is natural that one's immediate reaction is to evade or suppress the cul-turally anomalous as much as possible. This is in fact the reason for the ex-istence of what anthropologists have termed *taboo*. As Mary Douglas and Lévi-Strauss have shown, the object of a taboo is the anomalous, that which violates one's established categories.[18] The anomalous is taboo because, as an exception to one's categories, it constitutes a threat to them; the anomalous is the dangerous. It is a threat, for were it no longer perceived as an exception and at variance with the normal, one's categories would, perforce, be other than they are; they would be destroyed. For example, in all societies incest is generally taboo, for were it not, the social fabric and the patterns of kinship would be drastically disrupted.[19] Similarly, the "sacred" is also taboo, for it is a threat to one's profane, everyday existence; to see God face to face is, as the Bible says, to die. When one does have dealings with the sacred, one always takes the necessary safeguards to protect oneself from being contaminated by it.[20] As one anthropologist observes, "Much primitive religion is apotropaic; what is sought is the turning away of spirit, not its nearer approach." And he remarks more generally:

> Much primitive ritual expresses the necessity to keep separate things that ought to be kept separate; humans and spirits, male and female, senior and junior, left hand and right hand, inauspicious and auspicious. *It is almost as though the category distinctions which every culture sustains were regarded as hard-won gains, which must be emphasized and reaffirmed in ritual lest they fall into disuse, and primal chaos return.*[21]

The taboo reaction is basically a mechanism of self-defense. By isolating or expelling the anomalous through taboo, one removes the threat to one's belief system (or one's profane mode of existence in human community) and enables it to continue to function. This is why for so many peoples, and not only primitive ones, what is supremely taboo are other cultures. It is the reason for speaking of "foreign devils," "infidels," the "unclean," the "heathen," the "barbarians." The taboo reaction is a means of responding actively to the anxiety and disgust arising out of the experience of the culturally anomalous (which is always perceived as the naturally anomalous); it is one way of resolving a "paradigm crisis." The result, however, is not an understanding of what is other, not an enlarged, new understanding, but rather the mere reinforcement of one's previous understanding, of one's habitual belief system. This type of response to an alien belief system results in a dogmatic and inflexible intolerance of what is other. To the degree that the taboo reaction is normal and universal, human understanding is naturally dogmatic.

If a culture is sufficiently assured of its beliefs and confident in their explanatory power, it may not simply dismiss the foreign culture, as the Japanese did for two centuries from 1637, when all foreigners were banned from the country and several thousand Japanese Christians were massacred at Shimabara, to 1854, when Commodore Perry forced the reopening of the country (the only exception to this hermetic closure being the allowance once each year of one Dutch ship into Nagasaki). Instead it may seek to carry through the understanding process to the point where it can make sense of the alien belief system. This is the course adopted by Western science.

The science of anthropology attempts to explain or understand the beliefs and practices of primitive peoples. If it is to succeed in this task, it must eventually formulate certain theoretical notions or models of a highly generalized sort capable of ordering, and thus explaining, the wealth of disjointed field data. As Evans-Pritchard says:

> The social anthropologist discovers in a native society what no native can explain to him and what no layman, however conversant with the culture, can perceive—its basic structure. This structure cannot be seen. It is a set of abstractions, each of which, though derived, it is true, from analysis of observed behavior, is fundamentally an imaginative construct of the anthropologist himself. By relating these abstractions to one another logically so that they present a pattern he can see the society in its essentials and as a single whole.[22]

These remarks make clear that to the degree anthropology seeks to be a science, its mode of procedure is basically no different from that of any other science (or any other belief system): observable phenomena are made intelligible—are explained—by means of certain theoretical constructs invented for just this purpose. And these constructs are not the ones employed by the native people. Quite to the contrary, the theoretical constructs of anthropological science have the native beliefs as their object. The anthropologist does not want, like the native, to explain immediate experience by means of magical forces or spiritual entities but instead wants to explain these very beliefs about experience. In explaining these explanatory beliefs the anthropologist necessarily deprives them of their own explanatory power; he explains them away. The anthropologist cannot, qua anthropologist, believe in the reality of magical forces, for were he to do so, he would cease to be a scientist and would become a sorcerer. Science can understand magical powers only if it denies their very existence. This is why Evans-Pritchard says, "Witchcraft is imaginary and a man cannot possibly be a witch." Because science and sorcery are rival and incompatible interpretations of experience, the scientist qua scientist can understand sorcery only if he can translate this belief system into his own. The social anthropologist will thus tend to look upon magical power as something purely imaginary and accordingly will seek to explain witchcraft in terms of a different kind of basic underlying reality. "The witchcraft belief, and the persecution of witches," he will, for instance, say in a typically reductionist way, "are a response to social and psychological strains. The more exactly we can identify those strains, the better we can hope to understand the response."[23]

It may be the case that to translate an alien system of belief into scientific terms will oblige the scientist to revise his own system and enlarge it so as to enable it to deal better with the "data" to be explained (he may, for instance, have to allow for the existence of something he previously denied, such as mental telepathy). This is indeed what has happened in anthropology over the last century; the present-day anthropologist is on the whole much less naive than his predecessors, and anthropology today is much less crudely reductionistic than it formerly was. Yet it is still essentially reductionistic, for to explain and understand anthropologically something like sorcery means to interpret it or make it intelligible in the light of the theoretical constructs of science, in the light, as Evans-Pritchard says, not of native beliefs but of the imaginative constructs of the anthropologist himself.

Science does perceive the other as other; it does seek to understand the other, but this understanding inevitably results in a reduction of the other to the same. A scientific explanation of sorcery "defuses" sorcery and deprives it of its explanatory power. One leading social anthropologist candidly remarks:

> It is indeed a most important part of the social anthropologist's job to try to understand the distinctions consciously made by the people whose culture he is studying, but evidently his analysis may, and indeed must, go further. In the last resort their categories must be conceived in terms of ours, if they are to be intelligible to us at all.[24]

Thus although the scientific reaction to anomaly is markedly different from the taboo reaction, the end result is curiously similar: whether one actively ignores the anomalous or curiously investigates it, the result in both cases is to alleviate the threat posed by the anomalous other and render it inoffensive. This is frankly recognized by one anthropologist: "Anthropological understanding is a way of making the world feel safer, a way of extending the edge of order so that we can comfortably say that people are fundamentally the same everywhere and that 'cultural differences' are merely something like different mental images of the same basic reality."[25]

It could thus be argued that to understand another culture or a belief system such as sorcery by means of science is to misunderstand it. This is true in one sense but not in another. It is true if by understanding is meant empathetic understanding, understanding an alien belief system in the same way as its own adherents understand it. It is not true if it is taken to imply that no real understanding at all has occurred here. The alien belief system has been understood to the exact degree that it has served to provoke a heightened awareness in us who understand it scientifically. By means of this confrontation with the other, our own particular self-understanding has been transformed. By translating the world of magic into the world of science, by transforming it, we have transformed our own world, which is to say that we have gained a better understanding of it.[26] And yet the fact remains that our world, though transformed and enlarged, is the same world as before. Although by means of science we have broadened our horizons and widened our world, we have not escaped from our world into another in such a way as to understand this other world from within.

The question thus arises, How does one ever break out of one's world? This question is usually asked when one is talking about a superstitious world view. The devices by which a belief system such as magic protects itself from outside challenges and reinforces its tautological status are known, but it is not usually recognized that the scientific world view is every bit as "closed" and "imprisoning."[27] The question is thus a universal one. How in general can one pass from one belief system to another, from one world to another?

The example of learning a foreign language furnishes perhaps the best model of what is involved in coming to understand an alien culture or belief system as its members understand it. Whorf has described and diagrammed the process.[28] If the student of, say, French is to master the language so as to speak it as its native speakers do, he must overcome or escape from the patterns that command the formation of English sentences. The sound and form patterns that govern the speaking of his native English must be made to disintegrate, and he must learn in their place different patterns, which form the basis of French. Should he form some understanding of French without having also abandoned (in the sense of "bracketing" or "putting out of play") his own linguistic patterns, he will merely have learned bad French.

This example illustrates the necessary condition for the understanding of any alien system from within. In all cases it is necessary that one abandon one's own categories before one can master, or understand, foreign ones. Understanding another culture or belief system as other means, therefore, learning how to operate in the system with the same instinctive ease that its native adherents do. It means, in short, learning a new habit. If and when one has succeeded in thinking naturally and automatically in the alien categories, in interpreting without reflection his experience according to, say, the structure of the language or the tenets of magic, he can be said to understand this language or system. In this case he has actively achieved a passive understanding of the alien system; he has gone native; he has actually become, for instance, a sorcerer. On the basis of this newly acquired passive understanding, he is in a position to achieve active understanding in terms of the system itself. He may, for instance, use a foreign language creatively and become a genuine thinker in that language, furthering its own internal development.

"Understanding another culture" thus has two basically different meanings. On the one hand it can mean understanding the other system in terms of one's own. Here the most that can be achieved is the widening of one's native world view, which is also to say that here the "other" is necessarily ingested into and reduced to the "same." On the other hand, it can mean understanding the other *as* other—that is, acquiring a new habit, a new and different way of interpreting reality, which is to say that here one exchanges one system for another. The situation is thus that of an either-or: either one remains within one's own cultural reality or one escapes from this reality, but only to be confined within another reality.[29]

The worlds of magic and science are incommensurate and cannot be fused in such a way as to gain access to a world that would be "truer" or "more real" than either one alone. The plurality of realities cannot be "totalized" in such a way as to form a Totality—a cosmos, a unified and fully intelligible Reality. A totalization of realities is no more possible than is a totalization of perspectives. A bilingual, just as a bicultural person, is and must be something of a linguistic and cultural schizophrenic. He lives in one or the other world but never in the two at the same time and in the same way. The condition for participating in one is letting go of one's hold on the other. The two are discontinuous; entering into one means leaving the other behind.[30] As one anthropologist observes in regard to intercultural understanding:

> We can enter in some degree into other people's ways of thought, and we can attain some understanding of their beliefs and values, but we can never see things *exactly* as they see them. If we did we should have ceased to be members of our own culture and gone over to theirs.[31]

If, therefore, it is impossible ever to escape from one limited world view without at the same time taking up another with its own particular limitations, if, that is, it is impossible ever to transcend all cultural and linguistic limitations in such a way as to understand directly not just *a* reality but Reality itself (if Reality cannot be the object of any particular belief system), what is the value of attempting to understand a reality other than one's own? If all realities or world views are equally relative, what does one gain in coming to understand another one? The answer is that in learning something about a world other than one's own, one may learn something about all possible worlds, about Reality itself, the analogically common element in all realities. The direct understanding of another world may provoke an indirect understanding of Reality.

Active, insightful understanding always involves the creative discovery of a new world or reality. In the case of intracultural understanding, it involves the construction of a new, enlarged reality on the basis of an old one. In the case of intercultural understanding, it involves exchanging a familiar (old) reality for a strange (new) one. In both cases one learns, by means of new theoretical constructs, to interpret one's lived experience differently from before. Thus what in both cases occurs in active understanding is a change of understanding, a change in one's habitual belief system. And because a change in belief always means a change in the object of belief and because the object of belief is a reality, a change in belief involves a change in reality.

This change is not exactly the same in both cases, however. In the case of intracultural understanding or, to be more precise, in the case where a change occurs within a given system of belief, the result is a new belief system, but this new system is not radically new or totally discontinuous with the previous system; it is, rather, a modification of it. When, however, another culture or a wholly different belief system is genuinely understood, the result is not merely a change in belief but a change of beliefs.

The first kind of conceptual change can be called a revolution in outlook, the second a conversion of outlooks. An example of the first would be the change that occurred in physical science in the first part of this century. The world of relativity theory and of quantum mechanics is vastly different from the world of classical Newtonian physics, and were Newton to return to the contemporary scene he would be at a loss to know what to make of the new physics. And yet, with suitable explanations, he could, and undoubtedly would, succeed in understanding the new physics, for it could be shown to him how it emerged out of his own system of belief through a series of inner transformations. He would be shown that the new physics does not reject his own out of hand as false but rather incorporates it into a wider system of belief, according it thereby its own limited validity. No great leap of faith would be required for Newton to understand modern physics, merely a change—a revolution—in that self-same outlook on the world that he was greatly responsible for instigating in the first place.

But a leap of faith would be required of Newton or any modern scientist were they to attempt to understand a belief system totally alien to science, such as magic or sorcery. Whereas Newtonian physics is not incompatible with modern physics, a belief in sorcery excludes a belief in the physicalistic world view. A scientist could become a sorcerer or shaman only by rejecting science as a whole and subscribing to sorcery or shamanism in its place—only if, therefore, he underwent a spiritual conversion. A conversion involves not merely the transformation of a world view but the substitution of one world view for another.

The result of a conceptual revolution is a more or less significant transformation in one's previously accepted belief system and thus in what one holds reality to be. The reality continues to be what it was before, however—merely one particular type of reality among many other possible types, merely one possible world out of a potentially infinite number of possible worlds. No amount of progress in science would ever enable it to claim that its reality is Reality itself, for there would always remain the possibility of alternate beliefs, such as magic. Similarly, in ideological (or ideational) conversion, when one comes to believe in another reality, this reality is also merely one among many. Because every belief system is tautological, no one can be shown to be any more true than any other. When one undergoes a conversion one simply shifts one's dogmatic allegiance from one particular reality to another. The French saying is fully appropriate here: *plus ça change, plus c'est la même chose.*

A relativistic skeptic or a metaphysical cynic might argue that it is impossible for us ever to achieve a genuine understanding of Reality—however this might be construed—and that the attempt to work out a nonrelativistic metaphysics is doomed to failure. He might wish to claim with the literary critic, Michel Beaujour, that a genuine understanding of Reality is "an impossible goal." "No one," he will say, "can altogether escape from his culture, for escape into an alternative subculture takes place along determined lines, and embodies the rules and values of the dominant culture in the very effort to reject them. Even individual escapes into madness, and the manifestations of folly themselves are coded within a given culture." Freedom, accordingly, is but a subjective illusion: "Freedom, if we define it absolutely as freedom from being involved in a game, merely is the dialectical moment when one game is being discarded, and the rules of the new game, which will necessarily replace it, are not yet experienced as rules, but as the waning of the former rules."[32]

The relativistic skeptic would most certainly be right if he claimed that all belief is, by its very nature, dogmatic and that it is impossible for any one belief system to transcend its inherent limitations so as to become knowledge of Reality itself. Indeed our whole line of argumentation so far justifies the skeptic's critique of rationalism. Is this to say, however, that man's ingrained desire for truth and for fundamental meaningfulness is merely a cruel, sadistic trick played on him by a blind and insensitive universe? Is mankind's quest for true understanding of what really is, merely, as Sartre claims, a "useless passion"?[33] Is it impossible for man ever to liberate himself from the illusions of understanding?

It might appear that the attempt to achieve greater understanding is pointless and that freedom is an illusion if it is the case that a change in understanding amounts to no more than a widening of the confines of one's culturally inherited conceptual prison or a shifting from one such prison to another. And yet insightful understanding is not without ontological value[34] for it is not impossible that while one is undergoing a conceptual revolution or conversion, one may, in the process and before falling back into a new belief system, get some glimpse of that Reality analogically common to all realities, thereby freeing himself from the illusions of understanding.

If it is true that understanding necessarily tends to misunderstand itself, then the first step in liberating oneself from the illusions of understanding would be to realize this. In order to gain some understanding of Reality, it would first be necessary to realize that all knowledge is merely belief and that no belief can be absolutely true, can be knowledge of Reality, since no belief can radically question itself. Only if we become aware of our beliefs as such—that is, our inveterate tendency to misunderstand things, our tendency to take the objects of our beliefs for Reality itself—could we possibly hope to free ourselves from dogmatism (dogmatism being the taking of one's beliefs seriously, uncritically).

The value of experiencing other belief systems and understanding the force of their own logic is that this can make us aware of the relativity of our own beliefs (that is, our beliefs as such). The experience of other belief systems is, as Whorf would say, the exception that proves the rule; it is what makes us actively aware of the basic tenets of our inherited beliefs, which we normally are not conscious of, which are usually only part of the unexplicit background of experience.[35] *Only when our native preconceptions are somehow violated or challenged may we become genuinely aware of them at all.* Another way of expressing this would be to say that because we are not normally aware of our beliefs or basic preconceptions, we are tricked by them and are naively led by them to believe that what they posit as real is indeed Reality itself. An awareness of the relativity of all beliefs can thus free a person from being the dupe of any one of them.

It is here that one can discern the undeniable value of relativism and the reason why it has existed since the time of Protagoras and before and continues to exist still, even though a thoroughgoing relativism is untenable and will always be unable to defend itself adequately against the criticism of self-contradiction leveled at it by rationalism. Relativism always has and always will find a response among thinking people, and the reason for this is suggested by the editor of Whorf's writings:

> One wonders, indeed, what makes the notion of linguistic relativity so fascinating even to the nonspecialist. Perhaps it is the suggestion that all one's life one has been tricked, all unaware, by the structure of language into a certain way of perceiving reality, with the implication that awareness of this trickery will enable one to see the world with fresh insight.[36]

Perhaps, indeed, it is only by becoming aware of the relativity of all belief that one can somehow escape from the trickery of any one belief and in this way gain some insightful, albeit indirect, understanding of that Reality analogously common to all realities, which is identical with none but is, so to speak, "glimpsed" when one manages momentarily to slip in between realities.

If a nondogmatic metaphysics is possible, if that is, it is meaningful to speak of "reality" in a nonrationalist context, Reality cannot be that which is the object of any one belief system but must instead be analogically common to all such systems. Being common to all but identical with none, it cannot itself be the object of a direct understanding. If it makes any sense to speak of a Reality that is somehow the same for all—and the reflections on analogy in the preceding chapter would seem to indicate as much—it must be said that Reality is that which we do not and cannot directly know, for what we know are merely particular realities.

Reality (with a capital "r") is not *a* world (of belief) and so the only possible means of understanding it is when, in some way or other, one slips in between worlds. This is possible, for the various worlds of human understanding (science, magic, and others) are not isomorphically related (and this is why perfect translation is never possible). Thus there are cracks and crevices between the worlds; there are, in the words of Malinowski, "gaps and breaches left in the ever-imperfect wall of culture which he [man] erects between himself and the besetting temptations and dangers of his destiny."[37] *It can only be through these cracks and crevices, these gaps and breaches between worlds or within a given world, that something like Reality reveals itself to man,* if indeed it does at all.

The important thing would therefore be to learn how to get to the crack between the different worlds. One writer observes:

> The real transpires through the stitches of discourse. Being irreducible to any of the given totalities which cover it over at the same time they announce it, it is situated in the in-between of discourse. . . . From the fact that one has access to the real only through a representational system, it follows that one will shape the real according to the code; but from the fact that several codes are in use in us and in society, it will follow that reality will never be reducible to the code.[38]

It is thus necessary to consider more carefully what occurs when, in the attempt to enter into another world, one inadvertently finds oneself in between worlds.

A remarkable testimony to what may befall someone dislodged from one belief system and yet unable to make a successful transition to another is found in the memoirs of T. E. Lawrence, *Seven Pillars of Wisdom.* Lawrence, better known to many as Lawrence of Arabia, sought deliberately and methodically to disengage himself from his native English and Oxfordian culture and to take on that of the desert Arabs. His understanding of Arab culture was undoubtedly facilitated by his own sense of unease in his native cultural skin. The illegitimate son of an Irish landowner, Lawrence's awareness of his own illegitimacy undermined his sense of identity and set an initial wedge between him and the Establishment in which he was brought up. Thus when Lawrence set off for Arabia he was already something of an alien in his own culture. And yet, in spite of this, he did not succeed in actually becoming an Arab, as he tells us in the following passage:

> In my case, the effort for these years to live in the dress of Arabs, and to imitate their mental foundation, quitted me of my English self, and let me look at the West and its conventions with new eyes: they destroyed it all for me. At the same time I could not sincerely take on the Arab skin: it was an affectation only. Easily was a man made an infidel, but hardly might he be converted to another faith. I had dropped one form and not taken on the other, and was become like Mohammed's coffin in our legend, with a resultant feeling of intense loneliness in life, and a contempt, not for other men, but for all they do. Such detachment came at times to a man exhausted by prolonged physical effort and isolation. His body plodded on mechanically, while his reasonable mind left him, and from without looked down critically on him, wondering what the futile lumber did and why. Sometimes these selves would converse in the void; and then madness was very near, as I believe it would be near the man who could see things through the veils at once of two customs, two educations, two environments.[39]

This extraordinary text merits careful scrutiny. As he tells us here, Lawrence did not succeed in taking on the Arab skin, yet the attempt to do so was not without effect: the unsuccessful attempt to become an Arab resulted in his finally ceasing to be a true Englishman. After the attempt he was no longer able to look at the West and its conventions in the same way as before; he came to see them "with new eyes." This is to say that he succeeded in becoming expressly aware of his own native preconceptions and beliefs, and the result of this was that it "destroyed it all for me." What Lawrence became aware of was the trickery of his native belief system. And in becoming aware of the trickery and relativity of his native beliefs, these beliefs lost their hold over him: it "destroyed it all" for him.

The necessary result was a "feeling of intense loneliness in life." In losing his naive confidence in his native beliefs, Lawrence also lost the comforting reassurance that comes from living in a world taken for granted in dogmatic innocence, for when a belief system is altered, so also must be the world that is the correlate of this system. In losing one belief system and in not being able to make a successful conversion to another, Lawrence found himself outside any world and also outside any believing community of men; he was alone, without a world, an alien to any and every world. Having transgressed the limits of his native world and having failed to enter into another, Lawrence was without any genuine home in the universe. He became a kind of cosmic nomad and could not but experience a feeling of intense loneliness, a loneliness more intense than any ever known by a solitary bedouin in the desert.

Lawrence tells us that along with this loneliness he also experienced "a contempt, not for other men, but for all they do." This too was inevitable, for as soon as one realizes the trickery of any and every belief system, he can no longer take them seriously and will hold them in a kind of contempt. However, the word *contempt* is a bit misleading; it would be better to speak of folly or vanity. All beliefs are seen to be only so much human folly as soon as their artificiality, relativity, and mere conventionality is perceived. When one sees that no belief system has Reality for its object, inevitably one is inclined to exclaim with the author of Ecclesiastes, "Vanity of vanities, all is vanity." A person such as Lawrence perceives the trickery of his native beliefs; he sees them for what they really are: illusions of the understanding. He sees that his beliefs and the realities they project are of no real importance.

This is a dangerous position to find oneself in, for in losing the naive confidence in one's beliefs, one also loses the mundane self-assuredness that allows for habit, for unreflective and efficient action within a given world. One ceases to be a man of the world. Such a one as this will be perceived as a threat by others, for one always feels threatened when one is not taken seriously. The outsider is a threat, for he is a living reminder of what people generally want to ignore: the relativity and artificiality of their basic beliefs. He embodies the threat of meaninglessness, of chaos, of the cosmic abyss. He provokes anxiety. The outsider is also the outcast. Like a foreign body in an organism, he will be isolated and expelled; he will be the object of a taboo reaction and, because he threatens a group's belief system, he will be declared mad. Because he has become acutely aware of the folly of all that people say and do, he may indeed take himself to be mad. Madness is the great threat to anyone who has lost his hold on the world, who has lost the stabilizing reassurance of unquestioned beliefs. Lawrence thus writes, "Madness was very near, as I believe it would be near the man who could see things through the veils at once of two customs, two educations, two environments."

The experience Lawrence is describing is one wherein madness threatens. Madness could be defined as the full-fledged experience of the absurd, of the chaos that underlies all of man's finite worlds; it would be the true experience of sheer meaninglessness. The experience Lawrence is recording is not, however, the experience of madness per se. Whatever may have befallen him subsequently, what he is describing here is not madness but anxiety. To be made concretely aware of the relativity and folly of all beliefs is to experience anxiety. Anxiety may result in madness, but it may also give rise to wisdom.

What exactly is anxiety, and what is its ontological significance? Probably one of the finest analyses of anxiety is the one undertaken by Heidegger, who was basing himself on Kierkegaard.[40] Anxiety, Heidegger tells us, makes us aware of the "utter insignificance" of everything within the world, of the "nothing" of the world, of the groundlessness of our everyday existence.[41] "Anxiety discloses an insignificance of the world; and this insignificance reveals the nullity of that with which one can concern oneself."[42] In anxiety one's environment, one's world, slips away, as does the reassuring support of others within that world. Anxiety takes away from one the ability to interpret and understand oneself "in terms of the 'world' and the way things have been publicly interpreted."[43] In short, anxiety "individualizes" and reveals one to oneself as *solus ipse*.[44]

The resultant feeling is, as Lawrence said, one of intense loneliness in life. Or, as Heidegger says, it is one of 'uncanniness.'' One experiences anxiety when one is caught in between worlds; anxiety is nothing other than the uncanny, unsettling feeling that arises when one is no longer at home in a world. It is the feeling that makes one realize that one is no longer at home in a world. Uncanniness (*Unheimlichkeit*), Heidegger says, means nothing other than not-being-at-home (*Nicht-zuhause-sein*).[45] In anxiety "everyday familiarity collapses." One is made concretely aware of the utter insignificance of one's particular world and of the groundlessness of the belief system one had previously accepted without question.

As Heidegger describes it, the experience of anxiety is negative. Anxiety destroys one's naive assurance in the way in which things have been publicly interpreted; it calls into question the common consensus that engenders and sustains a particular reality. Like a horrific nightmare, anxiety disrupts one's calm, dogmatic slumber. Because anxiety is disruptive, one's normal tendency is to avoid it as much as possible, but then one is merely entrenching oneself ever more inextricably in one's dogmatic belief, in the illusions of understanding; one is merely, as Heidegger would say, "tranquilizing" oneself. To adopt Heideggerian terminology, we could say that from a merely ontic point of view, anxiety is no more than a negative experience, which should indeed be avoided as much as possible. It has no necessary and indispensable role to play in regard to the understanding of a particular reality. From an ontological point of view, however, that is, regarding the understanding not of a particular reality but of Reality itself (or what Heidegger calls Being), anxiety is of the utmost importance; its role here is strictly positive. It is this positive role that Heidegger stresses in *Being and Time* since for him anxiety makes possible a resolute, authentic existence.

In a subsequent work Heidegger attempts to make more explicit the ontological implications of the experience of anxiety. In *What Is Metaphysics?* he argues that what anxiety (*Angst*) reveals is Nothing (or Nothingness—the *Nihil, das Nichts*). Nothing is not, however, Heidegger warns us, to be taken in a purely nihilistic or negativistic sense. Nor is Nothing a mere logical or grammatical privitive. It is, rather, the essential counterpart of everything that is; it is in fact the creative source of all that is. Heidegger refers to the classical, rationalist dictum, *ex nihilo nihil fit* ("nothing comes from nothing"), but he turns this around saying, *ex nihilo omne ens qua ens fit* ("every being, so far as it is a being, is made out of nothing"). Nothing is the creative "ground" out of which all things arise. To speak of Nothing is to speak of Being itself: Nothing is the veil of Being ("*Das Nichts als das Andere zum Seienden ist der Schleier des Seins*"). To experience Nothing in anxiety is to have a veiled experience of Being itself.

If one is seeking to understand not merely a reality but Reality itself, the experience of anxiety is the "narrow gate" through which one inevitably must pass. The narrowness of the gate forces one to divest oneself of one's cultural baggage and acquired presuppositions. Anxiety must be neither repressed nor evaded, for just as insightful understanding with regard to a particular reality arises only out of the experience of frustration, so an understanding of Reality is possible only through an experience of anxiety. Anxiety is liberating. It frees us from our involvements with a particular world and in so doing exposes us to the worldless source of all possible worlds. In anxiety our domestic world tends to fragment, and through the cracks and crevices that appear in the wall of culture we catch a glimpse of what the later Merleau-Ponty termed *l'être sauvage,* the wild, untamed being that underlies all cultural constructs:

> What are to me all the worlds? . . .
> I went and found Truth
> as she stands at the outer rim of the worlds . . .[46]

In anxiety understanding is actively at work. In anxiety one achieves an active understanding of Reality. Active or insightful understanding is, however, always transitory. Thus in the understanding of Reality, no less than in the understanding of a particular reality, insight transforms itself into a new mode of habitual praxis. Here there are two possibilities. The experience of anxiety, of the relativity of all cultural constructs, may be so terrifying and unsettling that one loses one's hold on the world, on a system of meaning, and lapses into madness. A debilitating silence overtakes and stifles one. One is overcome by anxiety and engulfed in speechlessness. There is, however, another possibility. If one neither flees from anxiety nor lets oneself be overcome by it but instead resolutely wrestles with it and vanquishes it, one may achieve an understanding of Reality which merits the name of *wisdom. La sagesse est toujours l'enjeu d'un combat.* Wisdom, Nietzsche said, "is a woman and always loves only a warrior."

Wisdom is the ontological counterpart of knowledge. Knowledge, an ontic term, arises out of frustration and curiosity and is the acquired mastery of a given belief system. Knowledge is basically know-how, the ability to move within and manipulate a particular universe of discourse; it is mastery of the rules of the game. Wisdom, on the other hand, arises out of anxiety and wonder and is the ingrained awareness of the limits of any and all belief systems. It is the existential, concrete realization of the relativity and folly of all belief systems, of all dogmatism, and of one's own innate desire to possess reality whole. It differs from madness, however, in that this awareness of folly is a controlled awareness. In wisdom one liberates oneself from the illusions of understanding in that one becomes aware of these illusions and attempts to hold them in check. One does not seek to rid oneself of them altogether, though, for one knows that without them one would be a stranger to any human world and could not communicate with others or live in their company. Alienated from all human community, one would be an *aliéné*, a lunatic.

Wisdom is not the same as knowledge, therefore, but neither is it merely the opposite or the absence of knowledge. It is, rather, the knowledge that what we think we know is only an insignificant part of what we do not know, of the great unknown. Wisdom is thus a special and unique form of knowledge; it is the true knowledge of the unknown, the knowledge of the limits of all knowing. Whereas ordinary knowledge is superstitious, wisdom—knowledge of the unknown—is ironic. Wisdom is the realization that Reality is always infinitely more than what it is ever actually known-as, that it always "means" more than what is ever merely said about it.

This realization may not be exactly comforting. It can in fact amount to, as one scientific writer puts it, a "horrific prospect," for it means that Reality can never, even in principle, be adequately known. It means even more: Reality is unknowable in at least as much as it can never be the circumscribed object of any belief system, can never be adequately expressed in any language, not even an ideal one. If all realities are relative and finite and are, moreover, a function of language, of a particular universe of discourse, Reality must necessarily transcend all language and, accordingly, all knowing. "If ideas and words are inextricably bound up with reality," the scientist Robin Horton says, "and if indeed they shape it and control it, then, a multiplicity of idea-systems means a multiplicity of realities, and a change of ideas means a change of things."[7] But although this view is not, as Horton admits, "particularly absurd or inconsistent," it is, nevertheless, "clearly intolerable in the extreme," for, as he recognizes, "it means that the world is in the last analysis dependent on human whim, that the search for order is a folly, and that human beings can expect to find no sort of anchor in reality."

But there must, Horton insists, "be some anchor, some constant reality." This is indeed what the rationalist, scientific mentality demands, but it is also what a genuine understanding of Reality knows to be impossible. If, in the words of C. G. Jung, man is such a "reason-monger," it is because he sees in the logician's reason the only line of defense between himself and the horrors of the great unknown. "He protects himself with the shield of science and the armour of reason. His enlightenment is born of fear; in the day-time he believes in an ordered cosmos, and he tries to maintain this faith against the fear of chaos that besets him by night." He strives "to construct a conscious world that is safe and manageable in that natural law holds in it the place of statute law in a commonwealth."[48]

Is this to say that reality is meaningless, an abyss of absurdity? To think this would indeed be horrific and would no doubt lead to madness. But once again, as is so often the case, we must refuse the rationalist's either-or: either reality is meaningful and fully determined in itself and is thus, ideally, knowable and expressible, or it is thoroughly meaningless and all human attempts to understand it are in vain and doomed to a dismal failure. We will be able to spell out the sense in which Reality both is and is not meaningful only when we have seen how creative understanding constantly violates and transcends the rationalist's either-or and the logician's law of excluded middle. This will be the task of the following two chapters. What we shall see is that human understanding or, more precisely, the human use of natural language, is "overdetermined," contains a "surplus of meaning," and that it is this *Mehrmeinung* or "meaning-more," as Husserl would say, this "intentional excess," we could also say, that is what is meant by "reality." As Steiner observes, "Language generates—grammar permitting, one would want to say 'language is'—a surplus of meaning (meaning is the surplus-value of the labour performed by language)."[49] Or as Merleau-Ponty could well have said, Reality is *l'excès du signifié sur le signifiant, l'excès de ce que nous vivons sur ce qui a été déjà dit* ("the excess of the signified over the signifier, the excess of what we live over what has already been said").[50] If one holds with Gadamer that "Being that can be understood is language,"[51] then one must also maintain that the true understanding of Reality or Being—wisdom—is inextricably bound up with a use of language that is "excessive" and ironic, a use that makes it mean more than what it ever actually says. It is, then, to a consideration of the creative use of language that we must now turn.

NOTES

1. W. James, *The Principles of Psychology* (New York, 1950), 1:114.

2. Ibid., p. 122.

3. A. Koestler, *The Ghost in the Machine* (London, 1970), p. 240.

4. In his very noteworthy article, "African Traditional Thought and Western Science," in B. R. Wilson, ed., *Rationality* (New York, 1971), Robin Horton defends the thesis "that in traditional Africa relations between common sense and theory are essentially the same as they are in Europe" (p. 142). Both here and in Europe the jump from common sense to theory occurs, he says, at the same point, "the point where the limited causal vision of common sense curtails its usefulness in dealing with the situation on hand" (p. 143). Horton sets forth eight propositions on the nature and function of theoretical thinking and shows how in every case

they apply as much to traditional African religious thinking as to science. The eight propositions are:

1) The quest for explanatory theory is basically the quest for unity underlying apparent diversity; for simplicity underlying apparent complexity; for order underlying apparent disorder; for regularity underlying apparent anomaly (p. 132).
2) Theory places things in a causal context wider than that provided by common sense (p. 135).
3) Common sense and theory have complementary roles in everyday life (p. 140).
4) Level of theory varies with context (p. 143).
5) All theory breaks up the unitary objects of common sense into aspects, then places the resulting elements in a wider causal context. That is, it first abstracts and analyses, then re-integrates (p. 144).
6) In evolving a theoretical scheme, the human mind seems constrained to draw inspiration from analogy between the puzzling observations to be explained and certain already familiar phenomena (p. 146).
7) Where theory is founded on analogy between puzzling observations and familiar phenomena, it is generally only a limited aspect of such phenomena that is incorporated into the resulting model (p. 147).
8) A theoretical model, once built, is developed in ways which sometimes obscure the analogy on which it was founded (p. 148).

5. Our culture is a more complex culture than traditional, non-Western cultures, for when we actively attempt to understand our experience (when we attempt to go beyond common sense) we are faced with an *embarras du choix* in the way of theoretical belief-systems; a host of *rival interpretive schemata* present themselves of our allegiance. In addition to magical explanations which still persist subterraneously among us (e.g., in the form of astrology), there are well-articulated religious systems (some of which are exotic imports from the East) which are thoroughly opposed to magic and, in addition, there is science which itself is intolerant of all other systems of understanding. Actually, though, this abundance, this plurality of rival theoretical systems is to our advantage, for it is capable of provoking in someone acutely aware of the different alternatives a higher form of awareness (understanding), in the same way that, as we shall see later in this chapter, inter-cultural confrontation can.

6. In his *Theories of Primitive Religion* (Oxford, 1971), E. E. Evans-Pritchard writes, "All observers who have made lengthy first-hand studies of primitive peoples are agreed that they are for the most part interested in practical affairs, which they conduct in an empirical manner, either without the least reference to supra-sensible forces, influences, and actions, or in a way in which these have a subordinate and auxiliary role" (p. 88).

7. One views an illness, for example, as if it were the effect of witchcraft, or one views a particular observable process as if it were the result of atomic interactions. Given the nature of consciousness, however—as belief—the "as if" is destined to be forgotten and to be reduced to a simple "is" (as when the scientist [Eddington] says that a table is really nothing solid but only a mass of insubstantial, swarming atoms). The world of imaginative, theoretical entities thereby becomes every bit as real as that of immediate experience—more real, in fact, since it is taken to be the cause of "this" world, which becomes a merely "phenomenal" world. A new reality has been created. As Horton, "African Traditional Thought," p. 141, remarks, "For whatever the philosophers say, people develop a sense of reality about something to the extent that they use and act on language which implies that this something exists."

8. Horton, "African Traditional Thought," p. 136. In his book, *Scientific Explanation* (Cambridge, 1968), R. Braithwaite writes, "All scientific thinking is general thinking concerned with connecting pieces of empirical knowledge with one another; theoretical concepts are only a particularly elaborate way of making these connexions, and theoretical terms only a particularly striking case of contextual meaning" (p. 85). In chapter 7 we shall consider the

question of the ontological status of theoretical entities (for example, the sense in which a theoretical entity such as an atom *is*).

9. I. A. Richards, *The Philosophy of Rhetoric* (New York, 1965), p. 125. The philosopher of science, N. Hanson writes, "We have had an explanation of *x* only when we can set it into an interlocking pattern of concepts about other things, *y* and *z*. A *completely* novel explanation is a logical impossibility. It would be incomprehensible . . . ; it would be imponderable, like an inexpressible or unknowable fact" (*Patterns of Discovery* [Cambridge, 1972], p. 54).

10. T. Kuhn, *The Structure of Scientific Revolutions* (Chicago, 1970), p. 24.

11. Ibid., p. 52.

12. Heidegger, *What Is Called Thinking?* (New York, 1968), p. 8.

13. Kuhn, *Structure of Scientific Revolutions*, pp. 52–53.

14. Ibid., p. 111.

15. F. Nietzsche, *Mixed Opinions and Aphorisms* (New York, 1964), no. 200.

16. W. Stevens, "Adagia," in *Opus Posthumous* (New York, 1957), p. 179.

17. One is reminded of Wittgenstein's remark in his *Philosophical Investigations* (Oxford, 1963), (par. 336): "This case is similar to the one in which someone imagines that one could not think a sentence with the remarkable word order of German or Latin just as it stands. One first has to think it, and then one arranges the words in that queer order. (A French politician once wrote that it was a peculiarity of the French language that in it words occur in the order in which one thinks them.)"

18. Cf. Horton, "African Traditional Thought," pp. 165, 168, and E. Leach, "Lévi-Strauss in the Garden of Eden," in E. Hayes and T. Hayes, eds., *Claude Lévi-Strauss, The Anthropologist as Hero* (Cambridge, Mass., 1970), p. 54.

19. In his book, *Les structures élémentaires de la parenté* (Paris, 1949), Lévi-Strauss argues that the reason why incest is universally prohibited is because it disrupts the nature and function of kinship systems. Because the exchange of women though marriage is the most basic way in which alliances are contracted between groups and among individuals, incest, which withdraws women from circulation, must be prohibited if these alliances, which maintain a society and allow for its survival, are to exist. Incest is taboo in primitive societies not because it is thought to be morally wrong but because it is socially absurd. Moreover, Lévi-Strauss argues that the prohibition of incest is the decisive factor in the transition from the state of nature to that of culture; men see the prohibition of incest as that which sets them apart from the beasts.

20. Cf. M. Eliade, *Traité d'histoire des religions* (Paris, 1968), sec. 6.

21. J. Beattie, *Other Cultures* (New York, 1968), pp. 233, 235 (italics added).

22. E. E. Evans-Pritchard, *Social Anthropology and Other Essays* (New York, 1964), p. 149.

23. P. Mayer, "Witches," in M. Marwick, ed., *Witchcraft and Sorcery* (Baltimore, 1975), p. 46.

24. J. Beattie, "On Understanding Ritual," in B. R. Wilson, ed., *Rationality* (New York, 1971), p. 254.

25. P. Riesman, "A Comprehensive Anthropological Assessment," in D. Noel, ed., *Seeing Castaneda* (New York, 1976), p. 47.

26. Although intercultural understanding of the sort described here does not and cannot provide an understanding of another culture or belief system that would correspond to this other system's own self-understanding, it does have a definite value, and this is that it furthers our own self-understanding. It enables us to escape from the stagnation of the perfectly closed system, a dead end to which all understanding tends as by a kind of epistemological entropy. In the next chapter we shall return to this question of conceptual entropy and shall see that it is precisely the function of metaphor to combat this entropy and to introduce freshness into a system that of its own inertia tends toward a state of rigid closure.

27. Although Polanyi does recognize the similarity between magic and science in this regard,

he does not draw the conclusion called for: that the terms *superstition* and *true* when applied to belief systems are purely relative. Most writers do not even go as far as Polanyi. For instance, the philosopher-anthropologists I. C. Jarvie and J. Agassi, who, after remarking, "We know that magic, being a doctrine about the occult, is compatible with all empirical experience and thus cannot be directly refuted," go on to ask "how individuals or communities ever do break out of the magical world-view" ("The Problem of the Rationality of Magic," in Wilson, *Rationality,* p. 190). Writers such as these fail to see that magical forces are no less or no more occult than scientific entities such as electrons. In both cases the theoretical constructs of the system are postulated entities that cannot be directly experienced and whose function it is to tie together experimental data so as to "explain" them. From a formal or transcendental-pragmatic point of view, the question as to how one breaks out of a magical world view is in no way different from the question as to how one breaks out of a scientific world view.

28. B. Whorf, *Language, Thought, and Reality* (Cambridge, Mass., 1972), pp. 224-25.

29. T. S. Eliot has made much the same observation: "To understand the culture is to understand the people, and this means an imaginative understanding. Such understanding can never be complete: either it is abstract—and the essence escapes—or else it is *lived;* and in so far as it is *lived,* the student will tend to identify himself so completely with the people whom he studies, that he will lose the point of view from which it was worth while and possible to study it. Understanding involves an area more extensive than that of which one can be conscious; one cannot be outside and inside at the same time. What we ordinarily mean by understanding of another people, of course, is an approximation towards understanding which stops short at the point at which the student would begin to lose some essential of his own culture. The man who, in order to understand the inner world of a cannibal tribe, has partaken of the practice of cannibalism, has probably gone too far: he can never quite be one of his own folk again" ("Notes towards the Definition of Culture," in his *Christianity and Culture* [New York, 1949], pp. 113-14).

30. It might nonetheless be objected that it is possible to combine the best features of two cultures or realities so as to constitute a culture or reality that is more comprehensive and closer to the true Reality than either culture or reality taken alone. This is not possible, however, and again the model of language shows why it is not. It is quite possible for two or more genuinely bilingual persons, ones equally fluent in, say, French and English, to speak among themselves in a "language" that is a strange mixture of French and English, understandable for them but incomprehensible to a mere Francophone or Anglophone. The speaking of such a "language" may in fact be a very enjoyable experience, no doubt because it allows one to feel that one is combining the most expressive elements of both languages. Such a mode of communication is not, however, a genuine language, for it can be spoken only by those who have already mastered English and French in their own right. It is indeed a mixture and not a real fusion; it is strictly parasitical on the two languages, and whatever life it has flows into it from them. The mixture of French and English in this way produces a sterile offshoot in the same way as does the mating of a horse and a donkey. This is not to say that a new language with a life of its own could not be formed in this way, by the fusion of two existing languages. This is quite conceivable, but should it occur what one would then have would not be a combination, a "totalization" of French and English, but a new language altogether. One would not have synthesized two languages into a more perfect one but would have created a third language alongside the other two; one would have merely added to the plurality of discrete languages.

31. Beattie, *Other Cultures,* p. 76.

32. M. Beaujour, "The Game of Poetics," in J. Ehrmann, ed., *Game, Play, Literature* (Boston, 1968), pp. 66-67.

33. J. P. Sartre, *Being and Nothingness* (New York, 1956), p. 615.

34. A distinction should be made between *ontological* and *ontic*, the first being used to refer to Reality and the second to reality.

35. Cf. Whorf, *Language, Thought and Reality,* p. 209.

36. J. B. Carroll, in the introduction to ibid., p. 27.

37. B. Malinowki, *Magic, Science and Religion* (New York, 1954), p. 81.

38. S. Latouche, "Totalité, totalisation et totalitarisme" *Dialogue* 13, no. 1 (March 1974): 81-82 (author's translation).

39. T. E. Lawrence, *Seven Pillars of Wisdom* (New York, 1935), chap. 1.

40. In note 4, chap. 6, division 1, of *Being and Time* (New York, 1962), Heidegger says, "The man who has gone farthest in analysing the phenomenon of anxiety . . . is Søren Kierkegaard."

41. Heidegger, *Being and Time,* pp. 231, 393.

42. Ibid., p. 393.

43. Ibid., p. 232.

44. Ibid., p. 233.

45. Ibid.

46. From a Gnostic text quoted by Hans Jonas, *The Gnostic Religion* (Boston, 1963), p. 91.

47. Horton, "African Traditional Thought, p. 157.

48. C. G. Jung, "Psychology and Literature," in *Modern Man in Search of a Soul,* trans. W. S. Dell and C. F. Baynes (London, 1966), pp. 187-88.

49. G. Steiner, *After Babel* (New York, 1975), p. 280.

50. M. Merleau-Ponty, *Signes* (Paris, 1960), p. 104.

51. H.-G. Gadamer, *Truth and Method* (New York, 1975), p. xxii.

6 METAPHOR AND IMAGINATION: I

Inquiry into human understanding has enabled us to discern the basic modes in which understanding occurs. All that now remains is to uncover the actual mechanisms at work in the understanding process. If all insightful understanding is essentially of a creative or transformational nature, it is incumbent on us to form a more detailed picture of how insightful understanding arises through the creative transformation of an accepted system of understanding.

The peculiar trait of human understanding is that it operates primarily in a linguistic medium. Man, the rational animal, is also the speaking animal. Both Peirce and Whorf insist that thought is intimately bound up with language. A good language, Peirce says, is not merely important to good thought, "it is of the essence of it."[1] "Expression and thought," he says, "are one."[2] This view contradicts what might fairly well be called the traditional view, according to which language is but the vehicle of thought. Just as the function of thought is to refer to a reality, which is what it is independently of thought, so the function of language is merely that of expression: language merely articulates pre-existent meanings and is not involved to any significant degree in the actual production of meaning. Because this rationalist view is unacceptable, it would seem that we must agree with Peirce that language is not external to thought but is rather (as he says) its very "woof and warp."

We should do so with reservations, however, for we should not let ourselves be saddled with what would merely be the opposite view to rationalism, the one that identifies thought with language or that reduces the former to the latter. Such a view leads directly into relativism, and relativism, as in the case of Whorf, is unable to account for the fact that translation between one thought or linguistic system and another, while never perfect, is nevertheless always possible. The discussion of analogy in chapter 4 seemed to indicate that there is something like a thought, or meaning-intention, that transcends the actual use of language and that can be expressed in many different ways. It is significant that James, who defends the existence of meaning-intentions, also claims that thought without language is "perfectly possible."[3] But, interestingly enough as well, James's subsequent remarks appear to concede that, if not words, then at least some kind of "system of imagery" is necessary if a diffuse and dimly felt "halo" of meaning is ever to crystallize and know itself. Thus, even if an intimate connection between thought and language is recognized, it can still be maintained that thought transcends language in some sense or other and that one can mean or intend more than what one actually ever says. Indeed only if language can, at times at least, "mean" more than it "says"—only if it is "overdetermined—is it meaningful to speak of an understanding of Reality that transcends any and all finite and relative systems of linguistically structured belief. However, if we are to understand this, we must begin by seeing how what could be called the event of meaning is inseparably bound up with the creative use and "abuse" of language. This will be the task of this and the following chapter. Only after this will it be possible to ask whether the event of linguistically generated meaning cannot itself be viewed as the occasion for what might be called the advent of a meaning—the meaning of Reality or being—which transcends the mere use of language.

Creative, insightful understanding involves the creative use of language in a very basic way. It is through metaphor that a system of linguistic meanings is enlarged and extended; metaphor is the locus of emergent meaning, of insightful understanding. Because all insightful or active understanding arises only on the basis and in the context of a prior, passive understanding, we must first inquire into the nature of semantic systems—into what constitutes an acquired and stable meaning—if we are to grasp what creative, metaphorical, analogical thinking and the emergence of new meaning consists in. In short, what is a language, such that it allows for the production of metaphors and the creation of new meanings?

Whenever man seeks to understand himself and his world, his understanding invariably tends to assume the form of a system. Nature becomes understandable when it is viewed in terms of physical systems, biological, ecological, supernatural, and other systems. The exact form these systems will take varies from culture to culture and from epoch to epoch. The Navajo, for example, do not categorize and systematize the plethora of living beings in the same way as does a Western biologist in his taxonomies, but categorize and systematize they do. As Lévi-Strauss points out, "Native classifications are not only methodical and based on carefully built up theoretical knowledge. They are also at times comparable from a formal point of view to those still in use in zoology and botany."[4]

It is in being systematized that nature first becomes genuinely meaningful, and thus, from this point of view, meaning in the fully determinate sense of the term is nothing other than structure and form. Nature is indeed meaningful precisely because it is categorizable. But because, as anthropology has shown, nature is systematizable in an indefinite number of ways, this means that it does not have a single meaning but rather an indefinite number of different meanings. Human understanding operates in a twofold manner: out of the confused reality of immediate experience wherein everything flows together and is, in a sense, everything else, the mind isolates out certain elements and separates one part of experience from another. These basic elements are themselves meaningless, however. The world becomes truly meaningful and understandable—indeed only first becomes a "world," a cosmos—when "particulars" are viewed in the light of "universals," of, that is, a set of overriding categories. The meaning of any one thing is nothing other than its position in a total system or structure. Such is what has come to be known as the structuralist view of meaning. Lévi-Strauss articulates it in the following way:

> It is obvious that the same characteristics could have been given a different meaning and that different characteristics . . . could have been chosen instead. . . . Arbitrary as it seems when only its individual terms are considered, the system becomes coherent when it is seen as a whole set. . . . Nevertheless when one takes account of the wealth and diversity of the raw material, only a few of the innumerable possible elements of which are made use of in the system, there can be no doubt that a considerable number of other systems of the same type would have been equally coherent and that no one of them is predestined to be chosen by all societies and all civilizations. The terms never have any intrinsic significance. Their meaning is one of "position"—a function of the history and cultural context on the one hand and of the structural system in which they are called upon to appear on the other.[5]

Nothing having to do with man is ever purely "by nature," *physei*, as Aristotle would say. Even such a seemingly natural thing as kinship relations is in fact thoroughly cultural. In an attempt to discover some sort of order in the chaotic social reality, people have always had recourse to the basic categories of biological relationship, and yet the curious fact is that these categories are differently perceived and differently defined in different societies, and thus they are in fact more cultural than natural, more invented than discovered. Just as the native speaker of a language tends to look upon his language as the direct articulation of the natural articulations of thought and reality, so the member of a society assumes that the kinship system operative in this society is merely an expression of natural, biologically determined relations between male and female, between siblings and generations. To call one's biological progenitor by the name father is, though, arbitrary (cultural and relative), since there are cultures where this term is reserved for one's maternal uncle who is, indeed, in all practical, social respects, the "father" of his sister's child. Kinship systems are in fact a prime instance of the cultural and structural character of meaning. Because they are a fundamental manifestation of the conceptual framework peculiar to a given culture, it is no accident that they are a matter of prime interest to anthropologists. And because they also reveal very well the structural character of language use, it is not surprising that linguists would take such a keen interest in kinship terminologies.[6]

This reference to terminology leads directly into the question of language itself. Perhaps the most important and far-reaching theory of modern linguistics is that the very machinery that allows for fully developed understanding and meaning—language—itself possesses the structural form of a system. At the beginning of this century the Swiss linguist, Ferdinand de Saussure, articulated this thesis in the following way:

> Language [*la langue*] is a system of interdependent terms in which the value of each term results solely from the simultaneous presence of the others. . . .

> Language is a system of signs that express ideas, and is therefore comparable to a system of writing, the alphabet of deaf-mutes, symbolic rites, polite formulas, military signals, etc. It is but the most important of these systems.[7]

What is of interest in these definitions is that they not only assert that a language is a system of signs, but they also set linguistic meaning in an immediate relation to other, nonlinguistic systems of meaning. Saussure in effect is implying that all human social or cultural life is regulated by meaning and that in all instances meaning is nothing other than a certain code regulating, in a purely formal way, the use of signs. Saussure in fact foresaw the possibility of a general science of meaning, which he termed *semiology* (from the Greek, *semeion,* "sign") whose function it would be to study "the life of signs within society."[8] "Linguistics," he said, "is only a part of the general science of semiology." Saussure did not himself pursue this insight, but his suggestion has been taken up by a host of others after him who have attempted to work out in more detail various branches of this general science of semiology (or semiotics, as it is generally referred to today). The French structuralist, Roland Barthes, for instance, has attempted to study such manifestations of social life as clothing fashions and eating habits on the model of language, itself conceived of as a structural system of meaning: clothing styles are "semiological," are meant to communicate a message.[9] And Lévi-Strauss himself was led to formulate his structural anthropology in a similar way.

What exactly is Saussure's view of linguistic meaning? In simple terms, the meaning of a word is nothing other than the role it plays in a semiotic system, the system itself being what is called a language (English, French, and so forth). Saussure makes a fundamental distinction between *langue* and *parole*. A *langue* is an impersonal and abstract code; it is the total system of signs and their meanings, and it is the same for all the members of a linguistic community. *Parole* or speech is the personal, subjective use that an individual makes of the linguistic code; as such it is of no direct interest to linguistics whose sole proper object is the *langue*. *Langue* or language (I shall henceforth use the English *language* to mean Saussure's *langue*) is an autonomous system of internal dependencies understandable in its own terms, with reference to nothing outside itself. The basic, meaningful units of language—words, roughly—are constituted and defined diacritically— that is, by means of their mutual oppositions within a closed system. Language is thus a system, and the value (meaning) of its basic units is determined solely by the place they occupy in this structure (just as the value or meaning of a piece in chess, such as a knight, is determined solely by its relation to and difference from all the other pieces in the game).[10]

For Saussure a word is not simply a sign that refers to a concept independent of it. A concept or meaning (that which is meant in a sign) cannot be separated from the sign itself (from the acoustical, material image). In order to make this more apparent, Saussure introduces a terminological distinction. A sign, he says, is intrinsically two-sided; it is composed of two elements, which can be separated only in theory. These two elements he calls the *signifier* (*le signifiant*) and the *signified* (*le signifié*), the first corresponding to what is ordinarily called the image and the second to the concept or meaning. In saying that these two elements are inseparable, Saussure is claiming that the meaning of a word is inseparable from that word itself; it is, so to speak, the other, "invisible" side of the visible (or audible) image. Signifier and signified are like two sides of a single sheet of paper.[11]

Just as the signified is but the diacritical counterpart of the signifier, so also a given signifier is but the diacritical counterpart of all the other signifiers that together make up a language (a linguistic code). This latter, diacritical relation constitutes the semantic value of a sign and, as a consequence, its meaning. The concept or meaning is simply the expression of the interplay of one sign with all the others of the system. A given sign is the particular sign it is for the simple reason that it is different from all the other signs of a language. Thus in a language there is, basically, nothing but differences, without, Saussure says, any positive terms.[12] For Saussure, meaning is a purely contextual affair.[13]

This view, which might well appear counterintuitive (after all, is not the meaning of a word something eminently positive?), gains in plausibility when one considers what is involved in what we actually do when we wish to find out the meaning of a word and consult a dictionary. How does a dictionary define a word? It does so not, as might be thought, by giving the concept or meaning of a word or sign but by simply listing a number of other signs that can be substituted for the original one and can be used in its stead. Thus a dictionary is helpful only if one already knows the use of one or more of these other terms, or synonyms. Nowhere in a dictionary does one encounter pure "meanings"—only other words. And these words are all self-referential; one word is "defined" by means of another, and the second by means of a third, and so on, such that in going through the dictionary one turns about in a circle and may end up with the word one initially started out from. "In a monolingual dictionary," one linguist writes, "every word is defined in terms of other words in the language. But if the user does not know the meaning of any of the words, the whole thing is defining in a circle."[14] The dictionary is thus a closed system, and it thereby illustrates the systematic and tautological character of language itself. As Merleau-Ponty remarks, "We always have to do only with sign structures whose meaning, being nothing other than the way in which the signs behave toward one another and are distinguished from one another, cannot be set forth independently of them"[15]

The view put forth by Saussure is counterintuitive because we are not ordinarily aware of the semiotic (diacritical) character of meaning. If we were and if the object of our awareness were the signifiers themselves, we would lose sight of the signified, of the meaning of signs. A sign has meaning for us precisely because it is transparent; we are not aware of it as such but only of the meaning that it serves to generate. The signifier or word immediately transcends itself in the signified, in its meaning, and effaces itself before it, such that when one speaks one naturally believes that one has to do with a world of translinguistic meaning, whereas in fact one is doing nothing more than manipulating with the ease of instinctive habit a particular linguistic, semiotic code, which, like a musical score, refers ultimately to nothing other than itself. As Merleau-Ponty says:

> We think that language is more transparent than music because most of the time we remain within the bounds of constituted language, we provide ourselves with available meanings, and in our definitions we are content, like the dictionary, to explain meanings in terms of each other. . . . But in fact, as we have said, the clearness of language stands out from an obscure background, and if we carry our research far enough we shall eventually find that language is equally uncommunicative of anything other than itself, that its meaning is inseparable from it.[16]

The comparison of language with music is very instructive. One composer comments:

> It must not be forgotten that, for the composer, notes, chords, melodic intervals—all the musical materials—are far more real, far more expressive, than words; that let us say, a "leading tone" or a chord of the subdominant are for him not only notes, but sensations, full of meaning and capable of infinite nuances of modification; and that when he speaks or thinks in terms of them he is using words which, however obscure and dry they may sound to the uninitiated, are for him fraught with dynamic sense.[17]

A musical note, like a word, is full of meaning because it is "capable of infinite nuances of modification." In music, as in language, it is not the isolated unit but the *enchaînement* of different units that is important; a single musical chord, like an isolated word, has meaning only to the degree that it evokes other chords and in this way is part of an overall semiotic system: "It will lead the composer on, through the force of its own momentum or tension, to other phrases, other motifs, other chords."[18]

Correspondingly, in the case of actual writing, an author is often guided not by a set of predefined ideas but by the "music" of the words themselves, by a certain rhythm that determines the actual words, as the writer is drawn along by it. "Again sometimes when I am writing," a poet remarks, "the music of the words I am trying to shape takes me far beyond the words, I am aware of a rhythm, a dance, a fury, which is as yet empty of words."[19] That elusive something called inspiration could in fact be defined as sensitivity to the guiding music of words. In literature, no less than in music, the act of expression rests on the sense of hearing.

It is impossible to separate the sensual (linguistic signs) from the intellectual (linguistic meanings). One thinks not with pure meanings but with words, mere sounds and marks. Thought is nothing but the manipulation of signs, and the illusion of pure thought is possible only because the peculiar nature of a sign is that when its use is known and mastered, it is, like a trustworthy tool, totally unobtrusive and supremely transparent. When expressing one's thoughts, one is no more aware of one's words than one is aware of a hammer when pounding a nail. The word, like the tool, is naturally unobtrusive; only thus can it function as an expression of recognizable meanings. At times, however, one can become more or less expressly aware of the properly semiotic character of all meaning. In certain instances it is possible to recall the kind of magical qualities certain words had for us when we were first learning them and were fascinated with their sheer sonorous qualities. One of the functions of the poet—an individual who has a social license to play with words—is to make us more appreciatively aware of the sonorous qualities of words that we have long since ceased to notice. One can achieve for oneself a similar experience by simply repeating a given word over and over long enough. There comes a moment when the word suddenly appears strange, perhaps humorous, certainly meaningless. What is happening in such a case (better known to children than to adults) is that one is *seeing* the word for itself; the word loses its normal transparency and becomes mysteriously opaque. Such an experience brings one face to face with the fundamental arbitrariness and underlying opacity of all established meaning.

Saussure recognized that language is a structure or system of diacritically determined values even on a level below that of its fundamental units of meaning, its signs or words:

> The conceptual side of value is made up solely of relations and differences with respect to the other terms of language, and the same can be said of its material side. The important thing in the word is not the sound alone but the phonic differences that make it possible to distinguish this word from all others, for differences carry signification. . . . a segment of language can never in the final analysis be based on anything except its noncoincidence with the rest. . . . The foregoing principle is so basic that it applies to all the material elements of language, including phonemes.[20]

The truly basic building blocks of a language, of meaning, are not words but individual sounds, what linguists call phonemes, single sounds that can be represented by definite symbols. Thus the word *cat* is composed of three phonemes which, in accordance with the International Phonetic Alphabet, would be written: /k/, /æ/, /t/. *Car* differs from *cat* not in one but in two phonemes: /k/, /a/, /r/. The phonemes that form the repertory of a given language are always of a fixed number, although they may vary somewhat due to differences between regions, between classes and generations. English operates with about forty-five phonemes, French with thirty-one, Castilian with twenty-four, American Spanish with twenty-two, Italian with twenty-seven, Hawaiian with thirteen. Of the hundreds of sounds the human being is capable of emitting, each linguistic community selects only a very small number, between roughly a dozen and five dozen, which it deems important; it ignores the rest, and a member of one community will not even recognize a distinct sound uttered by the speaker of another community if it is not a recognized sound in his own language. One always translates phonetically a foreign language into one's own. As Saussure observed, "Each language operates on a fixed number of well-differentiated phonemes."[21] A sound (a potential phoneme) is meaningful (can function as a signifier or part thereof) only to the degree that it forms part of the finite phonetic system of a given language. Once again and on the most basic level, we observe the selective and structural or systematic character of human understanding at work.

Not only are the phonetic elements of a language strictly limited, but they operate in accordance with a structural or combinary schema that rigidly prescribes the ways in which they may be combined to form words. In any language only certain combinations of phonemes are allowable. The rules governing the combination of phonemes are inflexible. They are, of course, in regard to any given language, purely arbitrary; possible combinations have nothing to do with the intrinsic difficulty or ease involved in pronouncing them. In fact there is no such thing as intrinsic difficulty of pronunciation. What to an English speaker is a strange and unpronounceable series of letters is natural in another language, and the reverse is true as well. Any series of letters is pronounceable as long as it conforms to the phonetic schema of the language. The following schema or formula for the construction of a monosyllabic English word (in standard midwestern American) was worked out by Benjamin Lee Whorf:[22]

The interpretation of this schema need not concern us here. What is of note is that it—and others like it—aptly demonstrates that the rules governing the formation of English words can be clearly expressed, and in expressing them it demonstrates that such rules do indeed exist. As Whorf points out, his formula, like all other good formulas, has predictive power:

> A new monosyllable turned out, say, by Walter Winchell or by a plugging ad-man concocting a name for a new breakfast mush, is struck from this mold as surely as if I pulled the lever and the stamp came down on his brain. Thus linguistics, like the physical sciences, confers the power of prediction. I can predict, within limits, what Winchell will or won't do. He may coin a word *thrub,* but he will not coin a word *srub,* for the formula cannot produce a *sr.* A different formula indicates that, if Winchell invents any word beginning with *th,* like *thell* or *therg,* the *th* will have the sound it has in "thin," not the sound it has in "this" or "there." Winchell will not invent a word beginning with this latter sound.[23]

Thus, although these phonetic rules allow for no individual freedom, only if we conform to them do we, as speaking subjects, have the chance of saying anything meaningful, or properly unmeaningful. Even nonsense verse conforms to them. Lewis Carroll's "Jabberwocky" may be semantic nonsense or linguistic madness, but it is madness with a phonetic (as well as a grammatical) logic. Just as the nonsense words of an American seven year old conform to the schema, so also do Carroll's *toves, gyre,* and *wabe.* A modern poet who refuses to respect and follow these rules would be lost in a hopeless and sterile protest against the limits of meaning.

Although no two languages have the same phonetic schemata or even the same grammatical schemata, we should not be overly hasty to generalize from this to a vague linguistic relativity principle and, like Whorf, claim that what is said in one language is so thoroughly determined by the underlying schema of this language that it cannot be expressed properly in another language. We must continue to maintain that the criterion for meaningfulness is translatability. Any utterance that is meaningful in one language can be translated into a meaningful utterance in another. Poetry is no less translatable than prose; it is only more difficult to translate successfully. Even nonsense statements can be translated into the appropriate nonsense of another language, provided that they are correctly formulated in the first place. It is no accident that one speaks of "brilliant" translations of the feats of the Dong and the Snark, but what does this mean if not that the translator has hit upon a way of expressing the same meaning (or unmeaning) in a different way in another linguistic code? "Jabberwocky" becomes in French "Le jaserroque"—a brilliant translation indeed, the more one thinks about it.

> 'Twas brillig, and the slithy toves
>   Did gyre and gimble in the wabe,

becomes:

> Il brilgue: les tôves lubricilleux
>   Se gyrent en vrillant dans la guave.

The two utterances are obviously different, and yet the latter does seem to be analogously the same as the former, if one compares the way the French words relate to French schemata to the way the English words relate to the schemata of English. Whorf is right in maintaining that the meanings generated by one language are never univocally the same as or identical with those generated by a different language.

With these linguistic considerations in mind it is possible to formulate a coherent argument against the proper meaning superstition, the rationalist belief that the meaning of a word is determined by something extralinguistic, by an independently existing concept or state of affairs in reality. Whorf's views call for a radical modification, amounting in fact to a rejection, of the Fregean distinction between sense and reference. If it is true that a language refers to nothing but itself, then the reality that the rationalist speaks of and wants to use as an independent criterion for assessing the meaningfulness of language is in fact no such thing. The so-called referent of language, reality, is in fact what it is only in terms of and by means of language. A reality or world is nothing more than the correlate of beliefs, the objectification of belief; it is a semantic construct. "Reference," it must then be said, is actually a function of "sense." And since the sense of words is determined diacritically, by the sole interplay of words among themselves, sense is inseparable from what Frege called "coloring" or what others would call the connotative value of words (in opposition to their denotation—Frege's "reference").

If one wishes to account for established meanings or even for the way in which new meanings arise, one need look no further than the purely linguistic and semiotic basis of linguistic meaning. It is one of the underlying theses of modern linguistics that language can be explained in terms of itself; no reference need be made to the so-called extralinguistic elements of thought and reality. On another level, meaning can be accounted for in terms of conventional use alone. In the following section we shall see how new meanings arise by means of the "misuse" of words, of a linguistic code. The genuinely curious fact about language becomes apparent only when the semiotic account of meaning and the linguistic conception of language as a finite and closed system of material signs has been accepted. Although, as structural linguistics tells us, language refers to nothing but itself and is in this sense dense and opaque like a material object,[24] by means of it we are able to lead a life of meaning, a "spiritual" life, over and above mere material or biological existence. As Merleau-Ponty remarked, "Like the weaver, the writer works on the wrong side of his material. He has to do only with language, and it is thus that he suddenly finds himself surrounded by meaning."[25]

We never have access to pure thoughts or meanings or to a reality uncontaminated by language and which in fact is not itself constituted by means of language. Thought amounts to no more than the manipulation of material signs, and yet, by this finite, limited means, we are able to intend an unlimited, infinite Reality, which transcends all particular realities or universes of discourse and is their common, underlying source. This is the true mystery of language. Linguistically, meaning can be accounted for in terms of language itself; there is no mystery *in* language, but, as Paul Ricoeur insists, there is a mystery *of* language.[26] This mystery has to do with the elusive element of intention, with, that is, the preverbal, lived-through experience underlying all expression, which we encountered in chapter 4 when we came up against the limits of the relativist and conventionalist account of linguistic meanings and to which we shall return in chapter 8 as the ultimate horizon for determining the meaning of Reality.

One of the advantages of approaching the question of the meaning of meaning from the point of view of modern linguistics and of adopting a structuralist or semiotic view of it is that it enables us to bypass the age-old and by now profitless dispute as to whether the meaning of words is determined merely by convention or by nature. This is the *nomos-physis* debate over the "correctness of words" (ὀρθότης ὀνομάτων), which raged in the time of Socrates and has continued mainly unchanged down through the ages.

Against certain sophists and rhetoricians who argued that the meaning of words is completely arbitrary and, for this reason, they said, have no correspondence to reality, Plato wrote in his *Cratylus* that the meaning of words is prescribed by nature and that when a new word is coined it should be made to fit the concept it is intended to express and should conform to the precise nature of the thing talked about. Distinctions between and among words should correspond to natural distinctions between things, to natural kinds (εἴδεα). In short, for Plato things have names, or should have names, that rightly and naturally belong to them. It is important "to put the true natural name of each thing into sounds and syllables and to make and give all names with a view to the ideal name."[27] Different natural languages may use different phonetic materials, but they all express, or should express, the same ideal form (recall Aristotle's remarks on thought and language referred to in chapter 1). The name, Plato says, anticipating Wittgenstein and his picture theory of meaning, is the representation (μίμημα) of a thing; it is like a portrait, only it is an audible rather than a visual likeness: "the name, like the picture, is an imitation";[28] "primitive names may be compared with pictures." When one assigns the wrong name, this is falsehood. And just as in painting the basis for the resemblance between image and thing is the resemblance that certain pigments in nature have to the thing imitated, so the basis for resemblance between word and thing lies in the basic elements of the word, its letters. For instance, ρ expresses rapidity, motion and hardness; λ expresses smoothness and softness. Unfortunately not all words are composed of letters that resemble their object; the meaning of these words has to be a matter of convention: "Words should as far as possible resemble things, but I fear that this dragging in of resemblance . . . is a shoddy thing, which has to be supplemented by the mechanical aid of convention with a view to correctness. For I believe that if we could always, or almost always, use likenesses, which are perfectly appropriate, this would be the most perfect state of language."[29] Plato, it would seem, is dreaming of an ideal language. All in all, Frege, Russell, and modern logicians with their insistence on "correctness of reference" are in a direct line of descent from Plato.[30]

But with the semiotic model in mind, it is possible today to see that the standard issue being debated is spurious. It is vitiated by an underlying and unacceptable presupposition that both parties to the dispute tend to accept uncritically: that there is indeed a determinate reality that words may or may not correspond to. But if it is true, as modern linguistics implies, that the reference of language—what is called reality—is itself a function of language, then it is not true that the meaning of words need be either arbitrary and artificial, and thus in fact "meaningless" (in that there is no correspondence or correct reference to reality here), or that they be naturally determined and thus truly meaningful. No language can be said to be any more or any less correct than another, for there is no single reality universal to them all. The issue of correctness does not arise, and no language is any more artificial or natural than any other. All languages are both artificial and natural, for they are all quite adequate for dealing with the world in which one lives and thus in this respect correctly designate it, and this for the simple reason that the world that they refer to is ultimately relative to the language in question. As Plato would say, every language does articulate the "natural" differences between things, but what Plato and contemporary logicians fail to see is that these natural differences ultimately are an expression of the internal differences or oppositions between the words of the language themselves.

In the debate over the correctness of names, Plato was vehemently opposed by the rhetorician, Antisthenes, a pupil of Socrates who was present at his death, but an arch-opponent of the rationalist Plato who attempted to claim the Socratic succession for himself. Antisthenes has been called the first nominalist, for, as the historian W. K. C. Guthrie says, "he denied the existence of those forms or essences of particular things, which Socrates sought to define and Plato was already proclaiming as independent realities."[31] It is reported that Antisthenes once said to Plato, "I see a horse, but I don't see horseness," to which Plato could do no better than to reply, "No, for you have the eye with which a horse is seen, but you have not yet acquired the eye to see horseness."[32] Can one see an essence? Does the essence "horse" look anything like a real horse? Is not rather the essence of things—what they are, are said to be—a function of language and its use? Antisthenes clearly is anticipating the thesis we are attempting to defend: that the essence of a thing is merely a disguised and rigidified analogy. To say what something is is merely to draw an analogy and to say what it is like. A definition or an essence is a metaphor taken literally. Aristotle tells us that Antisthenes "and other such uneducated people" denied that one can "define" things (in the Platonic sense).[33] "They said that the 'what' cannot be defined (for the definition so called is a 'long rigmarole') but of what *sort* of thing, e.g., silver, is, they thought it possible to explain, not saying what it is, but that it is like tin." One defines a thing not by stating its so-called essence but by saying what it is like. Along with Protagoras, Gorgias, Diogenes the Cynic, Sextus Empiricus, and Montaigne, we have, it would seem, discovered within the wider tradition of Western thought another ally in our battle against the main-line tradition of rationalism.

In Plato's ideal language there would be a natural correspondence between words and things, which is to say that the meaning of words would not be determined by mere convention and in this sense would not be arbitrary or artificial. Plato's views on language and reality and the relation between the two are a direct anticipation of the views of Russell on the isomorphic relation between an ideal language and reality. But by a curious semantic twist, the ideal language Plato speaks of and which he calls natural today would be called artificial. The old *nomos-physis* issue has been transformed in our time by the creation of "artificial" or "formalized" languages and thus becomes the issue of artificial versus natural languages. Today when one speaks of an artificial language, one means what Plato meant by a natural language, and what is meant in both cases is an ideal language.

In contemporary terminology, natural languages are those such as French or English spoken by a community of people in their daily dealings with their world. Even a language such as Esperanto, which is an artificial creation, qualifies as a natural language since it is meant to play exactly the same role as do existing natural languages and is in fact patterned after the structure and vocabulary of the major Western languages. An artificial language, on the other hand, is not only artificially invented but is devised with specific and limited purposes in mind. Unlike a natural language that serves diverse purposes in the daily lives of people, the function of an artificial language is to serve as perfect a vehicle as possible for one purpose only: expressing "information" about the world. The essential difference between the two sorts of language does not lie in the fact that natural languages are not a product of conscious reflection whereas artificial languages are. There is in fact no such thing as a truly natural language, for all linguistic meaning is a matter of convention and in this sense is artificial. Rather the difference between the two lies in the degree of formalization characteristic of the semiotic system in question. All languages, natural as well as artificial, are structured systems, but artificial languages are much more systematic than natural languages. It is essential to an artificial language that the rules of the system be explicitly formulated.

An artificial, formalized, or logistic language is a semiotic system wherein the rules governing the use of signs or symbols (vocabulary and syntax) are strictly specified and allow of no exception. These rules are of two sorts. *Semantic* rules specify the meaning or reference of the signs themselves. The basic requirement here is univocity. As Russell says, "A logically perfect language . . . has single symbols which always have a definite and unique meaning." Each symbol must refer to one thing only; its "meaning" must be precise and unambiguous. In comparison, the words (symbols, signs) of natural language are notoriously vague, ambiguous, and imprecise, since one word may refer to many different and unrelated things (what is here called a "thing," itself one of those ambiguous terms of natural language, Russell calls a "simple," an expression that betrays his Platonic prejudice that reality is divisible into distinct "kinds"). *Syntactical* rules prescribe how and in what order these symbols may be combined. The result is that in a "logically perfect language" one can immediately tell, from the form of the proposition, whether it is valid. As the logician I. M. Copi remarks, "There must be certain rules according to which some expressions will be derivable from other expressions in virtue of their forms or structures or shapes, without any attention having to be paid to their meanings.''[34] In other words, recourse to an artificial, formalized language relieves one "of the need to *think* about the actual propositions involved in distinguishing between valid and invalid arguments, since he can differentiate between them on the basis of differences in their *formulations,* which are open to direct visual or auditory inspection.''[35] In a formalized language everything is "out in the open," and there are no hidden elements or *sous-entendus* as is more often than not the case in natural language (formal languages are "literal" and allow for no irony), such that, as Copi so aptly says, one is in effect dispensed from having to think here. One has only to follow routinely the explicit rules of the code. In an artificial language meaning is an all-or-nothing affair; either a proposition is meaningful or it is not. There is no room for thought-provoking nonsense; the very notion would be a logical absurdity.

The result is that whereas natural languages are dynamic, artificial languages are static. The meaning of an utterance in natural language is often fluid and capable of further development because the meaning of words is ambiguous or polyvalent, but the meaning of the propositions of an artificial language are fully determinate and thus incapable of further development. This indeterminate character of natural language allows for the fabrication of metaphors (metaphors do not exist in logic), which introduces ever greater meaningfulness. The basic feature of new metaphors is that they cannot be predicted in advance and are genuinely free and creative. This is another way of saying, with Copi, that in regard to natural language "any rules which may be formulated are merely descriptive of past usage, not prescriptive for the future.''[36] Formalization does not generate increased, new (insightful) understanding; it serves only to systematize already acquired understandings. As Copi points out, "The axiomatic method is primarily a method for introducing *order* into an already developed field.''[37]

It could thus be said that formal or artificial languages are dead languages (is this perhaps why computers, which are certainly not living beings, are capable of "speaking" and "understanding" them?), whereas Sanskrit, classical Greek, and Latin are still much alive. A formalized language represents something like the state of entropy toward which all understanding tends when it expresses itself in the form of a system. By "entropy" we mean here stagnation and inertia. When applied to human understanding as such the term does not mean what it means in thermodynamics; it signifies not a degree of disorder in a system but a state of perfect order—order being expressive of pure synchronicity immune to the unsettling effect of diachronicity, that is, time. (Time is always the great enemy of order, but at the same time it is the essential characteristic of life. Cultures die when they become so rigidly systematized as not to allow for free, imaginative transformation.) An artificial language is the dead end toward which a natural language is always tending but from which it continually escapes anew thanks to metaphor, the effect of metaphor being to combat and overcome entropy.

It might be argued, however (as Copi does), that formal languages are capable of generating metaphors. Or a philosopher of science of the logical positivist sort might maintain that scientific discoveries are made by the use of formal calculi expressive of a deductive system. Both views are wrong—the first because it misrepresents metaphor and the second because it ignores the role that metaphor and analogy play in science. What then is metaphor?

If it can be determined what metaphor is and how it functions, it should be possible to see how human understanding functions and what creative insight actually consists in. Insightful understanding is inseparable from creative expression, and this occurs when an existing language is made to express something never before expressed in that language. *Metaphor* is the name for this process. The preceding section, which attempted to set forth a contextualist view of meaning, provides the context in which metaphor becomes understandable, for a metaphor is a certain way of using words that amounts to a "misuse" of them in terms of accepted use. Metaphors set up new meanings by altering existing systems of meaning.

A metaphor is a figure of speech that's a play on words. It is not, however, merely one figure of speech among many, as a traditional rhetorician might say, but coincides with the basic mechanism of all discourse, which gives rise to insightful understanding. As one writer remarks, "Metaphor is as ultimate as speech itself, and speech as ultimate as thought."[38] To speak of metaphor involves all of the problems of self-reference and circular implication involved in speaking about speech or attempting to understand understanding. The meaning of the word *metaphor* is itself metaphorical. *Metaphor* is the transliteration of μεταφορά, which derives from the verb μεταφέρειν, a combination of the words φέρειν ("to carry") and μετα ("beyond, across"). "To carry beyond" or "across" in Latin is *transferre,* whence derives *translatio.* A metaphor translates an old experience into a new one; in so doing it *transports* us into a new meaning. In this it illuminates (furnishes insight); it casts the old and familiar into a new and strange light and thereby endows it with a new meaning.

Metaphor is the essential mechanism of all insightful understanding, for genuine understanding—thinking—occurs whenever we successfully make the transition from what was formerly known to what was unknown. Understanding stems from a paradigm crisis, from an experience of puzzlement and frustration, and consists in the translation of one belief system into another or in the widening of a belief system and in the transportation from the old to the new. As W. T. Jones remarks:

> Whenever we encounter something novel in experience, something that none of the standard available descriptions quite fits, we can allay our curiosity only by misusing one of these standard descriptions—by twisting and distorting it into a new and "far-fetched" use, which exploits a hitherto unseen similarity.[39]

This is a perfect description of metaphor. Metaphor is nothing other than the misuse of a current idiom, a distorting of a literal, habitual meaning that makes evident previously unnoticed relations or similarities. To be able to see something as an instance of something else is what is meant by understanding (to understand is to interpret). Insightful understanding occurs when a language or system of meaning is stretched beyond its limits. Metaphor functions by extending a literal meaning; it explains the new and strange by linking it up with and likening it to what is already known, to what is old and familiar. To coin a metaphor is to sally forth against the unknown, to capture it, and force it back within the bounds (clôture) of a belief system. It is precisely by means of its misuse of a current idiom and its semantic impertinences that a metaphor has as its effect the setting up of new, enlarged semantic pertinences. It is in this interaction between the strange and the familiar that active understanding lies.

In his remarkable and ground-breaking work, *The Philosophy of Rhetoric,* I. A. Richards coined the terms *vehicle* and *tenor* to describe what he calls the "two halves of a metaphor."[40] The semantic vehicle is the already known; the semantic tenor is the unfamiliar or the less known. The "meaning" of the metaphor results from the interaction of the two "halves."[41] A paraphrase of Longfellow will do as an example: "People are (like) ships which pass in the night."[42] The tenor here, or what the metaphor is about, is the human condition, the relation between human beings. This is something less well known or understood than the experience many of us have had and the rest can easily imagine of ships passing one another in the night. By likening the less well known to the better known, we are able to see the former in a new light, and a new meaning is generated: "The co-presence of the vehicle and tenor results in a meaning (to be clearly distinguished from the tenor) which is not attainable without their interaction."[43] The meaning of a metaphor lies in the in between; in passing over from the vehicle to the tenor we are made to see the tenor in a new light.

Bruno Snell is making much the same point as Richards and, like him, is pointing to the fundamental role of metaphor in understanding—and self-understanding—when he says that human action requires "comparison to achieve full expression":

It appears, therefore, that one object is capable of casting fresh light upon another in the form of a simile, only because we read into the object the very qualities which it in turn illustrates. This peculiar situation, namely that human behavior is made clear only through reference to something else which is in turn explained by analogy with human behavior, pertains to all Homeric similes. More than that, it pertains to all genuine metaphors, and in fact to every single case of human comprehension. Thus it is not quite correct to say that the rock is viewed anthropomorphically [as when the immobility of the boulder in the surf is interpreted as endurance, as a human being endures in the midst of a threatening situation], unless we add that our understanding of the rock is anthropomorphic for the same reason that we are able to look at ourselves petromorphically, and that the act of regarding the rock in human terms furnishes us with a means of apprehending and defining our own behavior. In other words, and this is all-important in any explanation of the simile, man must listen to an echo of himself before he may hear or know himself.[44]

Only by comparing something with something else, by, that is, making an analogy, can we actively understand the first thing, even, and especially, when the thing to be understood is ourselves.

The views of Richards and Snell constitute an interaction theory of metaphor. According to this theory, what is basic to metaphor is not the concrete image it may or may not produce in our mind but the way it alters our thought about something—that is, the properly semantic pertinences it sets up when diverse semantic regions or contexts are made to interact.[45] "In the simplest formation, when we use a metaphor we have two thoughts of different things active together and supported by a single word, or phrase, whose meaning is a resultant of their interaction."[46] Philip Wheelwright, too, recognizes that "the test of essential metaphor is . . . the quality of semantic transformation that is brought about."[47] But he goes beyond Richards; instead of merely pointing out the elements of a metaphor (vehicle and tenor), he analyzes the different modes in which semantic transformation occurs. These two modes he terms *epiphor* and *diaphor*, both referring to the "two main elements of metaphoric activity."[48]

Epiphor (a term Wheelwright borrows from Aristotle) expresses the basic characteristic of metaphor we have been considering, that of "outstretching," of semantic motion (*phora*) wherein the well or concretely known (the vehicle) is used as a means for saying something about something less known or more obscurely known (the tenor). Epiphor is the comparing of the unfamiliar with the familiar. Thus, *for there to be epiphor there must be an accepted, literal meaning (a semantic home base) used in an unusual way*. A good metaphor, in the sense of epiphor, enables one to perceive similarities between things formerly held to be utterly dissimilar; "the comparison comes as a shock which is yet a shock of recognition."

There is, however, Wheelwright claims, more to metaphor than just epiphor. There is another kind of semantic movement: diaphor. This is an element Richards had noted, without, however, giving it a special name and without drawing all the necessary consequences.[49] In diaphor new meaning is generated not by comparison (extension of meaning) but by sheer juxtaposition. As an example Wheelwright cites the following verse of Ezra Pound:

> The apparition of these faces in the crowd;
> Petals on a wet, black bough.[50]

The key characteristic of diaphor is that there is no apparent likeness (no "imitative or mimetic factor") between the two units of the metaphorical utterance (faces in the crowd; petals on a bough).

Diaphor is to be found in its pure state in nonimitative music and thoroughly abstract painting. It is "the sheer presentation of diverse particulars in a newly designed arrangement," "the balance or reconciliation of opposite or discordant realities." Diaphor, it could be said, is the factor at work in the fabrication of collages, where thoroughly heterogeneous elements are juxtaposed with striking effect and where the arrangement is not based on recognized likenesses but where, rather, a likeness or "natural" affinity between the elements is first instituted by means of the gratuitous juxtapositon itself.[51] This reference to the plastic arts is no accident. As Wheelwright himself suggests, diaphor corresponds to what Coleridge called the "esemplastic" imagination. Diaphor is the essential element in dada art and in surrealist poetry.

Wheelwright insists that diaphor is indispensable to all poetic utterances, but, as opposed to its presence in music, in language it rarely stands alone but is usually combined with epiphor. The image that presides over most metaphorical combinations is, as Wheelwright says, one "already charged with partly understandable meanings and shared associations." This is to say that an image lacking these shared associations and without connotative value works diaphorically.

Wheelwright's distinction between epiphor and diaphor is highly interesting and useful, for the notion of diaphoric synthesis can provide a means for linking that semiotic system which is language with that other semiotic system which is music and, in so doing, justify the contextualist or structuralist theory of meaning set out in the preceding section. We saw how Merleau-Ponty likened language to music. Basically the way that language signifies is the same way that music signifies; in both cases meaning is inseparable from sound and, indeed, consists in the mutual interplay of concrete signs or sounds. The name for this interplay is diaphor. It is a fact, as Merleau-Ponty himself recognized, that language seems to be different from music; it seems to be immensely more transparent, more expressive, and more "meaningful" than music. This difference can, however, be accounted for with the aid of the notions of diaphor and epiphor. Sheer diaphoric synthesis is what one normally tends to label as meaningless because the elements juxtaposed seem to have nothing in common; they do not carry with them a set of overlapping associations. But if this indicates anything at all, it indicates that what we do call "meaning" is nothing other than the "system of associated commonplaces," to use Max Black's felicitous expression, which have grown up around certain semiotic signs and which have become habitual.[52] Indeed the source of the meaningfulness of new, epiphoric metaphors lies in the interference between two established semantic contexts.

Wheelwright's notion of diaphor is so interesting because it can serve to support the thesis we will want to set forth later: that the resemblances between disparate objects that a metaphor calls attention to and makes us aware of are not so much "discovered" by means of metaphor as "invented." As Wheelwright says, "The essential possibility of diaphor lies in the broad ontological fact that new qualities and new meanings can emerge, simply come into being, out of some hitherto ungrouped combinations of elements."[53] "Resemblances" and "similarities" are what are engendered in the first instance by sheer, gratuitous juxtaposition (diaphor). The reason for this is easy to see if one accepts the view of understanding put forward in chapter 3 and which Richards sums up when he says that the "mind is a connecting organ, it works only by connecting and it can connect any two things in an indefinitely large number of ways."[54] What, on the basis of Gestalt theory, Merleau-Ponty says of perception in general is eminently true of the affinity between the elements of a metaphor:

> There are not arbitrary data which set about combining into a thing because *de facto* proximities or likenesses cause them to associate; it is, on the contrary, because we perceive a grouping as a thing that the analytical attitude can then discern likenesses or proximities. This does not mean simply that without any perception of the whole we would not think of *noticing* the resemblance or the contiguity of its elements, but literally that they would not be part of the same world and would not exist at all.[55]

The juxtaposition of disparate elements and contexts creates for the understanding a tension (puzzlement), which can be relieved only by its inventing a reason for the juxtaposition; the two different orders of experience reflected in vehicle and tenor must be related. Diaphor is *creative* of meanings, meanings that afterward can be extended and transferred to other realms by means of epiphor.

To return to metaphor in the traditional sense, as a transfer of meaning, it must indeed be recognized that there is more to most metaphors than the merely diaphoric element of sheer novelty. Novelty and linguistic oddity is one basic, indeed indispensable, characteristic of newly invented metaphors, but it is far from being the only one, for it is insufficient to account for the fact that most metaphors not only surprise us but are meaningful and understandable at once. Good inventive metaphors give not only a shock but a shock of recognition.[56] As Aristotle remarked, "Strange words simply puzzle us; ordinary words convey only what we know already; it is from metaphor that we can best get hold of something fresh."[57] How do metaphors do this?

Metaphor is defined traditionally as the substitution of one word for another, as, so to speak, a switching (transfer) of labels (names), but this definiton does not go nearly far enough. I. A. Richards holds that metaphor is not merely a shift of words but of interaction between thoughts, between semantic contexts. "Thought," he said, "is metaphoric, and proceeds by comparison, and the metaphors of language derive therefrom."[58] This insight has been further developed by Nelson Goodman. "An understanding of metaphor further requires," he says, "the recognition that a label functions not in isolation but as belonging to a family."[59] Words function never in isolation but always as members of a family or schema. The range of meaning of terms belonging to a family is what Goodman calls a "realm." "New metaphor typically involves a change not merely of range but also of realm"[60]—as when color words are applied to a sphere of noncolored objects such as feelings ("a blue mood"). Thus what occurs in a metaphor is the transfer not merely of words but of whole sets of contexts, of schemata, of conceptual frameworks, of categories.[61]

This is an important realization, for it can account for the properly heuristic value of good metaphors. Where one transports a schema to is purely arbitrary, but once the new territory has been chosen, the application of the alien schema is fully guided by rules. When we use terms from one domain (the vehicle) to describe another domain (the tenor), the way in which we apply the terms is determined or guided by the way in which we use them in their home territory. The habitual and antecedent use of terms serves as a guide when they are used in another realm to describe a less familiar subject matter. As Chaim Perelman observes, "Analogies are important in invention and argumentation because they facilitate the development and extension of thought. With the phoros [vehicle] as starting point, they make it possible to give the theme [tenor] a structure and to give it a conceptual setting."[62]

The essential affinity between metaphors and models thus becomes apparent, and it can be seen what it means to speak of metaphors as illuminating or insightful. Metaphorical language is illuminating and gives rise to new understanding in that it serves as a guide in the exploration of a new territory. In its epiphoric role of model, metaphor enables us to orientate ourselves and get our bearings in a new land. Metaphors are not merely decorative elements, therefore, which embellish talk about what is already known but are the very means whereby we first come to understand and orientate ourselves in the strange and unfamiliar. And this is what justifies one in speaking about the truth-value of metaphors. Metaphors are true in the proper sense of the term, if by truth we mean the ability of an idea or utterance to lead us from the known to the unknown. As William James says, "The essential thing is the process of being guided."[63] "New truth," he says, "is always a go-between, a smoother-over of transition."[64] Metaphors possess truth-value, therefore, because their essential function is to "carry us prosperously from any one part of our experience to any other part."[65] They are something, as James would say, "upon which we can ride." Metaphor is the vehicle of all insightful understanding, the source of all original truth.

But it must also be remembered that, like understanding in general, metaphorical understanding is relative. Just as insight transforms itself into unreflective, habitual praxis, so also do living metaphors transform themselves into dead metaphors, into literal truths that are taken for granted and no longer provoke surprise. Once the epiphoric transfer becomes a beaten track, living metaphor loses one of its essential elements: the diaphoric, or novelty and oddness. And as Ian Ramsey correctly observes, "What is not verbally odd is void of disclosure power."[66]

Although an open-minded rationalist like Aristotle might agree with much of what has been said here, particularly with the idea that metaphors have truth-value, nevertheless he would wish to maintain that metaphors are truthful in spite of their oddity because they point to something "objectively true" about the world, something that could be expressed in a straightforward way. Metaphorical creativity is merely a means of discovering objective truths; analogy is merely a means of getting at univocal universals. For the rationalist, a metaphor is a misuse of language, although one that sometimes has redeeming value. A metaphor is an equivocation. It is an equivocation (to use Aristotle's example in *Topics,* 107a17) when one speaks both of a musical note and a knife as being sharp, for a musical note and a knife belong to two different categories (quality and substance, respectively). In confusing a quality with a substance, one is violating categorical differences. A metaphor, to employ Gilbert Ryle's expression, is a kind of calculated "category mistake." It violates a conceptual taboo (and this is why scientists and especially logicians usually react, when they are thinking scientifically or logically, to metaphor with a kind of holy horror). It is, however, a justifiable or allowable mistake since, as the rationalist will argue, one can always restore the "proper" meaning of the term predicated ("sharp") by distinguishing between its different senses and locating the universal core, which is being applied analogously and improperly.

With this latter point we are, however, obliged to disagree, since it is a version of the proper meaning superstition. To say, as Aristotle does, that "metaphor consists in giving the thing a name that belongs to something else"[67] is to presuppose that there is a univocal core to the meaning of words and, moreover, that this universal meaning is determined by the nature of the things themselves. For a rationalist philosophy or a philosophy of essence (categories), metaphors must appear as equivocations, and in such a philosophy there must be a sharp difference between literal and metaphorical discourse, between proper and improper (though perhaps justifiable) expression. This difference between the two modes of discourse is only relative, however, and the expression *category mistake* is itself misleading when used to describe metaphor. It embodies, in the words of Richards, the "worst assumption—that metaphor is something special and exceptional in the use of language, a deviation from its normal mode of working, instead of the omnipresent principle of all its free action."[68]

If one is merely describing the use of metaphor by viewing it against the background on which it appears—the established, literal meaning of terms—then one can properly speak of it as a misuse of language and as a kind of category mistake.[69] But just as we saw that it was impossible to say that habitual understanding (the background of insight) is prior to insightful understanding in any absolute sense, so also here it must be realized that the literal meaning of terms is not absolutely more basic than the metaphorical meaning. The literal meaning is simply the one that has become habitual, which is to say that in its origin there is nothing "natural" or "proper" about it. It can therefore be wondered if metaphors do no more than merely link up already well-defined categorical sets. Does it not in fact have to be said that *the norms and categories that metaphor violates are themselves products of previous metaphors, which have become moribund?*

It is with a question similar to this that Goodman leaves us when he says, "The question why predicates apply as they do metaphorically is much the same as the question why they apply as they do literally."[70] He admits that he has "no good answer" to this question but suggests that perhaps it is because "there is no real question." His analysis of metaphor breaks off inconclusively at this point. The question of why things are said to have the properties they have and why they are the way they are is a question he says he is "content to leave to the cosmologist." At least Goodman does realize that with this question we come up against a properly cosmological or, to express the matter better, a properly ontological question. This should come as no surprise to us because questions about language are inseparable from questions about reality. The question Goodman leaves with and that English-language philosophy in general, with its traditional formalistic, antimetaphysical bias has neglected to pursue, is one we cannot afford to ignore.

Access to the ontological question from a consideration of metaphor is gained when we inquire into the reason for the similarities between things that metaphor is said to disclose. This question can be formulated in the following way: Is metaphor merely the means for discovering pre-existent relations between things, or is it rather the case that the likenesses that metaphor articulates are actually, in a very important sense, created by metaphor?

The rationalist position is well stated by Aristotle: "The greatest thing by far is to be a master of metaphor." So far, so good. But he goes on to say, "It is the one thing that cannot be learnt from others; and it is also a sign of genius, since *a good metaphor implies an intuitive perception of the similarity in dissimilars.*"[71] This is an unacceptable position, for it implies that metaphor involves the perception (by means of a special faculty called "genius") of objective similarities and relations that exist somehow *in rebus*. Moreover, these similarities could be expressed more directly and less ambiguously in literal language. Rhetoric is "concerned with appearances," and metaphor is really nothing more than decoration:

> We ought in fairness to fight our case with no help beyond the bare facts [note the unacknowledged metaphor]: nothing, therefore, should matter except the proof of those facts. Still, as has been already said, other things affect the result considerably, owing to the defects of our hearers. The arts of language cannot help having a small but real importance, whatever it is we have to expound to others: the way in which a thing is said does affect its intelligibility. Not, however, so much importance as people think. All such arts are fanciful and meant to charm the hearer. Nobody uses fine language when teaching geometry.[72]

Hobbes, a Puritan who believed in the virtues of plain style and, like other Puritans in general, was singularly devoid of imaginative ability, is merely drawing out Aristotelian rationalism to its ludicrous conclusion when he says:

> In demonstration, in counsel, and all rigorous search of truth, judgment does all, except sometimes the understanding have need to be opened by some apt similitude, and then there is so much use of fancy. But for metaphors, they are in this case utterly excluded. For seeing they openly profess deceit, to admit them into counsel or reasoning were manifest folly.[73]

A position with more nuances is that of Max Black who says, "It would be more illuminating in some . . . cases to say that the metaphor creates the similarity than to say that it formulates some similarity antecedently existing."[74] But even this is not a fully satisfactory position, for although it is more qualified than the former ones it does not represent a clear-cut, decisive alternative to the rationalist position, and it is just such an alternate theory that we are looking for and need. In particular, Black does not sufficiently distinguish between living (creative) and dead (decorative) metaphor and does not recognize that rationalism speaks only of the latter (in the case of living, genuinely innovative metaphor the similarity is always "created"). If it is recognized that in a sense everything in nature is like everything else or, as Anaxagoras said (fr. 18), "in everything there is a portion of everything," it must be recognized that there can be no antecedent reason for comparing any one particular thing than any other (except force of habit) and that, accordingly, the similarities a metaphor expresses are not merely brought to light by metaphor but are actually constituted by it.

A theory more responsive to our needs is the one set forth by Gadamer, who speaks of the "fundamental metaphorical nature" of linguistic consciousness.[75] "The well-known stylistic device of the metaphor," he says, "is only the rhetorical form of this universal—both linguistic and logical—generative principle." Universal concepts are actually the products of analogical thinking and speaking, he maintains ("the living metaphorical nature of language, on which all natural concept formation depends"). Logic, however, loses sight of this fact, of "the intimate unity of speech and thought" and proceeds to hypostatize meanings and to endow them with an objective existence. It loses sight of the fact that metaphor and analogy are the origin of the concepts and essences that scientific discourse claims as its special, independent objects.[76] A position such as Gadamer's would seem to require the abandonment of the rationalist notion that there are objective essences that language merely articulates. Language is, rather, the creative source of essences, of genus and species, of "objective" relations.

Paul Ricoeur is pursuing much the same line of thought when he speaks of his "most extreme hypothesis, that the 'metaphoric' that transgresses the categorial order also begets it."[77] He writes:

> The idea of category mistake brings us close to our goal. Can one not say that the strategy of language at work in metaphor consists in obliterating the logical and established frontiers of language, in order to bring to light new resemblances the previous classification kept us from seeing? In other words, the power of metaphor would be to break an old categorization, in order to establish new logical frontiers on the ruins of their forerunners.
>
> Advancing still another step, can we not hypothesize that the dynamic of thought that carves its way through already established categories is the same as that which engenders all classification? . . . one can propose that the figure of speech we call metaphor, and that appears first of all as a phenomenon of deviation in relation to an established usage, is homogeneous with a process that has given rise to all the "semantic fields," and thus to the very usage from which metaphor deviates. The same operation that lets us "see the similar" also "teaches the genus."[78]

If one accepts such a hypothesis, as we do, one can no longer, without inconsistency, maintain that the essential function of language is, as Russell maintains, to refer to an extralinguistic reality. What one normally takes to be the objective referent of language is in fact the correlate of a dead metaphor. Reality (in the usual sense of this term) and essences are nothing other than metaphors that are taken literally and are believed in. "Reality," as Wallace Stevens says, "is a cliché from which we escape by metaphor."[79]

It thus appears that a theory that recognizes the fundamental metaphorical nature of linguistic consciousness and sees in the metaphor and in analogical thinking the origin of all objective similarities calls for an appropriate metaphysics. If language and understanding are vitally and thoroughly metaphorical, Reality itself—that expressed and understood by means of living metaphor—must be fully alive and must, like metaphorical discourse, transcend all established classifications and logical categories. To the analogy of language and understanding must correspond an analogy of being. If we take the metaphor seriously, we must inevitably ask, as Ricoeur does, "What actually is reality?" Do we still know what reality and truth mean? One of the merits of Wheelwright's study of metaphor is that it does not hesitate to draw some of the ontological conclusions that seem called for.[80] We shall have to do the same once we have completed our survey of the nature and scope of human understanding.

I stated above that a consideration of metaphor would likely have a retro-effect on the notion of analogy. For the rationalist, analogical predication is based on resemblances, and, as one considers the propriety of such predication, three types can be discerned. In a descending order of propriety they are: analogy of attribution, analogy of proper proportionality, and metaphorical analogy. In attempting to understand either being (Aristotle) or God (Saint Thomas), analogy of attribution is said to have the greatest cognitive or truth-value and metaphorical analogy the least. If, however, the rationalist belief in objective essences or categories is rejected and it is maintained that objective relations and analogies are themselves the products of analogical discourse and specifically of metaphorical discourse, then the order of importance among the three types of analogy must be reversed. It is this "reversal" that we propose to attempt in this section. To do so it will be necessary to take note of some additional features of metaphorical discourse.

Traditionally metaphorical analogy is distinguished from analogy of proper proportionality in that the latter is held to be based on genuine, objective resemblances between the things talked about, whereas the former is not. Metaphor is thus an analogy of improper proportionality. To speak metaphorically of a "smiling meadow" is a roundabout way of saying, "The field in the beauty of its flowering is like to the beauty of the human

smile by proportionate likeness."[81] A rationalist account of metaphor reduces it to a kind of simile, and the "like" of a simile in turn is interpreted
in a strictly logical sense as expressing an identity of relation.

In reducing analogical likeness to logical identity, the rationalist also reduces analogy of proper proportionality to analogy of attribution. Just as
he seeks to spell out the exact literal sense of a term used metaphorically, so
also he attempts to specify the exact nature of the relation between the two
proportions in an analogy of proper proportionality. If, for instance, one
predicates being of God and says that as a person exists, so also in a somehow analogous way does God, but if one wishes to add—as one must in theology—that the term *exist* is used here in neither the same way nor in totally
different ways, that it is applied at the same time in similar and dissimilar
senses, the rationalist may remark that this way of speaking occasions considerable difficulties from a logical point of view. And indeed it does. It is
thus perfectly understandable that both Aristotle and Saint Thomas should
favor analogy of attribution when talking about being or God.[82] After
remarking how Thomas comes to emphasize analogy of attribution in his
later writings, Frederick Copleston expresses good logical sense when he
says:

> Some Scholastics have maintained that being, for example, is predicable of
> God and creatures only by analogy of proportionality and not by analogy of
> attribution. Without, however, wishing to enter on a discussion of the value of
> analogy of proportionality as such, I do not see how we could know that God
> has any perfection save by way of the analogy of attribution. All analogical
> predication rests on the real relation of likeness of creatures to God, and it
> seems to me that the analogy of proportionality presupposes analogy of pro-
> portion or attribution and that the latter is the more fundamental of the two
> kinds of analogy.[83]

That rationalism tends to reduce all forms of analogy to analogy of attribution (wherein the term predicated is accorded a univocal, unambiguous
meaning) serves to demonstrate, negatively, that the increase in logical exactitude gained in this way is paid for by an inability to make sense of
metaphorical analogy and of analogy of proper proportionality in their own
right. For rationalism it is impossible that metaphor be anything else than
an improper use of words (the substitution of one word for another), having
at the most merely decorative value. If, however, the properly heuristic
function of metaphor is recognized, the rationalist position becomes
untenable because it is unduly constrictive. Contrary to rationalism,
therefore, it must be maintained that metaphorical "likeness" is prior to
and more basic to the life of understanding than logical "identity." A genuine metaphorical analogy is irreducible to any other form of analogy.[84]

One cannot take metaphor to be an analogy of improper proportionality without presupposing "propriety" as the basic criterion of meaning—that is, without becoming a victim of the proper meaning superstition and without reducing analogy of proper proportionality to analogy of attribution. To suggest, with Copi, that formalized languages are capable of generating metaphors is simply to confuse metaphorical analogy with analogy of proper proportionality and to view the latter as a variant of analogy of attribution. The only "metaphors" that an artificial, dead language would be capable of producing would be artificial, dead ones (of the merely decorative sort)—dead because as an expression of an already systematized, habitual understanding, they would be incapable of generating new, insightful understanding and could never serve to revolutionize the conceptual, categorical system that produced them. Such metaphors would be stillborn. This is to say that metaphors are based, as the rationalist would have it, on pre-existent similarities to the exact degree that they are dead metaphors.

All logicist accounts of metaphor tend to lose sight of the basic, indispensable element of living, innovative metaphor: the diaphoric, gratuitous juxtaposition of terms, which cannot be explained in terms of antecedent likeness but is itself generative of such likeness. All good metaphors have a kind of "take-it-or-leave-it" quality. This is not to say, though, that they cannot be paraphrased. They must have this quality if one is to speak of them as having meaning, for only that is meaningful which can be translated. Our criterion for saying that a newly invented metaphor is meaningful is that we can construct glosses on it and can interpret what it says in terms of the categories operative in an established system of linguistic meaning. A good metaphor will generate a good deal of commentary. It is productive of further discourse, and this in fact is our criterion for assessing the worth of metaphors. But a good metaphor is never fully translatable; no one interpretation will ever exhaust its suggestiveness, and far from ending up with a purely literal paraphrase, one will usually find that in the attempt to paraphrase the original metaphor one is led to invent further ones.[85]

Unlike logical formalization, which only structures what one already knows, a good metaphor can serve as the means for new insight and increased understanding because it always "says more than it says." Good metaphors, like provocative symbols, are overdetermined.[86] They are of the very essence of creative language, whose function it is to give rise constantly to the various structured worlds in which people live. "A 'closed' syntax, a formally exhaustible semantics, would be a closed world," George Steiner remarks. "New worlds are born between the lines." And thus, as Steiner also says, "Ambiguity, polysemy, opaqueness, the violation of grammatical and logical sequences, reciprocal incomprehensions, the capacity to lie—these are not pathologies of language but the root of its genius. Without them the individual and the species would have withered."[87]

Just as human understanding is of two basic kinds—habit and insight—so also is human discourse. To use Wheelwright's terms, there is the "steno-language" (closed, block language) of either everyday, unimaginative discourse or of logic (the difference between the two being that the latter is closed by stipulation), and there is the "tensive" language of living metaphor. The two differ not as much in kind as in degree: "The former may be conceived roughly as the limit toward which language tends as its connotative fullness and tensive aliveness diminish."[88]

One of the most significant differences between these two types of language is that unlike steno-language, which is meant to be taken in a straightforward and literal way as the unqualified statement of a state of affairs, the tensive language of metaphor is indirect and intrinsically qualified. Metaphorical language has a kind of built-in self-destructing mechanism that prevents it from being taken in literal earnestness or dead seriousness. The metaphorical "is" is "tensive"; metaphorical language is playful language where the "is" always includes an implicit "is not," for to see something as something else (my loved one as a rose, man as a wolf) requires at the same time a realization that the one thing is not the other thing (if this is not realized, the metaphor ceases to be a metaphor). To say that something is like something else is to say that it both is and is not that other thing.

The tensive language of living metaphor is thus a language that says that something both is and is not something else and refuses to be understood in terms merely of the logician's either-or. It transcends all of the so-called laws of logic: identity, contradiction, excluded middle. As the Spanish storyteller signals the beginning of his story with the phrase, *Aixo era y no era* ("It was and it wasn't"),[89] or, as in Turkish at the other extremity of the Mediterranean one says in a similar situation, *Bir var mış bir yok muş* ("Once there was, once there wasn't"), so also a good metaphor refuses to be taken literally. In doing so it cancels out what it says in such a way as to merely show what it means. At the moment in metaphorical discourse when language achieves its greatest expressiveness, it reaches beyond itself and says nothing but merely hints. As Heraclitus said of the Oracle at Delphi, it "neither speaks out nor conceals, but gives a sign." By means of its elusiveness, metaphor discloses the mystery of being. The reality it speaks of both is and is-not.

This is-and-is-not feature of metaphorical discourse characterizes everything Saint Thomas has to say about God. When, for instance, in a supposed analogy of attribution, he says that God is wise, he invariably qualifies this assertion by saying that divine wisdom is not the same as human wisdom. Because God is infinitely perfect and humans are constitutionally imperfect, there cannot be a perfect relation or likeness (proportion) between a human attribution and a divine one; *inter finitum et infinitum non est proportio,* as Nicholas of Cusa was later to say. Thus the creature in his wisdom is at one and the same time both like and unlike God. This kind of is-and-is-not of theological analogy signals that the real mode of analogy at work here is metaphorical analogy, which is trying to hide the fact from itself. Thomas, whose goal was to raise theology to the level of a science, could not have admitted that his discourse was metaphorical, given his rationalist view of metaphor, as an analogy of improper proportionality. He would have thought that to recognize the metaphorical character of his language about God would be to deprive it of all truth-value.[90]

There is thus more to Thomas's practice than filters through into his rationalist theories: the net result of all of his statements about God is no different from metaphorical discourse about God. In both cases the important thing is not what the analogy says but what, by means of it saying, it shows. The peculiarity of metaphorical language is that it reaches beyond itself; what the metaphor does rather than what it says (literally) constitutes its meaning. The "meaning" of metaphorical discourse is nothing other than the practical transformation it brings about in the speaking and listening subject, the orientation it communicates to understanding. That this is precisely what is all important in Saint Thomas's talk about God is well brought out by Etienne Gilson:

> All these judgments direct our understanding toward the same goal, the direction of which is known to us but which, because it is at infinity, is beyond the reach of our natural forces. For we do not attain it by multiplying the affirmative propositions which denote it. But yet to make these propositions is neither to waste our words nor our efforts because *it is at least to turn ourselves toward Him.*[91]

In other words, if they are taken to be literally affirmative propositions, Thomas's utterances about God do not succeed in expressing their object and thereby fail to be meaningful. If, however, they are viewed in another light, in regard to what they succeed in doing for our understanding of God, which is to say, our relation to God, they are successful for they serve to "turn ourselves toward Him." It is as metaphors that they have truth-value.

Thus like all other good metaphorical language, the important thing about Thomas's language about God is not so much what it says, but what, by means of this saying, it does. Thomas's practice, as described by Gilson, is a perfect illustration of one feature of analogical, metaphorical discourse, as Perelman pointed out: "One special technique is to use several phoroi [vehicles] to make a single theme [tenor, such as God] understood. Such a procedure emphasizes the inadequacy of each phoros [vehicle] taken separately but *at the same time impresses a general direction on thought.*"[92] In this regard it is interesting to note that Thomas's technique is not all that different from the one used by Heidegger in his later work where he employs different metaphors to express Being. The net result is that the different metaphors cancel themselves out, in such a way as to provoke "an experience with language," which has as its effect "a transformation of thinking."[93]

In the end one seems to detect underneath Thomas's positive rationalist theology and his Aristotelian ancestry an undercurrent of negative theology and a certain affinity with Dionysius when the latter says, "While He possesses all the positive attributes of the universe (being the Universal Cause), yet, in a more strict sense, He does not possess them, since He transcends them all; wherefore there is no contradiction between the affirmations and the negations, inasmuch as He infinitely precedes all conceptions of deprivation, being beyond all positive and negative distinction."[94] Only metaphor can reveal God as He truly is, as something totally surpassing our ability to understand what He is. As Thomas himself says, "God's existence is the same as His substance, and as His substance is unknown so also is His existence."[95] As far, at least, as human understanding goes, God both is and is not.

In the end Thomas came to "know that Unknowing, which is enshrouded under all that is known and all that can be known."[96] Even before he underwent the strange and unknown experience during the celebration of Mass on the feast of Saint Nicholas in the year 1273, which put an end to his writing and which led him to say to his secretary, "All that I have hitherto written seems to me nothing but straw," he had written in the *Liber de Veritate Catholicae Fidei contra errores Infidelium (Summa contra Gentiles): Tunc enim solum Deum vere cognoscimus quando ipsum esse credimus supra omni id quod de Deo cognitari ab homine possibile est* ("For then only do we know God truly when we believe Him to be above everything that it is possible for man to think about Him").[97]

The link between analogical and metaphorical predication, on the one hand, and negative theology (or ontology), on the other, cannot be overemphasized, as we shall indeed see when in chapter 9 we attempt to spell out the ontological implications of our theory of human understanding.

Taking the metaphor as a model, it is possible to specify the nature of the creative act. Like metaphorical thinking, creative thinking is essentially analogical. Creative insight arises when two hitherto unrelated frames of reference or "systems of associated commonplaces" are made to, or happen to, interact. "Not that one is the first to see something new," as Nietzsche says, "but that one sees as *new* what is old, long familiar, seen and overlooked by everybody is what distinguishes truly original minds."[98] Creativity lies not in what one sees (as if it consisted in the "discovery" of new "facts") but in how one sees. The essence of the creative act, as of the metaphorical process, is to take what "custom had bedimmed" (Coleridge) and infuse it with a new light. All understanding is interpretation, is a seeing-as, and creative understanding is simply seeing something otherwise than before.

People do not exist in a void. To be is to be in a world, and to understand is to conform to or to transform a particular reality. All understanding, and thus all creative understanding, is culture and history bound. Unlike the divine act of creation, the human creative act never arises out of nothing. Strictly speaking, therefore, people never create or invent anything at all—radically, *ex nihilo*. They are limited to working with the elements they already possess in some way or another. What happens in the creative act is that one rearranges one's system of understanding. The painter, for instance, subjects his vision of things to a "coherent deformation" (Malraux), and the writer shakes up "the linguistic or narrative apparatus in order to tear a new sound from it."[99] As Merleau-Ponty also remarked:

> It is essential to what is true to be presented first, last, and always in a movement which throws our image of the world out of focus, distends it, and draws it toward fuller meaning. It is thus that the auxiliary line introduced into a diagram opens the road to new relations. It is thus that the work of art operates and will always operate upon us—as long as there are works of art.[100]

Creative work is, to use the expression of Lévi-Strauss, a kind of *bricolage*—a tinkering around with the inner arrangement of a system. The heart of this process is analogy: seeing a likeness between hitherto disparate elements and combining them anew, restructuring a system of categories. Meaning is nothing other than pattern or arrangement, and new meanings are generated by rearranging the elements of a system. Pushed to its limits, this repatterning can produce an altogether new system.

Thus one way of characterizing the creative act is to say that it involves the undoing of a current system and the rearrangement of its constituent elements in a new pattern. Although this would be correct of some instances of creative thinking, it would not be of all or, for that matter, of the most interesting, for it must be remembered that the "facts" are what they are only in terms of the system, or, as one anthropologist remarks, "an element, in passing over from one context to another, tends to have its character made over to fit the new setting."[101] There is no such thing as brute "information," which is merely structured in different ways. Alchemy, for instance, differs from chemistry not, as is usually and naively thought, in that it imposes a different (and superstitious) interpretation on the same "basic facts" that chemistry also seeks to explain. In reality, it deals with an entirely different set of "facts"—alchemic "matter" is totally different from chemical "matter"—and this is why all attempts to reduce alchemy to primitive chemistry are misguided and incapable of enabling one to understand properly what exactly alchemy is and how it can continue to exist alongside modern chemistry.[102]

The notion of *bricolage* must therefore be nuanced: when one "tinkers" with a system in such a way as to alter its basic categorical structure, it is the "facts" themselves that are transmuted. "New" facts emerge as soon as one changes one's categorical lenses. The creative rearrangement of a system itself is enough to generate new "information." When our way of viewing the world is changed, so also is the world that is there to be viewed. As Wallace Stevens aptly remarks, "Metaphor creates a new reality from which the original appears to be unreal."[103]

The notion of contextual meaning is essential for an understanding of the creative act. Creative insight is "a disclosure associated with a tangential meeting of two diverse contexts."[104] One should not, however, be too quick to equate context with linguistic context unless one is prepared to take language in a very broad sense as designative of any semiotic system. James hesitated to reduce thinking to language, though he did recognize that some sort of symbolism or imagery is necessary to thought. The case of Einstein can serve to show that while creative thinking may not, in its formative stage, necessitate the use and manipulation of words, it does require signs of one sort or another and consists in their systematic interplay.

Einstein possessed a very vivid visual imagination, and for him an operative concept was nothing other than a particular image that, turning up in many different series of images, served to connect and structure them. He did not arrive at his theories by means of mathematical calculation; this came only later once he had already visualized the arrangement of the theory.[105] The important thing here is not that he thought with images but that his thought consisted in the systematic ordering of these images. What is important is not the existence of an isolated image (any more than an isolated word) but its recurrence. By this an image (like a word) functions as a linguistic concept, a *verbum mentis*. A concept expresses a recognizable and recurrent pattern.

The net effect in Einstein's case of mental bricolage was that he was able to perceive inconsistencies in contemporary physics that were nonexistent for others and, once having done so, was able to reconcile them through a restructuring of the entire system of physics. The historian of science, Gerald Holton, remarks:

> A . . . creative use of apparent opposites can be found in Einstein's contribution to quantum physics, centering on the wave-particle duality. It really is the hallmark of Einstein's most famous contribution that he could deal with, use, illuminate, transform the existence of apparent contradictories or opposites, sometimes in concepts that had not been widely perceived to have polar character. One need only think of his bridging of mechanics and electrodynamics,

energy and mass, space coordinates and time coordinates, inertial mass and gravitational mass.[106]

Arthur Koestler has coined the term *bisociation* to refer to this fundamental characteristic of the creative act, the merging of disparate contexts, and the seeing a likeness or affinity where before only insignificant difference was perceived. Referring to Einstein as well he writes:

> From Pythagoras, who combined arithmetic and geometry, to Newton, who combined Galileo's studies of the motion of projectiles with Kepler's equations of planetary orbits, to Einstein, who unified energy and matter in a single sinister equation, the pattern is always the same. The creative act does not create something out of nothing, like the God of the Old Testament; it combines, reshuffles and relates already existing but hitherto separate ideas, facts, frames of perception, associative contexts. This act of cross-fertilization—or self-fertilization within a single brain—seems to be the essence of creativity, and to justify the term "bisociation."[107]

Viewed in terms of the system of understanding out of which it arises, the creative act always involves a kind of "category mistake." *Cogito,* Koestler observes, come from *coagitare,* "to shake together."[108] Creative thinking is "the coagitation or shaking together of already existing but previously separate areas of knowledge, frames of perception or universes of discourse."[109] Creative vision, like metaphorical vision, is a "stereo-vision," a sudden seeing of something in the mixed light of two equally systematic but mutually incompatible (because habitually unassociated) universes of discourse or frames of reference. From this it follows that creative insight is a very transitory phenomenon.

An interesting feature of Koestler's treatment of creativity is the way he relates and distinguishes three types of bisociation: the comic, the scientific, and the artistic, which he labels, respectively, the HAHA! reaction, the AHA reaction, and the AH . . . reaction. Comedy is the collision of two different contexts, science is their fusion, and art (and ultimately mysticism) is their juxtaposition or coexistence. [110] The three reactions form a continuum and merge into one another, yet at either end of the spectrum, the comic and the artistic have this in common that the syntheses they effect are not cumulative in the way scientific ones tend to be but rather are such that they need to be effected ever anew. This is precisely what accounts for the quasi-timeless character of art. But in all three cases insightful understanding fades once the interaction between contexts ceases to surprise. Creative visions transform themselves into clichés.

This is why creative thinking is not logico-deductive thinking. The latter is a skill, a habit, a permanent characteristic of understanding. The basic rule here is that of discipline: one should confine oneself to a particular universe of discourse and not shift back and forth from one to another. From the point of view of logic, creative metaphors quite rightly are labeled "category mistakes." But the result of logico-deductive thinking is that by means of it we never come up with anything "new" but only spell out more clearly and redundantly what was already implicitly contained in our starting point. Deductive thinking (like Kuhn's "mopping-up" operations in science) is merely the amplification of a given frame of reference. Creative thinking proceeds in a different direction; it does not *amplify* what was already known but *merges* two hitherto unrelated frames of reference. It consists in what Koestler calls "thinking aside" and is, in the terms of the psychologist, Edward de Bono, "lateral" thinking as opposed to "vertical" thinking.[111] The result of creative insight is to set up a new starting point, which routine thinking will then build upon. (Compare Kuhn's distinction between extraordinary and normal science.) Creative thinking thus obeys the rules not of logic but of analogic; it consists not in the elimination of the ambiguities in a system (in such a way as to make it more "systematic") but in their exploitation (in such a way as, ultimately, to undo the system and set up a new one in its place).[112]

The art of thinking not logically but analogically and of playing with ambiguities in such a way as to undo old worlds and set up new ones, new universes of discourse, new objects of belief, is the art of imagination. A perfectly ordered system or a perfectly logical language would be one that left no room for the play of the imagination and could no longer serve to generate new, insightful understanding. As polysemy is the necessary condition for metaphor, so ambiguity and paradox is the indispensable basis for all creative insight. A formalized language is highly efficient when it is merely a matter of handling information already acquired or new information that can easily be sorted into the logical pigeonholes of the language. But a formalized language is incapable of responding to radically new situations where it is necessary for understanding to restructure itself radically if it is to overcome the challenge.

A fundamental, and thus highly instructive, analogy can be drawn between linguistic or belief systems, on the one hand, and biosystems or ecosystems, on the other. In the case of the latter, it is known that the system, whether it is the human body or a colony of bacteria, is a much less efficient system than the artificial ones designed or capable of being designed by engineers. Artificial systems can be constructed that surpass in efficiency any natural system, and the temptation is great, in our increasingly technologically planned, "rationalized" society, to "improve" upon nature (for example, by devising new, superproductive strains of wheat). There is a great danger in this, however, for it is precisely the "inefficiency" of living systems that accounts for their long-range survival ability. What nature strives for is not the maximum of efficiency but a trade-off between effi-

ciency and survival ability. In the short run, a certain amount of inefficiency is the necessary condition for a system's resilience and long-range
survival. It is the same with language: ambiguity in the use of words—which
must give rise to a certain amount of misunderstanding in communication
(inefficency)—is the necessary condition for linguistic evolution and for the
furthering of understanding.

From a purely descriptive standpoint, this is all that need be said to characterize the creative act. The great merit of this kind of approach is that it
accounts not only for the creative act but also, at one and the same time, for
the object of creative understanding. From a reflective-pragmatic point of
view, *to describe the act of understanding is to account for the constitution
of what is understood.* If the "referent" of language is a "function" of the
linguistic "meaning," and if the latter is a matter of context and structure,
then one is not obliged, after accounting for the creative act, to account for
what, in the traditional rationalist view of these matters, is and must remain
highly mysterious: the fact that by means of creativity one *"discovers"*
something "objectively true" about the "real world." This is no longer a
problem since it can now be seen that what language supposedly refers to is
inseparable from language. To use language creatively is *eo ipso* to en-
gender a new semantic construct, a new reality, a new object of belief.

Nevertheless, there is a further element in the creative process, indeed an
indispensable one, but it cannot be accounted for by the purely contextual
or semiotic mode of analysis adopted in this chapter. Various creative alternatives arise by the sheer manipulation of an accepted system and by the
merging of different contexts. But what inclines one to opt for one particular creative alternative and to reject others? In virtue of what is judgment
exercised here? What motivates one in deciding that a particular creative alternative arrived at through the process described above is "interesting,"
"promising," "worthwhile," "good," and that certain others are not? The
only possible answer to this question is that the alternative chosen seems to
fit experience better or to express better what it was that one wanted to say
in the first place, To "want to say" something—*vouloir dire*—is to mean
something. The basic element in the creative process is one that does not appear overtly and is not open to direct observation and description; it is the
preverbal or, more precisely, presemiotic meaning-intention that precedes
and motivates all discourse and that all discourse is ultimately about. This is
the element that makes of creative expression something more than a mere
bricolage of signs and makes of meaning and freedom something more than
mere subjective illusions. It is what allows for something like a liberation
from the illusions of understanding and from the tyranny of theories that
masquerade as facts.

Chapter 8 will examine the meaning-intention and the relation between
theory and experience, but before this can be done it is necessary to advance

one step further in the analysis of creative understanding by inquiring into the nature of scientific understanding. It is no mere chance coincidence that scientific discoveries were able to serve as examples of the creative act, for, like art, science is one instance of creative understanding. But if this is so, how is it that there should exist within our culture a crisis of understanding and that science and the humanities should find themselves in conflict? If science is also a creative enterprise, why should it enter into conflict with other modes of creative discourse, such as religion? This is what needs to be determined.

NOTES

1. C. Peirce, *Collected Papers* (Cambridge, Mass., 1931-1958), 2:220.

2. Peirce to Lady Welby, December 1, 1903, in P. Wiener ed., *Charles S. Peirce: Selected Writings* (New York: Dover, 1966).

3. W. James, The *Principles of Psychology* (New York, 1950), 1:266.

4. C. Lévi-Strauss, *The Savage Mind* (Chicago, 1956), p. 43.

5. Ibid., pp. 54-55.

6. For Lévi-Strauss anthropology is a "branch of semiology." He says that we should view "marriage regulations and kinship systems as a kind of language, a set of processes permitting the establishment, between individuals and groups, of a certain type of communication. That the 'message' in this case, should be the *women of the group,* who are *circulated* between clans, lineages, or families, in place of the *words of the group,* which are *circulated* between individuals, does not at all change the fact that the essential aspect of the phenomenon is identical in both cases" *(Structural Anthropology,* [New York, 1963], p. 61; translation corrected).

7. F. de Saussure, *Course in General Linguistics* (New York, 1959), pp. 114, 16 (translation corrected).

8. Ibid., p. 16.

9. R. Barthes, *Mythologies* (Paris, 1957), as well as his "Eléments de Sémiologie," *Communications,* no. 4 (1964).

10. Saussure says, "Just as the game of chess is entirely in the combination of the different chesspieces, language is characterized as a system based entirely on the opposition of its concrete units" (*Course,* p. 107). "A game of chess is like an artificial realization of what language offers in a natural form" (ibid., p. 88).

11. Saussure says, "Language can also be compared with a sheet of paper: thought is the front and the sound the back; one cannot cut the front without cutting the back at the same time; likewise in language, one can neither divide sound from thought nor thought from sound" (ibid., p. 113).

12. Ibid., p. 120.

13. Saussure writes, "Two signs, each having a signified and signifier, are not different but only distinct. Between them there is only *opposition.* The entire mechanism of language . . . is based on oppositions of this kind and on the phonic and conceptual differences that they imply" (ibid., p. 121).

14. Y. R. Chao, *Language and Symbolic Systems* (Cambridge, Mass., 1974), p. 68.

15. M. Merleau-Ponty, *Signs* (Evanston, Ill., 1964), p. 42.

16. M. Merleau-Ponty, *Phenomenology of Perception* (London, 1962), p. 188.

17. R. Sessions, "The Composer and His Message," in B. Ghiselin, ed., *The Creative Process* (New York, n.d.), p. 47.

18. Ibid., p. 48.

19. S. Spender, "The Making of a Poem," in Ghiselin, *Creative Process,* p. 124.

20. Saussure, *Course,* pp. 117-19.

21. Ibid., p. 34.

22. B. Whorf, *Language, Thought and Reality* (Cambridge, Mass., 1972), p. 223.

23. Ibid., pp. 229-30.

24. To say that language refers to nothing but itself is simply a way of expressing one consequence of the structuralist understanding of language. For structural linguistics, language (like, indeed, all scientific subject matters) is a closed system (such that the "meaning" of the terms of the system—lexical units—is constituted diacritically, in terms solely of the mutual oppositions among them). Linguistics can thus consider that this system, language, has no outside. For a succinct account of the presuppositions of structural analysis see Paul Ricoeur, *The Conflict of Interpretations* (Evanston, Ill., 1974), pp. 81-83.

25. Merleau-Ponty, *Signs,* p. 45.

26. Ricoeur, *Conflict,* p. 77. See also my article, "Ricoeur et la non-philosophie," in *Laval théologique et philosophique* 29 (October 1973).

27. Plato, *Cratylus* (New York, 1961), 389d.

28. Ibid., 431.

29. Ibid., 431c.

30. This is recognized by Gadamer who, along with his work in hermeneutics, is well known for his studies in the philosophy of Plato; Gadamer writes:

> Plato's discovery of the ideas conceals the true nature of language even more than the theories of the sophists, who developed their own art (techne) in the use and abuse of language.
>
> Even where Plato, pointing forward to his dialectic, moves beyond the level of the discussion in the *Cratylus,* we find no other relation to language than that already discussed there: language is a tool, an image that is constructed and judged in terms of the original, the objects themselves. Thus even when he does not assign to the sphere of words (onomata) any independent cognitive function and calls for the transcending of this sphere, he keeps to the framework of reference within which the question of the "correctness" of the name presents itself. Even when (as in the context of the seventh *Letter*) he does not accept a natural correctness of names, he still retains resemblance (homoion) as the criterion: the image and the original constitute for him the metaphysical model with which he considers everything within the noetic sphere. Hence the critique of the correctness of names in the *Cratylus* is the first step in the direction at the end of which lies the modern instrumental theory of language and the ideal of a sign system of reason (*Truth and Method,* [New York, 1975], pp. 369, 378).

31. W. K. C. Guthrie, *A History of Greek Philosophy* (Cambridge, 1969), 3:214.

32. The story comes from Simplicius. Diogenes Laertius relates a similar tale about Diogenes the Cynic, a pupil of Antisthenes (D.L., VI, 53). Diogenes, it will be recalled, was the one who presented Plato with a plucked chicken after Plato had defined man as a "featherless biped."

33. Aristotle, *Metaphysics,* trans. W. D. Ross, in *The Basic Works of Aristotle* (New York, 1941), 1043b23.

34. I. M. Copi, "Artificial Language," in P. Henle, ed., *Language, Thought and Culture,* (Ann Arbor, 1965), p. 100.

35. Ibid., pp. 99-100.

36. Ibid., p. 117.

37. Ibid., p. 115.

38. J. M. Murry, cited by Wheelwright, *Metaphor and Reality* (Bloomington, Ind., 1973), p. 69.

39. W. T. Jones, *The Sciences and the Humanities* (Berkeley, 1967), p. 120.

40. I. A. Richards, *The Philosophy of Rhetoric* (New York, 1965), pp. 96ff.

41. "In the simplest formulation, when we use a metaphor we have two thoughts of different things active together and supported by a single word, or phrase, whose meaning is a resultant of their interaction" (ibid., p. 93).

42. Henry Wadsworth Longfellow, *Tales of a Wayside Inn, "Elizabeth,"* IV.

43. Richards, *Philosophy of Rhetoric* p. 100.

44. B. Snell, *The Discovery of the Mind* (New York, 1960), pp. 200-01.

45. Richards is quite insistent on rejecting the empiricism-influenced view that the function of metaphor is to conjure up a mental image ("the evil influence of the imagery assumption"). The metaphor is to be understood in terms not of mental images but of semantic meanings. The function of language is to bring together regions of experience that can never combine in sensation. Cf. *Philosophy of Rhetoric,* pp. 16, 98ff. 130-31. Perelman, for his part, writes:

> To conceive metaphor as derived from analogy and analogy as a confrontation of relations seems to us the most effective way of combating at the theoretical level the error—justly stigmatized by Richards—of regarding metaphor as imagery. . . . Any analogy—unless, like allegory or parable, it is confined within a rigid form—turns into metaphor quite spontaneously.

> Metaphor, an analogical fusion, fulfills all the functions of analogy itself. In certain regards it works even better, because it strengthens the analogy; the condensed metaphor integrates it into the language. (*The New Rhetoric* [Notre Dame, Ind., 1969], pp. 402-03, 410.)

46. Richards, *Philosophy of Rhetoric,* p. 93.

47. Wheelwright, *Metaphor and Reality,* p. 71.

48. Cf. ibid., chap. 4.

49. Cf. Richards, *Philosophy of Rhetoric,* pp. 123-27.

50. Other examples cited by Wheelwright, *Metaphor and Reality:*
> My country 'tis of thee
> Sweet land of liberty
>> Higgledy-piggledy my black hen
> (an anti-patriotic verse of the 1930's)

> Toasted Susie is my ice-cream
> (Gertrude Stein)

51. Cf. the remarks of Max Ernst, a master of surrealist painting:
> What is the mechanism of collage?

> I think I would say that it amounts to *the exploitation of the chance meeting on a nonsuitable plane of two mutually distant realities* . . . or more simply, *the cultivation of systematic moving out of place* on the lines of André Breton's theory: *Super-reality must in any case be the function of our will to put everything completely out of place. . . .*

> A complete, real thing, with a simple function apparently fixed once and for all (an umbrella), coming suddenly into the presence of another real thing, very different and no less incongruous (a sewing machine) in surroundings where both must feel out of place (on a dissecting table), escapes by this very fact from its simple function and its own identity; through a new relationship its false absolute will be transformed into a different absolute, at once true and poetic; the umbrella and the sewing machine will make love. The mechanism of the process seems to me to be laid bare by this very simple example. Complete transmutation followed by a pure act such as the act of love must necessarily occur every time the given facts make conditions favourable: *the pairing of two realities which apparently cannot be paired on a place apparently not suited to them.* ("Inspiration to Order," in Ghiselin, *Creative Process,* p. 66).

52. This is to say that in diaphoric metaphor one cannot, to use Paul Henle's words, specify "the property in virtue of which the transfer takes place" (Henle, "Metaphor," p. 173). But for Henle, as for Aristotle, one should be able to do so in the case of metaphor. "There must be an initial similarity between [the literal and the figurative elements] to make the metaphor possible" (ibid., p. 191). This insistence on initial similarities and conditions of possibility expresses Henle's "iconic" definition of metaphor as the representation of a likeness: "We are led to think of something by a consideration of something like it, and this is what constitutes the iconic mode of signifying" (ibid., p. 177). Epiphor does require, it is true, a prior categorical system (which will make for likenesses), but the precise nature of this system is arbitrary. An "iconic" theory of metaphor is misleading, since it implies that the similarities on which a metaphor builds have something objective and necessary about them.

53. Wheelwright, *Metaphor and Reality,* p. 85.

54. Richards, *Philosophy of Rhetoric,* p. 125.

55. Merleau-Ponty, *Phenomenology,* p. 16.

56. Nelson Goodman writes: "Metaphorical force requires a combination of novelty with fitness, of the odd with the obvious. The good metaphor satisfies while it startles" (*Languages of Art* [Indianapolis, 1968], p. 79).

57. Aristotle, *Rhetorica,* trans. W. R. Roberts, in *Basic Works,* 3:1410b.

58. Richards, *Philosophy of Rhetoric,* p. 94.

59. Goodman, *Languages of Art,* p. 71.

60. Ibid., p. 72.

61. "A whole set of alternative labels, a whole apparatus of organization, takes over new territory. What occurs is a transfer of a schema, a migration of concepts, an alienation of categories. Indeed, a metaphor might be regarded as a calculated category-mistake" (ibid., p. 73).

62. Perelman, *New Rhetoric,* p. 385. Max Black is getting at the same idea when he writes:

> The effect, then of (metaphorically) calling a man a "wolf" is to evoke the world-system of related commonplaces. . . . Any human traits that can without undue strain be talked about in "wolf-language" will be rendered prominent, and any that cannot will be pushed into the background. The wolf metaphor suppresses some details, emphasizes others—in short, *organizes* our view of man. . . . Or take another example. Suppose I am set the task of describing a battle in words drawn as largely as possible from the vocabulary of chess. These latter terms determine a system of implications which will proceed to control my description of the battle. The enforced choice of the chess vocabulary will lead some aspects of the battle to be emphasized, others to be neglected [notice how this reflects the revealing/concealing nature of human understanding discussed above in chapter 3], and all to be organized in a way that would cause much more strain in other modes of description. The chess vocabulary filters and transforms: it not only selects, it brings forward aspects of the battle that might not be seen at all through another medium (*Models and Metaphors* [Ithaca, 1962], pp. 41-42).

This entire text exemplifies, in the case of metaphor, the general traits of understanding discussed in chapter 3.

If the logic of the vehicle serves as a guide in the exploration of the tenor, certain semantic traits of the tenor have a retroeffect on the vehicle, which is to say that the relation between the two is a two-way relation, a genuine interaction. This was the point made above by Snell. Perelman also observes:

> Interaction between terms of an analogy is what often makes it possible to fit into the phoros [vehicle] elements which would be without significance if the theme [tenor], which gives them significance, were not in mind. . . . Sometimes the influence of the theme on the phoros is such that certain elements of the phoros undergo modification. . . . Often the terms of the phoros will be endowed with qualities that are the product of the imagination, but bring them nearer to the theme. An example is the attribution of the faculty of speech to animals in fables. *(New Rhetoric* pp. 378-79).

63. James, "Pragmatism's Conception of Truth," in *Pragmatism and Other Essays* (New York, 1963), p. 94.

64. James, "What Pragmatism Means," in ibid., pp. 29-30.

65. Ibid., p. 28.

66. I. T. Ramsey, "Models and Mystery," in W. Shibles, ed., *Essays on Metaphor* (Whitewater, Wisc., 1972), p. 165.

67. Aristotle, *Poetics*, trans. I. Bywater, in *The Basic Works of Aristotle*, Ch. 21, 1457b7. One finds in the *Oxford Dictionary* the same rationalist definition of metaphor (as the substitution of an improper for a proper name): "The figure of speech in which a name or descriptive term is transferred to some object to which it is not properly applicable." In contrast, the definition given in *Webster's New World Dictionary of the American Language* appears much more neutral and is decidedly less objectionable: "a figure of speech in which one thing is likened to another, different thing by being spoken of as if it were that other; implied comparison, in which a word or phrase ordinarily and primarily used of one thing is applied to another."

68. Richards, *Philosophy of Rhetoric*, p. 90.

69. For there to be epiphor there must be an accepted, literal meaning (a semantic "home base") that is used in an unusual way.

70. Goodman, *Languages of Art*, p. 78.

71. Artistotle, *Poetics*, chap. 22, 1459a5 (emphasis added).

72. Aristotle, *Rhetoric*, III, 1, 1404a5.

73. T. Hobbes, *Leviathan* (Indianapolis, 1958), 1:8.

74. Black, *Models and Metaphors*, p. 37.

75. Gadamer, *Truth and Method*, pp. 389ff.

76. "What originally constituted the basis of the life of language and made up its logical productivity, the spontaneous and inventive seeking out of similarities by means of which it is possible to order things, is now pushed to the side and instrumentalized into a rhetorical figure called metaphor. The struggle between philosophy and rhetoric for the training of Greek youth, which was decided with the victory of Attic philosophy, has also this side to it, namely that the thinking about language becomes the object of a grammar and rhetoric that have already recognized the ideal of scientific concept formation. Thus the sphere of linguistic meanings begins to become detached from the sphere of things encountered in linguistic form" (ibid., pp. 391-92).

77. Ricoeur, *Rule of Metaphor*, p. 24.

78. Ibid., pp. 197-98 (translation corrected); cf. also pp. 230-31. For a critical analysis of Ricoeur's treatment of metaphor, see G. B. Madison, "Reflections on Paul Ricoeur's Philosophy of Metaphor," *Philosophy Today* 21 (Winter 1977).

79. W. Stevens, "Adagia," *Opus Posthumous*, p. 179.

80. Wheelwright says, for instance:

> Reality, as distinguished from the intellectual artifacts that often usurp the name, is neither object nor subject, neither matter nor mind, nor can it be limited to any other philosophical category; it is That to which every such category tries to refer and which every philosophical statement tries to describe, always from an intellectual point of view and always with ultimate inadequacy (*Metaphor and Reality*, pp. 166-67).

> From the contextual and perspectival character of reality it follows that the nature of reality is intrinsically and ultimately hidden from any finite exploration. . . . Reality is ultimately problematical, not contingently so; for to grasp and formulate it, even as a set of questions, is to fragmentize it. There is always, in any inquiry, something more than meets the eye, even the inner eye; the permanent possibility of extending one's imaginative awareness has no limits. A person of intellectual sensitivity is plagued by the sense of a perpetual Something More beyond anything that is actually known or

conceived. A wise beginning for any large inquiry is to entertain the postulate that reality, or a goodly part of it, is not obvious and discoverable by overt public methods of investigation, but is latent, subtle, and shy (ibid., p. 172).

81. Saint Thomas, *Summa theologiae* (Alba, 1962), I, 13, 6. After saying that "metaphor consists in giving the thing a name that belongs to something else," Aristotle says that this transfer of substitution of names may be of four sorts: from genus to species; from species to genus; from species to species; on grounds of analogy. The rhetorical tradition labeled these transfers "tropes" ("turnings" of language away from literal use) and distinguished among various kinds—simile, synecdoche, metonymy—reserving, with good reason, the term *metaphor* for the last trope mentioned by Aristotle, where analogy is the basis for the "substitution." Aristotle's example of this last is: "As old age (D) is to life (C), so is evening (B) to day (A). One will accordingly describe evening (B) as the 'old age *of the day*' (D + A)—or by the Empedoclean equivalent; and old age (D) as the 'evening' or 'sunset *of life*' (B + C)" *(Poetics,* chap. 21, 1457b).

82. In regard to Aristotle see Ch. 4, n. 16, above.

83. F. Copleston, *A History of Philosophy* (Westminster, Md., 1962), 2:356.

84. Max Black points out: "Metaphorical statement is not a substitute for a formal comparison or any other kind of literal statement, but has its own distinctive capacities and achievements" *(Models and Metaphors,* p. 37).

85. Only in the case of trite metaphors, which are no more than decoration, is it the case that paraphrase or translation means giving the basic, literal sense that the metaphor communicates indirectly (which is to say also, spelling out the exact comparison or resemblance on which the metaphor is supposed to be based), for only here is it the case that a metaphor is the substitution of one word (improper, metaphorical) for another (proper, literal) that could have been used instead. A good, innovative metaphor, however, has no literal equivalent; it has, rather, a great number of possible literal interpretations (or "interpretants"). Here in fact is a convenient means for testing metaphors and determining their worth: if in paraphrasing a metaphor one can discover a literal sense and can thereby convert, without loss of meaning, the metaphorical meaning into a straightforward, literal one, one is dealing with nothing more than a dead metaphor (the paraphrase proves to be nothing more than a reconversion; it shows thereby that the metaphor in question was in its origin merely the conversion of a prior, though perhaps implicit, literal understanding of what is being said). It is therefore necessary to disagree strongly with Henle when he says, "There is no obstacle in principle to the adequate paraphrase of a metaphor though the difficulties may be very great in practice. They are least when the metaphor has become trite" *(Language, Thought and Culture,* p. 195). The last remark is an understatement. Any metaphor that can "in principle" be adequately paraphrased is a dead, trite metaphor and thus no real metaphor at all.

86. In *Metaphor and Reality,* chap.5, Wheelwright explores the relation between metaphors and symbols and argues that the former acquire a symbolic nature when they become capable of undergoing recurrence; "symbol is distinguished from metaphor by its greater stability and permanence" (p. 98). For his part, Perelman observes, "Such terms as *light, height, depth, full, empty,* and *hollow,* though borrowed from the physical world, seem to be endowed with value from the start. This may well be the case. But it could be that they have so often served in the past as elements of a phoros in analogies whose theme deals with the spiritual world, that it is no longer possible to detach from them the value derived from this role, as a consequence of interaction with certain terms of the theme" *(New Rhetoric,* p. 382; translation corrected). The latter hypothesis seems to us preferable; it avoids the need to have to posit Jungian-type archetypes and to have to posit a mysterious realm for them in the form of a "collective unconscious." If one still needs to account for the permanence and tenacity of certain symbols, one can do so in terms of their fit to preverbal, lived experience and in this way can avoid having to speak about the very dubious existence of unexperienced (unconscious) and unexpressed yet well defined meanings.

87. Steiner, *After Babel* (New York, 1975), pp. 228, 235.

88. Wheelwright, *Metaphor and Reality,* p. 17.

89. As mentioned by Ricoeur, *Rule of Metaphor,* p. 224. For Ricoeur's comments on thè is-and-is-not of metaphor, see pp. 6-7, 214-15, 223-24, 248, 255-56, 296-97, 306.

90. For Thomas the predication of a name of God is metaphorical and improper if the term refers primarily to a material quality. *Stone,* for instance, "signifies a material being, and names of this kind can be applied to God only in a metaphorical sense." Words, however, like *being, good,* and *living,* signify perfections, which in themselves transcend any limited mode of being. These names can be predicated "substantially" and "properly" of God (albeit "imperfectly" since as regards not what they signify but their mode of signification [modus significandi] they are finite and human and, in this sense, improper). Cf. *Summa theologiae,* 1:13, 3-4, and *Summa contra Gentiles* (Turin, 1961), 1:30. In Chap. 9 we shall argue that metaphor is the only means for coming to understand something about nonmaterial being. The only thing that Thomas's nonmetaphorical, theological, scientific mode of discourse can tell us about God is how little we know and can say about Him.

91. E. Gilson, *The Christian Philosophy of St. Thomas Aquinas* (London, 1967), p. 110 (emphasis added).

92. Perelman, *New Rhetoric,* p. 391 (translation corrected and emphasis added).

93. The way Thomas tries to dissimulate the properly metaphorical nature of his discourse about God is by grounding his analogical predications in a Platonic metaphysics of participation: human perfections are not "mere" metaphors for divine perfections but have a "real" relation to them by way of ontological participation. But this is no more than a typical rhetorical (in the pejorative sense of the term) and argumentative device of rationalism, as Perelman has pointed out (*New Rhetoric,* pp. 393-94). It is an attempt to reduce analogy to identity.

94. Dionysius the Areopagite, *Mystica Theologia* (Surrey, 1941), chap. 1.

95. Saint Thomas, *Quaestiones Disputatae. De Potentia Dei* (Turin, 1953), 7, 2, ad 1.

96. Dionysius, *Mystica Theologia,* chap. 2.

97. Saint Thomas, *Summa contra Gentiles,* I, 5.

98. The great mathematician, Henri Poincaré, remarked:

> The mathematical facts worthy of being studied are . . . those which reveal to us unsuspected kinship between other facts, long known, but wrongly believed to be strangers to one another.
>
> Among chosen combinations the most fertile will often be those formed of elements drawn from domains which are far apart. Not that I mean as sufficing for invention the bringing together of objects as disparate as possible; most combinations so formed would be entirely sterile. But certain among them, very rare, are the most fruitful of all ("Mathematical Creation," in Ghiselin, ed., *Creative Process,* pp. 35-36).

99. Merleau-Ponty, *Signs,* p. 46.

100. Ibid., p. 78.

101. F. M. Keesing, *Culture Change: An Analysis and Bibliography* (Stanford, 1953), cited by Beattie, *Other Cultures,* p. 243.

102. Most accounts of alchemy are written by people who know what scientific understanding consists of but who do not have an inside understanding of alchemy. For a sympathetic presentation of alchemy that has the merit of having been written by someone who understands both science and alchemy, see Titus Burckhardt, *Alchemy* (Baltimore: Penguin Books, 1971).

103. Stevens, "Adagia," p. 169.

104. Ramsey, "Models and Mystery," p. 163.

105. Cf. G. Holton, *Thematic Origins of Scientific Thought* (Cambridge, Mass., 1963), pp. 368-69.

106. Ibid., p. 362.

107. A. Koestler, *The Ghost in the Machine* (London, 1970), p. 214. See also his earlier but more detailed work, *The Act of Creation* (London, 1970).

108. Koestler, *Ghost in the Machine,* p. 213.

109. Ibid., p. 226.

110. Ibid., p. 224.

111. E. de Bono, *Lateral Thinking* (New York, 1973).

112. De Bono writes: "Vertical thinking is selection by exclusion. One works with a frame of reference and throws out what is not relevant. With lateral thinking one realizes that a pattern cannot be restructured from within itself but only as a result of some outside influence. So one welcomes outside influences for their provocative action. The more irrelevant such influences are the more chance there is of altering the established pattern. To look only for things that are relevant means perpetuating the current pattern" (ibid., p. 42). "It is the willingness to explore the least likely pathways that is important for often there can be no other reason for exploring such pathways. At the entrance to an unlikely pathway there is nothing to indicate that it is worth exploring and yet it may lead to something useful" (p. 43). "Both inductive and deductive logic are concerned with concept forming. Lateral thinking is more concerned with concept breaking, with provocation and disruption in order to allow the mind to restructure patterns" (p. 49). "The two processes are complementary not antagonistic. Lateral thinking is useful for generating ideas and approaches and vertical thinking is useful for developing them" (p. 50).

7 METAPHOR AND IMAGINATION: II

In order better to discern the overall structure of human understanding and the relations between its different modes, such as science, art, and magic, the structure of scientific understanding needs to be further clarified, and it needs to be seen how science embodies the principal characteristics of creative or insightful understanding. In order to understand properly scientific understanding and how it is a form of creative understanding, it will be necessary to dispel some myths about science, ultimately the greatest myth of all: that science represents a form of understanding radically different from the artistic or the magical. This is the myth at work when one claims that whereas art has to do with "fiction" and magic is "superstition," science, on the contrary, produces *knowledge*—knowledge being defined, as it traditionally has been, as the adequate or true expression of the "real world." What needs to be determined properly is the true status of scientific statements about reality (or about experience).

Are scientific theories, or can they be said to be, true? Do scientific entities such as atoms really exist? What is their relation to products of artistic or magical understanding? Is it the case that the latter exist only "in the mind," whereas the former exist "in reality?" What indeed, we are once again led to ask, is truth, reality? To ask questions such as these is to engage in metaphysics, and metaphysics is possible only as the analysis of human understanding. What kind of understanding, then, is scientific understanding?

It is obvious that scientific statements legitimately could lay claim to knowledge (the true understanding of what reality really is) only if it could be shown that scientific statements are or can be "true." The most simple and naive, but also the most common, position taken in regard to the status of scientific utterances is to say that what makes for their specificity and what distinguishes them from other kinds of utterances, such as artistic or magico-religious ones, is that only they are capable of being verified. This is the position maintained earlier in this century with much ado and fanfare by logical positivism. It was soon realized, however, and by the positivists themselves, that this strong claim is in fact untenable and that no scientific theory can ever be decisively verified. It was realized that there can be no *ex-*

perimentum crucis, no experiment that can conclusively demonstrate the truth of a scientific theory. For although a given theory might appear to fit the facts perfectly (and thus provide a true explanation of them), it is always possible that another, as yet undreamed-of theory might do so even better.[1] The fact of the matter is that *there is no end to the number of theories capable of "explaining" an event,* and so that a given theory is in fact true can never be demonstrated.

Thus a somewhat watered-down version of positivism emerged that relinquished the verification principle and substituted for it the principle of falsification. Karl Popper has been a leading spokesman for this version of positivism.[2] If, however, it is true that no scientific theory can ever be decisively verified, it is also true that no scientific theory can ever be radically falsified. This is what chapter 3 attempted to show by comparing scientific claims with magical ones and exposing the scientific myth of the experiment. Polanyi, himself a scientist, has remarked, "The falsification of a scientific statement can, therefore no more be strictly established than can its verification."[3] If this is so and if scientific statements can be neither verified nor falsified to any greater or lesser extent than magical ones, what does it mean, what can it mean, to speak of truth and falsity in their regard?

To a considerable extent scientific theories are like old soldiers; they never die but simply fade away. As the history of science superbly demonstrates (the phlogiston theory in chemistry furnishes a perfect example), when scientific theories are abandoned, it is not because they have been shown to be false so much as because people have simply ceased to believe in them. In other words, to say that a theory has been falsified simply means—*in actual fact* (transcendentally-pragmatically speaking)—that there is no longer any significant number of people who believe in it; its proponents have been reduced to silence or have been deprived of their audience or have simply been replaced by a new generation of scientists who hold different theories. As Max Planck wrote in his autobiography, "A new scientific truth does not triumph by convincing its opponents and making them see the light, but rather because its opponents eventually die, and a new generation grows up that is familiar with it."[4]

A theory, therefore, is never falsified or refuted. One cannot properly discern the ontological status of scientific theories and entities so long as one does not adopt the point of view we have consistently sought to maintain (transcendental-pragmatic reflection) and which amounts to paying less attention to what scientists say they do and more attention to what they actually do (that is, to the pragmatics of scientific understanding). Scientists like to look upon science as some kind of self-subsistent entity in its own right ("Science," with a capital "s," *"la science")* and not as one mode of human belief. The error of logical positivism that separates science from other human activities and accords it a privileged status ("knowledge" as opposed to "belief") is possible only because the true nature of scientific understanding is deliberately ignored. The distorting prejudice operative here could be labeled *logicism*.

Logicism is a falsification (a mystification, it could even be said) of scientific understanding arising out of a critique of psychologism. Beginning especially with Frege and Husserl, psychologism (that position that holds that everything can be explained in terms of the "laws" of psychology alone and that accordingly reduces everything to the psychological makeup of the human mind) has come in for extensive, and well-merited, criticism,[5] such that today a standard rationalist argumentative putdown is to label a position "psychologistic." It is not usually realized that the position emerging from antipsychologism, logicism, is equally subject to criticism.

A typical version of logicism is the one put forward by Popper.[6] Popper denounces the confusion of psychological problems with what he calls "epistemological" ones and insists on the need to distinguish between the psychology of knowledge and the logic of knowledge. In formulating the matter thus, Popper distinguishes (correctly, we would say) epistemology from psychology, but only to confound it in turn with logic. In saying that the epistemology of science is concerned not with "questions of fact" but with "questions of justification or validity," he is presupposing precisely that which, for us, is at issue: the privileged status of science as knowledge of reality. This is fully apparent from the way in which he quite arbitrarily (and in a typical Cartesian fashion) distinguishes between subjective feelings of conviction and objective logical relations having to do with verification.[7] Truth, he says in effect, is an objective (logical) sort of thing, which has nothing to do with what people take ("feel") truth to be. Reality is what it is independently of what people believe it to be (and what they take or believe—"feel"—it to be is of no interest to epistemology, only to psychology). This is all merely a reworking of the basic rationalist prejudices. In a typically rationalist and dogmatic fashion, Popper is hypostatizing one mode of human understanding—the one called "logical thinking"—according it an absolute or "objective" status and linking it isomorphically with reality (and, concomitantly, he is devalorizing everything that is not logic, reducing it to a matter of "mere" feeling, just as Plato devalorized rhetoric in absolutizing what he called dialectic).

This is especially apparent in a recent work where he says outright that scientific knowledge has nothing whatsoever to do with what people actually think reality is.[8] It has nothing to do with beliefs, which he reduces to mere "mental states," as opposed, one must presume, to "real," "objective states of affairs"; it is concerned, rather, with the logical relations between statements or propositions that exist independently of the mental states of the people who make and believe the statements. Popper in fact goes so far as to say that there are three different worlds: the physical

world, the mental world, and, finally, "the world of theories in themselves
and their logical relations; of arguments in themselves; and of problem
situations in themselves."[9] As if arguments, like uttered words, could ever
exist apart from the people who argued and made statements, suspended in
the air like the frozen exhalations of arctic explorers one sees in comic
strips.[10] It is doubtful if one could find a more blatant case of Platonic-style
hypostatization than this "third world" theory of Popper's, and the
tendency at work here is the same dogmatic one to be found in mythical
thinking, which similarly hypostatizes words and endows them with a dis-
embodied life of their own transcending that of mere, perishable mortals.

A corrective for this rabid logicism is sorely called for, and the physicist
and historian of science, Gerald Holton, has provided one. Because a
theory can be effectively opposed only by means of another theory, and because all theorizing involves the making of distinctions, distinctions other
than those made by Popper are called for. Holton emphasizes a distinction
that most writers on science, and Popper in particular, persist in ignoring.[11]
What the latter do is to consider science as an established body of knowledge rather than as an ongoing activity that scientists engage in. In other
words, they commit what might be called the fallacy of abstraction by removing scientific discourse from the personal level of the working scientist,
where it originates and without which it could not exist, to a second level,
which Holton calls public science. Public science is the result of the way
scientists express themselves after they have formulated their theories and
are addressing themselves to fellow scientists, adopting an impersonal form
of expression. In expressing themselves in this way, scientists cover up the
actual working of scientific thinking, and writers on science, who are often
not themselves scientists, actually falsify the true nature of science when
they identify science with "public science" and overlook the fact that the
latter is an abstraction from actual fact. Holton writes:

> This distinction between the two meanings of the same word [*private science*
> and *public science*], which appears to be helpful in allaying some serious con-
> fusions in methodological discussions, is often not adequately made by those
> who analyze science. Scientists themselves are largely responsible for that con-
> dition; for in formalizing an individual contribution for publication, it is part
> of the game to cover up the transition from the private stage, to make the re-
> sults in retrospect appear neatly derived from clear fundamentals. . . .
> Months of tortuous, wasteful effort may be hidden behind a few elegant para-
> graphs, with the sequence of presented development running directly opposite
> to the actual chronology, to the confusion of students and historians alike.[12]

Public science, it could be said, is a game (a serious and important one, to
be sure), which has as one of its fundamental rules that it should never admit that it is a game. Science is a game that takes itself overseriously; it re-

fuses to admit that it too is a play of the imagination. To understand science properly, it is necessary to understand this. Unfortunately a philosopher of science like R. B. Braithwaite perpetuates the logicist's fallacy of abstraction and dissimulates the real nature of science and the real problems to which it gives rise when he defines science as "a deductive system . . . which is arranged in such a way that from some of the hypotheses or premises all the other hypotheses logically follow."[13] What Braithwaite is describing here is simply what scientists would like to think science is.

It is important that Holton's distinction between private science (S_1) or science in the making and public science (S_2) or science as an institution, textbook science, be retained. He points out how grave misunderstandings arise and pseudoproblems are perpetuated when this distinction is ignored. The most notable problem is perhaps the difficulty most writers have in reconciling "the apparent contradiction between the often 'illogical' nature of discovery and the logical nature of physical concepts."[14] That this is indeed only an apparent contradiction we shall see for ourselves in a moment, but that nonetheless there is a kind of paradox or inner contradiction at the root of the entire scientific enterprise we shall see as well in the following section (already our remarks about the peculiar nature of the scientific game directly suggest as much).

For a descriptive analysis of human understanding that does not illegitimately transgress the limits of experience (a transcendental, phenomenological analysis), it is impossible to separate the true and the false from what people believe to be true and false. What Popper calls the justification of theories (a business of "public science") amounts to no more than the solicitation and reinforcement of belief. This becomes readily apparent once one distinguishes between private and public science, but it is deliberately obscured by the logician's spurious distinction between the psychology and the logic of science.

Actually the logicist distinctions are, like Frege's distinction between sense and reference, no more than a rhetorical, argumentative device—useful, it must be admitted, and indeed quite clever, if one's purpose is to perpetuate rationalist dogmatism. To set up as a supreme principle the distinction between questions of fact and questions of justification or validity or the distinction between subjective feelings of conviction and objective logical relations having to do with verification and, ultimately, to hypostatize logic with some kind of "third world" theory allows the rationalist to save face when it is quite obvious to everyone that what he says does not correspond to anything in actual experience. The rationalist can argue that he is not doing "psychology" but rather "logic"; he is not claiming to describe what in fact is the case but what ideally must be the case if X is to count as Y (if science is to be true knowledge of reality). The rationalist will attempt to save himself by saying that what makes a statement scientific is not that it is, was, or ever will be "tested," but only that it is capable "in principle" of being tested. In arguing in this way, however, he is obviously violating one of his own logical rules. In defining science in terms of what it must be if it is to be what it is supposed to be, he is begging the question as to whether it actually is what it is supposed to be.

Our most strenuous objection to logicism at this point is that it forever renders impossible a realization of the creative nature of science. Logicists usually have nothing to say about scientific discovery, about science in the making. Braithwaite, for instance, recognizes that the history of science raises many interesting problems, such "as to what causes the individual scientist to discover a new idea, and as to what causes the general acceptance of scientific ideas." But since as a "philosopher" he is concerned only with "straight logical problems" and "problems of inductive logic or epistemology," he immediately goes on to classify these historical problems as involving "the individual psychology of thinking and the sociology of thought." It comes as no surprise when he says, "None of these questions are our business here."[15]

Writers such as Braithwaite may allow that creative imagination plays an important role in science in the framing of hypotheses, but even if they do so, typically they will say that this is not a concern for the "logic" of science, only for "psychology"; it has merely "subjective" as opposed to "objective" importance. However the scientist happens on his hypothesis (and more often than not by some inspired, imaginative insight, as the positivist may admit), the important thing is that these hypotheses are accepted or rejected (become "scientific") only through rigorous testing. Moreover, the hypothesis is merely a way of ordering facts or data which are "objective," "given," and unaffected by imagination. It is not necessary to repeat here what chapter 3 so much insisted on—the imaginative, creatively selective nature of perception (this effectively eliminates the myth of objective facts) but only to remark how on this view imagination is accorded a subordinate and extremely limited role. It intervenes only after the collection of data and before experimental verification (or falsification).

Not only is the imagination devalorized here and not accorded its due recognition, it becomes thoroughly illogical and thus thoroughly incomprehensible. Because the logicist equates serious thinking with logical thinking, he puts himself at a complete loss when it comes to understanding any form of thinking that is not logical in the strict or narrow sense of the term. Thus when Popper argues in the fashion described in the preceding paragraph,[16] he is forced to say that a " 'rational reconstruction' of the steps which have led the scientist to a discovery" has nothing to do with describing the processes of thought "as they actually happen; it can give only a logical skeleton of the procedure of testing." His view of the matter ("for what it is worth," as he appropriately remarks) is that "there is no such thing as a logical method of having new ideas, or a logical reconstruction of this process. . . . every discovery contains 'an irrational element.' ''[17]

Not only does this narrow view obscure the integral role that creative, imaginative thinking plays in science, it also, and more seriously, makes it impossible for any analysis of human understanding to appreciate how understanding functions; it makes it impossible to understand creative, imaginative thinking or active understanding (just as it makes impossible an understanding of metaphor). It makes for the ironic situation wherein a writer can entitle his book, *The Logic of Scientific Discovery,* and yet have nothing of any merit to say about discovery in science.

Once the logicist mystification of science is exposed and once it is realized that what the positivist-style philosopher takes to be science, (that is, public science, S_2) is in fact an abstraction from actual science, science in the making, and has a derived, secondary status in regard to it, then the origin of scientific theories and postulated entities becomes a truly vital question. A great deal of work on the creative, imaginative nature of the thinking that leads to scientific "discoveries" has been carried out in recent years, and it is not our intention to reiterate these findings here.[18] Our only aim has been to provide a context wherein they can assume their properly epistemological significance. Philosophers of science have often ignored this wealth of information, having relegated it to the field of mere "psychology." It may be of some interest, say they, in learning how scientists think, but it has no relevance to learning what science itself is, to the truth or falsity of scientific statements or the ontological status of scientific entities. This prejudice must be overcome if the properly epistemological significance of these findings is to be grasped and if it is to be seen that scientific discovery in particular, and creative, imaginative thinking in general, has a logic of its own. The logic of scientific discovery becomes truly meaningful only when logicism is overcome.

To be sure, the activity of framing hypotheses or theories (S_1) does not follow the laws of formal logic and is not a form of inductive or deductive reasoning, but this does not mean that it is therefore an "illogical" or "irrational " activity. As Norwood Hanson rightly observes:

> If establishing an hypothesis through its predictions has a logic, so has the conceiving of an hypothesis. To form the idea of acceleration or of universal gravitation does require genius: nothing less than a Galileo or a Newton. But that cannot mean that the reflexions leading to these ideas are unreasonable or a-reasonable.[19]

The logic at work here is not that of linear thinking but of lateral "thinking aside."

Science is no less a creative, imaginative endeavor than art, and if this is not seen, it is only because one is taking an abstraction for reality, S_2 for S_1, and ignoring the basic rule of the scientific game as it is played in the area of public opinion. An actual scientist such as Jacob Bronowski is, on the contrary, sensitive to the epistemological reality of science when he writes:

> There exists a single creative activity, which is displayed alike in the arts and in the sciences. It is wrong to think of science as a mechanical record of facts, and it is wrong to think of the arts as remote and private fancies. What makes each human, what makes them universal, is the stamp of the creative mind.[20]

Not only does Bronowski recognize the creative makeup of science and its essential affinity with art, but he also pinpoints exactly what it means to speak of creativity:

> I found the act of creation to lie in the discovery of a hidden likeness. The scientist or the artist takes two facts or experiences which are separate; he finds in them a likeness which had not been seen before; and he creates a unity by showing this likeness.[21]

> In the act of creation a man brings together two facets of reality and, by discovering a likeness between them, suddenly makes them one. The act is the same in Leonardo, in Keats and in Einstein.[22]

The essence of creative thinking is analogical reasoning, the kind of reasoning or thinking exemplified in its purest state in the living metaphor. What Holton calls *science in the making* (S_1) or Kuhn *extraordinary science* obeys the rules not of formal logic but of what we have called analogic. Scientific theories, like magical ones, are a product of human understanding, and they take their shape not because they succeed in being factual "pictures" of reality but because they, like everything else human, have been forged in the smithy of the imagination. As Bronowski so aptly remarks, "A concept is an imaginative creation."[23] Even in science where univocity and logical exactitude is an avowed goal, language retains an important degree of ambiguity. If it did not, scientific discoveries would cease to be made, for, without semantic ambiguity, there would be no means for seeing old concepts in a new light, which is what is meant by insightful understanding.[24]

It could be shown, for instance, how scientific models are structurally akin to metaphors. What is important in metaphor making is the semantic background out of which the metaphor (more specifically, the vehicle) is drawn, its home context. The logic governing the use of the vehicle in its home context serves to guide us when applying the vehicle in a less familiar context or realm. This heuristic or guiding function of metaphor—explaining the less known in terms of the better known, analogical reasoning—is none other than that belonging to models in science.[25] Comparing Western science and African traditional thought, Robin Horton observes:

> In the genesis of a typical theory, the drawing of an analogy between the unfamiliar and the familiar is followed by the making of a model in which something akin to the familiar is postulated as the reality underlying the unfamiliar. Both modern Western and traditional African thought-products amply demonstrate the truth of this. Whether we look amongst atoms, electrons, waves or amongst gods, spirits, and entelechies, we find that theoretical notions nearly always have their roots in relatively homely everyday experiences, in analogies with the familiar.[26]

Enough has now been said of the creative nature of scientific thinking. All that remains is to draw the necessary conclusions: if science is a genuinely creative and imaginative enterprise, then scientific entities, such as atoms, are, like witchcraft substance in magic, imaginative constructs, convenient fictions. As William James remarked three-quarters of a century ago, "It is . . . *as if* reality were made of ether, atoms or electrons but we mustn't think so literally."[27] Atoms or any other theoretical entity of science do not really exist—if (and only if, to speak like the logician) by reality we mean something more than a semantic construct, an object of belief (this "something more" being what in chapter 4 we called Reality). The illusions of understanding arise when understanding takes its creative, imaginative products literally. Then metaphor is not only used but also abused. Liberation from the illusions, indeed, the self-delusions of understanding, can occur, and understanding's alienation from its own creative self can be overcome only if literal-minded belief is overcome and the free play of the imagination is recognized.

If science is fully as creative and imaginative as art, why, ever since Plato, should the two have been set at odds with one another and why should there be such a problem of reconciling the new scientific-technological culture with our traditional humanistic culture? Is it perhaps because the appreciation of an artwork demands more imagination on the part of the spectator or reader than the understanding of a scientific theory? Perhaps art does leave more to the imagination than science does, but, even if so, this cannot be made out to be an essential difference if one does not mix the terms of one's comparison and does not compare artistic insight, which is a form of active or insightful understanding, with science qua established system, which is a form of passive understanding. It is only public science, S_2, that does not put much of a demand on one's imagination. The case is different with science in the making. To appreciate properly a novel scientific discovery of the past, for instance, one must be able to recreate for oneself the sense of wonder that overwhelmed the person who originally made the "discovery." One must re-create for oneself the sense of awe (the AHA! experience, as Koestler would say) that accompanies the sudden and unsuspected fusion of two previously unrelated frames of reference, which is to say that one must exercise one's imagination. Bronowski is surely right when he says:

> Science, like art, is not a copy of nature but a re-creation of her. We re-make nature by the act of discovery, in the poem or in the theorem. And the great poem and the deep theorem are new to every reader, and yet are his own experiences, because he himself re-creates them. They are the marks of unity in variety; and in the instant when the mind seizes this for itself, in art or in science, the heart misses a beat.[28]

Extraordinary science is as much an imaginative activity as is extraordinary art, and the appreciation of both requires the same kind of imaginative response. Wherein, then, lies their difference, and what grounds can the philosopher of science have for according science a special status over and above art? This question can be made more precise: How is it that the creative, imaginative character of science is so easily overlooked, such that science is taken to be a form of understanding of a radically different sort than art? Is it perhaps because science is torn by an inner contradiction? Hegel said that the consciousness of a contradiction produces an unhappy consciousness, and we know from Freud that more often than not the response to an unhappy, tormented consciousness is the fabrication of a false consciousness. We have encountered enough scientific mystifications in the course of our inquiry to suspect that this might be the case here.

In any event, we are certainly involved in a paradox. Bronowski has recognized this and refers to it as "the paradox of imagination in science." In trying to locate the difference between science and art he was led to say:

> Science is a different pursuit from poetry not in its execution but in its endeavor. For the endeavor of science is to resolve ambiguities by making what I have described as critical and decisive tests between alternatives. An experiment to this end is as beautiful and as imaginative as any line of poetry, but it puts its imagination to a different endeavor: unlike poetry it does not seek to exploit its ambiguities, but to minimize them. This is the paradox of imagination in science, that it has for its aim the impoverishment of imagination. By that outrageous phrase, I mean that the highest flight of scientific imagination is to weed out the proliferation of new ideas. In science, the grand view is a miserly view, and a rich model of the universe is one which is as poor as possible in hypotheses.[29]

Whether Bronowski is right in speaking of "critical and decisive" experiments we have ample reason to doubt, but what is true is that scientists do think of experiments in this way, and the express purpose of the experiment clearly is to eliminate ambiguity by making a decisive choice between alternative possibilities. Science is indeed different from art in, as Bronowski says, its endeavor or, as one might also say, its motivation or goal. The activity is basically the same, but the self-interpretation of the activity differs markedly, for in art "the imagination explores the alternatives of human action without ever deciding for one rather than another. And in this tense and happy indecision, and only in this, the work of art is different from the work of science."[30]

In the preceding chapter we were able to discern the mechanism of all creative, insightful understanding. Insight arises from the merging of disparate frames of reference. Thus the condition for insight is the existence of semantic ambiguity within a system of belief or universe of discourse. A language that would be perfectly unambiguous and exact could not serve as the medium for active understanding and could never allow for unexpected "discoveries," that is, imaginative insights. This is true of all understanding, of science no less than of art, but the peculiarity of the scientific endeavor is that it aims at that which, if it were attained, would put an end to any further (insightful) understanding: exactitude and unambiguity. The inner contradiction of science is that in taking itself to be objective knowledge, it denies that which it is: an exercise of the creative imagination. This is indeed a very curious state of affairs, which seems to suggest that were one to take the scientific interpretation of science at its face value, one would actually misunderstand not only science but all understanding.

How is it possible that science should so radically misunderstand itself? The fact that science is a prime instance of human understanding leads one to wonder if it is not possible that something in the working of human understanding inevitably tends to produce a false self-understanding. I believe that this is indeed the case and, further, that this "something" is an integral aspect of understanding itself, such that understanding's misunderstanding of itself is not only an error but a natural and quasi-inevitable one. In other words, the paradox of imagination in science is but the expression of a more fundamental paradox of imagination or of understanding in general.

Light is thrown on this paradox as soon as it is realized that the process at work in science is the same as the one found in the rationalist, "scientific" theology of Saint Thomas: the properly analogical and metaphorical nature of the thinking in question is glossed over and ignored, demonstrating, as Perelman says, that "the status of analogy is precarious."[31] "If the analogy is a fruitful one, theme and phoros [tenor and vehicle] are transformed into examples or illustrations of a more general law, and by their relation to this law there is a unification of the fields of the theme and the phoros." In all forms of understanding that lay claim to true knowledge of reality, all the way from primitive myth to modern science, the normal outcome is, as Perelman says, this: "Broadly speaking, outstripping an analogy [*le dépassement de l'analogie*] has the effect of making it appear as the result of a discovery, as an observation of what is, rather than as the product of an original creative effort at structuration." Why this should be so, we shall see shortly; for the moment let us take sufficient note of the fact.

The matter could be expressed somewhat differently by saying that in science the is-not, which inseparably accompanies every metaphorical and artistic utterance, is ignored and analogical likeness is made out to be something approaching mathematical identity. Although all scientific "explanation" involves the application of a model to the thing to be made intelligible, the "as if" of the analogy is generally forgotten and is transformed into a pure "is." For instance, researchers who attempt to understand humans by using models borrowed from cybernetics generally are led to say that they are basically nothing more than machines for processing information.[32] This dehumanizing and unacceptable conclusion is reached because the analogical likeness (in some ways a person is indeed like a machine) is surreptitiously transformed into a relation of identity. The reasoning at work here seems to be something like this: if there is a "true" likeness, it can only be because of an underlying identity of structure; a person and a machine must belong to the same general class and share in the same generic essence—"since likeness is based on agreement or communication in form" (*cum similitudo attendatur secundum convenientiam vel communicationem in forma*).[33]

What Perelman calls "the outstripping of analogy" is a feature of human understanding in general and of science in particular. Indeed, the forgetfulness of the irremediably analogical character of understanding (and of the irreducible character of analogy which is neither univocity nor equivocity) accounts for the present crisis in our culture: the conflict between science and the humanities. One can already see this forgetfulness taking on a rigidified form in Galileo, the founder of modern, mathematized science. Galileo claimed that the scientific method as he had worked it out afforded not only a novel way of looking at one's environing world but actually expressed the very nature of reality, and it was this extravagant claim that brought him into direct conflict with the Church. The true issues underlying this conflict have been so thoroughly obscured by apologists for science that today one unhesitatingly and with all the force of ingrained common sense takes Galileo to be something of a cultural hero battling against the forces of superstition and the dark ages. This is enough to justify taking another, less prejudiced look at the issue that brought Galileo before the Inquisition.[34]

Galileo's adversary in this affair was Robert Bellarmine, a cardinal of the Church and a philosopher of considerable merit. Contrary to received scientific dogma, Bellarmine never forbade Galileo to "teach or discuss Copernicanism in any way." Indeed the issue was not that of heliocentrism versus geocentrism, and Bellarmine did not attempt to defend Aristotle as if he were sanctioned by the Bible. Quite to the contrary, Bellarmine encouraged Galileo, a personal friend of his, to put forward and hold whatever theories he felt necessary in order to lend greater intelligibility to observable celestial phenomena and greater cogency to his mathematical calculations. His only stipulation, but a most important one, was that Galileo should expressly recognize that the Copernican theory was a "mathematical supposition" and not a literal statement of reality.

In this Bellarmine was reasserting a medieval view of the function of theory expressed by Saint Thomas[35] and recently re-expressed by the great French scientist, Pierre Duhem, that of "saving the phenomena." In this view a theory in science is justified if it serves to give a coherent account of the way observable phenomena appear to behave; but rational justification does not, in a case like this, mean literal truth (justification does not mean verification). Bellarmine was opposing not Galileo or modern science; the issue did not concern "facts" but the physicalistic interpretation of facts and, indeed, the very notion of what constitutes a "fact" and the relation between fact and theory. Against Galileo's attempt to endow his scientific theories with "the certainty of sense-perception" and his tendency to confound theory and experience, Bellarmine pointed out that "to prove that the hypothesis . . . saves the appearances is not at all the same thing as to demonstrate the reality of the movement of the earth."[36]

Bellarmine's view of the status of scientific theory is found in a modern philosopher of science such as Braithwaite. In talking about "the status of the theoretical terms of a science," Braithwaite insists that such terms (for example, *electron, proton*) do not describe directly observable entities but are "symbols in a calculus which is interpreted as an applied deductive system," and they do not have "any meaning apart from their place in such a calculus."[37] Braithwaite thus opposes the view of Russell, reminiscent of that of Galileo, that such terms can be "translated without loss of meaning into a sentence in which there occur only words which denote entities (events, objects, properties) which are directly observable."[38] The truth of the matter is that the relation between scientific theory and concrete experience is only indirect. Indeed there is an unbridgeable gap between theory and experience, such that no theory, even (or perhaps above all) a scientific one, can claim to express what reality really is. This is what Bellarmine recognized, at least implicitly, and what Galileo and, more recently, Russell, persisted in ignoring.[39]

It is regrettable that after Bellarmine's death, the Holy Office should have lost sight of the true philosophical issues involved in the now infamous dispute and should have adopted a repressive course of action against

Galileo, but this cannot alter the fact that the Church had reason and justification for opposing Galileo and the naive (though now generally accepted) interpretation he placed on his "discoveries." And it is regrettable that the scientists themselves should have persisted in falsifying the issues. Kepler, for instance, objected to the principle defended by Bellarmine of "saving the appearances" on the grounds that one cannot explain things by hypotheses that one believes false. But this is an outrageous distortion of the principle. It does not ask us to disbelieve scientific theories and hypotheses or deem them false but only to recognize their theoretical, nonempirical status. In this dispute Bellarmine showed so much more philosophical good sense than Galileo, Kepler, and a host of other Copernicans that Duhem was able to say "that it was Bellarmine . . . and not Galileo and Kepler who had grasped the precise significance of the experimental method."[40]

Although the cultural consequences of Galileo's error have been enormous—accounting to a large extent for our present cultural crisis of the conflict between science and the humanities and between science and religion[41]—the error itself was quite simple, and even natural. That great archeologist of Western consciousness, Edmund Husserl, located and unearthed the source of the error in the investigations he undertook late in his life into the genesis of modern science. In reflecting back on Galileo, Husserl's goal was, as one commentator expresses it, "to relive the tradition of which we are a part for the purpose of liberating us from the prejudices that are inherent in that tradition."[42]

Galileo had sought to discover certain knowledge of the world by applying to the world of everyday experience (the life-world, as Husserl called it) the exactitude of mathematics. Mathematics became the key to unlock the secrets of nature. This was an unprecedented and exciting development in human understanding, but what Galileo failed to see—and this is Husserl's point ("Galileo . . . is at once a discovering and a concealing genius"[43])— was that the mathematical-scientific method is not a description of nature but an interpretation of it and an abstraction from it.

Galileo's world—the world of science—is an abstraction from the concretely experienced world, for the only things about the world that are allowed to count here are rigorously measurable qualities, the so-called primary qualities (mass, extension, and so forth), not the so-called secondary qualities of things (color and taste, for example), even though the latter are inseparable from and basic to (primary in) our experience of the world. It is also an interpretation of the experienced world, for the abstracted "primary" qualities are equated with the ideal forms and shapes of geometry; experienced spatial relations are treated as if they were the ideal ones about which geometry speaks so that they may be treated with the same exactitude characteristic of geometry and, in this way, become the fit object of an exact science.

Galileo's mistake was to have forgotten the abstraction and interpretation involved in the constitution of the scientific object and to have equated the latter with the real world. Galileo did not realize the hypothetical and purely methodological significance of the new science but instead ontologized it. He took "for *true being* what is actually *a method*."⁴⁴ This oversight was destined to be itself overlooked, such that, as Husserl says:

> Even where we do not recognize the universal binding force and general applicability of the "exact" methods of natural science and its cognitive ideals, still the style of this mode of cognition has become so exemplary that from the beginning the conviction persists that objects of our experience are determined in themselves and the activity of cognition is precisely to discover by approximation these determinations subsisting in themselves, to establish them "objectively" as they are in themselves. . . . This *idea of the determinability "in itself" of what exists* and hence the idea that the world of our experience is a universe of things existing in themselves and as such determined in themselves is so much a matter of course for us that, even when laymen reflect on the achievement of knowledge, this "objectivity" is from the first accepted as self-evident. Thus it is presupposed as self-evident that the space of our world and the time in which what exists is encountered and in which our experience is situated are precisely *the* space and *the* time, which it is then the task of physicomathematical natural science to grasp exactly as they are in themselves.⁴⁵

If this naiveté (as Husserl says) is to be overcome and if we are to appreciate properly the place of science in human understanding, it must be remembered that physical science deals not with "realities" but with "idealizations." Scientific objectivities are, in fact, "nothing more than a garb of ideas thrown over the world of immediate intuition and experience, the life-world."⁴⁶ "It is because of the disguise of ideas that the true meaning of the [scientific] method" remains misunderstood.⁴⁷ It must be remembered that *the world of theory is not the world of concrete experience.*

> This actually intuited, actually experienced and experienceable world, in which practically our whole life takes place, remains unchanged as what it is, in its own essential structure and its own concrete causal style, whatever we may do with or without [methodological] techniques. Thus it is also not changed by the fact that we invent a particular technique, the geometrical and Galilean technique which is called physics.⁴⁸

Galileo's error was simply the natural human error of taking for reality one's own imaginative fictions.⁴⁹ Science, as we know it and as it views itself, could be said to be a form of "glorified" common sense, for all the doxic certainty that consciousness attaches to the world of everyday experience at the lowest level of perceptual common sense is here reinvested in the higher-level world of scientific constructions. In science consciousness pursues at a higher level of sophisticated naiveté its native dogmatic bent and indulges in its unlimited capacity for believing.

Here, then, is the reason for the "paradox of imagination in science" and for the "outstripping of analogy"; it is to be found in the very makeup of human understanding, in its native dogmatism.[50] In science the analogical character of understanding is covered over and forgotten because understanding is naturally dogmatic and seeks to endow its belief objects with all the status of reality. As Sextus Empiricus rightly remarked, "Dogmatic conception is the acceptance of a fact which seems to be established by analogy or some form of demonstration, as, for example, that atoms are the elements of existing things."[51] Dogmatism is the result of understanding's denial of its own creativity and analogical mode of operation. When he expresses himself in the forum of public science, the scientist aims at eliciting acceptance of his views; he wants others in the community of scientists to endorse his beliefs, and accordingly he has recourse to a variety of argumentative techniques whose sole object is that of persuasion.[52] As Holton said, it is "part of the game" to cover up the transition from private to public science and to reduce analogy to identity, for only in this way can the contested prize—knowledge, science, truth—appear to the contestants as a meaningful and worthwhile one. The name of this game is *rhetoric*.

In both art and science people search for an understanding of reality and seek to say something true about the world in which they live, and what both the artwork and the scientific statement have in common is that, wittingly or unwittingly, they demand to be believed. They seek to provide a convincing world view that affords the comfort of understanding; that is, they seek to persuade. A tragic drama, for instance, is effective as a piece of literature only if it succeeds in creating the illusion of reality, just as a theory counts as scientific only if people are convinced that it is or could be "objectively true." If rhetoric is defined as the "art or science of using words effectively in speaking or writing, so as to influence or persuade,"[53] then science, as much as literature or jurisprudence, is "rhetorical." All consciousness, it has been maintained, is belief, and art and science, as modes of expressive consciousness, are modes of inducing and maintaining belief. The successful artwork, just as the successful ("true") scientific theory, is a semantic construct which provokes belief.

To be sure, the rationalist maintains otherwise. Science, he says, has to do not with "belief" but with "knowledge." Unlike rhetoric, the object of logic or dialectic, science, is not the "likely" or the "probable" but the "certain," the "true." Rhetoric, as Plato long ago said, does not seek to convince by giving true reasons but only to persuade by concocting sham reasons. Rhetoric is clever talking whose sole goal is to "make the same thing appear to the same people now just, now unjust, at will.''[54] It is the knack of creating illusions that values probability or plausibility more than truth, plausibility being simply "that which commends itself to the multitude.''[55]

Plato recognized that the key element in both rhetoric and dialectic is the drawing of likenesses and the making of comparisons—analogical reasoning—but he insisted that in rhetoric, unlike the case in dialectic, the likenesses talked about are merely apparent (Plato likened rhetoric to cosmetics) and do not correspond to the real "nature of things." In arguing against rhetoric in this way Plato was led to formulate a number of conceptual dichotomies basic to his own rationalist philosophy: appearance versus reality, opinion versus knowledge, the plausible versus the true, rhetoric versus philosophy (science, or what Plato called "true rhetoric"). These dichotomies today form the cornerstone of the edifice of scientific-technological rationalism. They determine our idea of reason, of what is rational and what is not.

The result of our present inability to reconcile scientific-technological and humanistic priorities and our inability to apply science and technology on a global scale without simultaneously poisoning the inner wellsprings of cultures other than our own is a cultural crisis of the greatest magnitude; it is nothing other than a crisis in the idea of reason bequeathed to us by the ancient Greeks. It is our inherited idea of rationality, that idea that has formed the sustaining and guiding principle of Western culture for well over two millennia, which is now in a state of severe crisis.[56]

In response to the forces of irrationalism, which increasingly threaten to undo the cultural order, it is often argued that what we need now is a reaffirmation of the goal of reason, a renewed commitment to the ancient Greek ideals of truth and science (this is, for instance, the tack taken by Husserl in response to the breakdown of civilization in Nazi Germany). Scientific-technological reason, it is admitted more and more, has failed to provide for the good life, which had been expected from it. What is called for, so people say, is a "humanization" of the scientific-technological enterprise; science must be made to take greater account of human concerns.[57] What is not generally realized by those who take up this "open-minded" approach (widening out scientific reason so as to take account of human concerns) is that so far from coming to grips with the cultural problem of our times, it has not even grasped the essence of this problem. The problem is not that of finding a place for human concerns within the world of scientific fact and objective truth but is the much more far-reaching one of properly situating science within the whole of human creative endeavors.

If we wish to avoid anarchy and cultural chaos but also an even greater scientific-technological planification of society—which can mean only a greater bureaucratization of society and a greater dehumanization of people—the only practicable alternative is to reappraise our idea of what makes for rationality. We need to question our naive assurance in the primacy of logical thinking and the supremacy of "objective fact." It is not a question of finding a place for values in the world of fact, but of re-assessing the status of scientific fact, which is to say of scientific truth. Is scientific and logical truth the supreme truth? What is the relation between the logically true and the morally good? Could it perhaps not be the case that the latter takes precedence over the former? In any event, the myth of truth, as Nietzsche so strenuously insisted, needs to be called into question.[58]

The very basis of Western culture needs to be re-examined, for the notions of objective, universal truth and scientific knowledge form the very essence of our cultural tradition. We need an archeological investigation into the grounds of Western culture, of the kind undertaken by Husserl in the case of Galileo, but of a much more radical sort, in order to reach back to the original foundation and to question, in a way Husserl, a rationalist in spite of himself, would never have been capable of, the guiding presuppositions of the tradition.[59]

Just as Galileo's disputations with the Church and the reaction of early modern thinkers to this episode constitute in a way the origin of our present scientific culture, so at the basis of our rationalist tradition as a whole there lies a nearly forgotten episode, and, as in the case of Galileo, it is one that, when alluded to, is distorted in the light of ideas that gained the ascendancy as a result of it. This decisive episode was the battle that Plato waged against the Sophists or Rhetoricians. So thorough was Plato's victory that today the word *sophist* is synonymous with dishonesty and specious argumentation; *sophistry* designates any form of plausible but fallacious argument. The sophist, we say, is one who through slick talking can make someone believe that black is white; he is interested only in his own personal gain and, as Plato said of one of the greatest of Sophists, Gorgias, he respects probability more than truth, makes trifles seem important and important points trifles by the force of his language, dresses up novelties as antiques and vice-versa, and argues concisely or at interminable length about anything and everything.[60] Nothing could be further from the truth.

There are always two sides to a story, and when it is said that the issue at stake in Plato's battle with the Sophists or Rhetoricians (what generally all Sophists had in common is that they taught young men the art of expressing themselves) was whether greater respect should be paid to serving the truth rather than merely winning an argument at whatever costs and by whatever means, we are being given only Plato's side of the story. In fact nothing could have been less intended by a Sophist such as Gorgias than deliberately to encourage his students to utter falsehoods and cleverly deceive their listeners. Naturally any ability can be made to serve any end, good or bad, honest or dishonest, and the ability to argue in a rational and convincing manner is no exception. This Gorgias recognized. But this is not what is important.[61] Plato notwithstanding, Gorgias was not an opportunist and he did not profess disrespect for the truth. He simply believed that, as far at least as mortals are concerned, there is no such thing. This is a different matter altogether, and a serious philosophical one at that.

Plato's battle against the Sophists was the battle of a self-righteous dogmatist against tolerant skeptics. At stake was the role to be assigned to reason. The real issue was a fundamental epistemological and metaphysical one: the status of men's knowledge claims as to the ultimate nature of reality—that is, the status of "truth." The Sophists were Greece's first professional teachers, and they originated in response to the rise and spread of democracy, which made it important for citizens to learn how to express themselves well in the forum of public opinion (public opinion does not exist in an authoritarian state nor would it have existed in Plato's ideal Republic). Their aim was therefore practical: to teach abilities that would enable citizens to lead a good social life in a free society. In this the Sophists represented a distinct turning away from the thought and concerns of the first Greek thinkers, the cosmologists, whose prime concern was not human existence in the world and in society but the underlying structure of reality. The Sophists, on the contrary, felt that problems of human existence were more important than questions as to the ultimate makeup of matter, and they accordingly professed no interest in physical science. Their concern was people, not atoms. They were the world's first humanists.

And as keen observers of people, they were the first to take note of the fact that there are about as many "ultimate realities" as there are speculative philosophers and theorizers. Each theorizer, Gorgias remarked, thinks that he has the secret of the universe, but what one sees is only a host of theories pitted one against the other, each one more incredible than the other and placing ever greater demands on the imagination. As one modern rhetorician observes, "The concepts that men have formed, in the course of history, of 'objective facts' and 'obvious truths' have sufficiently varied for us to be wary in this matter."[62] Their suspicions aroused, the Sophists realized that what a person holds to be true about reality is in fact a belief that he may persuade others to accept also. Thus for any person the "true" is (pragmatically speaking) simply what he believes in, or, as Protagoras said, "What seems to each man *is* as far as he is concerned."

As a matter of sheer description nothing could be truer, and the recognition of this fact led the Sophists to conclude that *it is impossible to separate belief from knowledge or appearance from reality.* But if this is so, it is surely a vain pursuit to try to discover the nature of that unknowable reality that the dogmatists assert underlies all appearances. This is what motivated the Sophists to declare that such a reality does not exist (Gorgias wrote an ironic, anti-Parmenidean treatise, *On Non-Being*, in which he maintained that being is not) and that there is no absolute truth to be known. All truths, at least as far as people are concerned, are irremediably relative. Thus when Protagoras declared, "On every topic there are two arguments contrary to each other," he was not advocating the fabrication of differing arguments simply to confound one's listeners but was simply and honestly stating a fact readily apparent to any unbiased observer of the human comedy.

In recognizing the relativity of all truth and the inescapability of belief—in denying, that is, the existence of truth—the Sophists were more truthful than their dogmatic predecessor, Parmenides, and their archrival, Plato, the faithful disciple of the great Eleatic. And they were more tolerant of men's beliefs and respectful of their freedom also. Plato, the great believer in truth and science, did not hesitate to advocate that the rulers of his ideal state foster "noble lies" upon their subjects in order to persuade them of the truth of their own belief in the truth. It is important to take careful note of this curious fact, that the belief in the truth, its unequivocal oneness and universal, uniform applicability—a belief in the supremacy of science—is used to justify a totalitarian state of affairs whereas the relativism of the Sophists goes hand in hand with a democratic respect for the individual and his beliefs.[63] This is something that Plato's victory, the victory of truth and science, tends to make us forget.

One of the most significant differences between the Sophists' conception of philosophy and of the fitting use of reason and that of Plato and his successors (who succeeded in usurping the title "philosophy" for themselves) concerns the existence of contradiction and paradox in human thinking. In the wake of his teacher, Plato, Aristotle sought to ban contradiction from rational discourse, and to this end he formulated his famous principle of noncontradiction, which he asserted was "the most certain principle of all." According to this principle, "The same attribute cannot at the same time belong and not belong to the same subject and in the same respect"; or, in a less hypostatized manner, "it is impossible for any one to believe the same thing to be and not to be, as some think Heraclitus says."[64]

After asserting this supreme principle, Aristotle says that if, on the contrary, one perversely maintains that "of everything it is possible either to affirm or to deny anything," then, like Protagoras (Aristotle says), he must also maintain that all attributes are accidents and must accordingly "do away with substance and essence." But since Aristotle, after Plato, holds to the proper meaning superstition—that is, he believes that "not to have one meaning is to have no meaning" and that "it is impossible to think of anything if we do not think of one thing"—he maintains that substance must exist. But it is precisely this belief in the existence of an underlying, nonappearing, self-same, and unchanging essence or substance that Protagoras refused, with good reason, to accept. It is therefore not out of a lack of "education," as Aristotle implies, but with the best of reasons that Protagoras denied the possibility of unequivocal definition and maintained that of anything anything can be said (this is a corollary to the thesis that everything in nature is like everything else). Protagoras is not uttering "unintelligibilities," as Aristotle says, and is not behaving like a "vegetable" but is, on the contrary, making the best of human sense. It is only Aristotle's rationalist presuppositions and his restricting conception of rationality (one must say either yes or no; A cannot also be not-A) that prevents him from seeing this. It is no accident that Aristotle was unable to give a proper account of metaphor, for the peculiar characteristic of metaphor is that its affirmations are always qualified and the metaphorical "is" is at the same time an "is-not."

When, as in Aristotle's case, a narrow, highly logicist view of reason is accepted, the utterances of the Sophists must appear to be self-contradictory, senseless, and irrational. When, however, a wider, more comprehensive view of what makes for rationality is adopted, their arguments can be seen to be not only meaningful but highly cogent as well. For instance, when Gorgias asserts at the high point of his famous treatise on non-being that "nothing exists," he is, in the limited half-vision of the logician, uttering nonsense and is in fact saying nothing at all. But if one stops to consider not just what Gorgias is saying but also what he wants to show by means of what he says—if, that is, one looks for the underlying reasons for what he says—his paradoxical and ironic utterances become intelligible. Gorgias wished to refute the rationalist's (Parmenides') claim that under the shifting phenomena of experience is a self-identical, changeless nature of things, and he did this in the most effective of ways—not by pointing out logical loopholes in Parmenides' statements about unchanging being but by constructing a flawless logical argument of his own to the effect that being is not. He thereby concretely demonstrated that in terms of the rationalist's own reasoning it is as easy to prove the exact opposite of what they do. As Isocrates, a pupil of Gorgias and a contemporary of Plato as well as the latter's arch-enemy, said, what Gorgias showed "was that it is easy to trump up a false argument about whatever you like to put forward."[65]

In demonstrating this, Gorgias justified, *indirectly* (the only way it is possible to do so), his own anti-rationalist thesis: that truth is relative. As Sextus Empiricus points out, Gorgias's objective (as well as that of Protagoras) was to show that there is no indisputable criterion of truth.[66] Therefore when one views Gorgias's theories ("nothing exists") in the light of his intellectual practice, when, that is, one takes account of his own anti-rationalist conception of the role of reason and argumentation—according to which the purpose of reason and theory is not to discover the truth but to provoke a certain existential transformation in ourselves and in others[67]—one realizes that in terms of this wider function of reason Gorgias does not contradict himself but is eminently consistent.

Can one say as much for the rationalist? The Sophists and skeptics do not set much store by the so-called principles of identity and contradiction, they do not believe that they are instruments capable of ferreting out the secrets of nature, and yet they do not contradict themselves and are fully consistent when one takes account of their own view of the nature and scope of human reason. The rationalists, however, appeal to these principles, and they assert that they are the laws of reality itself, but when one considers what they say in the light of what they actually do, one inevitably detects a number of grave inconsistencies and contradictions. Plato does not hesitate, in the name of truth, to advocate falsehood and deception (the "noble lie"). Another inconsistency is that while castigating rhetoric and his rival Isocrates, Plato makes use of every rhetorical device he can think of. (One has only to read a Platonic dialogue and note the innumerable rhetorical devices Socrates used in an attempt to bludgeon his interlocutor into agreement or silence.) This fact in particular merits attention; what needs to be seen is that while opposing rhetoric in the name of science and while castigating belief in the name of knowledge, Plato was doing no more than practicing the art of rhetoric and was attempting to persuade people that his beliefs were better than those of his fellow rhetoricians. It is Plato and his pupils that Isocrates has in mind when he condemns those who talk abusively of the "art of speaking," not because they are ignorant of its power "but because they think that by decrying this art they will enhance the standing of their own."[68]

The rationalist's inconsistent practice actually substantiates the skeptical-humanist objection to rationalism: that as a theory it can exist only by presupposing precisely that which it claims to prove. The supreme value that the rationalist seeks to invest in logic and science is warranted only if they are indeed disciplines capable of discovering the truth about reality, and it goes without saying that truth can be discovered only if it exists in the first place—that is, only if reality is itself determinate and intelligible. But that reality is intelligible is something that neither logic nor science could every conceivably prove.

Science is, rather, an expression of one's prior faith in the intelligibility of reality. A scientist cannot, qua scientist, defend his commitment to science. When, therefore, the skeptical humanist questions the priority that the rationalist accords to science vis-à-vis all other cultural endeavors, the rationalist will react in one of two ways. He will either simply ignore the objections of the humanist, since, qua scientist, he cannot rationally respond to them, in which case he imperiously cuts off all further dialogue (all *logos,* all rational discussion), thereby undermining the only possible basis for a genuinely free society, freedom of discussion; or else he will respond to them. In the latter case two avenues of argument are open to him. First, he may attempt to defend science through rational argument of a general sort, through rhetoric, but in this case he is implicitly recognizing that there is a realm of rational discussion that is more basic than scientific-logical discourse, and this is enough to refute his own thesis as to the priority of science as a means of arriving at the truth about things. Or, second, he may attempt to refute the skeptic's arguments. But here again he must have recourse to rhetoric, since if science cannot justify itself, it also cannot refute arguments directed against it. What usually happens in this case is that the scientist falls into bad rhetoric, eristic. As in the case of Frege, he ends up by begging the question or by proceeding in a vicious circle. When this is pointed out to him he has no further choice, apart from withdrawing from the discussion altogether, but to engage in *ad hominem* attacks against his rhetorical opponent.

Is this not an exceedingly strange state of affairs? The believer in "science" and "knowledge" who disparages "rhetoric" and "opinion" can defend, or attempt to defend, his belief in science only by means of rhetoric. Not only does his practice give the lie to his theories, but it also, and significantly, serves to debase the art of discussion, rhetoric, by reducing it to pure eristic. By means of an *ad hominem* argument (unallowable on the rationalist's own grounds) the rationalist defends his own notion of truth by imputing a disrespect for truth on the part of his critic. One can well wonder, with Kierkegaard, "How does it happen that derision, and contempt, and measures of intimidation are pressed into service as the legitimate means of getting forward in logic, so that the consent of the reader is secured . . . because he is afraid of what acquaintances and neighbors will think of him if he does not agree to its validity?"[69]

Not only must the rationalist fall back on rhetoric when he seeks to defend science, the truth of the matter is that science itself is a form of rhetoric. This will become fully apparent if we consider what rhetoric is. Let us begin with Aristotle's classic definition: "Rhetoric may be defined as the faculty of observing in any given case the available means of persuasion."[70] One is tempted to substitute for "available" the term "appropriate," but this is perhaps not necessary since "in any given case" only certain means of persuasion are available or appropriate to use. Aristotle takes note of three kinds of rhetoric: political (deliberative), forensic (legal), and epideictic (ceremonial oratory). And to these should be added dialectic or scientific-philosophical argumentation, for the latter is a form of argumentation and therefore a "means of persuasion." Rhetoric is the art of persuasion through discourse. It is concerned not with any particular subject matter but with everything in general having to do with discourse and with forms of reasoning or arguing, for the purpose of argument is persuasion.[71]

Let us consider argumentative rhetoric. The subject matter of all argumentation is the likely, the possible, the problematic—in short, all that which is not absolutely certain and self-evident, for the latter is, by definition, that which people are generally agreed upon and thus have no need to argue over. The subject of argument is thus that over which people tend to disagree or concerning which there is no commonly held opinion, and the purpose of argument is to "discover the truth of the matter." Translated into straightforward terms this means that *the purpose of argument is to secure a common agreement as to how the matter shall be understood*—to arrive at an opinion or view of the matter that will be generally accepted or agreed upon (which will be persuasive, credible). As Peirce would say, the purpose of argument is the fixation of belief. Such a belief or opinion is what people call the "truth." If one has already arrived at some definite understanding of the matter for oneself, when one "argues for" a thesis—whether in the law court or the scientific congress—one is seeking to secure the agreement (assent) of others or, in more euphemistic terms, one is seeking to "convince others of the truth of the matter." This is also what is involved when one lays out a "demonstration," for a demonstration is one (rhetorical) way of securing assent.[72]

This is to say that all argumentation is directed to an audience (even if the audience is of only one and even if this one is one's self, "for the same arguments which we use in persuading others when we speak in public, we employ also when we deliberate in our own thoughts").[73] Hence it is important, if the argument is to be successful, if it is to be a "good" one, that it be geared to the audience to which it is directed. As Vico remarked, "The whole object of eloquence is relative to our listeners, and it is according to their opinions that we must regulate our discourse."[74] This is important to realize, for it shows that in rhetoric it is not a question, as Plato disparagingly puts it, of merely flattering one's audience but rather of taking account of their demands, expectations, and presuppositions. A scientist who did not play by the rules of the game when writing a professional article would not be heeded. Even God, when He addresses Himself to humans, speaks in human terms and assumes human form, or at least a form recognizable by man (the Incarnation, the Burning Bush). It is in this sense above all, and not merely in the sense of eloquence, that rhetoric is the art of speaking or writing well.

What is appropriate for one audience will not be appropriate for another. There is the wavering mob which needs decisive and not very refined exhortation; at the other extreme is the dispassionate audience of "all reasonable men." It is to this latter that the scientist and the philosopher address themselves, and here agreement or assent can be secured only if one's discourse is constructed in such a way as to appeal not merely (or not primarily) to emotion and prior prejudice but to certain formal rules. Let us take scientific discourse as an example.

The basic rules of the game in arguing scientifically are three. In the appropriate wording of one scientific writer, those "attributes that appear to facilitate the adoption of concepts and statements into the scientific body of knowledge" are abstractness, intersubjectivity, and empirical relevance.[75] *Abstractness* involves the independence of a "scientific" idea from any particular place and time, for, as it is supposed, only if an idea is independent of any particular cultural or temporal setting can it be applicable to any and all settings; only so can it be "universally true." *Universality* (a better term than *abstractness*) is in fact the basic rule for all so-called rational argument or truth. *Intersubjectivity* means that the key terms used in the argument must have a meaning exactly agreed upon by the audience; the goal in scientific argument is univocity, semantic exactitude. A scientific writer must draw key terms from a generally agreed-upon vocabulary and, in addition, must use them in a way rigorously prescribed by the scientific community (syntactical exactitude). Only if he conforms to these semantical and syntactical rules will his audience consider him to be saying something worthwhile, that is, scientific. *Empirical relevance* is peculiar to modern science. It means that for every claim put forward, the writer must be able to find some empirical fact to support it. Generally a scientist will be heeded only if he can point to a mass of laboratory, experimental, or statistical data. It does not matter that an experiment, like statistics (or the Zande poison oracle), can be made to "prove" just about anything one wishes; the important thing is that one be able to appeal to "empirical research" and invoke its support. Although Einstein was notoriously uninterested in finding or appealing to empirical "confirmation" for his theories, most scientists will generally not be favorably received by their audience if, like a philosopher (or an ancient scientist), they can only provide well-structured theories.

Such are the basic rules of scientific rhetoric. What science (in the modern sense of the term) shares with philosophy is the first requirement: universality. This is indeed the most basic rule for any rhetorical activity proposing to deal with what is objectively true and laying claim to knowledge (science in the traditional sense of the term). What needs to be seen is that the characteristic of universality does not make an argument any less rhetorical but only marks it off as a special kind of rhetoric.

The basic feature of all rhetorical discourse is that it is directed to an audience, which it seeks to persuade. However, the kinds of audience are many and varied, which means that different kinds of argument or persuasive discourse must be used with them. What characterizes Science (we shall use *Science* to designate both traditional dogmatic philosophy and modern science) is that it seeks to secure as large an audience as possible. A Scientific argument, it is claimed, is not directed to this or that class of people only or to these or those individuals—above all, it is not, as in the unscientific work of Kierkegaard, directed to the Individual—but to all people without exception, in their quality of "rational beings." Therefore it must transcend the specific differences between particular audiences.

Science attempts to transcend particularity by isolating one particular aspect of human understanding and declaring it "essential." This element is what it calls "reason." Because reason is supposed to constitute the "essence" of man, in addressing himself to "all rational men," the Scientist can say that he is in fact addressing himself to a universal audience.[76] Of course, all people tend to think that "normality" ("essentiality") is the possession of certain particular traits (traits characteristic of their particular culture or class), and in declaring the human norm to consist in the possession and exercise of what it calls "reason." Science is doing no differently; it is merely privileging one particular feature of all human understanding.[77]

What it is that constitutes "rationality" is, indeed, something of which Science tends to form a very peculiar notion. For Science the laws of rational thinking are those codified in logic (such that the most rigorous and Scientific form of reasoning is held to be deductive, syllogistic reasoning in which the laws of identity, contradiction, and excluded middle hold sway). But this conception of what constitutes rationality has certain curious consequences. For one, it makes of analogical, metaphorical thinking—by far the most widespread and basic form of human understanding—something irrational. For another, it makes for insurmountable problems when it comes to understanding other cultures; everything about human behavior that is not rational in the technological and scientific sense (such as religious behavior) can be viewed only as "primitive" and irrational or prelogical. Also, it has an extremely serious consequence that it removes "all rational justification from action based on choice, . . . thus making the exercise of human freedom absurd."[78] Therefore, the more Science seeks for universal invariance in its object, the more narrow and less "universal" that object in fact becomes.

What all of this shows is that Science's appeal to universal man or to "all reasonable men" is an appeal to merely one aspect of man, and a relatively peculiar one at that. It is in fact an appeal to one peculiar kind of man and one peculiar form of reasoning, the kind of reasoning found in the logician and in the computer but not in the poetic or religious man. Science, like rhetoric, has its audience, and what for it is truth is merely what "commends itself to the multitude" of people who equate rationality with logic. As Bruno Snell said, "The belief in the existence of a universal, uniform human mind is a rationalist prejudice."[79]

It is not just Plato but the entire Scientific, dogmatic project, therefore, that is self-contradictory. For while the Scientist castigates *ad hominem* argument, it is precisely this which he practices. Perelman pertinently remarks:

The natural or rational order [these terms should be written with quotation marks] is not independent of all audiences, but is adapted to the universal audience and the rationality attributed to this audience. . . . One overlooks the fact that such notions as clarity and simplicity which form the basis of the rational order were developed psychologically, and, later, made absolute. In fact, rational argument is simply a particular instance of argumentation *ad hominem*—the one we have termed argumentation *ad humanitatem*.[80]

This reflection on the nature of rhetoric has served to demonstrate that what since Plato has been called philosophy or what today is called science, far from being of a different order than rhetoric, is itself a branch of rhetoric. To realize this is the sine qua non for reconciling science and the humanities and for grappling with the problem of other cultures. Scientific truth must be shown, and must be seen, to be a purely relative affair and to be a matter of opinion; if it is not, one cannot rationally oppose its cultural imperialism.[81] The great danger of rationalism and the logicist view of things, which sets up a rigid dichotomy between the "likely" and the "true," "appearance" and "reality," and according to which reality has an "essential nature" that in principle is knowable, provided one has access to the proper rational method, and the principal reason for our opposition to it, is that, when translated into the concrete realm of action (and this is the only "logical" thing to do), it makes for an inflexible and totalitarian state of affairs. In the rationalist view, truth is what demands to be acknowledged; it is what "all reasonable men" must agree to. What this means is that when the truth is implemented in the moral or political realm, individuals, as functionaries of the truth, will use persuasion or force to attempt to coerce all others into conformity with the truth (for the truth, being timeless and self-same, is that which must be conformed to). Only the truth about the dogmatic myth of truth can genuinely serve to make men free or, at least, to safeguard their freedom. As the philosopher of science, Stephen Toulmin, noted, although with a different point in mind, "The road from nice points about logic and idiom to the most difficult problems of conduct is not, after all, such a long one."[82]

If one's goal is to understand human understanding and what human understanding claims to understand, reality, one must inquire into that which lends credibility to any given "truth" or knowledge claim about reality. One must focus one's attention on the means themselves by which people are made to think or are persuaded, and thus come to believe, that reality is of such and such a sort. All our lives we have been taught a description of the world (this is the function of education, which is, as the anthropologist would say, a means of enculturation), and thus what we ordinarily take to be reality is in fact nothing other and nothing more than a kind of cultural construct imposed on our immediate experience. As Husserl observed, "The world of our experience is from the beginning interpreted by recourse to an 'idealization.' "[83] The persuasiveness of this learned interpretation "causes us to interpret the world of our experience always according to the sense of this garb of ideas thrown over it, as if it were thus 'in itself.' "[84] The world is such-and-such and so-and-so only because we have been trained to see it thus. As Whorf remarked "We cut up and organize the spread and flow of events as we do, largely because, through our mother tongue, we are parties to an agreement to do so, not because nature itself is segmented in exactly that way for all to see."[85] What guarantees the "objectivity" of truth and the "reality" of the world is the common consensus of the culture in which we live. Reality is a cultural, semantic construct or, as Husserl says, "The world is a meaning, an accepted sense."[86]

Whorf has attempted to show how the language we speak shapes our world view. But what is decisive in determining a world view is not just the grammatical structure of one's language but also—indeed above all—the way in which this language is used.[87] There are different modes of discourse, the principal ones being science, myth, and poetry (literature), and what they have in common is that they are all means of persuasion and thus are, in this sense, "rhetorical." This is not always readily recognized and merits a moment's consideration.

We have already attempted to show the intimate relation between dialectic and rhetoric; as a mode of persuasive argumentation dialectic is in fact a mode of rhetoric. But what about so-called epideictic rhetoric? What relation is there between, say, a funeral oration and a political speech or a legal brief or a philosophical-scientific argument? Is not oratory more a matter of "eloquence" than of persuasion? Oratory admittedly is a form of what is called "literature." If, then, it can be seen that it is also rhetoric in the strict sense of the term (a form of persuasive argumentation), the case for including literature along with science as a mode of persuasive argumentation will have been strengthened.

It is true that a funeral oration or a eulogy for an outstanding citizen does not attempt to solicit an audience's acceptance of certain intellectual theses about the makeup of reality or a political course of action to be undertaken or the guilt or innocence of a citizen, but it does solicit agreement from an audience, which is the central feature of all rhetoric. Oratory (a church sermon is a perfect example) seeks to reinforce the commitment on the part of the audience to certain cultural values. This is a key feature of oratory that Perelman has emphasized: "The speaker tries to establish a sense of communion centered around particular values recognized by the audience, and to this end he uses the whole range of means available to the rhetorician for the purposes of amplification and enhancement [*pour amplifier et valoriser*]."[88] It is thus evident that the orator is in fact an educator who teaches something even more basic than "facts": the basic values of a culture. Oratory is persuasive rhetoric.

Oratory, though, is only one branch of literature. What about that form of literature that Aristotle assigns not to rhetoric but to poetics? What is the relation between rhetoric and "poetry" or what today we would call fictional literature (play, novel, poem)? Gorgias said that tragic fiction is but rhetoric in verse form, and he had a point, for, like a good argument, fiction is successful only if it manages to make itself accepted by its audience. To do this it must, as one would formerly have said, be a convincing "imitation of reality." It must appear to be "true to life." What is peculiar to art and what distinguishes it from history is, as Aristotle noted, that it is not in spite of the artist's free inventions that art communicates a convincing truth about (imitates, represents) reality but precisely because of them.[89] To borrow an expression from Aristotle, we could say that in general fictional literature is "the art of framing lies in the right way."[90] The artist is not interested in "facts" and in correctly depicting them, but he *is* interested in reality, that is, in the universal, the essential meaning of things, and it is this which he seeks to communicate to his audience.

But, of course, art does not really imitate or represent anything at all. Nor is it, as the aesthete would have it, merely the expression of the artist's own inner landscape. Rather, art creates a new reality, one in regard to which, as Wallace Stevens would say, ordinary reality seems unreal. But science too creates its own reality. Atoms are semantic constructs in regard to which the things of ordinary experience, such as macroscopic tables and chairs, appear to be unreal or, at least, of a lesser reality. A literary fiction must succeed in creating the illusion of truth and reality, and, like a scientific theory, it wants to be believed. It is no accident that the ancient Greeks considered the poets to be their true teachers, at least until Plato denounced the poets as liars. Poetry too, therefore, is a form of rhetoric whose purpose in general is to produce objects for human belief.[91]

This approach to the varying modes of human discourse from the unifying point of view of rhetoric enables us to see something truly basic about language in general. What primarily characterizes human language is not its ability to communicate information, for even computer language can do this, even better in fact (more precisely, unambiguously) than can human language. Indeed, there is no such thing as simple, objective information; information or facts are a product of interpretation and exist only within a particular frame of reference or universe of discourse.[92] Now it is by means of language, whether scientific or artistic, that the kind of semantic construct that people call a "world" (reality) emerges as an object of belief and of a common consensus. The unique feature of human language is thus its power to create worlds. "Language," Steiner says, "is a constant creation of alternative worlds."[93] Language is persuasive; it seeks to persuade us of the truth of what it says, and what it says is reality (a world).

This world-projective ability of language is especially manifest in the metaphor which, we know by now, is the motor element in all language which says something new. It is on "the living metaphorical nature of language" that, as Gadamer said, concept formation depends. And since what a concept refers to is an essence (and since the "referent" of language is a function of its "sense"), the essence of things, or the interwoven tissue of concepts that people call reality, is engendered through the metaphorical use of language. The essence of metaphor is the juxtaposition of terms from two different semantic realms—that is, the making of a comparison or the drawing of a likeness. The mode of understanding at work here is thus analogy. When one speaks of original, creative understanding from the point of view of language, one will speak of analogical language (metaphor); when one speaks of creative understanding from the point of view of the kind of thought processes involved, one will speak of analogical thinking. As Richards says, "*Thought* is metaphoric, and proceeds by comparison, and the metaphors of language derive therefrom."[94] The proper name for metaphorical thought is *imagination*.

Philosophers have always recognized that imagination is the synthesizing faculty of the mind. Its function is to combine and associate; it is, as Plato would say, "the art of using similarities."[95] To the imagination thus conceived, philosophers have traditionally opposed another faculty: judgment. Judgment has to do not with combining and synthesizing but with dividing and classifying. Its function, in the words of Plato, is to "divide things into their kinds and embrace each individual thing under a single form."[96] In other words, judgment defines. As well as opposing imagination (or fancy) and judgment, the rationalist tradition has also always subordinated the former to the latter, for how, the rationalist rhetorically asks, could one possibly draw a correct likeness between two things if he did not first know the specific nature of each: "But can anyone possibly master the art of using similarities . . . unless he has knowledge of what the thing in question really is?"[97]

This is a typical instance of the rationalist inversion syndrome, of the rationalist's inveterate tendency always to get things backward. For "what a thing really is," its essence, is merely a statement of what it is like; it is, in short, a believed-in, dead metaphor. Just as language is not first of all descriptive and then only afterward inventive but instead creates by analogy those "essential" classifications or categories in terms of which it afterward draws further analogies (which ultimately transform the categorical structure), so also human understanding in general is, at its basis, imaginative. If the primordiality of metaphor in language is recognized and if the intimate link between language and thought is further recognized, one cannot but recognize also that the imagination is the omnipresent and primordial principle of all understanding.

Just as what is peculiar to the metaphor is the semantic pertinences it sets up when two different semantic contexts are made to interact and not, as is so often thought, the concrete images it may give rise to, so also the imagination, at least in the case of humans, is not primarily a faculty for associating sense images, and thus a lower faculty than intellection, but is, through and through, semantic. It has to do not with sense impression but with semantic meanings.

If this is not generally recognized,[98] it is due to the overwhelming but thoroughly regrettable influence that Aristotle has had on our intellectual tradition. On the whole, philosophers have never properly understood the importance of imagination, for they have followed in the footsteps of Aristotle and have relegated the imagination to a chapter in their treatises on psychology. They have taken the imagination to be that lower faculty, which men share with the brutes, whose business it is to coordinate and reproduce sense impressions. To be sure, this is consistent with the basic rationalist prejudice that there exists "in itself" a fully determinate reality and that the function of human understanding is to form a correct picture of this reality (the function of the imagination, qua *sensus communis,* being to fit together the fragmentary bits of information received through the different, individual senses into one unified picture).

Our inquiry into human understanding has led us, however, to see that this view of things is not tenable. The traditional assessment of the imagination must therefore be revised. If, as we would maintain, what people believe reality to be is a semantic construct, then all understanding that is genuinely insightful is also imaginative. It is by means of the imagination that ideas and theories are woven together to make new theories and that theory and experience are linked together in such a way as to produce what we call "knowledge." The imagination is the means whereby we understand reality.

Thus just as metaphor is not merely one figure of speech among others, so also the imagination (which one might wish to define as the faculty for producing metaphors) is not merely one faculty among others. Rather as Wallace Stevens says, "Man is the imagination or rather the imagination is man."[99] All of the worlds that people claim to know through art, science, myth, or metaphysical speculation on the "nature of things" spring forth from their fertile imaginations. The imagination is the source of all that we call "reality." Science is myth, and myth is believed poetry. What is called "reality" or "objective truth" is a fiction whose fictional nature has been forgotten. As Nietzsche remarked:

What therefore is truth? A mobile army of metaphors, metonymies, anthropomorphisms: in short a sum of human relations which became poetically and rhetorically intensified, metamorphosed, adorned, and after long usage seem to be a notion fixed, canonic and binding; truths are illusions of which one has forgotten that they *are* illusions.[100]

This should not be taken in a nihilistic sense to mean that scientific enti-ties such as atoms and electrons or mythical entities such as angels and demons are not real but are mere "fictions," products of the imagination only. This is precisely what must not be said, for to do so would be to fall once again into the rationalist's trap. The notion of a mere fiction makes sense only if one supposes that there exists some absolute standard as to what is real and what is not (that is, it presupposes the appearance-reality dichotomy), and it further implies that the imagination, as opposed to "per-ception" and "intellection," has nothing to do with understanding or apprehending what is real (presupposed here is the belief-knowledge dichotomy). But the notion of an absolute standard (or criterion, as Sextus would have said) is a rationalist notion. The electron *is* real—when one is doing physics and is participating in this particular world view. An electron is real to the degree that this notion plays a vital and indispensable role within the universe of discourse of physics, and its reality does not go be-yond this. As James so admirably said, "Each world *whilst it is attended to* is real after its fashion; only the reality lapses with the attention."[101] Truth and reality are nothing absolute but are relative to one's belief systems.

Liberation from the illusions of understanding is possible only when, as Nietzsche would say, the truth about truth is known, only when one comes to know that what the dogmatist calls knowledge is a convenient fiction. When the rationalist myth of truth is exposed, the entire edifice of ra-tionalist reason collapses: "Just as, when the foundation of a wall col-lapses, all the super-structure collapses along with it, so also, when the substantial existence of the true is refuted, all the particular inventions of the logic of the Dogmatists are included in the refutation."[102]

When man the world maker becomes explicitly aware of his creative, playful cosmic-constitutive activity, he must appear to himself as something exceedingly uncommon and the power of his language, analogous to the divine word in that it too is capable of calling worlds into being, something uncanny. All the human worlds are only so many semantic constructs, the mythical other-worldly world as much as the scientific this-worldly one. The person who stops to take note of this strange situation may begin to wonder whose puppet he is (if the person is also a Christian he will be reminded of the passage in Genesis, "God created man in his own image, in the image of God created he him"; for the Christian, the greatness of man stems from his, admittedly imperfect, participation in the divine creativity). If each world is true, what truth is it which thus reveals itself in the fact that man is even so much as able to play his various world games? What is the origin and significance of the world game itself? With these questions is opened up the field of a nondogmatic metaphysics that no longer constructs worlds but which takes as its theme the world-constitutive activity itself.

We have now completed our survey of the nature and scope of human understanding. Before we can proceed to draw out its ontological implications and presume to say something about that Reality which is analogically common to all realities, we must take account of one last, and crucial, objection, which the rationalist surely will not fail to raise. This objection, if not properly countered, could be devastating to our entire project of working out a nondogmatic metaphysics. The objection could be phrased something like this: If we maintain that all discourse about reality is not scientific (in the usual, dogmatic sense) but rhetorical, that is, has to do not with "objective truth" but with belief, if all understanding is "imaginative," is not what we have said about understanding a fiction also—a merely subjective view of our own, which may or may not be persuasive but which cannot claim to be true? What is the status of our own theory about the limits of all theory? Are we not finally being caught up in an ultimate self-contradiction, a self-refutation? Have we not cut the ground from under our feet, or, to vary the metaphor, in our refusal to be shipwrecked on either the Scylla of rationalism or the Charybdis of relativism, have we not, wittingly or unwittingly, scuttled our own vessel?

NOTES

1. Interestingly this view was already expressed by Saint Thomas in speaking about the rational justification of ideas; it is the second kind of reasoning that he mentions in the following passage:

> Reasoning may be brought forward for anything in a two-fold way: firstly for the purpose of furnishing sufficient proof of some principle, as in natural science, where sufficient proof can be brought to show that the movement of the heavens is always of a uniform velocity. Reasoning is employed in another way, not as furnishing a sufficient proof of a principle, but as showing how the remaining effects are in harmony with an already posited principle; as in astronomy the theory of eccentrics and epicycles is considered as established, because thereby the sensible appearances of the heavenly movements can be explained; not, however, as if this proof were sufficient, since some other theory might explain them (*Summa theologiae* [Alba, 1962], I, 32, 1, ad. 2).

We cannot agree that there are some principles that can be demonstrated with "sufficient proof" (let alone the uniform velocity of the planets). All principles purporting to describe the nature of reality are of Saint Thomas's second kind; they are "posited," taken on faith—even the highest rational principle of all, the principle of reason itself (*principium rationis sufficientis*).

2. Popper says: "Theories are, therefore, *never* empirically verifiable. . . . But I shall certainly admit a system as empirical or scientific [note Popper's way of equating these two terms] only if it is capable of being *tested* by experience. . . . not the *verifiability* but the *falsifiability* of a system is to be taken as a criterion of demarcation. . . . *it must be possible for an em-*

pirical scientific system to be refuted by experience" (The Logic of Scientific Discovery [New York, 1968], pp. 40-41).

3. M. Polanyi, "The Creative Imagination," *Chemical and Engineering News 44* (April 1966):111.

4. M. Planck, *Scientific Autobiography and Other Papers* (New York, 1949), pp. 33-34, cited by T. Kuhn, *The Structure of Scientific Revolutions* (Chicago, 1970), p.151.

5. One of the best argued critques of psychologism is the one found in the Prolegomena to E. Husserl's *Logical Investigations* (London, 1970).

6. Popper, *Logic of Scientific Discovery*, pp. 30ff.

7. Cf. ibid., pp. 44, 46.

8. Popper, *Objective Knowledge* (Oxford, 1972).

9. Ibid., p. 154.

10. In contrast to Popper, Polanyi shows much better sense when he says: "Nothing is a problem or discovery in itself; it can be a problem only if it puzzles and worries somebody, and a discovery only if it relieves somebody from the burden of a problem" (*Personal Knowledge* [Chicago, 1958], p. 122). The contrast in titles of these two books of Popper (*Objective Knowledge*) and Polyani is worth noting.

11. Holton, *Thematic Origins of Scientific Thought*, pp. 19ff, 100ff, 387ff.

12. Ibid., p. 388.

13. Braithwaite, *Scientific Explanation*, p. 12.

14. G. Holton, *Thematic Origins of Scientific Thought* (Cambridge, Mass., 1973), p. 20.

15. Ibid., pp. 20-21.

16. Popper, *Logic of Scientific Discovery*, pp. 31-32.

17. In his attempt to make of literary criticism a "science" and in accordance with his positivist-style conception of science, E. D. Hirsch is led to take up a position very similar to that of Popper; see his *Validity in Interpretation* [New Haven, Conn., 1967]. Just as Popper says that "there is no such thing as a logical method of having new ideas" and that the epistemology of science is concerned with questions of testing only, so Hirsch says that the interpretation of texts (hermeneutics) has nothing to do with "understanding" or "construing" a text, that is, apprehending its meaning. This is a matter of "psychology" and therefore is not a concern for hermeneutics, which is or should be a *science,* in the hypothetico-deductive (positivist) sense of the term. "The exigencies of validation," Hirsch says, "should not be confused with the exigencies of understanding. . . . Every interpretation begins and ends as a guess, and no one has ever devised a method for making intelligent guesses. They systematic side of interpretation begins where the process of understanding ends. Understanding achieves a construction of meaning; the job of validation is to evaluate the disparate constructions which understanding has brought forward" (p. 170). And brought forward in an "inspired," irrational way! "Conflicting interpretations," he also says, "can be subject to scrutiny in the light of the relevant evidence, and objective conclusions can be reached. . . . Devising subsidiary interpretive hypotheses capable of sponsoring probability decisions is not in principle different from devising experiments which can sponsor decisions between hypotheses in the natural science" (p. 206). For a critique of Hirsch's "scientific" hermeneutics, see my "Eine Kritik an Hirschs Begriff der 'Richtigkeit,' " in H.-G. Gadamer and G. Boehm, eds., *Die Hemeneutik und die Wissenschaften* (Frankfurt: Suhrkamp Verlag, 1978).

18. An extensive and usefully organized bibliography of works dealing with analogical-metaphorical thinking in science—with creative thinking in science—can be found in W. H. Leatherdale, *The Role of Analogy, Model and Metaphor in Science* (Amsterdam, 1974).

19. N. R. Hanson, *Patterns of Discovery* (Cambridge, 1972), pp. 71-72. T. Kuhn writes: "If history or any other empirical discipline leads us to believe that the development of science depends essentially on behavior that we have previously thought to be irrational, then we should conclude not that science is irrational but that our notion of rationality needs adjust-

ment here and there" ("Notes on Lakatos," in R. Cohen and R. C. Buck, eds., *P.S.A. 1970, Boston Studies in the Philosophy of Science* 8 [1971]:144). I am borrowing this citation from Carl Hempel who referred to it in a paper on the analytic and pragmatic approaches to scientific rationality given at the international symposium, "Rationality To-day," held at the University of Ottawa, October 1977, the proceedings of which were published under the title *Rationality To-Day/La rationalité aujourd'hui* (Ottawa: Presses de l'Université d'Ottawa, 1979).

20. Bronowski, *Science and Human Values*. p. 27.

21. Ibid.

22. Ibid., p. 51.

23. J. Bronowski, *The Identity of Man* (Garden City, N.Y., 1971), p. 47.

24. As Bronowski recognizes; cf. ibid., pp. 49-50:

> There is no way to avoid some ambiguity in every human language and, in spite of appearances, the language of science is not an exception. The concepts which form the critical words in its vocabulary mean much the same thing to every user, and yet they do not mean quite the same thing. If they did, then no one could begin to think of a fresh relation. . . . Imagination takes advantage of ambiguity, in the language of science as well as in the language of poetry. . . . the language of science cannot be freed from ambiguity, any more than poetry can: ambiguity lies in the very texture of all ideas. In spite of its tidy look, the structure of science is no more exact, in any ultimate and final sense, than that of poetry.

For his part, Braithwaite is getting at much the same point when he writes:

> It is only in theories which are not intended to have any function except that of systematizing empirical generalizations already known that the thoretical terms can harmlessly be explicitly defined. A theory which it is hoped may be expanded in the future to explain more generalizations than it was originally designed to explain must allow more freedom to its theoretical terms than would be given them were they to be logical constructions out of observable entities. A scientific theory which, like all good scientific theories, is capable of growth must be more than an alternative way of describing the generalizations upon which it is based, which is all it would be if its theoretical terms were limited by being explicitly defined (*Scientific Explanation* [Cambridge, 1968], p. 76).

This is enough to discredit the operationalist view of science as expressed by P. W. Bridgman.

It would not be out of place to comment here on prediction. It is said that a good theory should not only explain what is already known but should also be able to predict what is yet unknown. Just as in the sibylline remarks of the Oracle at Delphi, it is the ambiguity in scientific utterances that accounts for their predictive value. Prediction amounts to no more than this: being able to apply a model to new instances over and above the original ones it was designed to "explain." *Predictive value is nothing other than the ability certain models, like good metaphors, have of being extended in unforeseen and unforeseeable ways.* And a model has predictive value only if it is not rigidly exact but contains a certain amount of semantic ambiguity.

The fact that a scientific theory enables one to make "predictions" does not constitute a verification of the theory, if by verification one means a demonstration of the theory's correspondence to reality. All it shows is that the theory is a good one, as far as theories go.

25. In addition to Leatherdale's *Role of Analogy, Model and Metaphor,* which surveys the literature on the question, one should consult Max Black's excellent essay, "Models and Archetypes," in *Models and Metaphors* (Ithaca, N.Y., 1962), esp. pp. 231ff. Besides pointing out in a masterful way the relation between models and metaphors, Black observes: "Perhaps every science must start with metaphor and end with algebra." And in concluding he insists, like us, on the common imaginative character of both science and art:

If I have been on the right track in my diagnosis of the part played in scientific method by models and archetypes, some interesting consequences follow for the relations between the sciences and the humanities. All intellectual pursuits, however different their aims and methods, rely firmly upon such exercises of the imagination as I have been recalling. Similar archetypes may play their parts in different disciplines; a sociologist's pattern of thought may also be the key to understanding a novel. So perhaps those interested in excavating the presuppositions and latent archetypes of scientists may have something to learn from the industry of literary critics [this is the exact opposite of what Hirsch is doing]. When the understanding of scientific models and archetypes comes to be regarded as a reputable part of scientific culture, the gap between the sciences and the humanities will have been partly filled. For exercise of the imagination, with all its promise and its dangers, provides a common ground. If I have so much emphasized the importance of scientific models and archetypes it is because of a conviction that the imaginative aspects of scientific thought have in the past been too much neglected. For science, like the humanities, like literature, is an affair of the imagination.

26. R. Horton, "African Traditional Thought and Western Science," in B. R. Wilson, ed., *Rationality* (New York, 1971), p. 146. Horton goes on to point out correctly how, whether it be a case of positing scientific entities or of fabricating gods, the "theoretical model, once built, is developed in ways which sometimes obscure the analogy on which it was formed" (p. 148). This is an important feature of all good, provocative (heuristic) models, metaphors, and analogies: they have, as Mary Hesse remarks (*Science and the Human Imagination*), a life of their own, so to speak, or, again, in an attempt to make them applicable to new situations, one will "tinker" (*bricoler*) with them. The result is that a new, extended, higher-level understanding emerges as the basis for further theoretical constructions, more remote still from the original, usually common-sense, analogy of the beginning.

It is this basic feature of metaphorical or analogical understanding that accounts for what is called progress in knowledge (whether in science or theology).

Also, because analogical thinking of this sort is what actually guides "research" and allows for theory development, one can easily understand why scientists, like oracle operators, do not easily abandon their working models or "root metaphors" or, as Kuhn would say, their "paradigms," when new "facts" seem not to fit into the framework of the model and are accordingly "explained away." In other words, the curious practice of explaining away anomalous data, which has been noted by unbiased observers of science, becomes understandable when a theory of understanding of the sort argued for here is adopted.

27. W. James, "Pragmatism's Conception of Truth," in *Pragmatism and Other Essays* (New York, 1963), p. 95. In another article ("Pragmatism and Common Sense") James says, speaking of scientific entities: "It is *as if* they existed; but in reality they are like co-ordinates or logarithms, only artificial short-cuts for taking us from one part to another of experience's flux. We can cipher fruitfully with them; they serve us wonderfully, but we must not be their dupes" (*ibid.*, p. 84).

28. J. Bronowski, *Science and Human Values* (New York, 1965), p. 20.

29. Bronowski, *Identity of Man*, p. 51.

30. Ibid., p. 64. And as Koestler noticed, the fact that a scientific innovation involves the "fusion" of two different frameworks whereas art is their "juxtaposition" (making thereby for a "tense and happy indecision") is basically what accounts for the "cumulative" appearance of science as opposed to the "timeless" character of art; see Koestler, *The Ghost in the Machine* (London, 1970), p. 224.

31. C. Perelman and L. Olbrechts-Tyteca, *The New Rhetoric* (Notre Dame, Ind., 1969), sec. 86, pp. 396–97.

32. See my articles, "Le postulat d'objectivité dans la science et la philosophie du sujet," *Philosophiques* 1 (April 1974), and "The Possibility and Limits of a Science of Man," *Philosophy Forum* 14 (1976).

33. Saint Thomas, *Summa theologiae,* I, 4, 3.

34. The remarks that follow amount to no more than a sketch of the undertaking that is called for. The Galilean episode constitutes a kind of long-forgotten traumatic experience at the birth of our modern tradition, and benefit would surely be had from our submitting to a kind of psychoanalytical re-enactment of it.

35. See n. 1, above.

36. Cited by H. Arendt, *The Human Condition* (Chicago, 1958). p. 260.

37. Braithwaite, *Scientific Explanation,* p. 51.

38. Ibid., p. 53.

39. The motive behind the Church's opposition to Galileo and the one behind our own opposition to scientific mystification seem to be much the same; as Polanyi says (albeit unsympathetically), "The conventionalist theory of science, current in the late Middle Ages, was meant to deny science access to reality" (*Personal Knowledge,* p. 146, n. 1). Actually, it would be more correct to say, any direct access to reality, where "reality" is taken to be something more than just an object of belief, that is, "Reality." Only if Reality is something more than what science believes it to be can the cultural imperialism of science and technology be avoided and also something like Christian faith be possible.

40. Cited by Polanyi in ibid. It is interesting in this regard to take note of modern continuations of this dispute between Bellarmine and Galileo. After asserting the "indirect" nature of theoretical terms in science, Braithwaite voices the inevitable question: "If the theoretical terms of a science are not explicitly definable, but instead are implicitly defined by the way in which they function in a calculus representing a scientific deductive system, in what consists the 'reality' of the entities which these theoretical terms denote?" (*Scientific Explanation,* p. 79). Braithwaite quite sensibly remarks that the best procedure is to avoid "saying either that a theoretical concept exists or that it does not exist" (p. 81). More explicitly:

> For a physicist, to think about ψ-functions is to use the symbol ψ in an appropriate way in his calculus. When he has explained this appropriate way, there is nothing further to say upon what the propositions expressed by the formulae containing ψ are about. *Once the status within a calculus of a theoretical term has been expounded, there is no further question as to the ontological status of the theoretical concept* (pp. 81-82; emphasis added).

Cadinal Bellarmine would not, I think, have disagreed.

41. We can sympathize with the motives behind the protest of the fundamentalists against the scientific theory of evolution. They rightly object to the way evolution is taught, as if it possessed greater truth-value than the religious account of the origin of humans. Of course we cannot agree with their counterclaims—that science is wrong and that their own, rather naive beliefs constitute the literal truth. Both the evolutionists and the fundamentalists are wrong in taking their beliefs literally and are guilty of unrestrained dogmatism, of "dogmatic rashness," as Sextus Empiricus would say.

42. D. Carr, *Phenomenology and the Problem of History* (Evanston, Ill., 1974), p. 120.

43. E. Husserl, *The Crisis of European Sciences and Transcendental Phenomenology* (Evanston, Ill., 1970), sec. 9, h, p. 52.

44. Ibid., p. 51.

45. E. Husserl, *Experience and Judgment* (Evanston, Ill., 1973), sec. 10, p. 43.

46. Ibid., pp. 44-45. Similarly, James speaks of "toutes les inventions explicatives, des molécules et des ondulations éthérées, par example, qui au fond sont des entités métaphysiques" ("La notion de conscience," in *Essays in Radical Empiricism* [Gloucester, Mass., 1967], p. 211).

47. Husserl, *Crisis,* sec. 9, h, p. 52.

48. Ibid., pp. 50-51.

49. The error of Galileo the scientist is also the habitual error of the logician who has, as Husserl says, "superimposed an idealization of what is given originally, an idealization which

has its source in exact science (but which is no longer understood as such)" (*Experience and Judgment,* sec. 10, p. 45). Husserl's view on the relation between scientific and logical theory, on the one hand, and lived experience, on the other, finds a striking confirmation in the quite independent (one presumes) work of a recent Anglo-Saxon philosopher of science, Stephan Körner, *Experiment and Theory* (London, 1966).

50. The phenomena of the "paradox of the imagination" and of "the outstripping of analogy" are tied up with another curious phenomenon of the life of understanding having to do with truth and which Bergson and Merleau-Ponty referred to as "le mouvement rétrograde du vrai" ("the retrograde movement of truth") (see my study, *The Phenomenology of Merleau-Ponty* [Athens, Ohio, 1981], p. 137). (James also speaks of the "quasi-paradox" having to do with the retroactive character of truth in the latter part of his essay, "Humanism and Truth," in *Pragmatism and other Essays.*) When, after thinking about a matter and puzzling over it one finally "hits upon the truth" (more precisely, what one takes to be the truth), this "truth" always appears to one not as the consequence but as the cause of one's looking for it, as something that actually preceded one's thinking and called it forth in the first place. (We may recall Perelman's observation quoted above: "Broadly speaking, outstripping an analogy has the effect of making it appear as the result of a discovery, as an observation of what is, rather than as the product of an original creative effort at structuration.") What is happening here is that consciousness or understanding posits subsequently as its basis and "motivation" that which it arrives at only through its own operations. This actually amounts to saying that here understanding is not being truthful to itself about itself and is dissimulating from itself its own creativity. The curious thing is that it is in the name of truth that all of this is done.

51. Sextus Empiricus, *Pyrrhoniarum hypotyposeon* ("Outlines of Pyrrhonism") (Cambridge, Mass, 1967), 1:147.

52. "Though each [party to a paradigm dispute] may hope to convert the other to his way of seeing his science and its problems, neither may hope to prove his case. The competition between paradigms is not the sort of battle that can be resolved by proofs" (Kuhn, *Structure of Scientific Revolutions,* p. 148).

53. *Webster's New World Dictionary of the American Language.*

54. Plato, *Phaedrus,* in *The Collected Dialogues of Plato* (New York, 1961), 261d.

55. Ibid., 273b.

56. See my article, "Pour une dérationalisation de la raison," in Th. F. Geraets, ed., *Rationality To-Day/La rationalité aujourd'hui* (Ottawa, 1979).

57. This is the line taken by the more "open-minded" participants in the 1971 Ciba Foundation symposium, *Civilization and Science, in Conflict or Collaboration?* (Amsterdam: Associated Scientific Publishers, 1973). Other participants do no more than attempt to exonerate science of any guilt in the current "technological crisis" and worry over whether the growing public disenchantment with science will result in a cutback in research funding.

58. Or, as Thomas Kuhn was led to remark as a result of his analysis of what in science is called "progress": "We may . . . have to relinquish the notion, explicit or implicit, that changes of paradigm carry scientists and those who learn from them closer and closer to the truth" (*Structure of Scientific Revolutions,* p. 170).

59. Concerning Husserl's residual rationalism, see my article, "Phenomenology and Existentialism: Husserl and the End of Idealism," in F. Elliston and P. McCormick, eds., *Husserl: Expositions and Appraisals* (Notre Dame, Ind., 1977).

60. Plato, *Phaedrus,* 267b. A typical view of the Sophists, still not uncommon today, is the one alluded to by Henry Sidgwick in 1872: "They were a set of charlatans who appeared in Greece in the fifth century, and earned an ample livelihood by imposing on public credulity: professing to teach virtue, they really taught the art of fallacious discourse, and meanwhile propagated immoral practical doctrines. Gravitating to Athens as the Prytaneion of Greece, they were there met and overthrown by Socrates, who exposed the hollowness of their rhetoric, turned their quibbles inside-out, and triumphantly defended sound ethical principles against

their pernicious sophistries" (cited by W. K. C. Guthrie, *A History of Greek Philosophy* [Cambridge, 1969], 3:11).

Another typical view is the following one, found in a book geared to the educated masses: "Le sophiste est celui qui recourt systématiquement, pour aboutir à ses fins, à des arguments trompeurs qui n'ont de validité que l'apparence et qu'on appelle sophismes. Ainsi la sophistique est une dialectique, qui, indifférence à la vérité, se met au service des intérêts de celui qui l'emploie, prête à prouver le pour après avoir prouvé le contre" (P. Foulquié, *La dialectique* [Paris, 1969], p. 15).

61. In contrast to Plato, Aristotle did not hesitate to dismiss this objection as irrelevant: "And if it be objected that one who uses such power of speech unjustly might do great harm, *that* is a charge which may be made in common against all good things except virtue, and above all against the things that are most useful, as strength, health, wealth, generalship. A man can confer the greatest of benefits by a right use of these, and inflict the greatest of injuries by using them wrongly" (*Rhetoric*, I, 1, 1355b3–7). Aristotle is here reiterating an observation previously made by Plato's arch-opponent, Isocrates (*Nicocles, 3–5*).

62. Perelman, *New Rhetoric,* sec. 7, p. 33.

63. Guthrie speaks of "Protagoras's invincible respect for the democratic virtues of justice, respect for other men's opinions and the processes of peaceful persuasion as the basis of communal life, and the necessity of communal life to the very survival of the human race" (*History of Greek Philosophy,* 3:268).

64. Aristotle, *Metaphysics,* in R. McKeon, ed., *The Basic Works of Aristotle* (New York, 1941), 1005b10ff. All of the following quotations are drawn from chap. 4, bk. 4.

65. Isocrates, *Helen* (Cambridge, Mass., 1966), 4. This, it might as well be noted as it serves to illustrate the thought of the countertraditionalists, is basically the same tactic that the seventeenth-century skeptic, Pierre Bayle, uses to deny the existence of extension (so as to lend support to Zeno's denial of motion)—not that Bayle (in this respect unlike Zeno who was, after all, a dogmatist) refused to go along with the commonsense view as to the existence of extension; he simply wished to show, by concocting some very convincing arguments, that the opposing philosophical arguments as to the existence of extension cannot themselves be proven or justified. In this way he sought, like others within the counter-tradition, to expose *the limits of reason.* See remark G of the article on Zeno of Elea in P. Bayle, *Dictionnaire critique et historique* (Indianpolis, 1965).

66. Sextus Empiricus, *Adversus Mathematicos* (Cambridge, Mass., 1967) VII, 65ff.

67. P. Aubenque says of Gorgias's conception of the function of discourse:

Ce que suppose l'argumentation de Gorgias, c'est le caractère substantiel, fermé sur soi, du discours. Mais s'il ne permet pas la *communication,* puisqu'il n'a rien à communiquer, du moins autorise-t-il et facilite-t-il la *coexistence* avec autrui. . . . Ainsi entendu, le traité *Sur le non-être* ne viserait pas à établir l'impossibilité du discours, mais seulement la specificité de son domaine, qui est celui des relation humaines, et non celui de la communication de l'être. . . . Le discours, étant lui-même un être, ne peut exprimer l'Etre. . . . Le langage n'est pas dévalorisé pour autant, mais, n'étant pas le lieu de rapport significatifs entre la pensée et l'être, il ne peut être que l'instrument de rapport *existentiels* (persuasion, menace, suggestion, etc.) entre les hommes" (*Le problème de l'être chez Aristote* [Paris, 1962], pp. 103-04).

Gorgias's thesis about the incommunicability of being is an anticipation of Kierkegaard's notion of indirect communication. One commentator of Kierkegaard's observes: "La communication de la vérité consiste non pas à transmettre un contenu objectif, mais à mettre les individus dans des dispositions subjectives telles qu'ils puissent atteindre, par un approfondissement intérieur, leur propre vérité personnelle. Le rapport direct entre esprit et esprit étant impossible, la communication directe de la vérité est à exclure" (J. Nguyên Van Tuyên, *Foi et existence selon Kierkegaard* [Paris, 1971], p. 101).

68. Isocrates, *Antidosis,* 258. Cicero was expressing a similar thought when he said: "What

impressed me most deeply about Plato in that book [*Gorgias*] was, that it was when making fun of orators that he himself seemed to me to be the consummate orator'' (*De Oratore* [London, 1959], I, 11). One could say of Plato what Isocrates says of those Sophists who claim that virtue can be taught and that man can achieve a scientific knowledge of what he ought to do, so as to achieve happiness, that "they are on the watch for contradictions in words but are blind to inconsistencies in deeds" (*Against the Sophists*, 7).

69. S. Kierkegaard, *Concluding Unscientific Postscript* (Princeton, N.J., 1941), p. 102.

70. Aristotle, *Rhetoric*, in McKeon, *Basic Works*, I, 2, 1356b26.

71. I do not think that Aristotle would have any great objection to this way of defining rhetoric (although he would not care for what it can be taken to imply, namely that dialectic is a branch of rhetoric and not the other way around, as he asserts: cf. ibid.). For he does say: "I mean that the proper subjects of dialectic and rhetorical syllogisms are the things with which we say the regular or universal Lines of Argument are concerned, that is to say those lines of argument that apply equally to questions of right conduct, natural science, politics, and many other things that have nothing to do with one another" (ibid., I, 2, 1358a10).

72. Contrary to Aristotle, who holds that technical argumentation and the use of long chains of reasoning remove an argument from the sphere of rhetoric—which is only appropriate to "persons who cannot take in at a glance a complicated argument" (ibid., I, 2, 1357a)—it must be asserted that the use of complicated, technical argumentation does not make an argument any less "rhetorical"; it only means that the (rhetorical) argument in question is intended not for a general public but for a specialized audience.

Aristotle's rather bizarre statement at 1355a5, "Persuasion is clearly a sort of demonstration, since we are most fully persuaded when we consider a thing to have been demonstrated," would make much better sense were it changed to read: Demonstration is clearly a sort of persuasion, since we are most fully persuaded when we consider a thing to have been demonstrated.

73. Isocrates, *Nicocles*, 8. It is in terms of the audience in question that one can best situate dialectic in relation to rhetoric. In the large sense, rhetoric covers all forms of argumentation (and thus includes dialectic), but in a more restricted and specialized sense it signifies a long, continuous discourse, and the latter is usually utilized only when one's audience is of some magnitude. When, however, one is arguing with a single person (or a small number of people), a long discourse is not usually appropriate. Instead one will answer the questions of one's interlocutor and attempt to reply to his objections as one goes along. Dialectic is the name for this kind of dialogue. (A dialogue may in turn be of two kinds: it is a heuristic dialogue when both parties to the argument are motivated by a common desire to arrive at a conclusion, undetermined at the outset, which will be equally acceptable to both; it is an eristic dialogue when the goal of one or more of the participants is to dominate the other and constrain him to accept one's own predetermined conclusions.)

74. Cited by Perelman, *New Rhetoric*, sec. 5, p. 23 (translation corrected).

75. P. Reynolds, *A Primer in Theory Construction* (Indianapolis, 1971), p. 18; see also pp. 13-19.

76. Perelman writes: "Certain specialized audiences are readily assimilated to the universal audience, such as the audience of the scientist addressing his fellow scientists. The scientist addresses himself to certain particularly qualified men, who accept the data of a well-defined system consisting of the science in which they are specialists. Yet, this very limited audience is generally considered by the scientist to be really the universal audience, and not just a particular audience. He supposes that everyone with the same training, qualifications, and information would reach the same conclusions" (*New Rhetoric*, sec. 7, p. 34).

77. "Each individual, each culture, has thus its own conception of the universal audience. The study of these variations would be very instructive, as we would learn from it what men, at different times in history, have regarded as *real, true,* and *objectively valid*" (ibid., sec. 7, p. 33).

78. Ibid., sec. 10, p. 47.

79. B. Snell, *The Discovery of the Mind* (New York, 1960), p. 16.

80. Perelman, *New Rhetoric,* sec. 105, p. 507.

81. That the battle between Plato and the rhetoricians, Isocrates in particular, the battle, that is, between "rhetoric" and "philosophy" (as it was defined by Plato), was over the fundamental issue of properly situating scientific "truth" in the whole of our culture was recognized by Werner Jaeger: "What [Isocrates] was aiming at was universal culture, contrasted with one definite creed or one particular method of attaining knowledge, as preached by the Platonists. Thus, in the opposing claims made by both sides to ownership of the title 'philosophy', and in the widely different meanings given to the word by the opponents, there is symbolized the rivalry of rhetoric and science for leadership in the realm of education and culture" (*Paideia: The Ideas of Greek Culture* [New York, 1960], 3:49).

For a short history of some of the main episodes in the ongoing conflict between rhetoric and philosophy (science), see S. Ijsseling, *Rhetoric and Philosophy in Conflict* (The Hague, 1976). It would appear that today an increasing number of people are rediscovering the seriousness of the claims of rhetoric to true philosophy (if Plato claimed that scientific philosophy is the true rhetoric, rhetoricians have always claimed that persuasive rhetoric is the true philosophy). For what might be called a literary treatment of the issue see R. Pirsig, *Zen and the Art of Motorcycle Maintenance* (New York, 1975).

82. S. Toulmin, *The Uses of Argument* (Cambridge, 1969), p. 118.

83. Husserl, *Experience and Judgment,* sec. 10, p. 43. "For us the world is always a world in which cognition in the most diverse ways has already done its work" (ibid., sec. 8, p. 31).

84. Ibid., p. 45.

85. Whorf, *Language, Truth and Reality,* p. 240.

86. Husserl, *Cartesian Meditations,* p. 52, n. 1.

87. It may be the case that the basic categories of scientific thinking are an explicitation of the implicit categories of the Greek language in particular and of the Indo-European languages in general. We leave this question open. For a number of interesting remarks on this subject, see Snell, *Discovery of the Mind,* chap. 10.

88. Perelman, *New Rhetoric,* sec. 11, p. 51.

89. Cf. Aristotle, *Poetics,* chap. 9.

90. Ibid., 1460a20.

91. It must, however, be admitted that art, though it is a mode of rhetorical persuasion, does, like magic, have a peculiar status as a mode of human understanding and does differ from scientific rhetoric. The major difference is that in art one "believes without believing"; that is, the play of the imagination is recognized for what it is.

92. What is to count as "facts" or "data" is a function of the theory or system of belief that one holds: "Physical theories provide patterns within which data appear intelligible. They constitute a 'conceptual Gestalt'. A theory is not pieced together from observed phenomena; it is rather what makes it possible to observe phenomena as being of a certain sort, and as related to other phenomena. Theories put phenomena into systems" (Hanson, *Patterns of Discovery,* p. 90).

93. Steiner, *After Babel* (New York, 1975), p. 234.

94. Richards, *Philosophy of Rhetoric,* p. 94.

95. Plato, *Phaedrus,* 262b.

96. Ibid., 273e.

97. Ibid., 262b. The traditional devalorization of the imagination is amply typified in the following passage from John Locke's *Essay Concerning Human Understanding* (London, 1974):

> *Wit* lying most in the assemblage of *ideas,* and putting those together with quickness and variety, wherein can be found any resemblance or congruity, thereby to make up pleasant pictures and agreeable visions in the fancy: *judgment,* on the contrary, lies

quite on the other side, in separating carefully, one from another, *ideas* wherein can be found the least difference, thereby to avoid being misled by similitude, and by affinity to take one thing for another. This is a way of proceeding quite contrary to metaphor and allusion, wherein for the most part lies that entertainment and pleasantry of wit, which strikes so lively on the fancy, and therefore is so acceptable to all people: because its beauty appears at first sight, and there is required no labor of thought to examine what truth or reason there is in it. The mind, without looking any further, rests satisfied with the agreeableness of the picture and the gaiety of the fancy; and it is a kind of affront to go about to examine it by the severe rules of truth and good reason; whereby it appears that it consists in something that is not perfectly conformable to them (bk. 2, chap. 11).

98. Practically all accounts of the imagination in philosophical dictionaries and lexicons we have come across resemble in one way or another the following entry in *Dictionary of Philosophy,* ed. D. Runes (New York: Philosophical Library, 1942): "Imagination designates a mental process consisting of: (a) The revival of sense images derived from earlier perceptions (the reproductive imagination), and (b) the combination of these elementary images into new unities (the creative or productive imagination). The creative imagination is of two kinds: (a) the fancy which is relatively spontaneous and uncontrolled, and (b) the constructive imagination, exemplified in science, invention and philosophy which is controlled by a dominant plan or purpose." One cannot but note what this implies: the creative imagination in philosophy or science consists in nothing more than combining elementary sense impressions into new patterns.

99. W. Stevens, "Adagia," *Opus Posthumous* (New York, 1957), p. 177.

100. F. Nietzsche, *The Complete Works of Friedrich Nietzsche,* vol. 2: *Early Greek Philosophy and Other Essays* (New York: Russell & Russell, 1964); cited by Shibles, ed., *Essays on Metaphor* (Whitewater, Wisc., 1972), p. 5.

101. James, *Principles of Psychology,* 2:293.

102. Sextus Empiricus, *Pyrrhoniarum hypotyposeon* ("Outlines of Pyrrhonism") (Cambridge, Mass., 1967), II, 84.

8 THEORY AND EXPERIENCE

What then is the status of our own anti-rationalist theory? If we deny truth, how can we legitimately maintain that our theory is any better, any truer, than those of rationalism? Is not our position as untenable and as self-refuting as that of any thoroughgoing skepticism? But, then, is it really the case that skepticism is self-contradictory? In this chapter we shall argue that a proper skepticism need not be self-contradictory.

In order to defend the truth-value of our own theoretical alternative to rationalism, we shall have to tackle the question of the origin of meaning and determine how theory, and language in general, is related to lived, prethematic experience. Then we shall be able to respond to the ultimate rationalist objection to our own theory. We shall, in fact, see that a theory of human understanding of the sort argued for in this study—one that recognizes the limit of all human theorizing—is the only one capable of disclosing in a genuine, nondogmatic fashion the "meaning of being."

Our first task is to understand the relation between expression and experience. If we are to succeed in elaborating a non-rationalist view of this matter, we must reject one possible view of what accounts for the "meaningfulness" of language. This is the view that holds that the function of language vis-à-vis experience is merely that of "expression." Language simply expresses, or brings to the light of day (*ex-pressare*), meanings that exist prior to all language, or all expression. The essential business of language is to "refer" to or designate preverbal "meanings," and it is in terms of an utterance's "conformity" to these meanings that one will assess the truth-value of what is said. This is the typical rationalist view, which was discussed in chapter 1. It is, for instance, the view espoused by the early Husserl. Language is taken to be a sort of layer superimposed on experience, adding nothing to it: "The stratum of expression—and this constitutes its peculiarity— . . . is not productive."[1]

Language, however, is productive. As we saw in chapter 6, new meanings are generated through and by means of the creative manipulation of a semiotic system. To account for how meaning emerges and how it exists, one does not need to take into account anything more than the structure and use of language itself, and in this sense meaning is a purely intralinguistic affair. Meaning does not exist in any proper sense of the term before language (or some kind of semiotic code), and it is through the imaginative (metaphorical) use of language that new meanings are arrived at. Preverbal experience is not, therefore, meaningful "in itself"; the meaning that it is said to have is a consequence of the language one uses to speak about it.

The relation between language and what it is "about" (experience) is very peculiar. Experience is not simply external to language in the way the world is customarily thought to be external to language. For when we articulate an experience, what we say, our language, is felt to be nothing other than the experience itself, which has merely passed into words. Perhaps it could be said that language is something that accrues to experience or that experience expresses itself in language (such that language is the consciousness that experience has of itself). But it must still be remembered that without language, experience would be dumb, without meaning, in any concrete sense of the term.

This means that although the rationalist view of language (which subordinates expression to experience) is unacceptable, a merely "semiotic" account of linguistic meaningfulness (which separates expression from experience and ignores the latter) is not fully satisfactory as an alternative. A "semiotic" approach can account fully for the "how" of meaning, but because it does not consider the relation of language to what it is "about," preverbal experience, it cannot account for the "why" of meaning. Therefore it does not provide what one always expects from a theory: a sense of understanding. The latter requires that one also be able to account for the "why" of the phenomenon in question. One always wishes to ask, Why does one perceive this utterance as meaningful, as opposed to that other, semiotically correct utterance? And between two utterances that are meaningful, why is one perceived to be more felicitous than the other? What, in dealing with linguistically generated meanings, serves as our criterion of meaningfulness? If a "semiotic" approach accounts for the event of meaning, it does not, for all that, account for what could be called its *advent*.

What, then, is the "origin" of meaning? Whence derives the criterion of meaningfulness? Having rejected rationalism but having also recognized the limits of semiology, only one possibility seems to remain open: the origin of meaning and the criterion of meaningfulness is nothing other than our preverbal experience, the meaning-intention. By referring back to "what it was we wanted to say" we assess the propriety of what we do in fact say, of those meanings that are produced by means of language and would not have existed were not language what it is—a semiotic system capable of generating meanings by means of its own inner resources. One speaks in order to articulate a kind of felt "meaning" that precedes our speaking, but in speaking we are led, by the inner momentum of language, to produce specific meanings—in the proper, linguistic sense of the term—that go well beyond what we were aware of before turning to language.[2] Language is thus, as Merleau-Ponty would say, a creation, but it is a creation in a unique sense; it is a "creation which is at the same time an adequation, the only way to obtain an adequation."[3] This sounds like a paradox, but after our critique of rationalism we need no longer fear paradoxes; like good metaphors, they are the means of insightful understanding. Or, as Kierkegaard puts it, "This seems to be a paradox. However, one should not think slightingly of the paradoxical; for the paradox is the source of the thinker's passion, and the thinker without a paradox is like a lover without feeling: a paltry mediocrity."[4]

Preverbal, lived experience is latently or, to speak like the scholastic, "potentially" meaningful and serves as the criterion of assessing the meanings produced by means of language, but when we attempt with language to understand or come to grips with experience, we can never discover *a* meaning in it. Experience is quite simply, to borrow a term from psychoanalysis, overdetermined. It has not one meaning but an indefinite number of different possible meanings. Gadamer speaks of the "essential linguisticality of all human experience," and indeed there is nothing in experience that, in and by means of the speaking about it, cannot and does not become ever more meaningful.[5]

Thus, while language is grounded in experience and is itself the meaning *of* experience, no particular statement about experience at any particular time can ever be said to express it "adequately." A fortiori, no theory (which, to paraphrase Antisthenes, is simply a "long rigmarole") can ever claim to coincide with experience and to be *the* truth about it. There is an unbridgeable gap between theory and experience.

Unthematized, lived experience is mute and unintelligible: *individuum ineffabile est*. The particular (a given experience) becomes intelligible (meaningful) only by being subsumed under the universal, by being interpreted in the light of a conceptual schema or set of categories. This is, for instance, what on a basic level maxims and proverbs accomplish, as well as myths, which serve to draw a parallel between human actions and divine paradigms or exemplars, between, in other words, the particular and the universal. In so doing they lend meaning to the *hic et nunc*. On a higher level of conceptuality, it is also what science and speculative philosophy accomplish. We feel that we have begun to understand something only when we can say of it, "This is an instance of that" ("that" being some kind of general essence or a category of being). To do this is to apply to experience a conceptual schema. As Merleau-Ponty remarked, "Our existence is too tightly held in the world to be able to know itself as such at the moment of its involvement, and . . . it requires the field of ideality in order to become acquainted with and to prevail over its facticity."[6]

The less we verbalize experience and the closer we stay to it, the more certain we are of it; however, this certainty is a vacuous certainty. Certainty about *what?* We can become aware of the meaning of experience (the "what an experience means") only by articulating it; to understand it we must interpret it, and the more meaningful (or meaning-giving) the interpretation, the more it involves the application of theory to experience.[7] This increase in meaningfulness is paid for by a decrease in certainty. "Generally speaking," Braithwaite says, "a man will be much more prepared to bet at given odds on the lowest-level hypotheses in his rational corpus being the same after ten years than that the highest-level hypotheses will be the same."[8] As an interpretation becomes more highly theoretical, the distance between it and experience increases proportionately. (This is why art, which is less "theoretical" than science, endures, is "relevant" over a much longer period of time.) "There is a sort of balance between precision and certainty: one cannot be increased except to the detriment of the other."[9] In addition, *because experience is overdetermined* (can be interpreted in a limitless number of different theoretical ways, such as by magic or by science, and by different magical and scientific theories),[10] *no experience can ever be said unequivocally to call forth or prescribe any particular theory or type of theory about it,* and, conversely, no theory can ever be conclusively verified by experience.

In logical positivism the whole question of the verifiability and/or falsifiability of scientific theories hinges on the assumption that they, as opposed, for instance, to magical theories, are empirical. But our earlier comparison of magic and science is enough to show that science is no more or no less empirical than magic. Both magic and science postulate, as all genuinely explanatory theories must, unobservable entities (atoms, witchcraft substance) as the true causes of observable happenings, and both can appeal to observable events (predictions) as confirmations of their (nonobservable) theoretical constructs. In principle all theories about experience are empirical, for they are all taken by their adherents to be genuine explanations of experience.

Explanation means to make intelligible. To explain something is to make it understandable, and one understands something (in the sense of passive understanding) when one is no longer puzzled and perplexed over it. Puzzlement generally ceases when one is able to take that which is to be understood and fit it into a general system of belief (as one fits a piece into a jigsaw puzzle). To explain something is to link it up with things already understood, to relate it to other things already understood in that they are systematically interrelated. For instance, one explains an action on the part of a person by showing how it fits in with his general style of action or mode of behavior (and what one takes this general style to be is itself a product of interpretation). In this way the action in question becomes "logical"; one has given a reason for it when one has shown that it is part of a coherent pattern. In the realm of theory, this is often all that it takes to explain something, to overcome puzzlement. By linking the particular with the general, one succeeds in discerning what it is (it is an instance of such and such), and, having discerned this, one feels that one adequately understands it.

Sometimes, however, this is not enough in that it does not provide sufficient intellectual satisfaction. One feels a desire not only to know what something is but also why it is, and one will not feel that one has fully understood the thing until one can say that it is the necessary consequence (effect) of something else. In a case like this, it is necessary to give what is called a causal explanation. Causal explanation presupposes rational explanation in the sense described in the preceding paragraph (a cause is a kind of reason), but it goes further. One not only links up a thing to be explained with other things already understood (because they are already structured into a general pattern), but one also seeks to derive all these things from something that, while common to them all, transcends (or underlies) them. For instance, one shows how a particular action is not only "logically" related to other actions a person habitually performs—and thus "makes sense" (being part of a pattern, it is what one could have expected the person to do)—but how this action and the others as well all derive from a common source, such as a person's intention to pursue a certain course of action in the first place.

Intentions are sometimes called motives, and a distinction is often made between explanation in terms of motives and explanation in terms of causes, but this distinction, while valid, is irrelevant in the present context (we need not go into the difference between teleological and efficient causation). One gives a causal explanation of a natural event in the same way that one explains a person's behavior in terms of an underlying motive, that is, by attempting not just to link up the phenomenon in question with others that have already been systematically interrelated (due to the application of a conceptual schema) but by attempting also to derive all of the phenomena from an underlying something. The difference between commonsensical causal explanation and scientific (theoretical) causal explanation is that whereas in the former the cause is generally an observable phenomenon (all the lights in the room went out at the same time because the janitor pulled the main switch), in the latter the "cause," to the degree that it is truly "fundamental," is unobservable (the lights, the observable phenomena, went out because *electrons*, unobservable, theoretical entities, ceased to pass through the conducting wire; or else because of witchcraft).[11]

Thus, what in theoretical explanation is called a *cause* is not something that can be observed or experienced; it can only be inferred by means of the theory itself, which is to say that it is a theoretical construct. N. Hanson observes: "Causes certainly are connected with effects; but this is because our theories connect them, not because the world is held together by cosmic glue. The world *may* be glued together by imponderables, but that is irrelevant for understanding causal explanation."[12] When a scientist—or a magician, for that matter—says that something is the cause of something else, all he is in fact doing is interpreting an experience in the light of a theoretical system and is viewing the experience as a mere instance of a general law of nature postulated by the theory. "So it is not Nature that is uniform," Toulmin says, "but scientific procedure; and it is uniform only in this, that it is methodical and self-correcting."[13]

All people seek to discover reasons or causes that will explain their experience,[14] but since they interpret their experience by means of different conceptual schemata or theoretical systems, what they posit as the causes of a certain kind of experience will differ radically. As William James remarked, "Now the merely conceived or imagined objects which our mind represents as hanging to the sensations (causing them, etc.), filling the gaps between them and weaving their interrupted chaos into order are innumerable. Whole systems of them conflict with other systems."[15] The shaman and the scientist do not speak the same language, but they are nonetheless engaged in the same sort of activity: interpreting experience by means of theoretical constructs. The naturalness of "natural" laws and causes is totally relative to the type of rationally ordered system one uses to interpret an experience.

Let us consider in more detail the means whereby a theoretical construct is read into experience and itself becomes a believed-in, higher-level reality enjoying, as Galileo would say, all the "certainty of sense-perception." Theoretical terms (such as mass, energy, and mana) have the meaning they have because of the role they play and the place they occupy in an interwoven theoretical system. They are not descriptions of experience but, as Husserl would say, idealizations of experience (and the more formalized the system, the greater precision and exactness these terms have, in contrast to the vagueness inherent in the terms of more ordinary, everyday language, which is frankly metaphorical and paradoxical, and thus the more removed they are from the experience they purport to explain). How, then, can one, as one normally does, presume that in using them to elucidate an experience or observed phenomenon one is stating what the experience or phenomenon itself "really" is (for example, how can one presume to say that either unconscious states or physiological mechanisms explain what we actually feel or think)? In other words, what makes a highly theoretical, abstract, and idealized statement about experience "empirical" (from a purely formal point of view, psychoanalysis is as empirical a theory as brain physiology, and the basic concepts or causal entities of the latter are as "theoretical" as the former)? Obviously it is because one thinks that there is a direct (for example, causal) connection between the "reality" posited by the theory, the explicans (for example, brain mechanisms and unconscious states), and the experience to be explained, the explicandum. How is it that theory comes to be linked up and even equated with experience in this way?

Given the existence of a theory about experience, the procedure will be as follows: In order to make the concept empirically relevant one will derive from it what in science is called an operational definition, a statement as to what is to count as an experiential *equivalent* of the concept in question (a highly abstract theoretical concept may be translated into several operational definitions, which must all be systematically correlated). For instance, one will operationally define an electron as the presence in a cloud chamber of water droplets arranged in a certain pattern. If this is seen to occur, one will feel justified in saying that the phenomenon in question is really "an electron passing through the chamber." Similarly, an operational definition of the wrath of the gods would be the experience of unusual misfortune or violent meterological occurrences; a thunder storm becomes in this way a hieraphany, a revelation of the god himself. One does not and cannot see an electron or a god; one "sees" them, or, as Holton says, "the empirical matters of fact of modern science are not simply 'observed,' but are nowadays more and more obtainable only by way of a detour of technology (to use a term of Heisenberg's) and a detour of theory."[16] Of course, the "detour of theory" involved in seeing is not peculiar to modern science alone.[17]

The process at work here is what one philosopher of science, S. Körner, calls *identification*. One links up theory with experience by simply identifying a statement about observables (water droplets) with a statement about concepts (electrons). The important thing to note about identification, therefore, is that it is always an arbitrary procedure. Lower-level theoretical statements may perhaps be deduced from, and may therefore be said to be necessarily derived from, higher-level theoretical statements, but statements about direct experience cannot be logically derived from the lower-level theoretical statements. "No perceptual proposition," Körner says, "will be the last term in a deductive sequence. The theory will be linked to perception not by deduction but by identification. . . . The identification does not occur within the theory."[18] Identification is always an extratheoretical matter and results from a choice on the part of the scientist—and agreement among scientists—as to what shall be allowed to count as an instance of a theoretical concept. One freely chooses to view an experience as if it were the visible side of an invisible, underlying reality. This is to say, therefore, that theory is linked with experience not by logic (deduction or induction) but by analogic, by the imagination.[19]

This is to say also that, logically speaking, *there is an unbridgeable gap between lived experience and all the theories one can devise to explain it.* Empirical and theoretical discourse are, as Körner says, "logically disconnected."[20] If by "explanation" we mean something more than subsuming the particular under the universal (applying an interpretive schema to lived experience) in such a way as to provide a sense of understanding and intel-

lectual satisfaction (satisfaction being equivalent to the extinction of the felt
need to ask, Why?), if, that is, we mean actually discovering the true reason
why something really is what it is, then, in this strict, ideal sense, a law
about experience, being itself a theoretical construct, perhaps may be adequately explained—by being linked up with higher-level, more comprehensive laws within a given theoretical system (physics or theology)—but
because of the gap between experience and theory of whatever level, no
experience can ever be explained. One cannot build a logical bridge across
the gap between theory and experience, but one can and does constantly
cross over it, by a leap of the imagination. All the theories we devise to explain experience are imaginative constructs of our own. We may call them
"explanations" if we like, but we must realize that the experience in question could be explained in any number of different, equally logical or rational ways. Even in science, as Pierre Duhem pointed out, "we can make
an infinity of different formulas or distinct physical laws correspond to the
same group of facts. . . . any other law representing the same experiments
with the same approximation may lay as just a claim as the first to the title
of a true law or, to speak more precisely, of an acceptable law."[21]

Experience is not, as Luther said of the Bible, *sui ipsius interpres.* Like a
dream it is not self-explanatory, and any explanation of it is not it. Being (or
what we have called Reality) is not identical with meaning. There is more in
experience than is ever dreamed of in any speculative philosophy or world
view, and it is this "intentional excess," this something more, which is what
is meant when we speak of the "meaning of being."

The greatest illusion of all occurs when this is overlooked. Dogmatism
arises out of the forgetfulness of the "essential abyss between experience
and logically structured theory"[22] and consists in mistaking a theory for
what the theory is about. The mistake is the one that the psychologist, for
example, makes when, through identification, he confuses a theory about
experience with the experience itself. James detected this mistake and called
it the Psychologist's Fallacy. It is the "inveterate habit"[23] the psychologist
has of confusing "his own standpoint with that of the mental fact about
which he is making his report."[24] In order to understand our experience, we
have no choice but to fabricate theories about it, but we deceive ourselves
when we take the theory to be identical with the reality it serves to make
intelligible.

In a more general way, what could be called the Theorist's Fallacy is the
confusion of a method or doctrine with the very reality it is about. It is, as
Husserl said of Galileo, taking for true being what is only a method. In accordance with its methodological postulate of universality, dogmatism assumes that a body of scientific (or other) theory is, with suitable modifica-
tions, applicable throughout all of experience and that if something or other
cannot be thus explained (for example, "mental" experiences, such as that

of freedom, which resist behavior measurement) it simply does not exist and is "meaningless" (and this is why dogmatism always involves reductionism and cultural totalitarianism).

A nondogmatic use of theory, on the other hand, would be one that seeks to counteract the Theorist's Fallacy by constantly recalling to our attention the essential abyss between experience and all theory. Such a use of theory would be one that is not only conscious of the illusions of understanding but that is also, in being conscious of them, free from them. Its whole purpose would be to liberate us from the illusions of understanding. Such a liberation, it is true, necessitates a veritable acesis of understanding. Understanding must renounce its idols of truth and of science; it must realize that its desire for a "correct" understanding of what things "in themselves really are" is illusory. It must realize that what is called science or knowledge is but the name for an ensemble of techniques, techniques that may be extremely helpful in enabling one to come to grips with experience and to orient oneself in the world in which one lives but which cannot legitimately claim to be anything more.[25]

"We are born to seek after truth," Montaigne remarked, "to possess it belongs to a greater power." Science or knowledge is an attribute of the gods, not of humans. The only genuine knowledge that human understanding is capable of attaining is the knowledge of its own limits, the knowledge, that is, of the ultimate impossibility of Knowledge. The entire raison d'être of non-dogmatic theorizing is, in the words of one outstanding non-dogmatist, that it "discloses the scientific approach to the world in its own limited validity and denounces the tyranny of willing by the means of science and technology as the clash of reason with itself. There is no claim of definitive knowledge, with the exception of one: the acknowledgment of the finitude of human being in itself."[26]

As a result of our attempt to overcome the rationalist tradition—*the* tradition in Western thought—we have been led into a position of skepticism. Skepticism, though, it is always said, is self-contradictory and self-refuting. To say that nothing is true, so the objection goes, is at least to affirm one truth, and so the affirmation refutes itself. If knowledge is impossible, as the skeptic maintains, then the skeptic cannot, on his own grounds, claim to know even this much. Is not the only consistent skeptic the one who, like Cratylus, refuses to say anything at all? And in waving his finger back and forth in answer to questions, was not even Cratylus inconsistent in that he continued to use body language? Skepticism cannot be argued for, and thus it does not even count as a theory. The skeptic is he who places himself outside of the *logos,* outside of language and reason.

More precisely, when one says that all knowledge is belief and is historically and culturally conditioned (such that there is no one "true" world that is identically the same for all), is he not making a statement that claims to be universally valid and therefore contradicts what it says? In short, if we define the dogmatist as one who believes he has discovered the truth—"Those who believe they have discovered [the truth] are the 'Dogmatists,' specially so called—Artistotle for example"[27]—are we not ourselves guilty of dogmatism? The answer is quite simply, no.

The rationalist inevitably lands himself in inconsistencies, amounting in fact to a *reductio ad absurdum* of his doctrine. The dogmatic attempt to achieve true knowledge leads to difficulties that cannot be resolved. The genuine non-dogmatist does not contradict himself but is actually, like Gorgias, eminently consistent. When the non-dogmatist says that all knowledge is belief and is "prejudiced," he is not merely making a prejudiced statement of his own because he is not claiming that the dogmatist is wrong in his affirmations about what reality really is and therefore is not maintaining, even implicitly, that he has an understanding of reality which is the true one. He is in fact not saying anything direct about reality at all. He is not saying that there is or there is not a true reality, which different beliefs may correspond to, more or less. The dogmatist and the non-dogmatist are not talking about the same things, and the dogmatist can attempt to refute the non-dogmatist with the kind of objections set out above only because he supposes that the non-dogmatist is talking about the same thing as himself. The dogmatist invariably misunderstands the non-dogmatist (and fails to grasp the true nature of skepticism) because he is speaking from a standpoint that the non-dogmatist has managed to transcend. Non-dogmatic statements are made from a "transcendental" standpoint.

While the dogmatist talks in a direct, straightforward, and naive way about reality and, in so doing, posits theoretical, nonobservable entities as the explanation of observable phenomena, the non-dogmatist deliberately refuses to do so. He abstains from taking up the path of idealization and from putting forward knowledge claims about reality. He does not speak about what reality is in itself but only about what people say and believe reality is. This is to say that the object of his discourse is a kind of second-level object; he does not speak about what all belief or knowledge is a belief in or a knowledge of, "reality," but only about belief and knowledge as such. All non-dogmatic statements are reflective and presuppose what Sextus Empiricus called the *epoche,* the suspension of judgment, or what phenomenology calls the *reduction,* the suspension of belief.

The non-dogmatist suspends his belief in "the non-evident objects of scientific inquiry,"[28] and thus "whereas the dogmatizer posits the things about which he is said to be dogmatizing as really existent, the Skeptic does not posit these formulae in any absolute sense." He does not make "any positive assertion regarding the external realities," those said to underlie and be the reason or cause for "appearances" or experience.[29] Because all the statements of the non-dogmatist are made from a "reduced" standpoint and because he is not talking about reality as such but, in a reflective mode, about people's knowledge claims about reality, their meaning is fundamentally different from those of the dogmatist, and it is for this reason that all of the dogmatic objections simply do not apply.

To put into play the *epoche* is not, however, an easy task; "the 'suspensive' way of thought" is not an easy way to find or to follow.[30] It is, in fact, "unnatural" and goes against the whole grain of understanding, for understanding is naturally dogmatic, is belief, and invariably posits what it understands, its creative constructs, as reality itself. To transcend dogmatism so as to liberate oneself from the natural illusions of understanding necessitates a long and arduous battle of understanding against itself, a demanding acesis of belief, and Pascal was perhaps right when he said, "An absolutely thoroughgoing Pyrrhonian has never existed."[31]

But if liberation is to be achieved to some degree, there is no choice but to oppose one's ingrained tendency to believe, for in order to form a true understanding of what understanding is and of what one understands, it is necessary to describe what is understood precisely as it is understood, and for this it is necessary to refrain from the normal acceptance of one's belief objects, this being incompatible with understanding what is understood or meant precisely as it is meant. One cannot, for instance, understand what scientific understanding truly is or what the ontological status of scientific entities is if one does not bracket the question of their reality and focus instead on the way scientific understanding actually does function.

As with all active understanding, it is the experience of an "anomaly" that first propels one to embark on the suspensive way of thought. The anomaly in this case is nothing other than the difficulties created by the rationalist or dogmatic attempt to achieve a knowledge of reality. This is why a non-dogmatic theorizer like Sextus devotes the major part of his energies to pointing out the inner contradictions of rationalist arguments and the insuperable difficulties engendered by them.[32] And it is why he, like other skeptics in general, points out how different and often incompatible beliefs are equally possible and have in fact been held by people of different times and cultures.[33] Skepticism "is the result of setting things in opposition."[34] It is the result of concretely coming to realize what Sextus calls the "equipollence," that is, the equal validity and rationality, of beliefs that nevertheless are opposed to one another.

When one sees this, one sees also that one theory is "no more"[35] true than another: "no one of the conflicting judgments takes precedence over any other as being more probable."[36] "The main basic principle of the Sceptic system is that of opposing to every proposition an equal proposition; for we believe that as a consequence of this we end by ceasing to dogmatize."[37] This is why we ourselves have attempted to play off magic against science: not to demonstrate the superiority of one over the other but simply to bring out the dogmatic character of both, and of understanding in general. "So whenever I say 'To every argument an equal argument is opposed,' what I am virtually saying is 'To every argument investigated by me which establishes a point dogmatically, it seems to me there is opposed another argument, establishing a point dogmatically, which is equal to the first in respect of credibility and incredibility.' "[38]

To say that one belief system is "no more" true or likely than another is "not a piece of dogmatism, but the announcement of a human state of mind which is apparent to the person experiencing it."[39] It is the announcement of something that is readily apparent to any unbiased observer of the human comedy. Indeed the whole purpose of nondogmatic argument is to expose what in chapter 5 was referred to as the folly of human beliefs.[40] For only if we become aware of the folly of belief can we manage to slip in between beliefs so as to become aware of our believing as such. And only if we realize the relativity of all belief systems can we possibly become aware of that which is analogously common to them all: Reality. Since the dogmatic makeup of understanding prevents it from properly understanding itself, a suspension of belief is the only means for achieving a genuine self-understanding.

Indeed once one has managed to suspend one's believing, a whole field of investigation opens up: the field of human experience and belief in their different modalities. It must be emphasized that the suspension of belief is not its elimination. Human consciousness is naturally belief and thus cannot cease to be such, but—and this constitutes its uniqueness—it can, in a self-reflective mode of consciousness, become conscious of itself as belief. To do so is to cease naively to ontologize one's beliefs. It is, in other words, to become aware that the realities that one posits and cannot but posit are nonetheless posited realities, correlates of belief, and not Reality itself. After the *epoche* one believes, so to speak, without believing. One neither affirms nor denies the objects of one's beliefs; one does not "certify" them, as Husserl would say, but neither does one dispute them.[41]

This is what Sextus calls *aphasia* or nonassertion: "What, as we say, we neither posit nor deny, is some one of the dogmatic statements made about what is non-apparent."[42] "We say that our belief is a matter of simply yielding without any consent."[43] Or, as Husserl says, in describing the phenomenological reduction:

> It is not a transformation of the thesis into its antithesis, of positive into negative. *Rather is it something quite unique. We do not abandon the thesis we have adopted, we make no change in our conviction,* which remains in itself what it is. . . .And yet the thesis undergoes a modification—while remaining in itself what it is, *we set it as it were "out of action," we "disconnect it,"* "bracket it." It still remains there like the bracketed in the bracket, like the

disconnected outside the connexional system. We can also say: The thesis is experience as lived, *but we make "no use" of it.*[44]

If the object of dogmatic utterances is the nonapparent, is, in other words, theoretical, nonobservable entities taken to be the reasons or causes of what is observable, of experience, the object of non-dogmatic utterances is that which is apparent and self-evident. It is experience itself as it is lived and the theories devised to explain it. The "criterion," as Sextus says, of non-dogmatic utterances is what appears: "Our aim is to indicate what appears to us."[45] Now what, after the *epoche,* is apparent in human understanding is its actual working: human understanding as it posits theoretical entities in order to account for its own basic self-awareness. Because the statements of people and the various rhetorical means by which they defend them are apparent or evident, *truthful statements can be made about them.* The non-dogmatist can, therefore, make true statements and not contradict himself in doing so.

The skeptic, as Sextus says, states only what appears to him. He does not, as the dogmatist does, make the additional claim that what appears to him could not, in itself, be otherwise than it appears to be. The skeptic, in other words, does not make any transexperiential knowledge claims and, moreover, does not view knowledge rationalistically as the correct representation of what something is in itself. " 'We admit the apparent fact,' say they, 'without admitting that it really is what it appears to be.' . . . We merely object to accepting the unknown substance behind phenomena." The skeptic "holds to phenomena alone," and his criterion is the apparent or self-evident.[46] In the case of the theory of human understanding we have defended, we have not attempted to say what understanding really is in itself and what it must be for any and all possible thinking beings but only how it appears to be in the case of all known human communities of all known times and places. The skeptic is concerned not with what must be the case if such and such is to be universally true and invariant, but only with what is the case, as it is manifested in his experience of it. And what he experiences most of all is the gap, in his own life of understanding and in that of others with whom he has come into contact, between theory and experience. A non-dogmatic theory is thus a very special kind of theory; it is a theory about the discrepancy between theory and experience.

The object of this theory is not, therefore, experience itself; the non-dogmatist does not attempt to say what exactly experience is or means. The theory is, rather, a theory about theory (about "dogmatic statements made about what is non-apparent"). Its object is the interpretation of experience accomplished by all straightforward, dogmatic theorizing. It is this kind of second-level theoretical status that removes non-dogmatic theory from the objection of self-contradiction leveled against it by the dogmatist. For whereas the normal, dogmatic function of theory is to interpret experience in such a way as to say what it is, we do not attempt to do so; our only aim is to call attention to the fact that all understood experience is an already interpreted experience. Non-dogmatic knowing, therefore, is not simply a seeing-as but rather a seeing-that, a seeing that all ordinary, nonreduced seeing is a seeing-as.

As the suspension of belief, the *epoche* is the suspension of the kind of inner dialogue we are constantly pursuing, interpreting our experience to ourselves as we go along and persuading ourselves that our experience is indeed such as it appears to be in the light of the interpretive schema which has become a second nature to us. By means of the *epoche* one attains to something like a pure seeing, a seeing that is not merely the imposition of an interpretive schema on experience. What one sees is precisely the as-if, imaginative character of ordinary seeing and "knowing." In normal, nonreduced, straightforward living, we are not aware of the as-if character of our knowing, of the fact that all seeing is a seeing-as. Speaking of "the firmest and most universal of all our habitualities, the world," and of "this hidden positing of the world and this bond to being," Husserl says: "Only if we become conscious of this bond, *putting it consciously out of play* . . . do we achieve perfect purity. Then we find ourselves, so to speak, in a pure world of imagination, *a world of absolutely pure possibility*."[47] What one sees after the *epoche* is the imaginative character of all understanding. And in seeing this one can see also that whether reality in itself (whatever that might mean) is of a determinate sort, this is something that can never be known. Therefore it would be and is folly to attempt to know it, to achieve (as Husserl nevertheless attempted) a Science of Reality.

Perhaps, as one of the greatest dogmatists of all time, Descartes, claimed, there is one thing which can be genuinely known: the *sum,* the fact that I exist—for the very attempt to doubt my existence is sufficent proof of it. But this certainty is a blind certainty. The "I am" may be certain, but this does not mean, as Descartes naively and dogmatically assumed, that clarity and distinctness are the criteria of truth (such that whatever I can conceive of clearly and distinctly necessarily exists and is true), for there is nothing clear about my existence itself.[48] It may be clear that I am, but what I am is not. The meaning of my existence is shrouded in mystery.[49] The more, in fact, I theorize about my existence in an attempt to explain and understand it, the more I become aware of it as something fundamentally opaque and resistant to my attempts at understanding. I become aware of that characteristic of my existence that Heidegger termed *Befindlichkeit:* my simply "being there" in the world, "thrown" into it, as it were. Through reflection I come across myself as "already there," and the sheer, brute facticity of my being there blots out any apparent "why" or "wherefore" for this factual state of affairs. "The pure 'that it is' shows itself, but the 'whence' and 'whither' remain in darkness.''[50] Even if a human being ''is 'assured' in its belief about its 'whither', or if, in rational enlightenment, it supposes itself to know about this 'whence,' all this counts for nothing as against the phenomenal facts of the case,'' for one is brought before the ''that-one-is'' of one's ''there,'' which, Heidegger says, ''stares one in the face with the inexorability of an enigma.''[51] James, too, was aware of this when he wrote, ''After all that reason can do has been done, there still remains the opacity of the finite facts as merely given.'' There is no one point of view or interpretation in terms of which experience and lived reality become thoroughly intelligible; as James says, ''the universe is wild.''[52]

In the last analysis, therefore, what the *epoche* teaches and what one sees in becoming aware of one's beliefs as such is *the opacity of the fact*. The skeptical critique of dogmatism discloses the veritable human state. It is the state Pascal described in his *Pensées:*

> This is our true state; this is what makes us incapable of certain knowledge and of absolute ignorance. We sail within a vast sphere, ever drifting in uncertainty, driven from end to end. When we think to attach ourselves to any point and to fasten to it, it wavers and leaves us; and if we follow it, it eludes our grasp, slips past us, and vanishes forever. Nothing stays for us. This is our natural condition, and yet most contrary to our inclination; we burn with desire to find solid ground and an ultimate sure foundation whereon to build a tower reaching to the Infinite. But our whole groundwork cracks, and the earth opens to abysses.
>
> Let us therefore not look for certainty and stability.[53]

Alexis de Tocqueville was echoing Pascal when he wrote:

> The nature of man is sufficiently disclosed for him to know something of himself, and sufficiently obscure for all the rest to be plunged in thick darkness, in which he gropes forever, and forever in vain, to lay hold on some completer notion of his being.[54]

The ''greatness and the wretchedness of man,'' as Pascal would say, lies in the fact that he is able to know enough to know that he can never know the true meaning of his existence.

Is this to say, however, that the results of the *epoche* are merely negative? Is the suspensive way of thought only destructive? Does the *epoche* achieve nothing positive?

When one attempts to discern the positive value of skepticism, one possibility immediately presents itself. Skepticism is useful and necessary, it will be said, because it serves to make people critical of their beliefs and compels them to seek new and better formulations of the truth. The skeptic is a gadfly and a challenger who forces scientists and other searchers after the truth to admit to the falsifiability of their beliefs and to submit them to constant re-examination and not to rest content with easy answers. In this view skepticism is actually a major dynamic force in intellectual history and a vital stimulus in human progression from superstition to critical knowledge.[55]

Although it is obvious that skepticism does play a vital role in the development of critical and positive knowledge, this is not the main effect intended by the skeptics themselves. The skeptic does not view his objections to dogmatic systems of belief as merely one moment, to use a Hegelian term, in the system's inner progression from thesis to antithesis to a renewed, higher-level synthesis. There is indeed a place for skepticism within a belief system, but this kind of skepticism is not a threat or a challenge to the system itself. It is not, therefore, a genuine skepticism, a non-dogmatism. But what then, from the skeptic's own point of view, can possibly be the positive value of skepticism? In order to deal with this question let us attempt to discern better the various reactions possible to the skeptic's "setting of things in opposition."

The first is that whereby the dogmatist attempts, in answer to the skeptic's critiques, to shore up his own dogmatic arguments so as to make them immune to criticisms addressed against them. This reaction is, according to the skeptic, totally profitless, for the fundamental complacency of the dogmatist (his belief that the truth does indeed exist) has not been significantly disturbed.

The skeptical critique can begin to have its desired effect only when, as a result of "setting of things in opposition," one comes to see the relativity and groundlessness of one's habitual beliefs and, in addition, "the equal validity of [all] opposing arguments."[56] This is anything but a comforting realization. It is, in fact, the "dark night" of the understanding. The state of mind produced by a successful skeptical critique is anxiety.

With anxiety different paths are opened up. One may—and this is the normal reaction—simply flee from anxiety and what anxiety discloses—the relativity of all knowledge claims—and re-ensconce oneself in the comforting oblivion of dogmatism. This is the path of bad faith. It produces the false consciousness that characterizes all militant dogmatism. Or one may freely confront anxiety and do battle with it. Here the way splits off in two further directions. One may lose the battle and, overcome with the realization of the folly of all belief systems, succumb to madness. Or one may win the battle and achieve a kind of knowledge—the knowledge of the ultimate impossibility of Knowledge—which can be called wisdom.

The wise person is he who has learned who he is and who knows his place in nature, who knows what he is: a person and not a god. Wisdom is genuine self-understanding freed from the dogmatic illusions of understanding, an understanding, therefore, of the limits of understanding. What is here called wisdom is what Sextus termed *ataraxia:* unperturbedness or quietude. It is also what others have called peace of mind.

Traditionally (or counter-traditionally), the suspensive way of thought is said to be composed of three stages. First comes the skeptical critique of dogmatic arguments (Sextus listed various kinds of arguments or "tropes" to be used by the nondogmatic dialectician or arguer[57]), whose effect is to show the "equipollence" or "equality in respect of probability and improbability" of various beliefs. As Diogenes says, "They would first show the ways in which things gain credence, and then by the same methods they would destroy belief in them. . . . They showed, then, . . . that the probabilities on both sides are equal."[58] The purpose of all this is to lead one to perform the *epoche,* to suspend one's beliefs freely. The epoche is the means whereby, as we would say, anxiety is confronted and overcome. And third, following upon the *epoche,* "like a shadow," comes *ataraxia.*[59] "For the Sceptic, having set out to philosophize . . . , so as to attain quietude thereby, found himself involved in contradictions of equal weight, and being unable to decide between them suspended judgment; and as he was thus in suspense there followed, as it happened, the state of quietude in respect of matters of opinion."[60] Because the state of *ataraxia* corresponds to a very great extent to what we would like to call a genuine understanding of Reality, let us attempt to describe it in more detail and from a somewhat different vantage point.

The *epoche* is the suspension of judgment or belief (all belief is "judgmental" in that it posits as real what it is a belief in). By means of the *epoche* one overcomes belief—not in the sense that one ceases to believe (for this would be to cease to be conscious) but in the sense that after the *epoche* one "believes without believing." This is to say that the *epoche* is not a doubt (or a denial). To doubt something is still to believe; doubt, in the sense in which we are using the term, is negative belief, belief that such and such is not the case. Doubt, moreover, is always intrasystematic; it is an integral part of an overall system of belief. But the purpose of the *epoche* is to suspend belief altogether. The *epoche* is thus not negative in that it is not a doubting, but also its positive value does not lie in that it achieves a belief or knowledge claim immune to doubt. Rather the intended positive value of the *epoche* lies in the lesson it teaches: humility. This is the "telos" or end of the *epoche.*

By means of the *epoche* one comes to see that all of people's beliefs or knowledge claims are only so many feeble attempts to transcend the finitude of human being and knowing. *Ataraxia* is nothing other than the gentle, ironic realization of the insurpassably human character of all knowing and of the vanity and comedy involved in human attempts to transcend the limits of their condition so as to achieve a knowledge of reality, which would be that of the gods. Knowledge is always presumptuous, but wisdom is humble. The humility that the *epoche* teaches amounts to a reconciliation with the limits of understanding, the limits of the human condition. After the *epoche,* one continues to live as human beings must, following the customs of a given culture, participating in its beliefs and prejudices, but one does not give one's assent to them, one is aware of the *trickery of reason,* as Sextus says, and is thus not duped by it.[61] The *epoche* does not therefore remove one from the follies of human existence, but, in making one expressly aware of them and in reconciling one with them, brings them under control. "Quietude" is controlled folly.

The ultimate function and raison d'être of skeptical argumentation and theorizing is the overcoming of all theory, liberation from the illusions of understanding. This is why the skeptic does not take even his own antidogmatic theories seriously but believes, with Pascal, that "to make light of philosophy is to be a true philosopher." He believes that "the last step of reason is the recognition that there is an infinity of things which transcend it; it is nothing but weak if it does not go so far as to know that. . . . there is nothing more consonant with reason than this disavowal of reason."[62]

Skepticism, indeed, is not just a set of theories having no other purpose than to be opposed to those of dogmatism. Its ultimate goal is not to work out irrefutable theories; rather it seeks, by means of theory, to point out the gap between all theory and lived experience. In order to do this it must not take itself overseriously and must, indeed, destroy itself as theory: "While the dogmatizer posits the matter of his dogma as substantial truth, the Sceptic ennunciates his formulae so that they are virtually cancelled by themselves."[63] "Just as purgative medicines expel themselves together with the substances already present in the body, so these arguments are capable of cancelling themselves along with other arguments which are said to be probative."[64] After destroying others, skeptical theory "turns around and destroys itself, like a purge which drives the substance out and then in its turn is itself eliminated and destroyed."[65]

Thus our own use of theory in this study is not intended to "prove" or "demonstrate" any theoretical statements about reality or understanding but has instead the following twofold function: (1) to expose by means of dialectical argument the weakness of dogmatic or rationalist theories about reality and understanding and their own inner contradictions and (2) to show that an alternative, non-dogmatic view of reality and understanding is at least possible, that is, is fully rational. The non-dogmatic use of theory can prove nothing—not even that dogmatism is wrong—but it can at least serve to persuade us that a non-dogmatic view of this is coherent and rational and, in so doing, can free us from our native dogmatic allegiances.[66]

Non-dogmatic theory is fully coherent. And this coherence stems from the fact that its own theories ultimately cancel themselves out. Dogmatism has as its end the attainment of "truth," which is to say theoretical statements about experience that will be, ideally, final and definitive. This is why dogmatism is always inconsistent, for no theory, theoretically, can ever fully justify itself. In contrast, the raison d'être of non-dogmatic theory is not theoretical but practical. The purpose of theorizing here is not to arrive at a body of theoretical statements that can claim to be the "truth" (a system of knowledge); the aim of non-dogmatic theory is rather the cultivation of a certain concrete, existential attitude or practical disposition. When viewed in the context of the practice of which it is a part, non-dogmatic theory is supremely consistent and rational. Indeed if the critique of dogmatism succeeds in bringing one to suspend belief—that is, if it provokes a practical transformation in the one who theorizes—then it is, *ipso facto,* "true," for, as James so aptly remarked, "true is *one species of good.*"[67] What is good for living takes precedence over and in fact determines what is true for thinking.

The critique of dogmatism effectively undermines the claim of any belief system to have achieved a true understanding of what reality really is, for it shows that what people take reality to be is in fact relative to the way in which they "intend" it, to the particular universe of discourse through which they seek understanding. But non-dogmatism nevertheless is not a relativism (it is not a set of theses opposed to rationalism), and it does not make of "reality" a meaningless term, nor does it therefore exclude the possibility of metaphysics, the possibility of an understanding of Reality. The kind of metaphysics compatible with non-dogmatism is of a special sort. One could perhaps call it negative ontology, on an analogy with negative theology.

A non-dogmatic understanding of Reality is possible only when one realizes that what is usually called reality is a cultural construct, for then one realizes that what Reality must really be is something more than what it is ever known-as. To understand Reality as the something more is to understand it as transcending any particular understanding of it, when "understanding" is taken in its normal sense, as belief. In freeing us from the dogmas of belief, the *epoche* also frees us for a non-dogmatic understanding of Reality. Reality is that which we do not know and which, therefore, we can know truly only when, in the suspension of belief, we know it as a mystery. "The true problem," Heidegger said, "is what we do not know and what, insofar as we know it *authentically,* namely *as* a problem, we know only questioningly."[68]

To understand Reality as a mystery is not not to understand it. Quite the opposite; it is to understand it truly, for if there is any meaning at all to speaking of a Reality that is something more than the many finite interpretations of experience devised by people, then Reality can only be that which is always more than it is ever taken to be. This understanding is not, of course, as is the case with ordinary, nonreduced understanding, a theoretical knowing-as but is, rather, a practical mode of resolute existence. By means of the *epoche* one takes up a firm stand in openness to the mystery, in a realization that has become a way of life that, as Heidegger says, "there is much in being that man cannot master. There is but little that comes to be known. What is known remains inexact, what is mastered insecure."[69]

The entire raison d'être of the skeptical critique is to open us and to keep us open to the mystery. This task is never ending, for everywhere and always people have sought understanding by interpreting and idealizing their experience in such a way as to produce systematic, closed universes of discourse, and in attempting to "totalize" their experience—in attempting to discover *a* meaning in it—they have reduced Reality to the "total object" projected by their finite belief systems. Skepticism seeks to break down the naive acceptance of these systems in order to open up the possibility of an understanding of Reality as that which transcends all interpretations of it, as the unlimited.

The realization that Reality is always more than what it is known to be is not a deception nor does it give rise to indifference. On the contrary, it makes for the greatest possible challenge to human understanding. The Reality that is seen when one slips in between belief systems is the source of the greatest wonder, as well as the greatest terror. The mystery is a *mysterium fascinans et tremendum,* and the task of he who would seek to understand Reality while not losing his understanding of the one or many realities in which he must live and with which he must continue to deal is to balance the terror of the realization with the wonder of it. Terror is controlled and wonder predominates when one realizes that Reality is not meaningless but is, rather, infinitely meaningful and is thus an endless source of wonder and amazement.

Reality (capital "r") is meaningful in the same sense in which lived experience is meaningful. It does not have *a* meaning in itself that could ever be discovered and adequately expressed but becomes ever more meaningful in and through the imaginative creation of multitudinous worlds by people in their unending attempt to account for the fact of their own existence. Like human existence itself, Reality is overdetermined.

Is there anything more that can be said of Reality by a negative ontology than to say that it is always more than can ever be said about it? Or is it perhaps the case, as mystical thinkers have maintained, that ontological wonder does away with all discourse? If language is basically interpretive and if the *epoche* is the suspension of interpretation, does not the *epoche* also involve the suppression of language? How, after the *epoche,* can one continue to use language if, as the principle of linguistic relativity would have it, language is at the root of all belief systems? Is not phenomenologically reduced "seeing" or "knowing" necessarily wordless? The answer is

"No," if the "meaning" of Reality is like the "meaning" of experience, for then the relation between Reality and understanding would be of the same dialectical sort as that between experience and expression, where the latter is actually the meaning of the former. What Reality really is is a mystery, but this is something made manifest by means of language itself. The age-old question as to the "meaning of being" perhaps can best be accosted by considering the relation between Reality and creative expression as this relation is conceptualized by a genuinely negative ontology.

NOTES

1. E. Husserl, *Ideas* (New York, 1962), sec. 124, p. 321.

2. This important fact about the relation between experience and expression has been well noted by Eugene Gendlin. "To be able to be further schematized is a very striking characteristic of experience. . . . In the process of being *further* schematized, experiencing has no definite units, is responsive to any scheme, and is capable of being schematized by any other experience" ("Experiential Phenomenology," in *Phenomenology and the Social Sciences,* ed. M. Natanson [Evanston, Ill., 1973], p. 297). Gendlin pinpoints the key problem when he says:

> The crucial problem has two parts: (1) If experience is not like a verbal scheme and we do not wish to say that it is, then how can we say anything at all about it without imposing a verbal scheme? and (2) If we wish, in some way, to appeal beyond logical schemes to a sense of "experience" not yet organized verbally, in what way do we have such "experience" present and available for an appeal, and in what way does experience give "yes" or "no" answers, so that some statements will be "based" on it and some statements not? (ibid., p. 282).

Gendlin has dealt in an interesting way with this problem in his earlier book, *Experiencing and the Creation of Meaning* (Glencoe, Ill., 1962).

3. M. Merleau-Ponty, *The Visible and the Invisible* (Evanston, Ill., 1968), p. 197.

4. S. Kierkegaard, *Philosophical Fragments* (Princeton, N.J., 1971), p. 46.

5. When it is a question of interpreting the utterances of another person and, even more, the utterances of a person of another time and place or culture (a business called interpretation or hermeneutics), we can be said to understand them when we have seized hold of the meaning-intention they articulate. The way this is done is by the imagination; we freely vary the utterance and elaborate on it in such a way as to construct further utterances of meaning, which go beyond the original one. The process operative here is the same one to be found in metaphorical expression. As Gendlin observes, "Metaphor also describes the process one would go through to create (obtain, understand) [note the equivalence of these terms] the felt meaning [what we are calling the meaning-intention] that the person of the other culture already has as a recognition. It is possible to communicate (that is, lead a person to create) [note again the equivalence] metaphorically a felt meaning that the person has not previously had" (*Experiencing and the Creation of Meaning,* p. 223). All insightful understanding—whether it is understanding oneself or another—is creative (transformational, imaginative).

Once an understanding has been arrived at in this way, it is "tested"; not all understandings or meanings can be said to be appropriate to the utterance. That is, the understanding or meaning arrived at through imaginative variation must be not only "interesting" in its own right but must also serve to clear up difficulties having to do with the original. In any event, one can arrive at the "original" meaning (which is never univocally one but always multiple and overdetermined) only by "analogical reasoning," by the imagination. One understands an utterance, even one's own, only by developing it further (the meaning of the original is never merely the meaning consciously intended by the author, therefore; as with the "meaning" of an experience or of an action the meaning of a text goes beyond this).

6. M. Merleau-Ponty, *Phenomenology of Perception* (London, 1962), p. xv.

7. The main difference between scientific and artistic meaning giving is this: in art one thing, such as a human action, is made meaningful or intelligible by being compared to some other thing, such as the deeds of an archetypal hero. This comparison is always in respect to some supposed common feature both terms share; it is something that the archetypal figure is felt to exemplify in an eminent way. But in art, as opposed to science, this feature is not explicitly determined; *the theory in terms of which experience is made intelligible* is not fully spelled out, and thus art appears to be less "theoretical" than science. In art it is the reader or spectator who is called upon to fill in the in respect of which, the *tertium comparationis* (and it is in this sense that art "leaves more to the imagination" than does science), but is precisely this which makes of art, like science, a cognitive (and not, as the positivists would say, a merely "emotive") exercise of the understanding.

8. R. B. Braithwaite, *Scientific Explanation* (Cambridge, 1968), p. 359.

9. P. Duhem, *The Aim and Structure of Physical Theory* (Princeton, N.J. 1954), pt. II, chap. 5, sec. 5.

10. "It is not possible to limit in any *a priori* manner the number of theories which could be 'induced' from the evidence" (S. Körner, *Experience and Theory* [London, 1966], p. 192).

11. See Appendix I, "On Theoretical Explanation."

12. N. R. Hanson, *Patterns of Discovery* (Cambridge, 1972), p. 64; cf. also p. 90.

13. S. Toulmin, *The Philosophy of Science* (New York, 1960), p. 148.

14. "Whether or not all peoples employ a category which may be roughly equated with our 'causation' or even our 'mutual interdependence,' all human beings whom I have known or read about seem to go to considerable trouble to find and express 'reasons' for what they say and do. The giving of justifications which are 'rational' with reference to the logics of that culture seems to be one of the most universal of adjustive responses" (C. Kluckhohn, *Navaho Witchcraft* [Boston, 1967], p. 82, n. 6).

15. W. James, *The Principles of Psychology* (New York, 1950), 2:311.

16. G. Holton, *Thematic Origins of Scientific Thought* (Cambridge, Mass., 1973), pp. 53-54.

17. Writing in the early third century, Sextus Empiricus has in fact a great deal to say which is applicable to the "detour of theory" and the matter of operational definitions. In the second book of *Pyrrhoniarum hypotyposeon* (Cambridge, Mass., 1967) (cc. 10-11), Sextus attacks the epistemology of the Stoics, according to which true knowledge of reality can be obtained by means of signs or inferences which serve to connect what is evident and experienceable with what is not. An "indicative sign" is an object of experience that is supposed to prove the existence of something nonevident. What Sextus calls a "naturally non-evident" object is an object of thought (noetoi) that never appears of itself "but may be thought to be apprehended, if at all, owing to other things." An example of such an object of thought would be the atom. The stoics define an indicative sign as "an antecedent judgment, in a sound hypothetical syllogism, which serves to reveal the consequent." For example, if A, then B; A, therefore B; where A is observable and B is naturally nonevident and A is taken to be proof of the existence of B. Among other detailed criticisms, Sextus points out that this form of reasoning is guilty of circularity or of begging the question, for one must know that B (the nonevident) is true (exists) in order to determine whether the observable object, A, actually exists qua indicative sign of B, and one can know the nonevident, B, only by means of the evident, A.

18. Körner, *Experience and Theory*, p. 169.

19. Körner writes: " A hypothetico-deductive system is thus not directly connected with experience. In linking it to experience by 'identifying' some of its predicates and propositions with internally inexact empirical ones one is not ascertaining that they are identical, only treat-

ing them as if they were" (ibid., p. 90). Kant, it would seem, was getting at much the same thing with his notion of the pure a priori or productive imagination, whose function it is to link up the categories of the understanding with the manifold of sense impressions in such a way as to produce empirical knowledge.

20. Ibid., pp. xii, 63.

21. Duhem, *Aim and Structure,* pt. II, chap. 5, sec. 2.

22. Holton, *Thematic Origins of Scientific Thought,* p. 287.

23. James, *Principles of Psychology,* 1:278.

24. Ibid., p. 196.

25. And qua technique, magic may be just as effective as science. In his book, *The Mind Game: Witch Doctors and Psychiatrists* (New York, 1972), E. F. Torrey, of the U.S. National Institute of Mental Health, shows that the techniques of psychotherapy are in fact basically the same, whether they are those of a witch doctor or a psychiatrist.

26. H. G. Gadamer, "The Science of the Life-World," in A. T. Tymieniecka, ed., *The Later Husserl and the Idea of Phenomenology* (Dordrecht, 1972), p. 185.

27. Sextus Empiricus, *Pyrrhoniarum hypotyposeon* ("Outlines of Pyrrhonism"), I, 3.

28. Ibid., I, 13.

29. Ibid., I, 15.

30. Ibid., I, 209.

31. Pascal, *Pensées* (Paris, 1963), 434.

32. This is also Husserl's tactic in *The Idea of Phenomenology* (The Hague, 1964) and the means whereby he attempts to lead readers to perform the phenomenological reduction.

33. It is no accident that skepticism exists most notably in times of heightened extracultural awareness, such as the Hellenistic period, the early modern age of the great discoveries, and today.

34. Sextus Empiricus, *Pyrrhoniarum hypotyposeon,* I, 31.

35. Ibid., I, 188ff.

36. Ibid., I, 10.

37. Ibid., I, 12. Sextus is drawing out the implications of Protagoras's observation, "on every topic there are two arguments contrary to each other."

38. Ibid., I, 203.

39. Ibid.

40. The English translator of Sextus says, "The main task of the Sceptic is, in fact to expose the folly of every form of positive doctrine; and consequently the bulk of these works of Sextus is controversial" (*Outlines of Pyrrhonism,* p. vii).

41. Cf. Husserl, *Ideas,* sec. 32 (next to last sentence).

42. Sextus Empiricus, *Pyrrhoniarum hypotyposeon,* I, 193.

43. Ibid., I, 230.

44. E. Husserl, *Ideas,* sec. 31. In sec. 32, Husserl goes on to state the attitude that the phenomenologist who has performed the *epoche* will take toward the sciences:

> Thus *all sciences which relate to this natural world,* though they stand ever so firm to me, though they fill me with wondering admiration, though I am far from any thought of objecting to them in the least degree, *I disconnect them all, I make absolutely no use of their standards, I do not appropriate a single one of the propositions that enter into their systems, even though their evidential value is perfect, I take none of them, no one of them serves me for a foundation*—so long, that is, as it is understood, in the way these sciences themselves understand it, as a truth *concerning the realities* of this world.

45. Sextus Empiricus, *Pyrrhoniarum hypotyposeon,* I, 191.

46. Diogenes Laertius, *Vitae Philosophorum,* IX, 104–07.

47. E. Husserl, *Experience and Judgment* (Evanston, Ill., 1973), sec. 89, p. 351.

48. In his objections to Descartes, the Jansenist theologian and philosopher, A. Arnauld,

objected to Descartes's maintaining that consciousness is completely clear in regard to itself (that is, that it is fully conscious of itself). "But who does not see," he said, "that much may be in the mind, of the existence of which the mind is not conscious?" A perhaps ever more noteworthy objection is the one which immediately precedes this one. Arnauld wondered if perhaps Descartes was not guilty of circular reasoning in the way he linked together psychological certainty and ontological necessity. This particular argument came to be known as "the Arnauld circle":

> The only remaining scruple I have is an uncertainty as to how a circular reasoning is to be avoided in saying: the only secure reason we have for believing that what we clearly and distinctly perceive is true, is the fact that God exists.
>
> But we can be sure that God exists, only because we clearly and evidently perceive that; therefore prior to being certain that God exists, we should be certain that whatever we clearly and evidently perceive is true. (fourth set of objections in *The Philosophical Works of Descartes,* trans. Haldane and Ross [New York: Dover Publications, 1955], p. 92).

This objection of Arnauld's closely parallels in form Sextus's objection to the Stoic notion of "indicative signs" on the grounds that it embodies circular reasoning (cf. n. 17 above).

49. "For we admit that we see, and we recognize that we think this or that, but how we see or how we think we know not" (Diogenes Laertius, *Vitae Philosophorum,* IX, 103).

50. M. Heidegger, *Being and Time* (New York, 1962), sec. 29, p. 173.

51. Ibid., p. 175.

52. W. James, *The Will to Believe* (New York, 1956), pp. viii-ix. Cf. also p. 73: "The bottom of being is left logically opaque to us, as something which we simply come upon and find, and about which (if we wish to act) we should pause and wonder as little as possible."

53. B. Pascal, *Pensées,* ed. L. Brunschvicg (Paris, 1963), 72.

54. A. de Tocqueville, *Democracy in America* (New York, n.d.), vol. 2, bk. I, ch. 17.

55. This is a paraphrase of Richard Popkin's concluding remarks in his article, "Skepticism," in Paul Edwards, ed., *The Encyclopedia of Philosophy* (New York, 1967), vol. 7, p. 460.

56. Diogenes Laertius, *Vitae philosophorum,* IX, 101.

57. Cf. Sextus Empiricus, *Pyrrhoniarum hypotyposeon,* I, cc. 14-18.

58. Diogenes Laertius, *Vitae philosophorum,* IX, 78.

59. "The end to be realized they hold to be suspension of judgment, which brings with it tranquility like its shadow" (Diogenes Laertius, *Vitae philosophorum,* IX, 107).

60. Sextus Empiricus, *Pyrrhoniarum hypotyposeon,* I, 26. Cf. also ibid., I, 29: "The Sceptics were in hopes of gaining quietude by means of a decision regarding the disparity of the objects of sense and of thought [we would say, disparity of experience and theory], and being unable to effect this they suspended judgment; and they found that quietude, as if by chance, followed upon their suspence, even as a shadow follows its substance."

61. Ibid., I, 17: "We follow a line of reasoning which, in accordance with appearances, points us to a life conformable to the customs of our country and its laws and institutions, and to our own instinctive feelings." Ibid., I, 23: "Adhering, then to appearances we live in accordance with the normal rules of life, undogmatically, seeing that we cannot remain wholly inactive." Ibid., I, 226: "when we describe a thing as good or evil we do not add it as our opinion that what we assert is probable, but simply conform to life undogmatically that we may not be precluded from activity." Ibid., I, 231; "we live in an undogmatic way by following the laws, customs, and natural affections." Ibid., II, 102: "Not only do we not fight against living experience, but we even lend it our support by assenting undogmatically to what it relies on, while opposing the private inventions of the Dogmatists." Ibid., II, 246: "For it is, I think, sufficient to conduct one's life empirically and undogmatically in accordance with the rules and beliefs that are commonly accepted, suspending judgment regarding the statements derived from dog-

matic subtlety and furthest removed from the usage of life." Ibid., II, 235: "Accordingly, the Sceptic, seeing so great a diversity of usages, suspends judgment as to the natural existence of anything good or bad or (in general) fit or unfit to be done, therein abstaining from the rashness of dogmatism; and he follows undogmatically the ordinary rules of life, and because of this he remains impassive in respect of matters of opinion, while in conditions that are necessitated his emotions are moderate; for though, as a human being, he suffers emotion through his senses, yet because he does not also opine that what he suffers is evil by nature, the emotion he suffers is moderate."

62. Pascal, *Pensées*, 267, 272.

63. Sextus Empiricus, *Pyrrhoniarum hypotyposeon*, I, 15.

64. Ibid., II, 188.

65. Diogenes Laertius, *Vitae philosophorum*, IX, 76.

66. In answer to the objection that in attempting to prove the impossibility of knowledge the skeptic is contradicting himself, Sextus answers that this is precisely what the skeptic does not attempt to do. On the contrary, the skeptics

> will say that the argument against proof is merely probable and that at the moment it convinces them and draws them on to assent, but that they do not know whether it will still do so later on owing to the variableness of the human mind. For when our answer is framed thus, the Dogmatist will no longer be able to say anything. . . . just as, for example, fire after consuming the fuel destroys also itself, and like as purgatives after driving the fluids out of the body expel themselves as well, so too the argument against proof, after abolishing every proof, can cancel itself also. And again, just as it is not impossible for the man who has ascended to a high place by a ladder to overturn the ladder with his foot after his ascent, so also it is not unlikely that the Sceptic after he has arrived at the demonstration of his thesis by means of the argument proving the non-existence of proof, as it were by a step-ladder, should then abolish this very argument" *(Adversus Mathematicos, VIII, 473, 480-81).*

When Wittgenstein compared his propositions to steps ("He must, so to speak, throw away the ladder after he has climbed up it."—*Tractatus,* 6.54), he obviously was not expressing a new thought.

67. W. James, "What Pragmatism Means," in *Pragmatism and Other Essays* (New York, 1963), p. 36.

68. M. Heidegger, *An Introduction to Metaphysics* (New Haven, Conn., 1959), p. 206.

69. M. Heidegger, "The Origin of the Work of Art," in *Poetry, Language, Thought* (New York, 1971), p. 53.

9 THE MEANING OF BEING

In this book I have attempted to formulate a fundamental critique of rationalist or dogmatic thought, the dominant mode of thought in the Western tradition, and to this end we have focused on its underlying epistemological and metaphysical presuppositions: on its theories of understanding and reality. When one seeks to refute a theoretical outlook it is not usually enough, however, simply to point out its weaknesses, even though these may be extremely serious, for dogmatic tolerance (in the sense in which one speaks of the body's tolerance for drugs) knows practically no bounds, and one may still hold to a position in a general way (and extremely tenaciously at that) in spite of the fact that one has become increasingly aware of its shortcomings, and, indeed, it is often when one feels most threatened that one reacts in an inflexible and intolerant (in the proper sense of the term) fashion. This peculiar trait of human understanding (our indefatigable attachment to our beliefs) is well brought out in Thomas Kuhn's analysis of scientific revolutions when he shows how a scientist will not usually abandon a paradigm, no matter what anomalies may build up around it, unless he knows of an alternative paradigm that can take its place. It was for just this reason that Kuhn himself was unable to abandon the underlying rationalist epistemology of modern science, even though as a result of his investigations into the pragmatics of scientific understanding he came to perceive very acutely the deficiencies of that epistemology. "In the absence of a developed alternative," he wrote, "I find it impossible to relinquish entirely that viewpoint."[1]

The entire raison d'être of the skeptical critique of dogmatism is that it should enable us to relinquish entirely the conceptual framework of rationalist thought. To paraphrase Hume, it could be said that the trouble with skepticism in general is that while "it admits of no answer," it "produces no conviction." The reason it "produces no conviction" is that it does not put forward yet another object for dogmatic belief. The lesson to be drawn would seem to be that if the *epoche* is to be successful, it must not put an end to all theorizing and must not confine one to a position of total silence. On the contrary, after having put the *epoche* into play for himself, the non-dogmatist must continue to formulate theories about understanding and reality—for the sake of others who are victims of the disease of dogmatic rashness, as Sextus (a physican turned philosopher) would say, as well as for himself, since the suspension of belief never amounts to the elimination of belief and the temptation to dogmatize remains ever-present. The difference, however, between these theories and those of the dogmatist is that they are intended not to express the "truth" about what-is (they do not, for instance, attempt to say what experience means or to spell out the meaning of reality) but only to provide the necessary stimulus for abandoning dogmatic theorizing. If the skeptical critique is to be successful it must, for pedagogical or strategic reasons, provide an alternate epistemological and metaphysical theory. A non-dogmatic theory of human understanding has been formulated in the preceding chapters, and thus it remains only to sketch a corresponding theory of reality, a metaphysics.

To be sure, a non-dogmatic metaphysics cannot claim to be the "truth," but it can at least seek to be plausible; it is something that people can still "believe" in when they have suspended all their dogmatic beliefs. Thus this chapter will not attempt to state what Reality is in itself but will only spell out some of the implications that follow from the critique of rationalism. Having arrived at the end of our dialectical-skeptical critique, we need to determine what it can possibly mean to speak of Reality when all rationalist principles as to what constitutes meaningful discourse have been abandoned.[2]

When one becomes concretely aware of the multiplicity of languages and cultures, one may, as a consequence, realize the relativity of them all. When, for instance, a monolingual person learns a new language by actually living in a foreign culture, the naive confidence that he formerly placed in his native language will be disturbed. His own language will cease to be the unobtrusive and transparent medium for reflecting reality that it formerly was and will become problematic in its own right; he will become aware of it as such and will begin to wonder about it. If he pursues his reflections, he will see that there is no natural relation between words and things, and he may even see that there is indeed no such thing as distinct "things," which merely receive different names in different languages. The world itself (experience) is divided up differently in different languages, and these languages arrange the resultant basic elements in different configurations. As a result, he will see that what others take reality to be is relative to their own linguistic and cultural ways of "intending" it. Reality (with a small "r"), he will see, is cultural through and through. If he reflects on this in a theoretical way, he will be led to formulate some kind of theory of linguistic relativity.[3]

It is, however, when he takes up in this way the path of theory that his real difficulties begin, for how is one to conceive of relativity? How can one conceive of relativity? If all the culturally conditioned ways of speaking of ·

reality are relative, what are they relative to? Like the anthropologist who recognizes the fact of cultural relativity but who thinks he can transcend it by means of a value-free language, the person in question may believe that there is or can be a language that transcends cultural differences and is capable of expressing the univocal, self-identical core of meaning, which is simply expressed differently in different languages.[4] In this way the notion of an ideal language arises, and in our day and age, science claims for itself a universal, value-free, nonrelative status.

The notions of an ideal language and of a universal science are, however, illusory; they are merely refinements or sophistications of the same kind of dogmatic confidence that a monolingual person tends to place in his native language. For it can be shown—and this is the business of the skeptical critique—that no system of belief can justify its claim to certain knowledge of what reality really is, that is, its correspondence to reality. When any system attempts to justify itself, it inevitably falls prey to circular reasoning. Assuming, then, that the skeptical critique finally does lead one to let go of one's dogmatic thought habits, what theoretical possibilities still remain open?[5]

At this point the most tempting and usual of alternatives is to take up a position of relativism. Reality is intrinsically "relative"; there are a multitude of heterogeneous realities and language games with no common link between them. It is thus impossible to say what Reality—as opposed to the plurality of realities—really is. This position tends toward a kind of ontological nihilism, for, one will say, not only can Reality not be "said," but it is meaningless even to attempt to do so. The notion of Reality is meaningless; Reality simply does not exist.

But relativism constitutes a theoretical impasse. Rather than leading thought to a successful overcoming of dogmatism, it puts an end to thinking. Relativism is self-contradictory and cannot, with any consistency, be maintained. Just as academic skepticism, which holds that nothing can be known, refutes itself—because it implicitly affirms that at least one thing is knowable: that nothing is—and is, therefore, not really a genuine (Pyrrhonian) skepticism at all but only an absurd form of inverted dogmatism (is it not significant that academic skepticism held sway in the Platonic academy?), so all relativism is self-contradictory when it asserts, in what amounts to an absolute fashion, that nothing is absolute and that all is relative, when, that is, it asserts that reality is in no way one but is irremediably many. Not only does relativism as a theory refute itself, but it is contradicted by what relativists actually do, for they all, from time to time, communicate with people of different languages and cultures, different outlooks and belief systems. The fact that translation is always possible constitutes a practical refutation of relativistic theory. Finally, the fact that, theoretically, it is possible to say a great deal about different belief systems from the point of view of none in particular and to point out what is common to them all—as

we have in this study by means of our transcendental-pragmatic approach—
the fact that one can impartially speak about all belief systems is sufficient
refutation of the theses of relativism, for one could not do so if everything
that one said were relative to one particular belief system.

If, then, rationalism is unacceptable and relativism is impossible, what
are the viable theoretical alternatives? Since both of the former alternatives
have been rejected and it has yet been possible to say a great deal about all
belief systems, it would seem that we have only to articulate, on the level of
explicit theory, the implications of our own theoretical praxis. We would
then—without making any claims to definitive truth—have to say something like this:

There is what could be called a Reality that transcends all particular,
finite, realities. As transcending all realities it is identical with none, and yet
it is not purely and simply different from them, for then it would merely be
another particular, albeit higher-level, reality and would thus be, ideally,
the proper object of a kind of superscience. Reality is not the same as a reality (the natural object of human understanding), nor is it, as God is sometimes said to be, Wholly Other than what-is.

If there is such a "thing" as Reality, but if (given the makeup of human
understanding) in principle it can never be adequately known (in the sense
of positive knowledge), then we have no grounds for maintaining that Reality is determinate, that it has an essential makeup. Thus we must refuse one
major traditional alternative: to say that Reality does exist and is fully intelligible in itself but that people can never know it. This, of course, is a
version of the age-old Appearance-Reality distinction. And like the *nomos-
physis* controversy of the ancient Greeks, it serves only to confuse the issue.
The latter distinction was, as Aristotle points out, a widespread *topos* or argumentative device used to trap opponents in a paradox.[6] And an unfruitful
paradox at that, for it makes no sense to posit, as Kant did, a kind of unknowable *Ding-an-sich*. If we cannot know anything about *physis,* Nature,
or Reality, what right do we have to say even that it exists and that it is fully
intelligible in itself, though not for us?

The notion of transcendence, indispensable for conceiving of Reality,
needs to be refined. While transcending all realities (that is, while being identical with none), Reality is yet that which is common to and most intimate to
them all. Only the notion of analogy put forward in chapter 4 furnishes a
satisfactory way out of the *aporia* in which thought finds itself when it seeks
to overcome both rationalism and relativism. We need to conceive, as the
medievals would have said, of an analogy of being, an *anolgia entis*.

To the degree that anything can be said in a straightforward fashion
about Reality, it must be said that Reality is "analogous in itself" (the expression admittedly is awkward). The analogy here is one of proper proportionality and not of attribution, for there is no univocal core of meaning

to the term *Reality*. Reality is that which is analogously common to all realities.

Any given reality is simply the correlate of a belief. It is a "semantic construct," a function of the way in which people interpret their experience. Thus we must look for Reality—for that which is analogically common to all realities—in the very process of belief formation. The locus of Reality is creative expression.

Because understanding is naturally belief—that is, human understanding always takes its belief objects to be Reality itself and not what they really are, namely finite, relative "realities"—it is necessarily the case that Reality can never be a direct object of understanding. Reality is lost sight of at the very moment when it manifests itself in the fabrication of belief objects. Reality is necessarily elusive and can be "said," if at all, only indirectly. There can be no science of Reality.

Let us see if all of this can be made more concrete.

The term *Reality* is rather abstract and makes for difficulties in its own right. If we have had recourse to it, it is only because there is "something more" to what is meant by the term *reality* than simply the particular correlate of a finite world view (*a* reality). Other terms equally well could have been used to designate this something more: Being, Nature, World, the Unlimited, What-Is, the Transcendental Condition of Possibility of All That Is. If we have settled on *Reality* it is only because it seems to be more concrete than some (such as *Being*) or less restrictive than others (such as *Nature*). Still it is not easy to say exactly what we mean by it, but this is perhaps inevitable if it is indeed the case that Reality is nothing determinate in itself (is not *a* reality). But people always and everywhere speak of something like Reality, and the various isomorphs or versions of the term seem to have something in common. By *Reality* we mean to refer to what is common to all people, the comprehensive element in all comprehension, that which people presuppose when they experience a basic communion with their fellow beings that transcends all specific cultural differences.

Perhaps we could make some headway were we to ask what is most basic, most common and universal, and most characteristic of human existing and understanding. It would seem that what is most common and fundamental is not any specific view of things or any particular belief but rather a vague and often inarticulate question. The most basic thing about people is that they are vitally concerned about their existence, and their being is for them a question, the most momentous question of all. Always and everywhere people have puzzled over the fact of their existence and have sought to discover what it means that they are. Man is for himself the most wondrous and thought-provoking of all objects. As Tocqueville, the great observer, noted in the course of his reflections on the culture of the Americans:

I need not traverse earth and sky to discover a wondrous object woven of contrasts, of infinite greatness and littleness, of intense gloom and amazing brightness, capable at once of exciting pity, admiration, terror, contempt. I have only to look at myself. Man springs out of nothing, crosses time, and disappears forever in the bosom of God; he is seen but for a moment, wandering on the verge of the two abysses, and there he is lost.[7]

In their more reflective moments people inevitably ask, "What is the meaning of it all?" The title of one of Gauguin's paintings, *D'où venons-nous? Qui sommes-nous? Où allons-nous?* fittingly articulates the most basic of all questions and the most universal of human traits. "Where do I come from?" "Who am I?" "Where am I going?"—in short, "Why am I?"—is the question every person asks himself. The attempt to answer this question and to discern a meaning to life gives rise to myth, to religion, to art, as well as to science; it is indeed the original stimulus of all creative expression.

Thus it would seem that the question as to the "meaning of being" or the question as to "what reality really is" is simply a refined version of the question as to the meaning of life. The latter question, it would seem, is the practical equivalent of the former. When people speak about Reality, they are in fact speaking about their own experience and are attempting to make sense of the awareness they have of their own existence. We have no grounds at all for neatly distinguishing between Reality and our experience, and, indeed, for all practical purposes (transcendentally-pragmatically speaking) our lived-through, prethematic experience and Reality are one and the same.

When we talk about Reality we are actually talking about the reality of our own experience. Thus the problem of saying what Reality is and the problem of interpreting and articulating experience are but one problem, at least from a methodological point of view. Now when the question as to the meaning of Reality is seen to be a version of the question as to the meaning of experience, it becomes possible to say a number of things about Reality.

We have, indeed, only to say of Reality what in the preceding chapter we were led to say of experience. Reality has meaning in the same way that experience has meaning; it is not meaningful in itself but is what gives rise to meaning and what becomes meaningful in the attempt to express it and say what it is. The locus of Reality is creative expression. This statement needs, however, to be qualified.

Reality is not simply what, in creative expression, is said (this is rather *a* reality). It is also what remains unsaid. Reality is overdetermined; it is the intentional excess of what we want to say over what we in fact do say. It is "the excess of what we live over what has already been said." By Reality we mean that characteristic of our experience whereby it is overdetermined, can always be explicated further and which in our perpetual attempt at expression is generative of ever-increased meaningfulness. This is what is meant when one speaks of the "transcendence" of Reality. Reality transcends what is ever known or said of it, not in the sense that it is something other than this but rather that it is just precisely this open-endedness of acquired meaning, this excess of experience over expression.

And when we speak of the Reality of what is real, of "things," we mean not what the thing is or is taken to be (what traditionally is called its "essence") but the fact that it can be this or that or some other thing, depending on how we interpret it—or, to be more precise, depending on how we interpret our experience of the world. The Reality of a thing is its inexhaustible determinability.

One therefore achieves an understanding of Reality when, in the perception of any given thing, one sees that it *both is and is not what it is* (is believed to be), for the Reality of what-is lies precisely in its limitless possibility of being otherwise, in its not being what it merely appears to be for a given system of belief or interpretive framework. This is why we say that an understanding of Reality occurs when one slips in between realities or belief systems; one then appreciates the persuasive force of these two interpretations—for example, of an event as it is understood by magic and as it is understood by science—without dogmatically assenting to either one of them. One's believing having been suspended, one sees that what the thing or event in question really is is more than what it is taken to be.

Ever since metaphysics, or the search for the "meaning of being," has existed as a distinct theoretical enterprise, the notion of Reality (being, and so forth) has tended to be linked with the notion of the infinite. We have ourselves had the occasion to speak of the "infinite meaningfulness" of Reality. What, from a nonrationalist point of view, does the notion of infinity mean here?

Very often the notion of infinity simply serves to conceptualize our human experience of the limits of our knowledge. Because people, in dogmatic rashness, have always sought to transcend the finitude of their condition, they have posited as the object of their striving an infinite reality beyond the realm of appearance, a reality (such as Spinoza's Nature) that only partially reveals itself in experience. Perhaps the notion owes its existence to the fact that human understanding tends to function in a "binary" fashion (Alcmaeon of Croton, a disciple of Pythagoras, remarked that "most human affairs go in pairs"). To conceive of something one must conceive of nothing, to conceive of appearance one must conceive of reality, to conceive of the finite (to understand human existence) one must conceive of the infinite. The term itself, interestingly enough, is a privitive (not only in English but in all the philosophical languages of the West), which means that it lacks positive content and serves to refer only to what is other than human existence; the infinite is what man is not. Dogmatic understanding is never satisfied with indeterminateness, however, and attempts to form a positive understanding of the infinite, to convert the negative into a positive. In contrast to human imperfection and incompleteness, the infinite is perfect and complete; it is a perfectly articulated totality.

Dogmatic thinking works with unavowed images and concealed metaphors. For rationalist thought the perfect and most pleasing image is the circle, for the circle is without beginning or end and is complete unto itself. "Infinity" corresponds to the Greek, *to apeiron*, which in common parlance referred to circular or spherical shapes and, in particular, to rings without seams. When Hegel, the arch-rationalist, conceives of the infinite, he does so in terms of the archetypal image: the true infinite "is itself round," and it "organizes itself into a whole whose starting point again coincides with the final point."[8]

As knowledge becomes more aware of itself, it tends to assume the form of a circle, of a closed-off, self-subsistent system. Thus between positive knowledge and reality, rationalistically conceived as the infinite, there is a natural and predestined affinity or, as Leibniz, another superrationalist, would have said, a "pre-established harmony." Reality accordingly is the proper object of science; as the totality, it is the object of an absolute science in the Hegelian sense. What is rational is real, and what is real is rational. To be is to be intelligible. In itself, Reality is pure intelligibility, though it may not be fully intelligible for us. When the rationalist says that Reality is "potentially intelligible," he means that the meaning we discover in it was already there before our "discovery" of it.

Such is the rationalist conception of Reality and Infinity, which a non-dogmatic metaphysics must necessarily reject. It can affirm neither with rationalism that Reality is fully intelligible and meaningful in itself nor with rationalism's opposite, relativism, that it is absurd and meaningless. To interpret Reality is neither to discover a preexistent meaning, nor is it merely to project onto an amorphous "matter" an artificially constructed and merely "human" meaning. Reality can not be said to be meaningful in itself nor can it be said to be meaningless. All that can be said is that Reality is potentially meaningful, in the same way as is experience.

And just as the relation between experience and expression is not a relation between two distinct things but a very special kind of relation wherein what gets said is not other than but rather is the very meaning of experience itself, so it must be said that between Reality and our understanding of it there obtains a similar dialectical relation. When, therefore, in negative ontology one speaks of the "potential" meaningfulness (or intelligibility) of Reality, one does not mean what the rationalist means by the term: that all actual or expressed meaning is nothing but the unfolding of what was already there, the merely making explicit of what already existed implicitly.

Raising in effect the question of what exactly it means to speak of "po-

tential'' existence, James likens the relation between thought and experience
to the relation between the sculptor and his block of stone. He says that
while it is true that in one sense the figure that the sculptor brings into existence had existed in the stone from all eternity, only waiting to be released, it
must not be forgotten that an indefinite number of other figures ("a thousand different ones beside it") also existed in it potentially; "the sculptor
alone is to thank for having extricated this one from the rest."[9] Expression
does not therefore merely discover what was already there only waiting to
be discovered but is genuinely creative.

In another text, James, insisting that "in our cognitive as well as in our
active life we are creative," goes on to say:

> The import of the difference between pragmatism and rationalism is now in
> sight throughout its whole extent. The essential contrast is that *for rationalism
> reality is ready-made and complete from all eternity, while for pragmatism it is
> still in the making, and awaits part of its complexion from the future.* On the
> one side the universe is absolutely secure, on the other it is still pursuing its
> adventures.

And he quite appropriately concludes:

> *The alternative between pragmatism and rationalism, in the shape in which we
> now have it before us, is no longer a question in the theory of knowledge, it
> concerns the structure of the universe itself.*[10]

While it is true that though human understanding is creative it is not a
creation *ex nihilo,* it is also true that the meanings generated through imaginative thinking are never perfectly predictable in advance; they do represent
something genuinely "new." For the nondogmatist the history of human
understanding is not what it was for Hegel: the progressive realization or
unfolding of a predetermined scenario. Although one may always, in retro-
spect, link up the subsequent with the prior in such a way as to see the
former as necessarily deriving from the latter (this is of course an exercise of
the imagination, the synthesizing faculty, which is at work in all explanation
building), one cannot determine in advance the course of understanding.
"Predictions" are never true in advance; they are made true *post factum.*
To say that Reality is meaningful is not, therefore, to say that it does not
contain surprises. For the nondogmatist, Reality is not the object of a
Science but is a continual source of amazement and puzzlement, or frustration and wonder.

And when negative ontology says further that Reality is infinitely
meaningful, it does so again with an eye to the characteristics of expressed
experience. An experience gives rise not to just one expression (one mean-

ing) but to an indefinite or an infinite number of possible expressions; an experience can always be expressed further. As Gendlin notes, "Any datum of experiencing—any aspect of it, no matter how finely specified—can be symbolized and interpreted further and further."[11] Because all expressed experiences are open-ended and capable of infinite variation and development, Reality is similarly open-ended. The meaning of Reality is nothing other than the various ways in which it can be, and the ways in which it can be become manifest in the ways in which it can be said to be. The ways in which Reality can be spoken of are endless; there is an infinity of possible worlds or realities. Reality (capital "r") is, therefore, infinitely meaningful.

Obviously, "infinity" here does not mean a fully articulated totality but rather an indefinite, endless, essentially open and ongoing "process." A rationalist such as Hegel would call this kind of infinity a "bad" infinity, in contrast to his notion of complete determinateness and self-enclosure, which he labels a "good" infinity, for here there is no possibility of our ever arriving at an understanding of Reality that would be closed, immune to further revision; in principle knowledge becomes impossible.[12] But for us the rationalist's good infinity is the bad infinity; it is, as Merleau-Ponty said, "a congealed infinity."[13] The rationalist's "positive infinity" is a false infinity, an illusion of dogmatic understanding. When mortals attempt to conceive of the infinite positively and without restriction and due regard to the insurpassable finitude of their own understanding, they inevitably experience only a pseudo-infinity, one made to the measure of man and expressive of nothing more than his own frustrated wishes.

To recapitulate, our position enables us to avoid relativism and allows us to maintain that Reality is intelligible and "meaningful" while at the same time it circumvents rationalism through its insistence that Reality is not completely knowable, is not fully determinate in itself, such that it would be possible, if only in principle, to achieve an "adequate" knowledge of it, which would itself be determinate and fixed. To say that Reality is infinitely "meaningful" means only that it is inexhaustible and that the search for genuine self-understanding is without end. To the eternal enigma of human existence corresponds the boundless mystery of Being.

At its highest level of theorizing, non-rationalist thought thus provides an ontological justification for cultural diversity and linguistic pluralism. It reveals, within the limits of possible theory, why the search for an ideal language and for cultural monism is necessarily misguided. That people should speak in a multitude of tongues and hold to different imaginative world views is, in the final analysis, the most "natural" thing of all; it is the most fitting expression of Reality itself, a testimony to our basic freedom, which transcends all determinations, and, through this, to the freedom and indeterminateness of Reality. "The imagination is the liberty of the mind and hence the liberty of reality."[14]

In his book on language and translation, Steiner puzzles over a fact about language that is not usually given much consideration. In view of the physical uniformity of the human race, why is it that, when they seek to express themselves, people should use such an overwhelming diversity of languages?

> Translation exists because men speak different languages. This truism is, in fact, founded on a situation which can be regarded as enigmatic and as posing problems of extreme psychological and socio-historical difficulty. Why should human beings speak thousands of different, mutually incomprehensible tongues? We live in this pluralist framework, have done so since the inception of recorded history, and take the ensuing farrago for granted. It is only when we reflect on it, when we lift the facts from the misleading context of the obvious, that the possible strangeness, the possible "unnaturalness" of the human linguistic order strikes us. . . . Why does *homo sapiens,* whose digestive track has evolved and functions in precisely the same complicated ways the world over, whose biochemical fabric and genetic potential are, orthodox science assures us, essentially common, the delicate runnels of whose cortex are wholly akin in all peoples and at every stage of social evolution—why does this unified, though individually unique mammalian species not use *one* common language? . . . We do not speak one language, nor half a dozen, nor twenty or thirty. Four to five thousand languages are thought to be in current use. This figure is almost certainly on the low side. We have, until now, no language atlas which can claim to be anywhere near exhaustive. Furthermore, the four to five thousand living languages are themselves the remnant of a much larger number spoken in the past. . . . The mind must be complacent to regard this situation without a radical sense of perplexity.[15]

In an attempt to make sense of this strange phenomenon, Steiner alludes to Humboldt's reflections on language, which anticipate those of Sapir and Whorf:

> It is . . . in the nature of "spirit" to seek to realize, to energize into conscious being, all the modes of possible experience. This is the true cause of the immense variety of speech forms. Each is a foray into the total potentiality of the world. "Jede Sprache," writes Humboldt, "ist ein Versuch." It is a trial, an assay. It generates a complex structure of human understanding and response and tests the vitality, the discriminatory range, the inventive resources of that structure against the limitless potential of being. Even the noblest language is only *ein Versuch* and will remain ontologically incomplete.[16]

Speaking for himself, Steiner says:

> This is my main point. Man has "spoken himself free" of total organic constraint. Language is a constant creation of alternative worlds. There are no limits to the shaping powers of words, proclaims the poet. . . . In every fixed

definition there is obsolescence or failed insight. The teeming plurality of languages enacts the fundamentally creative, "counter-factual" genius and psychic functions of language itself. It embodies a move away from unison and acceptance—the Gregorian homophonic—to the polyphonic, ultimately divergent fascination of manifold specificity. Each different tongue offers its own denial of determinism. "The world," it says, "can be other." . . . The proliferation of mutually incomprehensible tongues stems from an absolutely fundamental impulse in language itself. I believe that the communication of information, of ostensive and verifiable "facts," constitutes only one part, and perhaps a secondary part, of human discourse. The potentials of fiction, of counterfactuality, of undecidable futurity profoundly characterize both the origins and nature of speech. They differentiate it ontologically from the many signal systems available to the animal world. They determine the unique, often ambiguous tenor of human consciousness and make the relations of that consciousness to "reality" creative. . . . Through language, we construct what I have called "alternities of being." . . . To a greater or lesser degree, every language offers its own reading of life. To move between languages, to translate, even within restrictions of totality, is to experience the almost bewildering bias of the human spirit towards freedom.[17]

An ideal language would in fact be "unnatural"—would not genuinely express Reality—for Reality does not have *a* meaning; it is infinitely meaningful. The teeming profusion of different languages reflects and is itself the most perfect expression of this incredible richness and prodigality.

This brings us, by way of conclusion, to the question of the relation of Reality and creative expression and to the question, raised at the end of the preceding chapter, as to whether it is possible to say anything meaningful about Reality.

If it is indeed the case that Reality is indeterminate, then it necessarily follows that it is not possible, even in theory, to say what it is that Reality really is. Reality, being indeterminate, has no essence—it is "above essence"—and thus cannot be defined (for a definition is simply the statement of what something is, of its "essence"). One could thus say of Reality what Scotus Erigena said of God: one cannot say what Reality is because Reality is not a what. This automatically disqualifies as a vain and illusory pursuit the age-old quest for a science of Reality—metaphysics in the traditional sense. When dogmatism is refuted, so also are the pretensions of speculative, systematic philosophy, which has as its goal positive knowledge of Reality. Ignoring the imaginative makeup of human understanding, traditional systematic philosophy does no more than construct *chateaux d'idées,* systems of ideas around some dominant metaphor taken in literal earnestness and not even seen to be a metaphor. Philosophical concepts that claim to express something about the essence of Reality or being are simply disguised metaphors or analogies. There is no such thing as a speculative or conceptual order of thought that transcends analogical thinking and carries within itself its own principle of autonomy.[18] Speculative philosophy is believed-in poetry, myth.

A non-rationalist metaphysics, aware of the illusions of understanding, is aware also of the utter impossibility of attaining to a positive knowledge of Reality. This impossibility is in fact its very subject matter; it does not attempt to say what Reality is but only that, as far at least as human understanding goes, it is unknowable. The only ontology compatible with the skeptical refutation of dogmatism is negative ontology, on the model of negative theology. Negative ontology is the knowledge of what we do not and cannot know of Reality. It is the knowledge of Reality as that which is, for human understanding, the great Unknown.

Because negative ontology is the knowledge of the limits of knowing, it is inevitable that it should realize itself "negatively," as essentially the critique of all positive claims to definitive knowledge, of dogmatism. The purpose of theorizing and argumentation here is not to build up a system of knowledge and a science of Reality but to expose the pretensions and limits of all those modes of understanding—magic, science, and speculative philosophy, among others—that strive after systematicity and positive knowledge. Thus negative ontology, in itself, has nothing to do with wordless mysticism. On the contrary, it is in its very essence linguistic and theoretical. If it were not linguistic, it would not even qualify as thought, for, as Nietzsche rightly observed, "We cease to think when we refuse to do so under the constraint of language."[19]

Since the illusions of human understanding are mostly linguistic in nature—semantic constructs believed in and taken to be Reality itself—they can be effectively overcome only by language. The cure for dogmatic rashness must be proportionate to and of like nature as its cause. If the basic function of language is to project worlds and to construct belief objects, negative ontology is the systematic misuse of language. In any event, the critique of dogmatism is, as Sextus says, effected by means of speech: "The Sceptic, being a lover of his kind, desires to cure by speech, as best he can, the self-conceit and rashness of the Dogmatists."[20]

Negative ontology is thus actually "positive" in its intentions. The destruction of dogmatism and the criticism of the pretensions of all finite belief systems that seek to reduce Reality to the totality projected by the system is the means whereby the "infinite meaningfulness" of Reality is safeguarded and the freedom and dignity of the human person, which lie in his irreducibility to the object of any finite universe of discourse—such as that of modern science—is preserved. There is something more to Reality or being and to human being than what is objectifiable in them, and the purpose of negative ontology is to remind us continually of this, to reopen us continually to that which transcends the closed universe of any and all belief systems. Negative ontology and the critique of dogmatism is a form of "logotherapy" whose goal is ontological openness and liberation from the illusions of understanding. Such an openness is the only truly effective cure for cultural imperialism and ideological totalitarianism.

What Reality really is cannot be said. But this does not mean that Reality is totally foreign to language, anymore than the fact that an experience can never be "adequately" expressed means that it is foreign to expression. The logician's law of excluded middle—his either-or—simply does not apply here. Reality may be unsayable, but it is not the case that the unsayable can in no way be said. Reality is limitless,. but it is reduced to manageable proportions when it is viewed in the light of our own experience. As far as our ability to understand goes, Protagoras was right in saying that man is the measure of things; our experience is the only means we have for sounding out the depths of being.

If the "meaning of being" is taken to be practically equivalent to the "meaning of life or experience," it is apparent that all attempts to express the meaning of existence are so many expressions of Reality itself. As the intentional excess or overdetermination of experience—its potentiality for being explicated even further and further—it is obvious that Reality is made manifest in and by means of creative discourse itself, in the very process whereby people freely construct particular belief systems. Of course, to the degree that people also assent naively to their belief objects and enclose themselves in their semantic universes, Reality, as that which transcends all realities, remains hidden from them. Thus language expresses or reveals Reality not so much by means of what it says—the overt meanings created by means of language—as by what it does. The "meaning of Reality" is, so to speak, the surplus value created by the use of language. One cannot say what Reality is, but in and by means of the creative use of language Reality shows something of itself.

Perhaps it will be said that the function of language is to make the absent present (this is the same as projecting a world), but, if so, what in this case language makes present is the irremediable absence of any definitive understanding of Reality. Language here reveals Reality as that which conceals itself, as the mystery. But although Reality can never be the object of an "essential insight" or *Wesenschau,* as Husserl would say, it is nonetheless always there on the margin of our perceptual field, when through language we fabricate and contemplate various "essences" or realities. Reality can be glimpsed only out of the corner of one's eyes, when one slips in between worlds.

It can therefore be said that the "revelation of being" is bound up with and made possible by a very special feature of human language that is peculiar to it: it is capable of expressing what transcends it. Because language allows for its own transcendence, it is capable of expressing that Reality which cannot be directly said. What this means in concrete terms can be seen in the way in which metaphor produces its effect, insightful understanding.

A metaphor does not "say" what it means, for what it actually says, its literal meaning, is precisely what it does not mean. The mode of metaphorical communication is indirect; there is no direct transmission of "information" here, in the way in which computers exchange information. When one truly means what one metaphorically says, one never wants to be understood by those by whom one wants to be understood (which is not always everybody) as meaning what one merely seems to mean. What one says metaphorically is not to be taken literally, at its accustomed face value, for when this happens one's true meaning has not been grasped. The meaning of a metaphor is not like the meaning of a straightforward referential proposition or a constative utterance; it is not what is apparently said but is, rather, what the utterance shows in transcending itself toward what is not said in the saying, and it is what the utterance does when it leads another person to recreate for himself a meaning analogous to the one intended by the maker of the metaphor. As Perelman observes:

> Furthermore, one may be obliged to invent the theme because, through inability to understnad the terms of the discourse in their literal sense, one is impelled to give them a figurative meaning and so to discover the theme and reinvent an analogy which will give the discourse its real meaning. . . . The reader must discover the theme, in other words, the *spirit* of the phoros that will correspond to the author's intentions. This quest can give rise to new creations of an ethical, aesthetic, or religious nature.[21]

And, it might be added, of a metaphysical nature as well. *A metaphor generates insightful understanding precisely because it forces one to be creative.* Metaphorical language thus does not really say or state anything at all. Rather it performs an extralinguistic, existential function in that it provokes a change in the way we view things, it brings about a transformation in our thinking. Its meaning lies entirely in its "perlocutionary force," in the effect the words have on us.

If the locus of Reality is creative expression, then Reality best reveals something of itself in the living metaphor. Insight into Reality occurs when in metaphorical discourse one slips in between established categorical systems and semantic realms and sees thereby that what one takes reality to be is something that could be otherwise.

Because Reality is not a reality, it is not possible to say anything directly about it. It is this impossibility that is thematized by negative ontology. Habitually, however, people feel the need to speak about that which concerns them, and what concerns them the most is the Reality of their existence. Metaphorical discourse is the only means available for speaking in a seemingly direct way about Reality while not falsifying it (that is, not reducing it to a mere reality). The reason is that only metaphorical discourse can say something about something without hypostatizing that about which it speaks. This is due to that unique feature of metaphorical predication, the fact that every genuinely metaphorical assertion is a qualified one and the metaphorical "is" always includes an "is-not." When we speak metaphorically about Reality, *and are aware that we are indeed speaking metaphorically,* we cannot but realize that Reality is something more than what, in the metaphor, it is said to be, that Reality both is and is not what it is said metaphorically to be.[22]

This is particularly evident in the case of the Nuer, a people of the south Sudan studied by Evans-Pritchard. They can, in a metaphor, say that a crocodile is *kwoth* or Spirit—their supreme ontological principle—without reducing the latter to the former and without meaning that Spirit, which for them is immaterial, is identical with a material body.[23] In fact, all of the Nuer conceptions of and actions toward the holy are metaphors, "imaginative constructions," as Evans-Pritchard says, and they do not make the mistake (so often made by "scientific" observers of them) of taking them literally and of confusing the symbol with what the symbol is meant to express and which transcends all determinations. As the anthropologist says:

> *Kwoth* [Spirit] would, indeed, be entirely indeterminate and could not be thought of by Nuer at all were it not that it is contrasted with the idea of *cak,* creation, in terms of which it can be defined by reference to effects and relations and by the use of symbols and metaphors. But these definitions are only schemata, as Otto puts it, and if we seek for elucidation beyond these terms, a statement of what Spirit is thought to be like in itself, we seek of course in vain. Nuer do not claim to know. They say that they are merely *doar,* simple people, and how can simple people know about such matters? What happens in the world is determined by Spirit and Spirit can be influenced by prayer and sacrifice. This much they know, but no more; and they say, very sensibly, that since the European is so clever perhaps he can tell them the answer to the question he asks. . . .

> When the purely social and cultural features of Nuer religion have been abstracted, what is left which may be said to be that which is expressed in the social and cultural forms we have been considering? It is difficult to give a more adequate answer to this question than to say that it is a relationship between man and God which *transcends all forms.* It is not surprising therefore that we cannot give any clear account of what for Nuer is the nature of God other than that he is *like* wind or air. . . . Spirit in itself is for Nuer a *mystery* which lies behind the names and the totemic and other appearances in which it is represented.[24]

What religious symbols are meant to express is something that is, not just accidentally, but essentially *"secretive,"* so to speak, and therefore can be communicated only indirectly, in metaphors and images. A similar situation obtains in the realm of art. There is indeed one particular feature of all good art that merits consideration.

Why is it that the poet hesitates to communicate in a straightforward way the "meaning" of his poem? Why is it that he even thinks that the meaning must not be said? The poem that speaks of the play of sunlight on the sea coast does mean more than just what it says: "The sea represents death and eternity, the land represents the brief life of the summer and of one human generation which passes into the sea of eternity." But, as Stephen Spender goes on to say:

> Let me here say at once that although the poet may be conscious of this aspect of his vision, it is exactly what he wants to avoid stating, or even being too concerned with. His job is to recreate his vision, and let it speak for itself. The poet must distinguish clearly in his own mind between that which most definitely must be said and that which must not be said. The unsaid inner meaning is revealed in the music and the tonality of the poem, and the poet is conscious of it in his knowledge that a certain tone of voice, a certain rhythm, are necessary.[25]

The meaning of the poem "should never be said and yet should shine through every image in the poem."[26]

Why this apparent refusal on the part of the poet to state clearly what he means? Why, in the words of Heraclitus, does the poet neither affirm nor deny but merely give a sign whose meaning is elusive? The poet's reserve is all the more remarkable in that it stands in marked contrast to the philosopher's compulsion to say everything he knows in as straightforward and clear a way as he can.

Is not the poet's restraint at least in part due to his knowledge that human existence and Reality are overdetermined and that they "mean" more than what they can be said to mean at any given time and from any given point of view? Is it not because he realizes that existence and Reality do not have a meaning but an indefinite number of different meanings? If poetry is capable of provoking in us the feeling that by its means we have achieved an insight into the meaning of life (of Reality), is it not precisely because it does not attempt to state in a univocal way this meaning but is content to merely evoke it? Heraclitus said that Nature likes to hide herself. Is not the poet's reticence the most fitting response to the self-dissimulation of Reality itself?

The poet is he who is uncommonly attuned to "the wholeness and the fullness of complete experience" and who knows that everything is "at the same time one thing and another thing, escaping the outlines of any one pattern applied in abstract analysis."[27] The poet expresses Reality by constructing a poem that communicates its meaning only indirectly and that, by means of the very elusiveness of its meaning, reflects the mystery of being it-self. Nature, like people, is withdrawing and secretive. This the poet knows, and his way of using language conforms to this realization. The poet is he who, in the true sense of the word, *respects* Reality (Nature) and the reality of the person. For to respect something is to accord it its due recognition by leaving it to its own unfathomable self.[28]

The religious person, the poet, and the negative philosopher all know more about Reality than does the speculative philosopher or the presumptuous scientist who vainly attempt to solve the "world riddle" and to state in a straightforwrd, literal way the meaning of being. While the approach of the three to Reality is different, their goal is much the same. The religious person, the poet, and the negative philosopher are joined in their realization that being or Reality transcends all determinations and that everything that one can say about it directly are metaphors that communicate their truth not so much by what they say as by what, in their saying, they do. The negative philosopher knows that even to say that Reality *is* (or that being *is*) is to speak metaphorically, for, strictly speaking, only realities are. We can properly say that Reality is only if we are aware that we are speaking metaphorically, for, in accordance with the ironic and paradoxical nature of metaphorical predication, we are then also aware that Reality both is and is not and that our speaking about it metaphorically is the best testimony to what it really is: always more than what is said of it.

Heidegger, who throughout the course of his life pursued but a single thought—the meaning of Being—was in the end able to write: "But is Being a thing? Is Being like an actual being in time? *Is* Being at all? . . . Being *is* not."[29] But let us leave the final word to that master of the metaphor, the poet: "Reality is not what it is. It consists of the many realities which it can be made into."[30]

NOTES

1. T. Kuhn, *The Structure of Scientific Revolutions* (Chicago, 1970), p. 126.

2. This is the most perilous part of our undertaking. It is well known that Sextus Empiricus does not set forth an ontology and that he in fact limits himself to criticizing the various ontologies of the dogmatists. It is even thought that skepticism is incompatible with ontology or metaphysics. I do not concur. I believe that skepticism implies an ontology—albeit one of a peculiar sort—and I believe, moreover, that the ontology to be set out in what follows is rigorously consonant with pyrrhonism.

3. On the usual attitude of the monolingual person, Y. R. Chao makes the following amusing but thoroughly true remarks:

> Monolingual persons take language so much for granted that they often forget its arbitrary nature and cannot distinguish words from things. Thus, primitive peoples often believed that putting a curse on somebody's name could actually harm his person. Persons unused to foreign languages tend to find something perverse in the way foreigners talk. Even Oliver Goldsmith could not get over the perversity of the French, who would

call a cabbage *shoe* instead of calling a cabbage *cabbage*. The story is told of an English woman who always wondered why the French call water *de l'eau*, the Italians call it *del'acqua*, and the Germans call it *das Wasser*. "Only we English people," she said, "call it properly 'water'. We not only *call* it 'water', but it *is* water!" This spirit of "it *is* water" shows how closely words and things are identified by the speakers, even though the relation is actually arbitrary. (*Language and Symbolic Systems*, [Cambridge, 1974], pp. 1-2).

4. Curiously enough, Whorf, the most famous advocate of linguistic relativity, was originally motivated by such an ideal. In an early text he speaks about working out a new, universal science of language and of "restoring a possible original common language of the human race or in perfecting an ideal natural tongue constructed of the original psychological significance of sounds, perhaps a future common speech into which all our varied languages may be assimilated, or, putting it differently, to whose terms they may all be reduced. This may seem at the present time very visionary, but it would be no more remarkable than what science has already done in other fields when it has got hold of sound principles to point the way, and I believe my work is tending to unfold such principles" (*Language, Thought and Reality* [Cambridge, Mass., 1972], p. 12).

5. The world *theoretical* should be emphasized, for one may always cease to dogmatize by simply ceasing to theorize. There are many "practical skeptics," but their's is not a philosophical position, and it does not therefore constitute a serious threat to dogmatic theory.

6. Aristotle, *De Sophisticis Elenchis,* in R. McKeon, ed., *The Basic Works of Aristotle* (New York, 1941), 173a7.

7. A. de Tocqueville, *Democracy in America* (New York, n.d.), vol. 2, bk. I, chap. 17.

8. Hegel, *Lectures on the History of Philosophy* (London, 1895), 2:367.

9. W. James, *The Principles of Psychology* (New York, 1950), 1:288.

10. W. James, "Pragmatism and Humanism," in *Pragmatism and Other Essays* (New York, 1963), p. 113.

11. E. Gendlin, *Experiencing and the Creation of Meaning* (Glencoe, Ill., 1962), p. 16.

12. An "empirical" scientist such as R. Calder belongs to the same dogmatic family as the idealist, philosophical scientist Hegel when he says: "Given the right question, properly posed, Nature will reveal the right answer in the course of time" (*Man and the Cosmos: The Nature of Science Today* [New York, 1969], p. 10). In contrast, Nietzsche wrote: "One should have more respect for the bashfulness with which nature has hidden behind riddles and uncertainties" (Preface to the 2d ed. of *The Gay Science* [New York, 1974], p. 38).

13. Merleau-Ponty, *The Visible and the Invisible* (Evanston, Ill., 1968), p. 169; see also my study, *The Phenomenology of Merleau-Ponty* (Athens, Ohio, 1981), pp. 215-16.

14. Stevens, "Adagia," *Opus Posthumous* (New York, 1957), p. 179.

15. Steiner, *After Babel* (New York, 1975), pp. 49-53.

16. Ibid., p. 83.

17. Ibid., pp. 234-35, 472-73.

18. For an attempt to throw light on the way logical and philosophical thinking emerged, historically, out of poetry in ancient Greece see B. Snell, *The Discovery of the Mind* (New York, 1960), chap. 9. Snell defends the thesis that "even 'abstract' thought never detached itself from the metaphors, but continued to depend on the crutches of analogy" (p. 199).

19. Nietzsche, *The Will to Power* (New York, 1968), sec. 522.

20. Sextus Empiricus, *Pyrrhoniarum hypotyposeon,* III, 280. Herein is to be found, Sextus goes on to say, the reason "why the Sceptic sometimes purposely propounds arguments which are lacking in power of persuasion":

> Just as the physicians who cure bodily ailments have remedies which differ in strength, and apply the severe ones to those whose ailments are severe and the milder to those mildly affected,—so too the Sceptic propounds arguments which differ in strength, and

employs those which are weighty and capable by their stringency of disposing of the Dogmatists' ailment, self-conceit, in cases where the mischief is due to a severe attack of rashness, while he employs the milder arguments in the case of those whose ailment of conceit is superficial and easy to cure, and whom it is possible to restore to health by milder methods of persuasion. Hence the adherent of Sceptic principles does not scruple to propound at one time arguments that are weighty in their persuasiveness, and at another time such as appear less impressive,—and he does so on purpose, as the latter are frequently sufficient to enable him to effect his object.

21. C. Perelman and L. Obrechts-Tyteca, *The New Rhetoric* (Notre Dame, Ind., 1969), sec. 84, p. 384.

22. *Mutatis mutandis,* what has been said here about metaphor being the most fitting means of expressing Reality applies also to other "intangibles" such as the self and God.

23. See E. E. Evans-Pritchard, *Nuer Religion* (New York, 1974), chap. 5.

24. Ibid., pp. 315-16, 320-21 (emphasis added).

25. S. Spender, "The Making of a Poem," in B. Ghiselin, ed., *The Creative Process* (New York, n.d.), pp. 116-17.

26. Ibid., p. 120.

27. B. Ghiselin, "The Birth of a Poem," in Ghiselin, *Creative Process,* p. 134.

28. This double meaning of the term *respect* is clearly reflected in the praxis of the Nuer. For them, respect *(thek)* "always contains the idea of avoidance" (Evans-Pritchard, *Nuer Religion,* pp. 179ff). To respect something is to accord it its due value or recognition by restraining oneself in one's dealings with it. *Respect is inseparable from deference.* This is perhaps enough to indicate that *the scientist can be said to have respect for the human person only if, at some point or other, he refuses to "understand" him scientifically.* Science, which is the attempt to know and control all things, obviously can have respect for nothing.

29. M. Heidegger, *On Time and Being,* pp. 3, 6.

30. Stevens, "Adagia," p. 178. Similarly, we can say, the Reality of the person does not consist in what he is but in his being always more than whatever we take him to be or categorize him as.

CONCLUSION: THE GOOD LIFE

It is our conviction that what is good for living takes precedence over and in fact determines what is true for thinking. Usually truth is said to be a property of statements about experience and reality. The making of statements presupposes the existence of a linguistic or conceptual frame of reference and is, to a greater or lesser degree, a matter of theorizing. The purpose of theory is to confer meaning on existence or experience and in this way to enable one to pursue a particular course of action in the world. Theory makes possible a way of life. It is therefore with respect to the mode of existence that a theory serves to generate and encourage that it is to be assessed. As Peirce says, "Thus we come down to what is tangible and conceivably practical, as the root of every real distinction of thought, no matter how subtle it may be; and there is no distinction of meaning so fine as to consist in anything but a possible difference of practice."[1]

A theory can never be conclusively proven; that is, it can never be demonstrated that one theory corresponds to "the real world" whereas another does not. Therefore it is impossible to demonstrate that rationalism is false, but this does not mean that the attempt to "refute" it is useless. On the contrary, it is essential that it be opposed, and it can be effectively opposed only on the level of theory.

The function of theory in general is twofold: to justify or make plausible, by means of persuasive argument or exposition, a certain way of conceiving of things, of existence and reality, and to discredit opposing theories. Thus although no theory can ever be "disproven," it is always possible to disqualify or discredit a theory. The way in which this can be done is itself twofold: one may show that the theory qua theory is unsatisfactory, that is, that the theoretical means used to advocate it are faulty; or one may discredit a theory by revealing its practical implications and showing that these are unacceptable because they conflict with or are hostile to what is or ought to be the case.[2]

Our critique of rationalism has operated in this twofold way. On the one hand I have attempted to show that the various rationalist theories as to what constitutes language, knowledge, and reality raise difficulties that these theories cannot overcome. Basically we have done nothing more than

314

employ in our own fashion the age-old dialectical tactics of skepticism, the most important of which are the so-called Five Tropes of Agrippa, a Pyrrhonian forerunner of Sextus Empiricus. (1) I have shown that science cannot demonstrate that, on the whole, it is any truer than magic. Both science and magic are, qua systems of belief, equally convincing—both are equally "verifiable" and neither is more "falsifiable" than the other—but both cannot be true, for they are incompatible. This is a version of the argument or trope based on discrepancy or conflict between opinions (*ho apo tes diaphonias*). (2) I have shown that rationalism (and science) rests on certain presuppositions that it cannot itself justify; this is a version of the argument based upon regression ad infinitum (*ho eis apeiron ekballon*). (3) I have shown that magic and science are, qua systems, equally rational or "logical"; this is a version of the argument based on relativity (*ho apo tou pros ti tropos*). (4) I have shown that to the degree that rationalism attempts to justify itself as a system, it proceeds in a circle, using one ungrounded assumption to bolster another, equally ungrounded assumption; this is a version of the argument based on circular reasoning (*ho diallelos tropos*). (5) I have shown that if a vicious circle is to be avoided, it can be only by making an initial assumption that the system itself cannot justify; this is a version of the argument based on *petitio principii* or begging the question (*ho hypothetikos*). These are the main theoretical devices that I have used to discredit rationalist theory.

On the other hand, I have pointed out the practical implications of rationalism, which are unacceptable because they are in conflict with what ought to be the case. Technologism and cultural imperialism are the "logical" consequences of rationalism or the dogmatic belief in the possibility of a science of reality. Thus one of the functions of the critique of dogmatism is to show how the rationalist attempt to achieve a science of reality presupposes an entire constellation of concepts, whether or not any particular rationalist thinker is expressly aware of the fact. The apologist for science may, as an individual, be open-minded and tolerant, but this does not alter the fact that the ideal of science is opposed to that of freedom.

Science cannot serve as the basis for a genuinely free society, for, far from being "democratic" as some of its advocates wish to maintain,[3] science, by its very nature, makes for a dominating elite in exactly the same way as technology tends toward technocracy, or the dictatorship of those who possess knowledge of specialized techniques. Is it not, after all, only "logical" that those who know the "laws" of, say, economics should be allowed to direct the economy of the nation without interference from those who do not? Science and technology are in fact divisive for, of their essence, they create a gap between those who are in the know and those who, lacking this specialized knowledge, have only their own human instincts to rely on. Pierre Aubenque is correct when he says, "Science also separates man from man; it substitutes the transcendence of 'those who know' for the groping brotherhood of those who live in 'opinion.' "[4]

If one believes that science—understood in the strict sense as the true knowledge of what reality really is—is possible, one must also believe that reality itself is such as to be "knowable." This means that one must hold, if only in an unreflective way, that reality is absolute, that it is "what it is," fully determinate in itself. If it is to be the object of a systematic science— and there is no science that is not systematic—it must itself be "systematic." The world must be a cosmos, a well-structured totality. Optimism in the powers of reason to achieve a science of reality can justify itself only through the belief that the world is knowable, and it can be knowable only if it is a perfectly articulated whole. If the world is a cosmos, a *universus* (a unified whole), the universalist, totalizing pretensions of reason—the "presumption on the part of reason," as Merleau-Ponty would say—is fully vindicated, for in this case reason has only to discover and conform itself to the reason in things in order to achieve a science that mirrors the totality. Language has only to articulate the natural articulations of reality.

When, however, belief in the totality is translated into concrete practice in the social and cultural realms, it inevitably tends toward totalitarianism, the outcome of which is institutionalized terrorism.[5] To believe that there are absolutes and that man can, at least in principle, attain to a knowledge of them is, besides being extremely presumptuous, highly dangerous. This is why Protagoras, Gorgias, Isocrates, and others within the anti-rationalist, humanist tradition—the counter-tradition—consistently opposed the claims of the rationalists. As one modern-day humanist writes, alluding to Erasmus who at the outset of the modern period sought to expose the folly of the rationalists:

> There is one respect in which we too must abide by the principle of *humanitas,* even though we may not have the talent which makes men humanists. That is the esteem in which we must hold the dignity of man: a modicum of *humanitas* for which no particular talent is needed. The eternal absolutes which rule over us, especially justice and truth, unhappily often make us forget that the absolute which accedes to our understanding is not entirely absolute after all. On occasion they will even allow us to act as if we were the absolute embodied, to the great sorrow of our fellow-men. At that point, morality turns into dynamite, and the explosion increases in violence as more and more men come to believe that it is their duty to follow the absolute. Finally, when it is agreed that certain institutions have come to represent that absolute, the catastrophe becomes inevitable. Then is the time to remind oneself that each and every human being has his own share of dignity and of freedom. All we require is a little courtesy, a bit of tolerance and, *o sancte Erasme,* just a dash of your irony.[6]

The goal of anti-rationalist, nonscientific, skeptical, humanistic thought is liberation. It is liberating because it teaches not specialized knowledge or techniques but the art of questioning all things, even those things that those in the know hold to be self-evident and immune to doubt. It recognizes that true wisdom is not a matter of specialized knowledge and that accordingly all people have, in principle, equal access to the source of wisdom and are, in principle, equally qualified to raise questions concerning matters of vital concern to them. By instilling in people a critical attitude, it allows for that perpetual vigilance without which freedom is impossible, and it gives to people the means of safeguarding the personal autonomy and dignity which is theirs by virtue of their being reflective beings. It seeks, in what may unfortunately prove to be a vain attempt, to combat that tyranny which stems from the dominance of science and technology: the tyranny of universal and uniform "truth." A scientifically ordered and technologically controlled society is one in which pluralism of opinion—of "truth"—is suppressed and in which all those who do not endorse the opinions of those in the know are ostracized by denying them any intellectual respectability. When not themselves controlled, science and technology make possible and in fact encourage political repression. The "free exercise of a scientific analysis" is, quite simply—as B. F. Skinner, the advocate of a scientific utopia ("Walden Two"), himself implicitly recognizes—incompatible with a recognition of human freedom.[7]

Historically the ideal of freedom may well become ever more of a meaningless notion in that it ceases to correspond to anything in concrete praxis, but this does not alter the fact that if people are to be genuinely freed from the limiting constraints of any particular universe of discourse or belief system, such as science or technology, the only way is by their becoming aware of the limits of all belief systems. By showing that all so-called knowledge (science) is in fact belief and by exposing in this way the illusions of understanding, the skeptical critique seeks to reveal to people that infinite openness that transcends all finite determinations. When one realizes that Reality is always more than what it is merely believed to be or is known as, one is not likely to be duped by any partial belief masquerading as knowledge of the totality. To attempt to achieve mastery and control over the great unknown and the basic contingencies of life through science and technology—to attempt to realize the scientific ideal of becoming, as Descartes put it, "maîtres et possesseurs de la nature"—is the height of human folly, but realizing the folly of the attempt to know and control all things will bring it under control. When the scientific desire to know all things and the technological, promethean attempt to control all things—"the free exercise of scientific analysis"—is brought under control through a knowledge of the ultimate impossibility of definitive knowing, one is liberated from the conceptual imperialism of science and the practical tyranny of technology.

And in being so liberated, one is also freed for science and technology. Then it becomes possible to engage in that creative game which is science

and to use technology to make everyday living more efficient and comfort-
able while not at the same time letting oneself be enslaved by them. It must
be realized, though, that for our society as a whole this liberation will not be
easily achieved, if it is achieved at all. It requires nothing less than an
overcoming of more than two thousand years of Western thought—of the
entire rationalist tradition and, in particular, the myth of the supremacy of
objective truth.

Neither science nor technology can be "humanized,"[8] for science is not
"pure knowledge," which of itself would be "value free," but represents a
one-sided idea of what counts as valid understanding, and technology is not
simply a collection of tools and artifacts to be used however one pleases but
embodies a particular mentality for which value is nothing more than efficiency and cannot cease to be such without ceasing to be technology. To the
degree that a person is irreducible to a machine, the notion of a humanistic
science and technology is a contradiction in terms. Thus, if our culture is to
preserve human and social freedom as a meaningful ideal, it can do so only
by humanizing the scientists and technologists, not their disciplines.

It is thus apparent that while the skeptical critique of rationalist or dogmatic theory is itself a theoretical undertaking, it is theory with a practical
purpose. In fact, because freedom is not a theoretical but a practical concept, it cannot be theoretically proven; it can only be concretely exercised
and practically defended. But an important element in this practical defense
consists in theoretically discrediting those theories inimical to the practice of
freedom. Thus when this practical defense has recourse to theory, the ultimate rationale or justification for this theory is not theoretical but practical.

As in the case of Isocrates' conception of a humanistic education, which
he defended in opposition to Plato's ideal of a scientific education, the "criterion" that guides nondogmatic theorizing is of a moral and political nature; it is a certain conception of what constitutes the good life, the life most
appropriate for people. It is indeed skepticism that calls for and justifies a
liberal education, a mode of education whose goal is to "enable us to
govern wisely both our own households and the commonwealth"—in a
word, wisdom—for the supreme importance of this kind of education can
be appreciated only when one realizes that "it is not in the nature of man to
attain a *science* by the possession of which we can know precisely what we
should do or what we should say."[9]

And it is skepticism that is the staunchest ally of humanism. The critique
of dogmatism seeks to instill in one respect for the infinite openness of
being and recognition of the ontological mystery and thus, in this way, to
furnish a theoretical basis for the respect due a person. This respect stems
from a recognition of the mystery of the person, that is, from a recognition
that what a human being is is ultimately unknowable by science and uncontrollable by technology. This recognition is presupposed by any concept of

human dignity according to which the person is held to be an end in himself. And such a recognition is the only proper basis for a politics that would seek to safeguard the freedom and dignity of the citizen.

To be sure, it cannot be proven that freedom is a supreme good and as Dostoevski's story of the "The Grand Inquisitor" implies, it may well be the case that people prefer the comfort of their illusions to the uncertainty into which they are plunged when they are freed from them (the idea of freedom may not be, as Skinner would say, a very effective "reinforcer"). Be that as it may, my guiding purpose in this book was not to argue *for* certain values in the sense of showing why it is that people should be free or what it is that guarantees their dignity; my overriding purpose was, rather, to argue against those positions and outlooks that I believe are inimical to these values. The theories of understanding and Reality set forth here were dictated by this tactical consideration; their justification lies in the fact that they provide a viable alternative to rationalist theories. And an alternative to the latter is necessary if the values of freedom and dignity are to be safeguarded.

Assuming that, in the moral realm, the "good" means something more and quite other than what is merely technologically efficient or expedient, moral beliefs can no more be proven than can religious beliefs. One can no more demonstrate the existence of an autonomous "I" than one can demonstrate the existence of the personal God of the Christian faith, the God, as Pascal would have said, not of the philosophers but of Abraham, Isaac, and Jacob. However, this does not mean that such (moral or religious) beliefs cannot be argued for and that consequently they are irrational. The ultimate purpose of the theory of human understanding set out and argued for in this book was to provide the theoretical context wherein it could make good rational sense to speak of the values of freedom and dignity, and I would hope that readers will have become convinced that this anti-rationalist theory is indeed rational, that it is theoretically consistent and plausible. Similarly I hope they will have come to see that rationalist theories of understanding and reality—wherein, ultimately, as in the case of scientific-technological thinking, it really does not make much sense to speak of the freedom and dignity of the person—are rationally suspect; even as theories, they are not as plausible as the alternative theory I have sought to defend. Thus, in criticizing rationalist theory, I have sought indirectly to defend my own moral convictions. It would be the task of another work to take matters further and to argue for these convictions in a more directly positive way.

If values are to be based on something more than arbitrary, subjective whim and if a ruinous decisionism is to be avoided in this area, it would seem that the following argumentative tactic (or something like it) is called for. One would have to show that if one holds to a rationalist conception of understanding, values such as freedom and dignity cannot be rationally defended; there can be no reason for believing in them, apart from the fact that one simply decides to do so, which is to say that there can be no good reason for doing so. One would then have to argue for an alternative conception of understanding. Having done so, one would then have to take the further step of showing that when understanding is conceived of in this non-rationalist way, a number of values, all having to do with the freedom and dignity of the person, can be rationally argued for—specifically by showing that they are necessarily implied by or are the actual conditions of possibility of nondogmatic understanding.

As far as the present work is concerned, its goal was twofold. It attempted to show that cultural imperialism (both within our own culture and between our culture and others) is a necessary consequence of an unqualified allegiance to the scientific-technological enterprise, and it attempted to show that the presuppositions of science and technology are those of philosophical rationalism; cultural totalitarianism is a result of the philosophical belief in the totality. Along with this, and in accordance with my belief that one theory can be effectively opposed only by means of another theory, it argued for an alternative conception of rationality or intelligibility—of, in other words, human understanding. Thus, to paraphrase Kant, this dialectical-skeptical attack on rationalism could be viewed as a prolegomenon to any future value theory.

Since the matter of religious belief has been brought up, it might not be inappropriate to conclude this inquiry into human understanding, its nature and its limits, with an observation on the relation between dogmatic belief, the skeptical critique thereof, and religious faith.

In attempting to show the relativity of all dogmatic beliefs, does not skepticism undermine religious belief as well? The answer is both yes and no. To the degree that "superstition" consists in the dogmatic allegiance to one's belief objects and is a failure to recognize that they are creative constructs relative to one's time and culture—and from this point of view science can be (and usually is) as superstitious as magic—it must be admitted that much of what passes for religion is indeed no more than superstition. Skepticism, which is antithetical to all dogmatic belief, is thus antithetical to all kinds of fundamentalist religions where myths are propounded and believed in literally and where these beliefs are used to repress those who do not share in them.

But a distinction must be made between belief and faith. True religious faith has nothing to do with human belief. Unlike belief, faith is humble and is the recognition of what one does not know. It is openness to that surpassing dimension of Reality called the "divine" or the "holy." The true Christian, for instance, has faith in God to the precise extent that he knows that whatever God be—and, strictly speaking, he does not even claim to know that God *is*—He is infinitely more than what human understanding can ever conceive Him to be. A genuine skepticism of the Pyrrhonian sort is not incompatible with religious faith, and, indeed, as one writer observes:

> Religious faith is so little at variance with skepticism that both are rather united by their common opposition to the presumptions of settled knowledge. . . . The skeptic and the believer have a common cause against the easy reading of history and its meaning. Their wisdom, like all wisdom, consists not the least in disillusion and resignation, in freedom from illusions and presumptions.[10]

Skepticism is in fact the greatest ally of religious faith, for if the latter is to be anything more than mere, secular ideology, it must, in a constant battle against the illusions of understanding, divest itself of all finite world views and claims to positive knowledge. As one Christian theologian points out:

> Faith needs to be emancipated from its association with every world view expressed in objective terms, whether it be a mythical or a scientific one. . . . The invisibility of God excludes every myth which tries to make him and his acts visible. . . . God withdraws himself from the objective view; he can only be believed upon in defiance of all outward appearance.[11]

In short, as Paul Ricoeur has observed, "An idol must die so that a symbol of being may begin to speak."[12]

Of course, a genuine religion is based on more than faith alone—on hope and love also. But in its insistence on the mystery of the human person, a mystery that is the source of his dignity, skepticism allows for a kind of love that is more than the expression of one's own self-interest, however enlightened it may be, and in exposing the limits of science and technology, it justifies a kind of hope that does not limit itself to what merely can be reasonably known and expected, that is free from dogmatic illusions and that is not a form of human, all-too-human wishful thinking. The skeptic, purely as such, knows nothing of the divine mysteries. He does not affirm them, it is true, but then neither does he deny them. His silence on these matters is not totally unlike that of the true believer, of, for instance, that of Saint Dionysius, traditionally one of the most respected of Christian theologians, who says, "The hidden Mysteries which lie beyond our view we have honored by silence."[13] When all is said and done, the skeptic's suspension of judgment and his way of answering, "Maybe,"[14] are not incompatible with the believer's conviction that with God all things are possible.

NOTES

1. C. Peirce, *Collected Papers* (Cambridge, Mass., 1931-1958), 5:400.

2. It should not be necessary to add that the expression "what is the case" is not to be taken in a rationalist sense as meaning what is "objectively" true, the way things "really are," and so forth. Rationalism indeed holds that theories are to be assessed according to their "correspon-

dence" to "objective fact." When, however, we speak of "what is the case," we are speaking from a transcendental-pragmatic point of view. We are not appealing to "objective" facts, existing apart from our experience of them, but are simply seeking to describe or discern the way things actually appear to be—the way they are—once we have suspended all beliefs about what things are "in themselves." If this methodological point is kept in mind, it will be seen that there is no contradiction involved in our way of speaking.

3. For instance, M. Polanyi in his *Science, Faith and Society* (Chicago, 1964).

4. Aubenque, *Le problème de l'être chez Aristote* (Paris, 1962), p. 263 (my translation).

5. One writer very pertinently notes:

> La réduction du vécu à la totalité par le processus d'abstraction aboutit à un véritable "totalitarisme" idéologique et en fin de compte, comme le montre Sartre, à un "totalitarisme" pratique qui peut même aller jusqu'au terrorisme avec le stalinisme.
>
> La totalité est toujours posée *a priori* et elle aboutit à éliminer la *particularité*. Toutes les particularités d'une période historique, d'une oeuvre, d'un événement sont dissoutes dans la totalité qui, comme chez Hegel, pré-existe à l'événement et lui donne sa finalité de l'extérieur. . . . Le fétichisme des concepts que Marx dénonçait chez Hegel est devenu une des caracteristiques du marxisme et trouve son aboutissement dans le fétichisme idéologique de la science que les marxistes partagent avec les positivistes de toutes sortes" (S. Latouche, "Totalité, totalisation et totalitarisme," *Dialogue* 13, no. 1 [March 1974]: 78).

A similar point was formerly made by Georges Gusdorf:

> L'impérialisme du système, qui se fait fort de donner raison de tout, se transforme facilement en un terrorisme, qui fait de la force pure et simple l'ultime raison de la Raison, ainsi que le montrait Georges Sorel à propos des idéologies rationalistes et optimistes de la Révolution française. Le rationalisme marxiste, là où il est parvenu au pouvoir, confirme parfaitement les vues de Sorel sur ce point" (*Mythe et métaphysique* [Paris, 1963], pp. 298-99).

In the latter half of his book Gusdorf makes many pertinent observations on the imperialism of scientific reason.

6. B. Snell, *The Discovery of the Mind* (New York, 1960), pp. 262-63.

7. Skinner says of the philosophy and literature of democracy, the doctrine of the rights of man, and concerted action of individuals against governmental tyranny: "The ubiquity and ease of expression of this attitude spells trouble for any science which may give birth to a powerful technology of behavior." The attitudes of people "dominated by the humanistic philosophy of the past two centuries" "have already interfered with the free exercise of a scientific analysis, and their influence threatens to assume more serious proportions" ("Some Issues Concerning the Control of Human Behavior," in Douglas, ed., *The Technological Threat* [Englewood Cliffs, N.J., 1971], pp. 123-24). One can only hope that Skinner is right in making this last remark and that their influence will indeed "assume more serious proportions." When Skinner speaks of "the free exercise of a scientific analysis," he means that science should be free from all external constraints, in particular from having to abide by human values (which, as he perceives, are extrascientific in origin and nature). In his reply to Skinner's article, Carl Rogers rightly points out that value decisions are no matter for science to handle and that if this is not clearly recognized "1984" will be upon us sooner than expected.

8. See my article, "Technics, Metaphysics, Politics," *Journal of Social Philosophy* 3, no. 1 (February 1972). In his article, "A Humanistic Technology" in C. Dechert, ed, *The Social Impact of Cybernetics* (Notre Dame, Ind., 1966), H. G. Rickover wrongly assumes that technology is a mere means and therefore does not realize the enormous difficulty in attempting to control it, but he does see very well the gravity of the problem—"how to limit power so men may be free"; "how to reconcile liberty and civilization"—and he recognizes also that a reaf-

firmation and extension of traditional humanistic education is indispensable. "Paradoxically, liberal education, which at one time we tended to regard as 'aristocratic,' is the very kind of education we now need most to preserve our 'democratic' way of life."

9. Isocrates, *Antidosis,* 285, 271.

10. K. Löwith, *Meaning in History* (Chicago, 1949), p. vi. Much the same point was made by the great skeptic, Pierre Bayle, in the article on Pyrrho in his *Dictionnaire historique et critique* (1697). Similarly, Pierre Charron, a disciple of Montaigne and a Christian skeptic of the sixteenth century wrote, "Cet aduis mien, qu'il leur plaist appeler Pyrrhonisme, est chose qui fait plus de seruice à la pieté et operation diuine, que tout autre qui soit, bien loin de la heurter: seruice, dis-je, tant pour sa generation et propagation, que pour sa conseruation" (*De la sagesse* [Paris, 1824], 2:310).

11. R. Bultmann, *Kerygma and Myth* (New York, 1961), p. 210.

12. P. Ricoeur, "Religion, Atheism, and Faith," in *The Conflict of Interpretations* (Evanston, Ill., 1974), p. 467.

13. Dionysius the Areopagite, *De divina hierarchia,* last line.

14. Sextus Empiricus, *Pyrrhoniarum hypotyposeon,* I, 194-96.

APPENDIX I:
ON THEORETICAL EXPLANATION

Explanation is of two kinds: commonsensical and theoretical. In turn, theoretical explanation is of two basic sorts (that is, "theory" can be taken in two general senses), the latter of which presupposes the former.

1. The interpretation of experience not in a commonsensical, unreflective way but rather in the light of interpretive principles that have been explicitly formulated and are consciously (though perhaps routinely) applied is an instance of what might be called *descriptive-nomological theory*.

Description is the characterization of a phenomenon in terms of certain general terms or concepts, and thus, since it presupposes or is the actual implementation of an interpretive, classificatory schema, there is no such thing as a "pure" description. All description is "theory-laden."[1] Also, description is not opposed to explanation (although many writers oppose these terms; S. Toulmin in *The Philosophy of Science,* is one) but is, rather, one kind of explanation, or one kind of making intelligible. One explains a phenomenon (descriptively) by showing that it is an instance of some general class or category of being, that is, by fitting it into a conceptual pigeon hole.

Descriptive ordering or explaining gives rise to what in science are called "empirical laws" as well as to "universal laws" (such as the law of universal gravitation). One explains a phenomenon by showing that it is an instance (logical consequence) of some law (descriptive-nomological theory) about nature. This is called axiomatic theory or deductive-nomological (D-N) explanation; one deductively subsumes some event or phenomenon under a general law (*nomos*). It is thought by many (including Braithwaite and Hempel) to be the strongest kind of explanation. Whether or not this is so, this kind of explanation is not by any means peculiar to science (in the modern sense) but can be found in varying degrees of explicitness in any kind of theoretical, explanatory belief system, such as magic or theology, although in these cases it does not appear in mathematical, quantitative guise. As W. James summarizes the matter, "Classification of things into extensive 'kinds' is thus the first step, and classification of their relations and conduct into extensive 'laws' is the last step, in their philosophic unification."[2]

A distinction is sometimes made between "laws" (what we have called empirical laws) and "theories" (what we have called universal laws); Kepler's laws of planetary motion and Newton's theory of gravitation are two examples. The big difference is that "laws" are supposed to be able to be confirmed by experience in a way that "theories" are not. But in fact the boundary line between the two is extremely fluid, and a change in "theory" can very well necessitate a change in a "law," without there being any "observational" or experimental motive for doing so (Kepler's "laws" were modified as a result of Newtonian "theory"). In a theoretical context, such as in science, the distinction among fact, law, and theory is not absolute but corresponds to the degree of interpretation involved. A fact is explained by being related to an empirical law and, in this way, to other facts, and an empirical law is explained by being related to a theory and, in this way, to other laws. Explanation is the search for unity (paradoxically, a theory points to an ever greater unity and simplicity in nature to the degree that, qua theory, it is ever more developed, complex, and sophisticated, that is, to the degree that it interrelates an ever larger number of facts, laws, and other theories). The language of facts changes more slowly than that of laws and that of law more slowly than that of theories, but development at the level of theory eventually alters the language of laws and facts in the way that theory in general retroactively modifies common sense.

2. Phenomena explained in sense 1 may be further explained by means of *causal theories*. Causal theoretical explanation (as distinct from causal commonsensical explanation) involves the use of theoretical, nonobservable entities that are postulated for just this purpose: in order to account for the "why" of the phenomenon. This kind of theory explains something by showing (or purporting to show) that it is the effect of something else that exists on a more basic level of reality. Therefore, to the extent that in theoretical explanation one posits unobservable entities to explain observable phenomena (as in the kinetic theory of gases one postulates microscopic molecules to account for the macroscopic behavior of gases), one is involved in causal explanation. This form of theory is well described by one English writer who says that in addition to classificatory explanation (or theory) there is

the business of devising scientific theories in the narrow sense, where the existence of altogether new and unfamiliar kinds of entity is supposed in order to explain the properties and behavior of what can be straightforwardly observed. The theorist in this sense adds to our knowledge of the world, not by discerning hitherto hidden patterns in the relationships and activities of known things, but by the discovery of altogether new kinds of things which constitute the fine structure of the familiar and straightforwardly observable. Thus molecules, atoms and electrons are invoked to explain the thermal, chemical and electrical properties of ordinarily accessible material objects, micro-organisms to explain the characteristic properties of the material of which living bodies are composed.[3]

It could be added that explanation or theory in sense 2 has a retroeffect on explanation in sense 1 (just as theory in general has a retroeffect on common sense). A new way of classifying material substances—explanation in sense 1—is made possible by atomic theory—in terms of these substances' nonobservable, underlying atomic structure.

The preceding can be schematized as follows:

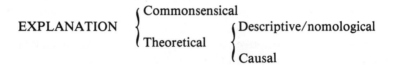

Theoretical explanation in sense 1 is what makes possible essences and natural order (law), explanation in sense 2 basic causal entities. These essences and laws (*rationes*) and entities (*causae*) are a product of creative understanding and are real only to the extent that they enable people to feel intellectually secure in their theoretical beliefs. Ernst Mach was quite correct when he said that the atomic theory was but a mathematical model for dealing with observable phenomena and that atoms were not real in the sense that the latter are. He was wrong, however, in thinking that scientific explanation should eschew theoretical entities, for the postulation of such entities is one of the prime means for the development of ever more comprehensive theories. Perhaps, therefore, science can exist only to the degree that scientists deceive themselves as to the true status of scientific entities. But again, perhaps an awareness of the purely as-if character of such entities would not interfere with their postulation and utilization and thus with the progress of science. To be sure, science, as it is generally conceived to be, is not, like a game, a matter of creative fantasy but of obsessional hallucination; it is more like the deadly games played by schizophrenics.

NOTES

1. Pierre Duhem, *The Aim and Structure of Physical Theory* (Princeton, N.J., 1954), pt. II, chap. 5, sec. 1.

2. William James, "The Sentiment of Rationality," in *The Will to Believe* (New York, 1956), p. 67.

3. A Quinton, *The Nature of Things* (London, 1973), p. 284.

APPENDIX II:
MAGIC, SCIENCE, AND RELIGION

The discussion of magic in chapter 3 essentially was a comparison of magic with science from an epistemological point of view (viewing the two as systems of belief) and was addressed to the widely held assumption that magic is a form of primitive science. This way of approaching magic served to bring out some important similarities that it shares with science (and vice-versa), but it also had the unavoidable effect of obscuring some of the crucial differences between these two types of understanding, which need to be emphasized.

To a great extent magic is indeed a form of primitive science, for, like science, magic attempts to furnish a coherent and total explanation of observed phenomena. Also, like science and technology, this "knowledge" is used to control the course of events. But magic also possesses a dimension totally absent from science and technology: a sacramental function. Magic is not only a means for explaining and controlling phenomena but also serves to reconcile man to what he cannot know and cannot control, ultimately to the fact of his mortality. "Witchcraft, oracles and magic," Evans-Pritchard observes, "attain their height of significance, as procedures and ideologies, at death."[1] This is certainly *not* the case with science and technology. The difference is worth reflecting upon.

Magic is like science, but it is also like religion, and science is not like religion (that some scientists, having lost their religious faith, reinvest all their religious enthusiasm in science does not alter the fact that science has nothing to do with religion). What exactly are the relations among magic, science, and religion?

For Frazer the differences were clear-cut. Magic is like science in that it holds that nature operates in accordance with fixed, immutable, and determinable laws; it is a human attempt to control events through a "knowledge" of these laws. When, higher up on the evolutionary ladder, humans realize that magic is ineffective, they turn to religion, which posits the existence of invisible beings who control nature according to their arbitrary whims. Since humans cannot hope to control events through their own powers, they must propitiate these beings and trust to their favors. "Thus in the acuter minds magic is gradually superseded by religion, which explains the succession of natural phenomena as regulated by the will, the passion, or the caprice of spiritual beings like man in kind, though vastly superior to him in power. But as time goes on this explanation in its turn proves to be unsatisfactory."[2] Humans now discover that magic was right after all in postulating natural laws; however, unlike magic, science does not merely project fanciful associations onto nature but discerns its actual workings, through "patient and exact observation." "Here at last, after groping about in the dark for countless ages, man has hit upon a clue to the labyrinth, a golden key that opens many locks in the treasury of nature."

Frazer's version of the matter (still widely held, if only in a thoughtless way) can no longer be accepted, and not merely because of its simplistic evolutionism and Victorian belief in "progress," for magic, religion, and science do not fall into the same category and therefore cannot be ranked in a linear or hierarchical order.[3] Magic is not merely an attempt to explain and control things (and thus, from this point of view, primitive science) and is not simply a prelude to religion but is *already, in one of its aspects, a form of religion*. And religion itself, for that matter, though ideally the manner in which people relate to that which transcends their understanding, is more often than not like magic in one of its aspects, an attempt to explain phenomena.[4] Believers often mistakenly consider religious myths to be a kind of scientific or rival scientific account of things (as when Genesis is read as an empirical account of the beginning of the world). But this is not the essential function of religious myth.

One might want to say that religious myth is a form of believed poetry, but it is nonetheless not believed in in the same way that scientific truths are believed in. To be sure, as in scientific explanation, the explicandum is lived experience (observable phenomena), and in order to give meaning to experience myth posits unobservable entities as an explicans (such as gods, or supernatural forces). But these entities are different from scientific entities in that they are not meant to be believed literally; they have a different kind of reality status from the theoretical entities of science. The superficial resemblances between mythological "explanation" and scientific explanation should not be allowed to obscure their fundamental differences.

A causal explanation in science "explains" a present state of affairs by deriving it from a previous state of affairs, and myth appears to do the same. Myth recounts what happened *in illo tempore, ab initio;* the present is given meaning (is "explained") by being linked up with an archetypal past.[5] But it would be wrong to see in myth only a recital of the past and an attempt to explain the present by linking it up with the past, for the "past" in myth is a different kind of past from the one of which science speaks. Its difference from the present is not simply that it is more remote in time, but it is essentially different from the present and exists on another level of being. It is sacred being as opposed to the profane being of the here and now, of everyday existence.⁶ The events and entities talked about in cosmogonical myths are transcendent entities and events. And because these events belong to "sacred history," which is a different kind of history altogether from "profane history," they can be and are indeed reactualized from time to time (in New Year's rites, for instance), whereas history as we moderns conceive it (profanely) is irreversible. When a primitive recounts a creation myth in a ritual context, he is not simply "commemorating" certain events of the bygone past but is actually repeating them and is making himself a contemporary of them (in the same way that the celebration of the Eucharist repeats the sacrifice of the Christ and makes it a contemporary event). As the anthropologists Hubert and Maus pointed out, mythical events take place outside of time or, to put it another way, throughout the whole extent of time; mythical time is not historical time.⁷

Myth expresses the realization that human existence is dependent upon beings or forces that transcend people in the here and now. But it might be objected that science also explains the existence of experienced things by purporting to show how they are dependent upon entities that "transcend" experience—that is, on theoretical, unobservable entities such as atoms. This is true, but an atom differs from a god in that an atom is taken to be something that exists in an empirical or natural sense, whereas a god is not. Nothing in science corresponds to the religious and mythical distinction between the natural (the profane) and the supernatural (the sacred), and this distinction is crucial to a proper understanding of religious myth. Myth expresses one's conviction that human existence can be properly understood only in terms of something not of this world; the meaning of mundane existence must be sought for not within the world but beyond it.

Related to this is another feature of myth. What myth expresses is the realization that man is not master of his own life and that the world, like life, is full of riddles and unfathomable mysteries.⁸ For mythical consciousness the basis of reality is something beyond all calculation and control. This is an essential difference in regard to scientific understanding. Mythical man is lord neither of nature nor of his own being, whereas the express goal of science and technology is to make men, as Descartes put it, "maîtres et possesseurs de la nature." Science seeks to achieve knowledge of and control over nature (in a scientific experiment knowledge is inseparable from control), whereas myth says that man is dependent upon a transcendent realm of being, which he can neither know nor control. The basic function of myth is, therefore, to point to this transcending dimension of existence. For in myth reality is something more than what it ever merely appears to be in everyday life.⁹

In myth man expresses his awareness of this something more in images and metaphors. The supernatural can be expressed only in terms of the natural, the invisible in terms of the visible, the other world in terms of this world. Divine transcendence, for instance, is expressed in terms of spatial distance; God is "above," in "heaven" (the sky). But mythical man is aware of the metaphorical nature of his statements and does not, unlike the scientist, take them literally. It must not be thought that primitive peoples are like children who believe in fairy tales, that they have a "prelogical" mentality (as Lévy-Bruhl would have said) and take their myths literally. That this is not the case is perfectly evident in the case of the Nuer, a neolithic people studied by Evans-Pritchard, of whose observations the following are typical:

> In the Nuer conception of God he is thus creative Spirit. He is also a *ran*, a living person, whose *yiegh*, breath or life, sustains man. . . . However, the anthropomorphic features of the Nuer conception of God are very weak and . . . they do not act towards him as though he were a man. Indeed, such human features as are given barely suffice to satisfy the requirements of thought and speech. If he is to be spoken about, or to, he has to be given some human attributes.[10]

> Within their system of religious thought things are not just what they appear to be but as they are conceived of in relation to God.
> This implies experience on an imaginative level of thought where the mind moves in figures, symbols, metaphors, analogies, and many an elaboration of poetic fancy and language; and another reason why there has been misunderstanding is that the poetic sense of primitive peoples has not been sufficiently allowed for, so that it has not been appreciated that what they say is often to be understood in that sense and not in any ordinary sense. This is certainly the case with the Nuer, as we see in this chapter and in many places elsewhere in this book, for example, in their hymns. In all their poems and songs also they play on words and images to such an extent that no European can translate them without commentary from Nuer, and even Nuer themselves cannot always say what meaning they had for their authors. . . . Lacking plastic and visual arts, the imagination of this sensitive people finds its sole expression in ideas, images, and words.[11]

This "metaphorical" character of myth is to be found in magic also, and it is what distinguishes a magical deed from a technological action. The magical performance is a living metaphor. Herein lies the essential difference between magic and technology and the reason why magic is not simply a less "efficient" way of doing the everyday sort of things technology does. Let us consider an example drawn from Tibetan spirituality, a mixture of shamanism and Buddhism, of magic and religion.[12]

In the secret lore of the Tibetan lamas there are countless stories of how lamaist masters float in the air and walk on water, how they resuscitate corpses (in a mysterious and rather gruesome rite called *rolang*), how they create animate objects by thinking them into existence, and innumerable other marvelous deeds. Of particular interest is the commerce with gods and demons (which are legion in Tibet). For example, a person with a firm belief in these fantastic creatures (and there is hardly a Tibetan who does not have such a belief) presents himself to a master with the intention of taking up a religious life and achieving liberation. The master directs the disciple to shut himself up and meditate on his *Yidam* or tutelary deity with the goal of compelling his *Yidam* to appear. The novice may spend months and even years calling upon the *Yidam*. Finally he informs the master that the *Yidam* has appeared, although only momentarily and in a rather hazy way. The master notes the progress but points out that a definitive result has not yet been achieved and orders his disciple to pursue his efforts. Again after a long time the novice succeeds in making the *Yidam* not only appear but remain in his hut. The master is satisfied but again orders the novice to carry on with his efforts: he must not only be able to see but also to touch the *Yidam* and compel him to bless him and speak to him. This is very difficult and few novices are successful. But those who are can actually feel the weight of the *Yidam's* hands as he blesses them and hear him speak. This is a very dangerous moment, for an *Yidam* that has been made to materialize must not be allowed to escape the confines of the hut, for he would then take revenge on the person who called him into being in the first place. But after the *Yidam* has been sufficiently trained, the novice may allow him to accompany him when he goes out. This is a very difficult feat to accomplish, for it is one thing for the *Yidam's* form to remain firm in the dimly lit hut and another for it to do so in the bright sunlight. Another selection among novices therefore occurs at this stage, for many *Yidams* flatly refuse to accompany their devotees out of doors. But to those disciples who are successful, the master informs them that they have reached the desired goal, for they now possess a permanent protector. Some disciples are indeed fully satisfied and spend the rest of their lives playing with their *Yidams*.

Others, overcome with agony, confess to their *guru* that in spite of all their strenuous and sustained efforts and in spite of their success, they have not been able to overcome all doubt and have not been able to rid themselves of the suspicion that the *Yidam* is really only a hallucination, a creature of their imagination. The master affects to be taken aback and orders the novice to begin his efforts all over again. Very much disillusioned but out of respect for his master, the novice perseveres nonetheless, although the effort proves finally to be hopeless. Again he returns to his master and makes the same confession of doubt. Indeed it is no longer a question of doubt; the novice is convinced that the *Yidam* is only a product of his imagination and does not "really" exist. The master is now able to give his final reply: "That is exactly what it is necessary for you to realize. Gods, demons, the whole universe, are but a mirage which exists in the mind, 'springs from it, and sinks into it.' "[13]

Thus the essential function of lamaist magic is to awaken in one the realization that "the worlds and all phenomena which we perceive are but mirages born from our imagination."[14] This constitutes the ultimate goal, *liberation*—liberation from taking for true reality what is only a product of the imagination. Magic, in this instance, is successful only if, by means of its fictional beliefs, one is enabled to transcend all superstitious belief. As with the metaphor, the truth of magic consists not in what it says or purports to establish but in what, by means of its myths and fictions, it does. Unlike science, magic is successful and gives rise to understanding only if, by its means, one succeeds in overcoming it. Magic places exorbitant demands on one's imagination in order that one may free oneself from entrapment in one's own imaginative creations. This points to an important difference between science and magic, and it can indeed be said that the successful scientist is like the "unsuccessful" magician; like the latter, the former is content to believe in and play with his conjured-up *Yidam* for the rest of his life.

Now, could it not be said that what in the Western religious tradition are called miracles have a similar function? Is not the miracle a living metaphor also? And does one not misunderstand miracles when one takes them "literally"?

In our literal-minded, scientific age even theologians tend to scoff at miracles or are at least so embarrassed by them that they prefer to ignore them. Modern "rational" theologians misunderstand miracles, and the reason is that their understanding of the world is, as is the case generally with educated moderns, that of science. For science, the world—nature—is a closed system, intelligible in terms of itself, wherein everything has a reason and a cause. If the world is indeed such as science conceives it to be, a miracle is nothing if it is not a suspension, indeed, a violation, of the laws of necessity, of natural cause and effect, a tearing asunder of the closed weft of time and space. If, like a modern theologian, one believes that science affords a true and definitive understanding of the natural world, one cannot believe in miracles so conceived, for from a purely scientific point of view, they are a logical absurdity, and because logic is the criterion of truth, they are a physical impossibility. The modern theologian therefore says that they are mere allegories; they are a crude, primitive, and naive way of saying something, not about reality, but about the human soul; their meaning is entirely "ethical," and this ethical significance can be extracted from the shell of mythology, processed, and set out in a straightforward, literal way that will not shock scientific sensibilities. Miracles must be "demythologized."

A miracle, however, is not an "allegory." It is a "metaphor," and real metaphors cannot be translated into straightforward, literal language. A miracle is not a roundabout way of uttering some "spiritual" or "ethical" truth about humanity; it is a direct way of saying something about reality.

To "demythologize" miracles therefore is to render them insignificant. One totally misunderstands miracles if one does not take them in all earnestness, as a way of saying something very important about reality itself, that very self-same reality over which science claims a monopoly. Strictly speaking, a miracle does not contradict science; it affirms rather that a scientific understanding of events is not the only possible understanding of them one can have. What in fact a miracle "says," in its own concrete way, is that there is a wholly other dimension to reality than that understood in either common sense or science, for both of which reality or nature is something explainable. The point of miracles is to jar our normal complacency and to make us see that reality is "not what it is" (this is the function of metaphor).

Both science and common sense provide for reassurance in that they enable us to feel that we understand the world in which we live. They make for a sense of mastery. But a miracle violates this understanding and enables us to understand reality differently: as something that escapes our understanding. A miracle is the eruption of the extraordinary in the heart of the most ordinary of things; it is a manifestation of the supernatural, that is, of a dimension of reality other than or transcending that one corresponding to everyday, "natural" experience. If one takes miracles in conjunction with myth, they can be said to be part of "a complex system of coherent affirmations on the ultimate reality of things, a system which can be taken as constitutive of a metaphysics."[15] The difference between this metaphysics and that implicit in science is that while for science and technology reality is what it is (principle of identity), for myth reality is not what it is. It is overdetermined and can therefore be expressed only metaphorically, through symbols and actions that are misunderstood when they are taken "literally."

No more, therefore, than a genuine metaphor can be given a literal paraphrase can a miracle be "demythologized" and made to be scientifically respectable. To attempt to do so is to attempt to make miracles less "shocking" for the modern mind. But like a good metaphor, a miracle is nothing if it does not shock us. This shock is a shock of recognition. The whole purpose of a miracle is to make us *see* the world to which we have grown accustomed in a new light: as the playground of a divine creativity that knows no bounds and for which nothing is impossible. As Saint Augustine said in book X, chapter 12 of *The City of God,* the existence of nature and man is the greatest miracle of all. If one does not accept the miracle at its face value, everything is lost, for then it cannot produce its effect: insightful understanding.

Nevertheless this does not mean that one should take the miracle literally. As with metaphor in general, there are two errors to be avoided here. The one is to take the miracle "allegorically" and to view it as simply a figurative way of communicating a message that can be translated into nonmythological terms, as expressing a speculative truth that can be abstracted from all concrete imagery. The other error is just the opposite: it consists of refusing to go beyond the manifest content of the miracle. The miracle, like the myth, is taken literally and is seen to be a contradiction to the "laws" of science. But as Saint Augustine said, miracles do not contradict the order of nature, only our restricted ideas about this order. The two errors are different forms of a single underlying error. They both take the miracle at its face value and then either reconcile it with science or oppose it to science. The essence of miracle, like that of metaphor, consists not in what it "says" or appears to be but in what it does to us who give ourselves over to it. Miracles and myths are like metaphors in that they are vehicles of understanding, and the meaning of a vehicle lies not in itself but in the fact that it enables us to get from one place to another.

Miracles are a form of magic, and magic falls under the heading of ritual. Myth must be understood in this context, as an integral part of ritual performance, understood as a self-transforming practice (myths are, for one thing, an important and indispensable part of magical curing rites). The fact that we moderns are accustomed to reading myths (in encyclopedias and manuals of mythology) is perhaps the prime reason for our inability to make sense of them (or, correlatively, for our frantic attempt to discover some hidden meaning in them, as for example in the psychoanalytic interpretation of myth). We have a distorted understanding of the myths that figure in Greek drama, for instance, because we look upon these dramas in a modern, "profane" way as "plays," whereas Greek drama was religious in origin and function and formed an integral part of religious festivals. Myth is not a theoretical account of things that simply masquerades as an improbable tale.

One of the merits of Malinowski was that he was aware of this. Unlike other anthropologists who viewed myth as a pseudoscientific attempt at explanation, Malinowski rightly insisted that myth "is not a savage speculation about origins of things born out of a philosophic interest."[16] Myth, as he saw it, is essentially bound up with the magical rite. Indeed he thought of it as the means whereby magic justifies ("vouches for") itself; "the myth," he said, "recounts simply the primeval miracle of the magic."[17] Myth "is engendered by the real or imaginary success of witchcraft."[18] In pointing out the "pragmatic" meaning of myth, his purpose was to emphasize the "deep connection between myth and cult." In this he was fully justified, for whatever he himself sought to make of this connection, it is true that the real meaning of myth consists not in what it overtly says or cryptically implies but in the role it plays as part of a religious or magical rite. Myth and ritual are inseparable.[19] Like metaphors, myths are misunderstood when one attempts to "demythologize" them in such a way as to extract from them a pure "intellectual content," which is then held to be the "real meaning" of the myth.

Mythical statements are, like metaphors (and, it might be added, zen *koans*), performative utterances whose meaning is nothing other than their "perlocutionary effect."[20] And myths, like metaphors, are essentially "secretive" in that they communicate their meaning only in a roundabout and indirect way, in terms of the transformation they manage to produce in our understanding of things (their "secrecy" does not derive simply from the reluctance a people usually has to communicating them to outsiders; rather this reluctance itself derives from an intuitive awareness people have that to relate their myths outside of their performative context is somehow a sacrilege and a falsification of the myth). Both myth and magic (miracles) are misunderstood when they are viewed in anything other than their ritual context. Only if one has an eye to this context can one hope to deal properly with the very tricky, but inevitable, question: Does the myth maker really mean what he seems to be saying? Does the magician or miracle worker really do what he seems to be doing?

We moderns inevitably fail to grasp the true significance of magic and myth because we look at these phenomena with the wrong mental spectacles and talk about them in the wrong language, thereby failing to bring them into proper focus. Our usual scientific, matter-of-fact way of reacting to shamanism, for instance, is to question whether the shaman really does what he claims to do. Does he really leave his body and wander about in another world in the heavens or at the bottom of the sea? Does he really converse with animals and learn secrets from them? Does he really become an animal himself? Is he really—physically—torn apart and put back together again during his initiation rite into shamanism? Our next reaction is to disclaim the whole business by saying to ourselves that the shaman could not possibly do all these things because they contradict what we take to be the laws of physics and biology. They are not possible in our world. We thus conclude that they are nothing but illusion and that the shaman is a mere trickster, thereby dismissing the whole business. If, however, we are really curious in a scientific sort of way, we will attempt to discover how, by means of what subtle tricks and sleight-of-hand, the shaman manages to manipulate, hallucinate, hypnotize, or otherwise pull the wool over the eyes of others and why he so manipulates them. Or else, if we are modern "demythologizing" theologians, we will attempt to discern a "higher spiritual meaning" in all this.

When, however, we have proceeded down this path of inquiry we have gotten so far away from the phenomenon itself that what we have to say no longer has any real relevance to the matter, and the mentality of these shamanistic peoples—what really happens during a shaministic seance—has become completely inaccessible to us. We are no longer communicating with the shaman, for we have translated his world into our own. We have analyzed the world of the shaman in terms of our own scientific categories of reality and illusion and have failed to notice, to see, what alone is essential: that the whole point of shamanism is to *call into question one's usual idea of what is real and what is not.*

The question, Does the shaman *really* do such-and-such? cannot be answered with a simple "yes" or "no," for the precise purpose of the shaman is to undermine our ordinary conception as to what constitutes reality. The question itself is made to undergo a strange transformation: after our encounter with the shaman, do we still know what reality really is?

The shaman plays a vital and indispensable role in his society. As a person in contact with the powers of "another" world—the sacred—and who manifests this other dimension of existence to his fellow men, he reveals to them and makes them aware of something that they normally tend to forget: the fabulous and marvelous character of existence. Perhaps we would understand the true significance of shamanism better were we not to concentrate so much on the shaman himself or his various claims as on the essential role that shamanism plays in those societies where it exists. To people lost in the everyday world of drudgery, hardship, and indifference—the profane—the shaman reveals to them their world in a different and exceptional light. A Sioux Indian describes the effect of a visionary ceremony in this way: "When the ceremony was over, everybody felt a great deal better, for it had been a day of fun. They were better able now to see the greenness of the world, the wideness of the sacred day, the colors of the earth, and to set these in their minds."[21]

And at the end of his treatise on shamanism, M. Eliade makes the following highly instructive remarks:

> It is difficult for us to imagine what such a champion [the shaman] can represent for archaic society. . . . Every truly shamanistic seance ends up by becoming a spectacle without equal in the world of everyday experience. Fire tricks, "miracles" such as the rope trick and the mango-tree trick, the exhibition of magical powers disclose another world, the fabulous world of the gods and magicians, the world where *everything seems possible,* where the dead return to life and the living die in order afterwards to be reborn, where the "laws of nature" are abolished and a certain super-human "freedom" is illustrated and rendered *present* in a striking manner. It is difficult, for us moderns, to imagine the resonance of such a *spectacle* in a "primitive" community. Not only do the shamanistic "miracles" confirm and fortify the structures of traditional religion but they also stimulate and nourish the imagination, make the barriers between dream and immediate reality disappear, open windows unto worlds inhabited by gods, the dead, and spirits.[22]

The shaman is a master of the techniques of ecstasy.[23] He is adept at removing himself from the world normally held to be the true one and at transporting himself into another world, which he evokes, calls forth, by

means of his own shamanistic and metaphorical use of language.[24] The shaman is a cosmic voyager; what he sees and shows is out of this world, and
his saying and doing transport his fellow men out of their ordinary, everyday world of banal reality.

Of course, we might want to say that the shaman does not "really" leave
this world; the world in which he takes his flight is not "another world,"
"more real" than this one. The shaman has his critics even in his own society. But these critics, like modern-day positivistic ones, miss the whole point.
They are blind and insensitive to what the shaman sees and shows. The whole
meaning of shamanism is that it upsets our usual interpretation of the world;
it transforms the ordinary world into something extraordinary and thereby
destroys for a time the illusion that the world of everyday life or what today
we call the physical world is the sole and basic Reality. Through fantasy and
imagination—creative expression—the shaman *irrealizes* what is ordinarily
accepted as real. He makes people aware that there are other possible
worlds, these "other" worlds being none other than this world viewed
otherly (as in Mahayanist Buddhism *nirvana* or supreme salvation is not
separated from *samsara* or the phenomenal world, but the first is discovered
in the heart of the second). In seeing the world otherly, we encounter and
transcend its limits in that we see it as a limited expression of the unlimited.

When ordinary, everyday belief in the world has been suspended in this
way, nothing in the world has changed, but the world itself has undergone a
radical transformation. It is no longer what it was, something taken for
granted, self-evident, banal, but has become supremely wonderful, problematic, and mysterious. What one now sees and understands is nothing
other than the miracle of existence. As the medicine man of the Oglala
Sioux stated in the passage quoted above, one sees the world afresh. Old
things appear new, familiar ones strange. It is as though one were seeing the
world for the first time; one sees that the way things are is the strangest
thing about them. Everything is new; it is as if everything had never happened before: "when the storm of vision has passed, the world is greener
and happier; for wherever the truth of vision comes upon the world, it is
like a rain. The world, you see, is happier after the terror of the storm."[25]

In our own secular times and culture, what is called magic—the art of the
theatrical magician—still manifests, if only in a decadent and vulgar way,
the essential function of all magic, which is that of making the extraordinary come to pass in the being of the world. Doug Henning, the only
magician ever to receive a grant from the Canada Council, said that he justified his request in this way:

> I told them magic was very important in our society. It instills people with a
> sense of wonder and makes them think. Magic is really everywhere. Life is
> magic. A flower blooming is magic. People want to know there is still some

mystery left. They want to know there are some things science and technology can't explain. The human mind has limits to what it can understand. But in magic, I take people outside those limits and show them the impossible.[26]

Magic is indeed everywhere. The function of the magician is to remind us of this. That, like a rabbit out of a hat, the world should have come to be out of nothing is itself sheer magic. The essential function of magic and myth is not, like science, to provide us with a certain interpretation of the world; it is to enable us to see that the world is something that transcends all pat interpretations. Magic and myth give rise not to knowledge but to wonder, to an awareness of the supreme mystery of being.

Generally and with due regard to the impossibility of distinguishing clearly and neatly between the two, it can be said that magic differs from religion in that its object tends to be more specific and the means for dealing with this end equally specific. It tends to be a kind of technique or a loose collection of techniques (although it is impossible to reduce it to this). Religion, however, has no specific object (although believers tend to localize their religious sentiments on specific objects such as particular saints or gods). It is generally fear of the unknown that provokes magic, whereas it is anxiety in the face of the unknowable that evokes religion. There does not seem to be any justification for maintaining that magic is prior to religion (and indeed one could argue that religion precedes magic and that people only first become human with the advent of religion, that is, when they experience anxiety in the face of their own death, when they encounter experientially the unknowable).[27] Again, magic, whose function qua primitive science and technology is to provide people with confidence and poise, tends as such toward optimism; it represents in a way the victory of optimism over pessimism, of confidence over doubt. Religion, on the other hand, though it too gives people poise and steadfastness (peace), goes beyond optimism and can survive all manner of adversity. Religion, in fact, enables people to live tragically, to accept the ultimate and inevitable failure of their life, their death, with a kind of impassioned indifference. Religious faith and hope is more than mere optimism and wishful thinking. Here faith is faith in spite of deception, and hope is hope in spite of adversity. This is why, from the point of view of science, technology, and common sense, magic and expecially religion must appear as folly, crude or sublime, divine or all-too-human, as the case may be.

As Malinowski recognized, the distinction between the sacred and the profane is indispensable for understanding primitive culture.[28] But Malinowski's way of situating magic, science, and religion in terms of this distinction is misleading.[29] He rightly locates science on the side of the profane or everyday, but he wrongly places both magic and religion on the other side, that of the sacred. The fact is that magic straddles the line and is ambivalent. To the degree that it is a kind of primitive science and is an attempt to know and control things (and Malinowski himself points out this aspect of magic and even calls it, after Frazer, a "pseudo-science"), magic belongs not to the sacred but, like science, to the profane. Conversely to the degree that magic enables people to reconcile themselves to the limits of their power (their "impotence," as Malinowski says), to overcome their dependence on their own available means of control (thereby affording them a means of controlling their means of control and of understandingly reconciling themselves with the unknowable), magic performs a properly religious function and belongs to the realm of the sacred.

What makes it difficult to understand the precise place of magic in primitive or non-Western cultures is that, unlike modern Western man who looks to science for all the answers to the problems of life and who sees in technology his only hope, "primitive" man does not put all of his eggs in one basket. Contrary to long-standing opinion (which recent anthropology has rectified), primitive man is not without what we would call science and technology. He possesses an incredibly rich knowledge of animal and vegetable forms of life and is a careful observer of nature (as in modern science, his observations are guided by an avid curiosity free from the dictates of practical necessity or immediate action), as well as a sizable body of practical know-how, or technology. But, unlike us, he does not think that science and technology are enough to insure the good life. He knows that there is something more to life, and in religion and magic he expresses this awareness in symbols and ritual. One reason why it is so difficult for us to appreciate how primitive people can be both very practical minded in their technology and superstitious in their magic is that our technology is not simply a more refined version of primitive (or, for that matter, medieval) technology but something altogether different. Modern technology is a total way of life; it is above all a certain mentality or way or relating to the world and to existence; it regulates our entire lives: politics, economics, and social relations. The only criterion it recognizes is the law of efficiency. This is not at all the case with primitive man. In his case, technology is indeed a mere means whose sphere of application and legitimacy is deliberately circumscribed; primitive man does not reduce the good to what is efficient. This is most important to keep in mind when dealing with the problem of other cultures, and indeed it may not be irrelevant to our own problem of the Two Cultures.

NOTES

1. E. E. Evans-Pritchard, *Witchcraft, Oracles and Magic among the Azande* (Oxford, 1937), p. 541.

2. J. G. Frazer, *The New Golden Bough* (New York, 1959), pp. 648-49.

3. Although Lévi-Strauss shows himself to be somewhat sympathetic to Frazer's view, he does admit that, properly speaking, magic and science are parallel systems.

4. Although he presents the relation between magic and religion in a misleading light, Lévi-Strauss does recognize that both imply each other, that there is no religion without magic and no magic which does not contain "at least a grain of religion."

5. M. Eliade, *Aspects du mythe* (Paris, 1963), chap. 1.

6. Cf. M. Eliade, *Le sacré et le profane* (Paris, 1965).

7. R. Hubert and M. Mauss, *Etude sommaire sur la réprésentation du temps dans la religion et la magie* (Paris, 1909), p. 192.

8. R. Bultmann, *Jesus Christ and Mythology* (New York, 1958), p. 19.

9. In religion what one understands is the limits of understanding, as the well-known historian of religion, G. Van der Leeuw notes:

> Le sens religieux de la chose est celui auquel ne puet succéder aucun autre sens plus large ou plus profond. C'est le sens du tout. C'est le dernier mot. Or, ce sens n'est jamais compris; ce mot n'est jamais prononcé. L'un et l'autre nous dépassent toujours. Le sens dernier est un mystère, qui se révèle toujours à nouveau et cependant reste toujours caché. Il désigne un progrès jusqu'à l'ultime limite, où l'on ne comprend plus qu'une chose, à savoir que toute compréhension se trouve "au delà." Le sens dernier est en même temps la limite du sens. . . . La religion, c'est une expérience vécue de la limite qui se dérobe au regard, c'est une révélation qui, par essence, est et demeure cachée. . . . Plus profondément la compréhension pénètre dans un phénomène, mieux elle "comprend," plus aussi il devient clair pour celui qui comprend que le fondement dernier de la compréhension n'est pas en lui-même mais en quelque chose "d'autre" qui d'au delà de la limite, le comprend. Faute de cette compréhension de valeur absolue, décisive, il n'y en aurait aucune. Toute compréhension "jusqu'au fond" cesse d'en être une avant d'avoir atteint le fond: elle se reconnaît comme étant comprise, au lieu de comprendre (*Le religion dans son essence et ses manifestations, phénoménologie de la religion* [Paris, 1970], pp. 663-66).

10. E. E. Evans-Pritchard, *Nuer Religion* (New York, 1974), p. 7.

11. Ibid., pp. 143-44.

12. The source for this material is A. David-Neel, *Magic and Mystery in Tibet* (Baltimore, 1965), who, a Buddhist herself, spent fourteen years wandering through the "Land of Snow" studying the practices of this people.

13. Ibid., pp. 283-87.

14. Ibid., p. 267.

15. M. Eliade, *Le mythe de l'éternel retour* (Paris, 1969), p. 13.

16. B. Malinowski, *Magic, Science and Religion* (New York, 1954), p. 88.

17. Ibid., p. 84.

18. Ibid., p. 85.

19. If anthropologists and other "scientific" observers have been baffled for so long by the highly complicated ceremonialism of the Hopi indians, it is because they were unable to see that it is in this way, in concrete practice, that they express their myths of the origin and destiny of mankind; with the Hopi myth and ritual form a united whole. Cf. F. Waters, *Book of the Hopi* (New York, 1974). Hopi religion, Waters observes, "is a belief whose core is not spoken, but expressed by the abstract ritualism and symbolism embodied in the great annual cycle of intricate ceremonies. This is what has made it almost impossible for whites to understand, and also so difficult for the Hopis themselves" (p. 411).

The following remarks made by a high priestess or *Mae de Santo* of Macumba, the indigenous Brazilian religion similar in some ways to Haitian voodou, in answer to questions put to her by a European interviewer also substantiates our thesis as to the inseparability of myth and ritual:

> Interroge nos fidèles: ils n'expliquent pas ce qu'ils font ou éprouvent. Et il n'est pas

nécessaire de tout expliquer. Beaucoup d' idées me passent par la tête. Mais je ne crois qu'en ce que j'ai expérimenté. Notre religion se pratique, elle ne s'étudie pas. Alors je ne comprends pas ton livre. Il est semblable à un chant dont on n'aurait que les paroles. Et je te l'ai dit: les rythmes sont l'essentiel (S. Bramly, *Macumba* [Paris, 1975], p. 152).

20. To borrow an expression from the English philosopher of language, J. L. Austin, *How to Do Things with Words* (Oxford, 1962), pp.101ff.

21. J. G. Neihardt, *Black Elk Speaks* (Richmond Hill, Ont., 1972), p. 163. In a different context, Pope Jean Paul II, during his June 1980 visit to France, addressing himself to the crowd of 500,000 faithful (official police estimate) who had come to Le Bourget to celebrate with him the eucharistic rite, spoke of that day as a "moment extraordinaire entre les moments ordinaires avant le retour à la banalité et au courage quotidien" (*Le Monde,* June 3, 1980, p. 11).

22. M. Eliade, *Le chamanise* (Paris, 1968), pp. 395-97 (my translation.)

23. Eliade subtitles his study, "Les techniques arcaiques de l'extase," and in it maintains that the ecstatic trance is the essential and distinctive trait of all authentic shamanism (cf. pp. 22-23).

24. "Quand il prépare sa transe, le chaman bat le tambour, appelle ses esprits auxiliaires, parle un "langage secret" ou le "langage des animaux," imitant le cri des animaux et surtout le chant des oiseaux. Il finit par obtenir un "état second" qui met en branle la création linguistique et les rythmes de la poésie lyrique" (ibid., pp. 396-97).

25. Neihardt, *Black Elk Speaks,* p. 159.

26. *Canada Magazine,* January 20, 1973.

27. The great, so-called world religions, which represent an extremely high degree of systematicity, are, to be sure, relatively recent developments in comparison with the age-old existence of magic. What they represent is indeed a decided development in culture, which is to say, in man's humanity. Nonetheless, genuinely religious elements are often to be found in even the most primitive of magical belief systems.

And in regard to the problem raised in the Preface to this book—the survial of primitive, that is, technologically underdeveloped, societies in an increasingly technologized world—it could be said that the chance such societies have of not so much merely surviving as transforming themselves in such a way as to preserve in the process a renewed self-identity is directly bound up with their being or not being able to transform archaic magical belief systems into genuinely religious outlooks.

28. Malinowski, *Magic, Science and Religion,* p. 17.

29. Cf. ibid., pp. 86ff.

BIBLIOGRAPHY

Aquinas, Saint Thomas. *Quaestiones Disputatae. De Potentia Dei*. Turin: Marietti, 1953.
———. *Liber de Veritate Catholicae Fidei contra errores Infidelium (Suma Contra Gentiles)*. Turin: Marietti, 1961.
———. *Summa Theologiae*. Alba: Editiones Paulinae, 1962.
Arendt, Hannah. *The Human Condition*. Chicago: University of Chicago Press, 1958.
Aristotle. *De Interpretatione*. Translated by E. M. Edghill. In R. McKeon, ed., *The Basic Works of Aristotle*. New York: Random House, 1941.
———. *De Poetica*. Translated by I. Bywater. In R. McKeon, ed., *The Basic Works of Aristotle*. New York: Random House, 1941.
———. *De Sophisticis Elenchis*. Translated by W. A. Pickard-Cambridge. In R. McKeon, ed., *The Basic Works of Aristotle*. New York: Random House, 1941.
———. *Metaphysica*. Translated by W. D. Ross. In R. McKeon, ed., *The Basic Works of Aristotle*. New York: Random House, 1941.
———. *Ethica Nicomachea*. Translated by W. D. Ross. In R. McKeon, ed., *The Basic Works of Aristotle*. New York: Random House, 1941.
———. *Politica*. Translated by B. Jowett. In R. McKeon, ed., *The Basic Works of Aristotle*. New York: Random House, 1941.
———. *Rhetorica*. Translated by W. R. Roberts. In R. McKeon, ed., *The Basic Works of Aristotle*. New York: Random House, 1941.
Aubenque, Pierre. *Le problème de l'être chez Aristote*. Paris: Presses Universitaires de France, 1962.
Augustine, Saint. *Confessions*. Translated by R. S. Pine-Coffin. Harmondsworth: Penguin Books, 1979.
Austin, John Langshaw. *How to Do Things with Words*. Oxford: Clarendon Press, 1962.
Bachelard, Gaston. *La formation de l'esprit scientifique*. Paris: Librarie philosophique J. Vrin, 1969.
Bambrough, Renford. "Universals and Family Resemblances." In G. Pitcher, ed., *Wittgenstein, The "Philosophical Investigations."* London: Macmillan, 1968.
Barrett, William. *The Illusion of Technique*. Garden City, N.Y.: Anchor Books, 1979.
Barthes, Roland. "Eléments de Sémiologie," *Communications*, no. 4. Paris: Editions du Seuil, 1964.
———. *Mythologies*. Paris: Editions du Seuil, 1957.
Bayle, Pierre. *Historical and Critical Dictionary*. Translated by R. Popkin. Indianapolis: Bobbs Merrill Co., 1965.
Beattie, John. "On Understanding Ritual." In B. R. Wilson, ed., *Rationality*. New York: Harper Torchbooks, 1971.
———. *Other Cultures*. New York: Free Press, 1968.
Beaujour, Michel. "The Game of Politics." In J. Ehrmann, ed., *Game, Play, Literature*. Boston: Beacon Press, 1968.
Beck, Lewis White. "The 'Natural Science Ideal' in the Social Sciences." In Robert A. Manners and David Kaplan, eds. *Theory in Anthropology*, Chicago: Aldine, 1968.

Bidney, David. *Theoretical Anthropology*. New York: Schocken Books, 1967.

Black, Max. *Models and Metaphors*. Ithaca, N.Y.: Cornell University Press, 1962.

Boas, Franz. "On Grammatical Categories." In D. Hymes, ed., *Language and Culture in Society*. New York: Harper and Row, 1964.

Bochenski, I. M. "On Analogy." *Thomist* 2 (1948): 424-47.

Braithwaite, Richard Bevan. *Scientific Explanation*. Cambridge: At the Press, 1968.

Bramly, Serge. *Macumba, Forces noires du Brésil*. Paris: Seghers, 1975.

Bronowski, Jacob. *The Identity of Man*. Garden City, N.Y.: Natural History Press,1971.

———. *Science and Human Values*. New York: Harper Torchbooks, 1965.

Bultmann, Rudolph. *Jesus Christ and Mythology*. New York: Charles Scribner's Sons, 1958.

———. *Kerygma and Myth*. New York: Harper Torchbooks, 1961.

Burkhardt, Titus. *Alchemy*. Baltimore: Penguin Books, 1971.

Burrell, David. *Analogy and Philosophical Language*. New Haven, Conn.: Yale University Press, 1973.

Caillois, Roger. *Les jeux et les hommes*. Paris: Gallimard (collection "Idées"), 1967.

Cajetan, Cardinal. *The Analogy of Names*. Pittsburgh: Duquesne University Press, 1959.

Calder, Ritchie. *Man and the Cosmos: The Nature of Science Today*. New York: Mentor Books, 1969.

Camus, Albert. *The Rebel*. Translated by Anthony Brower. New York: Vintage Books, 1956.

Carr, David, *Phenomenology and the Problem of History*. Evanston, Ill.: Northwestern University Press, 1974.

Cassirer, Ernst. *Language and Myth*. New York: Dover Publications, n.d.

Cicero. *De Oratore*. Translated by E. W. Sutton. Loeb Classical Library. London: William Heinemann, 1959.

Civilization and Science. 1971 Ciba Foundation Symposium. Amsterdam: Associated Scientific Publishers, 1973.

Chao, Yuen Ren. *Language and Symbolic Systems*. Cambridge University Press, 1974.

Charron, Pierre. *De la sagesse*. 3 vols. 12th ed. Paris, 1824.

Chomsky, Noam. *Language and Mind*. Enlarged ed. New York: Harcout Brace Jovanovich, 1972.

Copi, Irving M. "Artificial Languages." In P. Henle, ed., *Language, Thought, and Culture*. Ann Arbor: University of Michigan Press, 1965.

Copleston, Frederick. *A History of Philosophy*. Vol 2: *Mediaeval Philosophy, Augustine to Scotus*. Westminster, Md.: Newman Press, 1962.

David-Neel, Alexandra. *Magic and Mystery in Tibet*. Baltimore: Penguin Books, 1965.

de Bono, Edward. *Lateral Thinking*. New York: Harper Colophon Books, 1973.

Diogenes Laertius. *Lives of Eminent Philosophers* (*Vitae Philosophorum*). Translated by R. D. Hicks. Loeb Classical Library. Cambridge, Mass: Harvard University Press, 1972.

Dionysius the Areopagite. *The Mystical Theology and the Celestial Hierarchies*. Fintry, Brook, Nr. Godalming, Surrey: Shrine of Wisdom, 1949.

Duhem, Pierre. *The Aim and Structure of Physical Theory*. Translated by P. Wiener. Princeton, N.J.: Princeton University Press, 1954.

Eliade, Mircea. *Aspects du mythe*. Paris: Gallimard (collection "Idées"), 1963.

———. *Le chamanisme*. Paris: Payot, 1968.

———. *Le mythe de l'éternel retour*. Paris: Gallimard (collection "Idées), 1969.

———. *Le sacré et le profane*. Paris: Gallimard (collection "Idées"), 1965.

———. *Traité d'histoire des religions*. Paris: Payot, 1968.

Eliot, T. S. *Christianity and Culture*. New York: Harcourt, Brace, and World, 1949.

Ellul, Jacques. *The Technological Society*. New York: Vintage Books, n.d.

Ernst, Max. "Inspiration to Order." In B. Ghiselin, ed., *The Creative Process*. New York: New American Library, n.d.

Evans-Pritchard, E. E. "The Morphology and Function of Magic: A Comparative Study of

Trobiand and Zande Ritual and Spells." In J. Middleton, ed., *Magic, Witchcraft, and Curing*. Garden City, N.Y.: Natural History Press, 1967.

———. *Nuer Religion*. New York: Oxford University Press, 1974.

———. *Social Anthropology and Other Essays*. New York: Free Press, 1964.

———. *Theories of Primitive Religion*. Oxford: Oxford University Press, 1971.

———. "Witchcraft Amongst the Azande." In M. Marwick, ed., *Witchcraft and Sorcery*. Harmondsworth: Penguin Books, 1975.

———. *Witchcraft, Oracles and Magic Among the Azande*. Oxford: Oxford University Press, 1937.

Foulquié, Paul. *La dialectique*. Paris: Presses Universitaires de France (collection "Que sais-je?"), 1969.

Frazer, Sir James George. *The New Golden Bough*. Abridged ed. Edited by Theodor Gaster. New York: Criterion Books, 1959.

Frege, Gottlob. "Frege-Husserl Correspondance." *Southwestern Journal of Philosophy* 5, no. 3 (1974).

———. *Translations from the Philosophical Writings of Gottob Frege*. Edited by Peter Geach and Max Black. Oxford: Basil Blackwell, 1970.

Gadamer, Hans-Georg. "The Science of the Life-World." In A.-T. Tymieniecka, ed., *The Later Husserl and the Idea of Phenomenology*. Dordrecht: D. Reidel, 1972.

———. *Truth and Method*. New York: Seabury Press, 1975.

Garrigou-Lagrange, Reginald. *God, His Existence and Nature*. London: B. Herber Book Co., 1949.

Gendlin, Eugene T. *Experiencing and the Creation of Meaning*. Glencoe, Ill.: Free Press, 1962.

———. "Experiential Phenomenology." In M. Natanson, ed., *Phenomenology and the Social Sciences*. Evanston, Ill.: Northwestern University Press, 1973.

Ghiselin, Brewster. "The Birth of a Poem." In B. Ghiselin, ed., *The Creative Process*. New York: New American Library, n.d.

———. *The Creative Process*. New York: New American Library, n.d.

Gilson, Etienne. *The Christian Philosophy of St. Thomas Aquinas*. London: Victor Gollancz, 1967.

Gluckman, Max. "The Logic of African Science and Witchcraft." In Max Marwick, ed., *Witchcraft and Sorcery*. Harmondsworth: Penguin Books, 1975.

Goodman, Nelson. *Languages of Art*. Indianapolis: Bobbs-Merrill Co., 1968.

Gusdorf, Georges. *Mythe et métaphysique*. Paris: Flammarion, 1963.

Guthrie, W. K. C. *A History of Greek Philosophy*. Vol. 3. Cambridge: At the Press, 1969.

Hanson, Norwood Russell. *Patterns of Discovery*. Cambridge: At the Press, 1972.

Harris, Marvin. *The Rise of Anthropological Theory*. New York: Thomas Y. Crowell Co., 1968.

Hegel, G. W. F. *Lectures on the History of Philosophy*. Translated by E. S. Haldane and F. H. Simpson. London: Kegan Paul, Trench, Trübner, 1895.

Heidegger, Martin. *Being and Time*. Translated by J. Macquarrie and E. Robinson. New York: Harper and Row, 1962.

———. "The End of Philosophy and the Task of Thinking." In *On Time and Being*. Translated by J. Stambaugh. New York: Harper and Row, 1972.

———. *An Introduction to Metaphysics*. Translated by R. Manheim. New Haven, Conn.: Yale University Press, 1959.

———. *Poetry, Language, Thought*. Translated by A. Hofstadter. New York: Harper and Row, 1971.

———. *What Is Called Thinking?* Translated by F. D. Wieck and J. Glenn Gray. New York: Harper and Row, 1968.

———. "What Is Metaphysics?" Translated by R. F. C. Hull and Alan Crick. In Heidegger, *Existence and Being*. Chicago: Henry Regnery Co., 1949.

Heisenberg, Werner. *Physics and Beyond*. New York: Harper Torchbooks, 1971.

Hempel, Carl G. *Philosophy of Natural Science*. Englewood Cliffs, N.J.: Prentice-Hall, 1966.
Henle, Paul. "Metaphor." In Paul Henle, ed., *Language, Thought, and Culture*. Ann Arbor: University of Michigan Press, 1965.
Hirsch, E. D., Jr., *Validity in Interpretation*. New Haven, Conn: Yale University Press, 1967.
Hobbes, Thomas. *Leviathan*. Indianapolis: Bobbs-Merrill Co., 1958.
Holton, Gerald. *Thematic Origins of Scientific Thought*. Cambridge, Mass.: Harvard University Press, 1973.
Hook, Sideny. *Reason, Social Myth, and Democracy*. New York: Harper Torchbooks, 1966.
Horton, Robin. "African Traditional Thought and Western Science." In B. R. Wilson, ed., *Rationality*. New York: Harper Torchbooks, 1971.
Hubert, R., and Mauss, M. *Etude sommaire sur la représentation du temps dans la religion et la magie*. Paris: Alcan, 1909.
Huizinga, Johan. *Homo Ludens*. Boston: Beacon Press, 1970.
Husserl, Edmund. *Cartesian Meditations*. Translated by D. Cairns. The Hague: Martinus Nijhoff, 1960.
——. *The Crisis of European Sciences and Transcendental Phenomenology*. Translated by David Carr. Evanston, Ill.: Northwestern University Press, 1970.
——. *Experience and Judgment*. Translated by J. S. Churchill and K. Ameriks. Evanston, Ill.: Northwestern University Press, 1973.
——. *The Idea of Phenomenology*. Translated by W. Alston and G. Nakhnikian. The Hague: Martinus Nijhoff, 1964.
——. *Ideas*. Translated by W. R. Boyce Gibson. New York: Collier Books, 1962.
——. *Logical Investigations*. 2 vols. Translated by J. N. Findlay. London: Routledge and Kegan Paul, 1970.
Ijsseling, Samuel. *Rhetoric and Philosophy in Conflict*. The Hague: Martinus Nijhoff, 1976.
Isocrates. *Isocrates*. 3 vols. Translated by G. Norlin. Loeb Classical Library. Cambridge, Mass.: Harvard University Press, 1966.
Jaeger, Werner. *Paideia: The Ideals of Greek Culture*. 3 vols. Translated by G. Highet. New York: Oxford University Press, 1960.
Jahoda, Gustav. *The Psychology of Superstition*. London: Penguin Books, 1969.
James, William. *Essays in Radical Empiricism/A Pluralistic Universe*. Gloucester, Mass.: Peter Smith, 1967.
——. *Pragmatism and Other Essays*. New York: Washington Square Press, 1963.
——. *The Principles of Psychology*. 2 vols. New York: Dover Publications, 1950.
——. *The Will to Believe/Human Immortality*. New York: Dover Publications, 1956.
Jarvie, I. C. "Limits to Functionalism and Alternatives to It in Anthropology." In Robert A. Manners and David Kaplan, eds., *Theory in Anthropology*. Chicago: Aldine, 1968.
Jarvie, I. C., and Agassi, J. "The Problem of the Rationality of Magic." In B. R. Wilson, ed., *Rationality*. New York: Harper Torchbooks, 1971.
Jonas, Hans. *The Gnostic Religion*. 2d ed., Boston: Beacon Press, 1963.
Jones, W. T. *The Sciences and the Humanities*. Berkeley: University of California Press, 1967.
Jung, Carl Gustav. "Psychology and Literature." In *Modern Man in Search of a Soul*. Translated by W. S. Dell and C. F. Baynes. London: Routledge and Kegan Paul, 1966.
Kant, Immanuel. *Immanuel Kant's Critique of Pure Reason*. Translated by Norman Kemp Smith. London: Macmillan, 1963.
Kaplan, David. "The Superorganic: Science or Metaphysics." In Robert A. Manners and David Kaplan, eds., *Theory in Anthropology*. Chicago: Aldine, 1968.
Kierkegaard, Søren. *Concluding Unscientific Postscript*. Translated by D. Swenson and W. Lowrie. Princeton, N.J.: Princeton University Press, 1941.
——. *Philosophical Fragments*. Translated by D. Swenson. H. Hong, *revised trans*. Princeton, N.J.: Princeton University Press, 1971.
Kluckhohn, Clyde. *Navaho Witchcraft*. Boston: Beacon Press, 1967.

Koestler, Arthur. *The Act of Creation*. London: Pan Books, 1970.
——. *The Ghost in the Machine*. London: Pan Books, 1970.
Körner, Stephan. *Experience and Theory*. London: Routledge and Kegan Paul, 1966.
Köner, Stephan. *Experience and Theory*. London: Routledge and Kegan Paul, 1966.
Kuhn, Thomas. *The Structure of Scientific Revolutions*. Chicago: University of Chicago Press, 1970.
Lagueux, Maurice. "L'usage abusif du rapport science/idéologie." In *Culture et langage*. Cahiers du Québec, no. 11. Montréal: Hurtubise HMN, 1973.
Langer, Susanne K. *Philosophy in a New Key*. Cambridge, Mass.: Harvard University Press, 1974.
Latouche, Serge. "Totalité, totalisation et totalitarisme." *Dialogue* 13, no.1 (March 1974).
Lawrence, T. E. *Seven Pillars of Wisdom*. New York: Doubleday, 1935.
Leach, Edmund. *Lévi-Strauss*. London: Wm. Collins and Co., 1970.
——. "Lévi-Strauss in the Garden of Eden." In E. Hayes and T. Hayes, eds., *Claude Lévi-Strauss: The Anthropologist as Hero*. Cambridge, Mass.: M.I.T. Press, 1970.
Leatherdale, W. H. *The Role of Analogy, Model and Metaphor in Science*. Amsterdam: North-Holland Pub. Co., 1974.
Lévi-Strauss, Claude. *The Savage Mind*. Chicago: University of Chicago Press, 1966.
——. *Structural Anthropology*. Translated by C. Jacobson and B. G. Schoepf. New York: Basic Books, 1963.
——. *Les structures élémentaires de la parenté*. Paris: Presses Universitaires de France, 1949.
——. *Tristes Tropiques*. Translated by J. Russell. New York: Criterion Books, 1961.
Locke, John. *An Essay Concerning Human Understanding*. 2 vols. Edited by John W. Yolton. Everyman's Library. London: J. M. Dent and Sons, 1974.
Löwith, Karl. *Meaning in History*. Chicago: University of Chicago Press, 1949.
McLuhan, Marshall. *Understanding Media: The Extensions of Man*. New York: Signet Books, 1964.
Madison, Gary Brent. "Eine Kritik an Hirschs Begriff der 'Richtigkeit.' " In H.-G. Gadamer and G. Boehm, eds., *Die Hermeneutik und die Wissenschaften*. Frankfurt: Suhrkamp Verlag, 1978.
——. "Phenomenology and Existentialism: Husserl and the End of Idealism." In F. Elliston and P. McCormick, eds., *Husserl: Expositions and Appraisals*. Notre Dame: University of Notre Dame Press, 1977.
——. *La phénoménologie de Merleau-Ponty, une recherche des limites de la conscience*. Paris: Editions Klincksieck, 1973. English translation, *The Phenomenology of Merleau-Ponty*. Athens, Ohio: Ohio University Press, 1981.
——. "The Possibility and Limits of a Science of Man." *Philosophy Forum* 14 (1976).
——. "Le postulat d'objectivité dans la science et la philosophie du sujet." *Philosophiques* 1, no. 1 (April 1974).
——. "Pour une dérationalisation de la raison." In Th. F. Geraets, ed., *Rationality To-Day/La rationalité aujourd'hui*. Ottawa: Editions de l'Université d'Ottawa, 1979.
——. "Reflections on Paul Ricoeur's Philosophy of Metaphor," *Philosophy Today* 21, supplement to no. 4/4 (Winter 1977).
——. "Ricoeur et la non-philosophie." *Laval théologique et philosophique* 29, no. 3 (October 1973.).
——. "Technics, Metaphysics, Politics." *Journal of Social Philosophy* 3, no. 1 (1972).
Malinowski, Bronislaw. *Magic, Science and Religion*. New York: Doubleday Anchor Books, 1954.
Manners, Robert A., and Kaplan, David, eds. *Theory in Anthropology*. Chicago: Aldine, 1968.
Maritain, Jacques. *The Degrees of Knowledge*. New York: Charles Scribner's Sons, 1959.
Marwick, Max, ed. *Witchcraft and Sorcery*. Penguin Books, 1975.

Mayer, Philip. "Witches." In Max Marwick, ed., *Witchcraft and Sorcery*. Harmondsworth: Penguin Books, 1975.

Mead, Margaret, ed. *Cultural Patterns and Technical Change*. New York: Mentor Books, 1955.

Merleau-Ponty, Maurice. "Eye and Mind." In M. Merleau-Ponty, *The Primacy of Perception and Other Essays*. Edited by James Edie. Evanston, Ill.: Northwestern University Press, 1964.

———. *Phenomenology of Perception*. Translation by Colin Smith. London: Routledge and Kegan Paul, 1962.

———. *Signes*. Paris: Gallimard, 1960. English translation by R. McCleary, *Signs*. Evanston, Ill.: Northwestern University Press, 1964.

———. *The Visible and the Invisible*. Translated by Alphonso Lingis. Evanston, Ill.: Northwestern University Press, 1968.

Middleton, John, ed. *Magic, Witchcraft, and Curing*. Garden City, N.Y.: Natural History Press, 1967.

Montaigne, Michel de. "Apologie de Raimond Sebond." In *Oeuvres complètes*. Paris: Gallimard ("Bibliothèque de la Pléiade"), 1962.

Nadel, S. F. "Witchcraft in Four African Societies." In M. Marwick, ed., *Witchcraft and Sorcery*. Harmondsworth: Penguin Books, 1975.

Neihardt, John G. *Black Elk Speaks*. Richmond Hill, Ont: Pocket Books, 1972.

Nemetz, A. "Metaphysics and Metaphor." In R. Houde and J. Mullally, eds., *Philosophy of Knowledge*. Philadelphia: J. B. Lippincott, 1960.

Nguyên Van Tuyên, J. *Foi et existence selon Kierkegaard*. Paris: Aubier-Montaigne, 1971.

Nietzsche, Friedrich. *The Complete Works of Friedrich Nietzsche*. Vol 2; *Early Greek Philosophy and Other Essays*. Translated by M. A. Mugge. New York: Russell and Russell, 1964.

———. *The Complete Works of Friedrich Nietzsche*. Vol. 7: *Mixed Opinions and Aphorisms*. Translated by P. Cohen. New York: Russell and Russell, 1964.

———. *The Gay Science*. Translated by W. Kaufmann. New York: Vintage Books, 1974.

———. *The Will to Power*. Translated by W. Kaufmann. New York: Vintage Books, 1968.

Pascal, Blaise. *Pensées et opuscules*. Edited by L. Brunschvicg. Paris: Classiques Hachette, 1963.

Peirce, Charles Sanders. *Collected Papers*. 8 vols. Vols. 1-4, edited by C. Hartshorn and P. Weiss. Vols. 7-8, edited by A. W. Burks. Cambridge, Mass.: Harvard University Press, 1931-1958.

Perelman, Chaim, and Olbrechts-Tyteca, L. *The New Rhetoric, A Treatise on Argumentation*. Translated by J. Wilkinson and P. Weaver. Notre Dame, Ind.: University of Notre Dame Press, 1969.

Pirsig, Robert M. *Zen and the Art of Motorcycle Maintenance*. New York: Bantam Books, 1975.

Pitcher, George, ed. *Wittgenstein, the "Philosophical Investigations."* London: Macmillan, 1968.

Plato. *Cratylus*. Translated by B. Jowett. In *The Collected Dialogues of Plato*. Edited by E. Hamilton and H. Cairns. Bollingen Series LXXI. New York: Pantheon Books, 1961.

———. *Phaedo*. Translated by H. Tredennick. In *The Collected Dialogues of Plato*. Edited by E. Hamilton and H. Gairno. Bollingen Series LXXI. New York: Pantheon Books, 1961.

———. *Phaedrus*. Translated by R. Hackforth. In *The Collected Dialogues of Plato*. Edited by E. Hamilton and H. Gairno. Bollingen Series LXXI. New York: Pantheon Books, 1961.

———. *Theaetetus*. Translated by F. M. Cornford. In *The Collected Dialogues of Plato*. Edited by E. Hamilton and H. Gairno. Bollingen Series LXXI. New York: Pantheon Books, 1961.

Poincaré, Henri. "Mathematical Creation." In B. Ghiselin, ed., *The Creative Process*. New York: New American Library, n.d.

Polanyi, Michael. "The Creative Imagination," *Chemical and Engineering News* 44 (April 1966).

——. *Personal Knowledge*. Chicago: University of Chicago Press, 1958.

——. *Science, Faith, and Society*. Chicago: University of Chicago Press, 1964.

Popkin, Richard. "Skepticism." In P. Edwards, ed., *The Encyclopedia of Philosophy*. New York; Macmillan,1967.

Popper, Karl. *The Logic of Scientific Discovery*. 2d ed. New York: Harper Torchbooks, 1968.

——. *Objective Knowledge*. Oxford: Clarendon Press, 1972.

Quinton, A. M. "Excerpt from 'Contemporary British Philosophy.' " In G. Pitcher, ed., *Wittgenstein, the "Philosophical Investigations."* London: Macmillan, 1968.

——. *The Nature of Things*. London: Routledge and Kegan Paul, 1973.

Ramsey, Ian T. "Models and Mystery." In W. Shibles, ed., *Essays on Metaphor*.

Reynolds, Paul Davidson. *A Primer in Theory Construction*. Indianapolis: Bobbs-Merrill, 1971.

Richards, Ivor Armstrong. *The Philosophy of Rhetoric*. New York: Oxford University Press, 1965.

Rickover, Hyman G. "A Humanistic Technology." In C. Dechert, ed., *The Social Impact of Cybernetics*. Notre Dame: University of Notre Dame Press, 1966.

Ricoeur, Paul *The Conflict of Interpretations*. Edited by Don Ihde. Evanston, Ill.: Northwestern University Press, 1974.

——. *Freedom and Nature: The Voluntary and the Involuntary*. Translated by Erazin V. Kohak. Evanston, Ill.: Northwestern University Press, 1966.

——. "Husserl and Wittgenstein on Language." In E. Lee and M. Mandelbaum, eds., *Phenomenology and Existentialism*. Baltimore: Johns Hopkins Press, 1967.

——. *The Rule of Metaphor*. Translated by Robert Czerny. Toronto: University of Toronto Press, 1977.

Riesman, Paul. "A Comprehensive Anthropological Assessment." In D. Noel, ed., *Seeing Casteneda*. New York: G. P. Putnam's Sons, 1976.

Robinson, H. J. *Renascent Rationalism*. Toronto: Macmillan, 1975.

Russell, Bertrand. *An Inquiry into Meaning and Truth*. New York: W. W. Norton, 1940.

——. Introduction to L. Wittgenstein, *Tractatus Logico-Philosophicus*. London: Routledge and Kegan Paul, 1970.

Saler, Benson, "Nagual Witch and Sorcerer in a Quiché Village." In J. Middleton, ed., *Magic, Witchcraft, and Curing*. Garden City, N.Y.: Natural History Press, 1967.

Sapir, Edward. *Culture, Language, and Personality*. Edited by D. Mandelbaum. Berkeley: University of California Press, 1970.

Sartre, Jean-Paul. *Being and Nothingness*. Translated by H. Barnes. New York: Philosophical Library, 1956.

Saussure, Ferdinand de. *Course in General Linguistics*. Translated by W. Barkin. New York: Philosophical Library, 1959.

Schapara, Isaac. "Sorcery and Witchcraft in Bechuanaland." In M. Marwick, ed., *Witchcraft and Sorcery*. Harmondsworth, Middlesex, England: Penguin Books, 1970.

Sessions, R. "Problems and Issues Facing the Composer Today." In P. H. Lang, ed., *Problems of Modern Music*. New York: W. Norton, 1962.

Sextus Empiricus. *Adversus Mathematicos (Against the Logicians)*. *Sextus Empiricus,* Vol. II Translated by R. G. Bury. Loeb Classical Library. Cambridge, Mass.: Harvard University Press, 1967.

——. *Pyrrhoniarum hypotyposeon (Outlines of Pyrrhonism)*. *Sextus Empiricus,* Vol. I. Translated by R. G. Bury. Loeb Classical Library. Cambridge, Mass.: Harvard University Press, 1967.

Shibles, Warren, ed. *Essays on Metaphor*. Whitewater, Wisc.: The Language Press, 1972.

Skinner, B. F. *Beyond Freedom and Dignity*. New York: Alfred A. Knopf, 1971.

———. (with C. R. Rogers) "Some Issues Concerning the Control of Human Behavior: A Symposium." In J. D. Douglas, ed., *The Technological Threat*. Englewood Cliffs, N.J.: Prentice-Hall, 1971.

Snell, Bruno. *The Discovery of the Mind*. New York: Harper Torchbooks, 1960.

Snow, C. P. *The Two Cultures: and a Second Look*. Cambridge: University Press, 1969.

Steiner, George. *After Babel*. New York: Oxford University Press, 1975.

Stevens, Wallace. *Opus Posthumous*. New York: Alfred A. Knopf, 1957.

Tocqueville, Alexis de. *Democracy in America*. 2 vols. New York: Vintage Books, n.d.

Torrey, E. Fuller. *The Mind Game: Witchdoctors and Psychiatrists*. New York: Bantam Books, 1972.

Toulmin, Stephen. *Human Understanding*. Vol. 1. Princeton, N.J.: Princeton University Press, 1972.

———. *The Philosophy of Science*. New York: Harper Torchbooks, 1960.

———. *The Uses of Argument*. Cambridge: At the Press, 1969.

Van der Leeuw, G. *La religion dans son essence et ses manifestations, phénoménologie de la religion*. Paris: Payot, 1970.

Varine, H. de. *La culture des autres*. Paris: Editions du Seuil, 1975.

Vuillemin, Jules. "La raison au regard de l'instauration et du développement scientifiques." In Th. F. Geraets, ed., *Rationality To-Day/La rationalité aujourd'hui*. Ottawa: Editions de l'Université d'Ottawa, 1979.

Waters, Frank. *Book of the Hopi*. New York: Ballantine Books, 1974.

———. *Masked Gods: Navaho and Pueblo Ceremonialism*. New York: Ballantine Books, 1973.

Wheelwright, Philip. *Metaphor and Reality*. Bloomington, Ind.: Indiana University Press, 1973.

Whorf, Benjamin Lee. *Language, Thought, and Reality*. Edited by J. B. Carroll. Cambridge, Mass.: M.I.T. Press, 1972.

Wiener, Norbert. *Cybernetics*. Cambridge, Mass.: M.I.T. Press, 1961.

Wilson, Bryan R., ed. *Rationality*. New York: Harper Torchbooks, 1971.

Wilson, Monica Hunter. "Witchcraft-Beliefs and Social Structure." In M. Marwick, ed., *Witchcraft and Sorcery*. Harmondsworth: Penguin Books, 1975.

Winch, Peter. "The Idea of a Social Science." In B. R. Wilson, ed., *Rationality*. New York: Harper Torchbooks, 1971.

———. *The Idea of a Social Science and Its Relation to Philosophy*. London: Routledge and Kegan Paul, 1958.

———. "Understanding a Primitive Society." In B. R. Wilson, ed., *Rationality*. New York: Harper Torchbooks, 1971.

Wittgenstein, Ludwig. *The Blue and Brown Books*. Oxford: Basil Blackwell, 1958.

———. *Notebooks 1914-1916*. Oxford: Basil Blackwell, 1958.

———. *On Certainty*. New York: Harper Torchbooks, 1972.

———. *Philosophical Investigations*. Translated by G. E. M. Anscombe. Oxford: Basil Blackwell, 1963.

———. *Tractatus Logico-Philosophicus*. Translated by D. F. Pears and B. F. McGuinness. London: Routledge and Kegan Paul, 1961.

Wojciechowski, Jerzy A. "Science and the Multiplicity of Cultures." In *Filosofia* (Anais do VIII Congresso Interamericano de Filosofia e v da Sociedade Interamericano de Filosofia). 3 vols. São Paulo: Instituto Brasileiro de Filosofia, 1974.

Wolfe, Thomas. "The Story of a Novel." In B. Ghiselin, ed., *The Creative Process*. New York: New American Library, n.d.

INDEX

ϕ

4/N31 DWLT
MADISON